ONE WEEK LOAN

16 OCT 1997

12 FEB 1996

11 NOV 1997

8 OCT 1996
16 oct

11 DEC 1997
27 FEB 1998

25 NOV 1996

11 DEC 1996

4 MAR 1997

THE HAYMARKET SERIES

Editors: Mike Davis and Michael Sprinker

The Haymarket Series offers original studies in politics, history and culture, with a focus on North America. Representing views from across the American left on a wide range of subjects, the series will be of interest to socialists both in the USA and throughout the world. A century after the first May Day, the American left remains in the shadow of those martyrs whom this Haymarket Series honors and commemorates. These studies testify to the living legacy of political activism and commitment for which they gave their lives.

The Invention
of the White Race

Volume One:
Racial Oppression and Social Control

THEODORE W. ALLEN

V

VERSO

London · New York

First published by Verso 1994
© Theodore W. Allen 1994
Second impression 1995
All rights reserved

Verso
UK: 6 Meard Street, London W1V 3HR
USA: 180 Varick Street, New York, NY 10014–4606

Verso is the imprint of New Left Books

ISBN 0-86091-480-1
ISBN 0-86091-660-X (pbk)

British Library Cataloguing in Publication Data
A catalogue record for this book is available from the British Library

Library of Congress Cataloguing-in-Publication Data
A catalogue record for this book is available from the Library of Congress

Typeset in Times by Solidus (Bristol) Limited
Printed and bound in Great Britain by
Biddles Ltd, Guildford and King's Lynn

In memory of
Esther Kusic (1917–69)
who sold *Equality* in Yorkville

Contents

Acknowledgements

This work began as a spark of intuition in the charged ambience of the civil rights struggles of the 1960s. I am therefore above all inspired by that movement and its ongoing forms, and spurred on by the reminders of the "dream deferred" that I see every day in the generations of my Brooklyn neighbors.

Many individuals and institutions have assisted me during the decades spent working on this book. Space allows specific mention of only a few.

First, I acknowledge my obligation to two fellow proletarian intellectuals, Charles Johnson and William Carlotti, who cleared away ideological barnacles left from my previous moorings, and taught me to say, as Carlotti did, "I am not 'white'."

Jeffrey Babcock Perry – himself a historian and the biographer of Hubert Henry Harrison – has throughout been the individual most intimately acquainted with the development of the book's argument. He has been as ready to offer helpful criticism as the work progressed, as to defend its basic themes in the forum. As personal friend he has stood by me through the vicissitudes of my reckless domestic economy, as well as in my bouts with not always user-friendly computers. If this work had brought me nothing more, to have made such a friend would be reward enough.

It is to the hospitality of my beloved friend Dr. Edward Harden Peeples, of Richmond, veteran civil rights battler, that I am forever indebted for the opportunity to conduct my months of research of the Virginia records of the seventeenth and early eighteenth centuries.

I have been the beneficiary of the kind disinterested assistance of a legion of library-staff persons, including, but not limited to those of the following institutions: Alderman Library, University of Virginia; Cornell University Olin Library; the New York Historical Society; New York Public Library, Research Libraries; New York University Bobst Library and Law Library; and the Virginia State Library, Archives Division. I take this opportunity to express my gratitude to, and my affection for, the Brooklyn Public Library, my resource of first resort. I am obliged to BPL, not only for the regular services it provides, despite a decade and more of budget cuts, but for convenient access to the great store of individual titles, serials, periodicals, and microfilms, which it maintains from acquisitions of more prosperous times.

Though I have not been a part of the academic scene, a number of historians and others in that world have taken the time to offer me their criticisms at various stages of the work. I am grateful to them all, and particularly to Peter Bohmer, Michael Farrell, Gwen Midlo Hall, Noel Ignatiev, David Slavin, John W. Smit, James Turner, and, especially to Peter H. Wood for his detailed early-stage commentary. On their behalf, I enter a disclaimer of responsibility for the faults of the work, for which I alone am accountable.

My thanks go to Michael Sprinker for his initiative in promoting my book as a publishing prospect, and for his support and suggestions as the writing progressed. I cannot adequately express my appreciation to Pat Harper, the Verso copy-editor to whom the manuscript for the first volume of this work was assigned. By her patience and perseverance, and her willingness to shoulder a burden beyond that for which she would normally be obligated, Pat caused important clarifications to be made at various points of the manuscript.

Two generous grants – from the Rabinowitz Foundation and from Charles Knight, respectively – buoyed me up at critical moments as I paddled my way toward completion of the work. I hope the grantors will find their confidence in me justified at last.

Finally, I thank the Vidinha-Rothenhausen group who sustained me with unreflecting love.

Introduction

In this Introduction I criticize freely both "friend and foe", even as I have drawn
upon their research and insights to a great and obvious extent. I have tried to
remain aware that any unfairness could only weaken my own argument. I ask
indulgence for only one assumption, namely, that while some people may desire
to be masters, all persons are born equally unwilling and unsuited to be slaves.

In the broad division of historians into "psycho-cultural" and "socio-
economic" groups as I have defined them, I, of course, belong with the socio-
economic category – with them, but not altogether of them. I have tried to show
that one cannot rest content with the socio-economic case as it now stands,
because of serious compromising ambiguities and inconsistencies in it. This
book is intended as a contribution toward freeing the socio-economic thesis of
such weaknesses.

The doing of it, however, has led me to cast the argument in a new
conceptual mold. I approach racial slavery as a particular form of *racial
oppression*, and racial oppression as a sociogenic – rather than a phylogenic
– phenomenon, homologous with gender and class oppression. Second, in
considering the phenomenon of racial slavery I focus primarily not on *why* the
bourgeoisie in continental Anglo-America had recourse to that anachronistic
form of labor, slavery, but rather on *how* they could establish and maintain for
such a long historical period that degree of *social control* without which no
motive of profit or prejudice could have had effect.

I believe that the thesis here presented – of the origin and nature of the
so-called "white race," the quintessential "Peculiar Institution"[1] – contains the
root (from the seed planted by W.E.B. DuBois's *Black Reconstruction*) of a
general theory of United States history, more consistent than others that have
been advanced. Only by understanding what was peculiar about the Peculiar
Institution can one know what is exceptionable about American Exception-
alism; know how, in normal times, the ruling class has been able to operate
without "laborite" disguises; and know how, in critical times, democratic new
departures have been frustrated by *re*inventions of the "white race".

The Search for Beginnings

The liberating impulses set loose by World War Two, and the impact of the United States civil rights movement in particular brought official society for the first time in American history to acknowledge racism to be an evil in itself. Addressing itself to the problem of the nation's social policy, the presidential commission appointed in the wake of a number of insurrectionary anti-white-supremacy urban outbreaks of recent years concluded:

> Few appreciate how central the problem of the Negro has been to our social policy. Fewer still understand that today's problems can be solved only if white Americans comprehend the rigid social, economic, and educational barriers that have prevented Negroes from participating in the mainstream of American life.[2]

It was in this context that racial slavery became the central preoccupation not only of African-American historians, but of American historians in general. It had long been a truism of our social sciences that the historical roots of racism were traceable to the slave system. But that was a proposition that quickly deteriorated into a pointless tautology: European-Americans deny equal place to African-Americans today because European-Americans denied equal place to African-Americans in slavery times. This tautology could no longer be reconciled with a national consciousness in what some have ventured to call the Second Reconstruction.[3] If racism was an evil, historians were impelled to question the tautology, to examine the basis on which it rested, to understand not only that racism and slavery were connected, but to study the nature of that connection more deeply than before. What were the roots of the tautology, how did the imposition of lifetime hereditary bond-servitude, the quintessential denial of equal place to African-Americans, begin?

Striking parallels were to be seen between patterns of history and its interpretation. Just as consideration of the injustices imposed on African-Americans had for half a century been confined within the constitutional lines of the "equal-but-separate" doctrine, so European-American historians generally dealt with the subject of African-American bond-labor on the basis of an unchallenged assumption of a natural instinct for "racial" domination.[4] Just as the constitutional principle of racial segregation was challenged by Oliver Brown of Topeka and by Rosa Parks of Montgomery, the African-Caribbean historian Eric Williams challenged his profession with the proposition that "Slavery was not born of racism; rather racism was the consequence of slavery."[5] Just as Brown and Parks sent shock waves deep into the foundations of United States society, so did the Williams idea evoke a convulsive controversy in the field of American historiography.[6] Just as the forces of racism rallied on the "white-man's-country" premisses of the United States constitution to produce the Wallace movement, self-servingly called a "white backlash," so from the ranks of American historians there emerged a cohort of defenders of the basic validity of the old assumption of "natural" racism. Like the slaveholders who absolved themselves by putting the blame on evil British ancestors, or like those who today excuse their own defense of white-race privileges by noting that their ancestors never owned slaves, this avowedly "anti-liberal" contingent revels in condemning as "racism" every reference to "anti-blackness" that antedates the founding of Jamestown, the first permanent English settlement in America, in 1607, and then concludes on that ground that regrettably there is little, if anything, they or anyone else can do to change it. And just as in time the political scene came to be dominated by those who celebrate the battles won but forget that the war is just begun, so some historians claimed to rediscover a symbiosis of democratic freedoms and racial slavery.

The Origins Debate

In 1950, in an article published in the *William and Mary Quarterly*, Oscar and Mary Handlin planted the Williams banner most appropriately on continental Anglo-American soil, particularly that of seventeenth-century Virginia and Maryland. The Handlins argued that African-American laborers during the first four decades after their arrival, that is, up until 1660, were not lifetime hereditary bondmen and bondwomen; rather, their status was essentially the same as that of European-American bond-laborers, namely limited-term bond-servitude. Furthermore, the Handlins maintained, when a difference in the treatment of African-American and European-American laborers did emerge, it was by deliberately contrived ruling-class policy, rather than as the outcome of some inborn or preconditioned "race consciousness." The Handlins also briefly noted that in England's Caribbean island colonies, in contrast to those on the continent, the pattern of "race" privileges for "white" laborers, free or bond, did not develop. The root of this difference, they said, was the scarcity of land on which a free, or prospectively free, person of even modest means might subsist.[7]

The basic historical fact upon which the Handlins rested their thesis – the non-slave status of African-Americans in early Virginia – had long been established in the opinion of a number of the most eminent scholars in that field.[8] And at least one, John H. Russell, in 1913, charged that to contend otherwise was to make apology for the slave system.[9]

The Handlins therefore were renewing an old debate, but one whose time had come. Its implications for the rising anti-racism cause were of the utmost significance. If racism was historically prior and the oppression of the African-American was derivative, then the shadow of "natural racism" was cast over the prospect. On the other hand, if racism was derivative of ill-treatment of African-Americans in the form of slavery, then the hope was encouraged that racism could be eliminated from present-day American society by establishing equality for African-Americans. As Winthrop D. Jordan, who would emerge as one of the two foremost opponents of the Handlin thesis, put it: "If whites and Negroes could share the same status of half freedom for forty years in the seventeenth century, why could they not share full freedom in the twentieth?"[10]

The Psycho-cultural Argument

The issue began its evolution into a major controversy with the appearance in 1959 of an article by Carl N. Degler, "Slavery and the Genesis of American Race Prejudice," and a published exchange of letters with the Handlins in the following year.[11] In 1971 Degler elaborated his views in a book comparing social attitudes toward race and prejudice in Brazil and in the United States of America.[12] In 1962 Winthrop Jordan took his stand with Degler in "Modern Tensions and the Origins of American Slavery." In a series of subsequent journal articles, Jordan defended and developed the anti-Handlin argument. Then, in 1968, his main work appeared under the title *White over Black: American Attitudes Toward the Negro, 1550–1812.*[13]

Although Degler and Jordan deeply wished it otherwise, they were convinced all along that there was practically no possibility that "whites and Negroes could share full freedom in the twentieth" or any other century. "It is my conviction," said Degler, "that blacks will be ... discriminated against whenever nonblacks have the power and incentive to do so ... [because] it is human nature to have prejudice against those who are different."[14] Jordan understood the concept of race in exclusively genetic terms. He argued that "races are incipient species," but that the prevalence of interbreeding makes the full development of different race-species "very unlikely." Even so, he was convinced, and his study of "historical experience" confirmed his belief, that the white man's "blackness within" constitutes an insuperable barrier to finding "a way out of [racist] degradation."[15]

From the time of the first Degler article, the argument over the origin of slavery has been enriched by the contributions of scores of scholars representing the two fundamental lines of analysis: the Williams–Handlin socio-economic approach and the Degler–Jordan psycho-cultural approach.

Whether they avowed or merely tacitly accepted the gloomy Degler and Jordan premises, historians on the psycho-cultural side of the issue quite logically emphasized those aspects of the record that might serve to indicate that prior to 1660 African-Americans in Virginia and Maryland were held in a bondage and contempt worse even than that inflicted on the European-American bond-laborers. They also drew support from the works of pre-controversy historians who had tended to the opinion that in continental

Anglo-America the status of African-Americans was not significantly different in 1619 from what it was in 1719 or 1819.

Holding that the Handlins had erred by assuming that the subordination of African-American laborers could not have occurred until it was done by positive legislation, the psycho-cultural school easily found sufficient evidence in the records to demonstrate that the matter was at least more complicated than the Handlins had suggested. On the other hand, there was much evidence that in those early decades "Negro" was not simply another word for "slave."[16] Jordan himself was forced to concede that until at least 1640, "There simply is not enough evidence to indicate with any certainty whether Negroes were treated like white servants or not."[17] Small matter; the strategy of the psycho-cultural school would depend not upon direct frontal assault, but upon encirclement and inferential attack from the rear.

If racial discrimination were the consequence of slavery, said Carl Degler, then how could one account for the differences in the treatment of free African-Americans and of free African-Brazilians? Since both emerged from an initial condition of slavery, why was there a racist rejection in one case, and an assimilationist and positive attitude in the other? Why did Brazil provide an "escape hatch" of social mobility for the free African-Brazilian, while in America the African-American was systematically denied such opportunities? Or, from another perspective, if racism was a function of slavery, he asked, why was the free Negro in the USA obliged to cope with the same cruel racist exclusionism in the non-slave states as in the slave states?[18]

This contradiction could be avoided, said Degler, "only if we reverse our assumption as to which came first, slavery or discrimination ... and work on the assumption that discrimination preceded slavery and thereby conditioned it." Degler accordingly projected three theses: (1) "American race prejudice originated in the discriminatory social atmosphere of the early seventeenth century"; (2) "slavery in the English colonies was the institutionalization of [pre-existent] race prejudice"; and (3) "from the outset, as far as the evidence tells us, the Negro was treated as inferior to the white man, servant or free."[19]

Determined though he was to block the Handlins' passage, Degler stood on a slippery sill. His evidence was too little, and that little tendentiously selected. As evidence of the predominance of anti-Negro attitudes in England before the founding of the first Anglo-American colony, Degler cited the depiction of two Moorish characters in Shakespeare plays, Aaron in *Titus Andronicus* and the title character of *Othello*.[20] But if one proceeds consistently with this exegesis, it is possible to find implications quite contrary to those inferred by Degler. Shakespeare's Aaron is black and villainous; Othello is black and noble. Since Othello appeared ten years after Aaron, might we not, by Degler's logic, infer that this indicated a growth of respect and a reduction of contempt in the English attitude toward Africans? It seems pertinent, if we develop the subject along this line, to point out the transformation undergone by the character of the Moor in Shakespeare's hands. In the original Italian play, the Moor is simply a weak-minded cowardly murderer, uncomplicated by any redeeming quality. Othello, on the contrary, was made a tragic hero, said to be modelled on the real-life Earl of Essex, and in literary power and pathos ranking with Lear.[21] Othello's flaw was not his color but his male ego, made to pass for some part of "honor" and surely calculated to evoke universal sympathy from the English male audience. It may be worth noting that Degler's sense of audience appreciation of Othello is not one the American slaveholders would have shared. An English traveler to Charleston, South Carolina about 1807 found that there "*Othello* and other plays where a black man is the hero of the piece are not allowed to be performed."[22]

Or again, were contrary opinions and attitudes with respect to Negroes, as expressed by some of Shakespeare's contemporaries, to be ignored for want of iambic pentameter? Take Sir Francis Drake. At least three times in the 1560s, Drake (under the command of his kinsman John Hawkins) participated in the premature first English interloper venture in the African trade to the Americas, selling captive Africans into bondage in the Caribbean and on the Spanish Main.[23] A few years later, in 1572–73, this time under his own command, Drake returned to the Spanish Main to conduct a campaign of privateering raids. After an initial setback, the English decided on a basic strategy of alliance with the Maroons (or Cimarrons) of Panama, self-liberated former African slaves and their freeborn descendants, some three thousand in all, living in a number of independent settlements, "growne to a nation, under two Kings of their owne."[24] The English and the African-Panamanians, in mutual sympathy for the particular aims of each in the common anti-Spanish cause, worked, suffered, rejoiced and fought side by side and, according to Drake, "These Symerons during all the time that wee were with them, did us continually good service ... and they would shew themselves no lesse valiant then [than] industrious and of good judgement." On parting there were exchanges of gifts, including silks and linens, from the English in token of friendship and appreciation; the English also burned their small ships in order to leave the precious ironwork, nails etcetera, for the Maroons (iron was worth more to the Maroons than the gold and silver so eagerly sought by the English and other Europeans).[25] Richard Hakluyt, the English visionary of exploration and colonization, generalized from Drake's Panamanian experience and proposed that the Straits of Magellan at the tip of South America be made an English stronghold against the Spanish, defended by a colony of Cimarrons.[26] Edmund S. Morgan, in his *American Slavery, American Freedom*, cited this record in order to argue that the defeat of such antecedent English attitudes was a necessary precondition for the eventual establishment of racial slavery in Virginia.[27] Certainly these facts do not conform to Degler's facile thesis that the origin of racial slavery is in part to be found in an English precedent of racial prejudice against non-Europeans.

One more example. When ship captain Richard Jobson in 1620 and 1621 made a trading voyage to Africa, he refused to engage in slave-trading because the English "were a people who did not deal in any such commodities, neither did we buy or sell one another or any that had our own shapes."[28] When the local dealer insisted that it was the custom there to sell Africans "to white men," Jobson answered that "They," that is, "white men," "were another kinde of people from us ..." Jobson's account was alluded to by Basil Davidson in *The African Slave Trade*, in which he argued that "European attitudes toward Africans in those early times displayed a wide range of contrast ... [but] they supposed no natural inferiority in Africans."[29]

For those who feel that a generalization about "the English attitude toward the Negro" must be attempted, it might be safer to see in the contrasting "Moors," Othello and Aaron, a reflection of a common ambiguity expressed by another Shakespeare contemporary and poet, Sir John Davies of Hereford:

Southward men are cruel, moody, mad
Hot, black, lean leapers, lustful, used to vaunt [boast]
Yet wise in action, sober, fearful, sad
If good, most good, if bad, exceeding bad.[30]

Even such a "balanced" view cannot be made to conform with the assumptions on which Degler chose to rest his case.

Finally, if ingrained English prejudices, institutionally evolved, predetermined the reduction of African-Americans to slavery, why should Degler not at least have indicated why equally apparent contemporary English anti-Irish and anti-Jewish biases did not eventuate in the enslavement of Irish and Jews?[31] The anthropologist Marvin Harris challenged Degler specifically on this question. "Ethnocentrism," Harris said, "is a universal feature of inter-group relations, and obviously both the English and the Iberians were prejudiced against foreigners, white and black." Proceeding from this generalization, Harris directly controverted Degler. In the Anglo-American colonies, said Harris, "the Negroes were not enslaved because the British colonists specifically despised dark-skinned people and regarded them alone as properly suited to slavery." Two historians who have devoted a great deal of study to the attitudes of early English colonialists, Nicholas P. Canny and P. E. H. Hair, have explicitly challenged Jordan on this question. Canny maintains that early colonial records of the fellowship between Anglo-American and African-American laborers in Virginia "greatly modify the opinions on seventeenth-century Englishmen's antipathy for people with black pigmentation advanced in W. D. Jordan, *White over Black*." Professor Hair, writing on the basis of sixteenth-century documents, argues that, "English opinions about Africans ... were more varied than has been suggested in works which set out to show that Anglo-African contacts in Elizabethan times were dominated by 'racialist' considerations." He too specifically mentions Jordan's *White over Black* as tending to this error.[32]

As I have noted, Degler recognized the fundamental significance of the contrast between the racist exclusionism faced by all African-Americans, free or bond, on the one hand, and the assimilationist policy with regard to African-Brazilians. This difference he ascribed to the difference between the cultural backgrounds of Iberia and England.[33] But no such cultural variation could be invoked to explain the difference in the positions of the free Negro in the British West Indies and in continental Anglo-America. Despite the explosive implications of this historic fact, Degler ignored it completely. The omission was especially deplorable since the Handlin article, which originally drew Degler to battle, had directed attention to differences between the Anglo-Caribbean and continental Anglo-America.

Worse still, Degler attempted to support his thesis by citations from the record of the short-lived (1630–41) English colony on Providence Island, located in the western Caribbean about 350 miles northeast of Panama. In the very record he cited, he completely neglected the dispute among the English colonizers of Providence Island over the legal and moral permissibility of attempting to hold Africans in lifetime servitude. In the end the colony had to be abandoned because of mutiny by the Negro laborers and the external pressure of the Spanish.[34]

Having insisted on the assumption that the origin of slavery depended upon the English colonists having come to the Americas with already indelible prejudices against "black men," Degler proceeded with a most explicit self-contradiction by asserting that slavery-producing prejudice "did not depend" on an imported mind-set but rather was fostered by the sight of Africans "as the cargo of the international slave trade ... those wretches newly spilled out of the slave ships!"[35] If the prejudices "originated long before slavery became legal" (and therefore long before the arrival in the Chesapeake of "slave ships" directly from Africa),[36] why intrude "fostering" (without a pretense of documentation) and, incidentally, hold the Africans responsible for it? Instead of racial prejudice causing slavery, here Degler was making slavery the cause of racial prejudice. In seeking to support his argument with both the *a priori* belt and the *post facto* suspenders, Degler instead rendered untenable the "reversal of assumptions" upon which his thesis depended.

Most regrettable of all, Degler was oblivious of the transcendental fact that, *whatever the state of English prejudices at that time*, any attempt to hold African laborers in lifetime hereditary bond-servitude was doomed by the African "prejudice" against it, as expressed by flight and rebellion.

Jordan scornfully distanced himself from "liberals on the race question ... uninterested in tired questions of historical evidence ... [who] could not easily assume a natural prejudice in the white man ... [because it] would violate their basic assumptions concerning the dominance of culture."[37] He took up the gauntlet of his own design: "If prejudice was natural there would be little one could do to wipe it out"; and his book, naturally called *White over Black*, was written to say a defiant "Amen."

With regard to the crucial question of the origin of racial slavery, Jordan believed he had found a way to save the psycho-cultural case from the "which-came-first" dilemma on which Degler had impaled himself.[38]

> Rather than slavery causing "prejudice" or vice versa, they seem rather to have generated each other. Both were ... twin aspects of a general debasement of the Negro. Slavery and "prejudice" may have been equally cause and effect, continuously reacting upon each other ...: a mutually interactive growth of slavery and unfavorable assessment, with no cause for either which did not cause the other.[39]

In thus conflating cause and effect, Jordan disposed of the dilemma by evoking a parthenogenetic unicorn called "the general debasement of the Negro." If, in the process, he abandoned the principle of chronological order by which the historian is bound to live, Jordan found a *cause* outside of time (at least, time as measured by the rhythms of recorded history) in instinct (or, at most, the unconscious). There, in an atavistic domain of aversion to black, of guilt as blackness, of blackward projection of guilt; there, in the pits of identity crisis, in the realm of dreams and symbols, Jordan said, was prefigured time out of mind the "unthinking decision" that produced racial slavery in Anglo-America.[40] So it was that Jordan contributed a book on the history of thought, the crux of which was an *un*thought choice.

As a corollary to the asserted instinctive drive to "debase the Negro," Jordan posited a psychological compulsion: "the need of transplanted Englishmen to know who it was they were." And what they were, he said, was "white": "white men had to know who they were if they were to survive."[41] This notion, Jordan avowed, was the thread that bound his study together. It was the old "germ theory" of American history decked out in up-to-date psychological trappings: before the Mayflower Compact, before the Petition of Right, before the Magna Charta, before the German-Saxon Hundred, there was the Word: White over Black, innate, ineradicable – a Calvinism of the genes, a Manifest Destiny of the White Soul.[42]

Historians are cautioned to avoid the vice of "presentism," that is, the assignment of motivations for behavior to suit current vogues without proof that those motivations actually figured in the needs and feelings of the people of the historic period under consideration. One common example of this error is that of casually classing Negroes in colonial Anglo-America as "slaves" from the first mention in 1619 on, decades before there is any justification in the record for such a generalization. On account of the inevitable deficiencies of the record, the tendency to this kind of error has to be guarded against, even when the subject is the objective, material world of actual places, persons, and events. But when, as in Jordan's book, the subject is the thoughts, reflections, attitudes of the observers of actual places, people and events, the danger is of a higher order of magnitude, because it involves the interpretation of interpretations.

As a citizen of the twentieth century, Jordan could look forward from his spaceship-in-time and see that the war to abolish slavery would be led by anti-abolitionists; that the war fought to strike the chains of slavery from the African-American would sow the seeds of a "white" imperialism; that even on the bank of the river of martyrs' blood the promise of equality would be repudiated after the Civil War, by a white-supremacist exclusion of Africans,[43] Asian-Americans, Mexicans, Indians and African-Americans. But the "trans-planted Englishmen" in the new republic where Jordan left them – perched on the Atlantic slope of a continent inhabited in its vastness by a non-European majority, and further opposed by a rival European power's ancient claim to much of that territory – they could not know what the future would hold with regard to "the Negro question," or "the Indian question," or "the Spanish-Mexican question." For all they knew, Spain would maintain its claim to Texas and the West, and the "Indians" would continue (perhaps with outside help) to preside over most of the rest of the continent.[44] At the same time, they were increasingly convinced that slavery would have to end, and that, whatever some of the literate, record-leaving "whites" might wish, schemes for colonization of African-Americans outside the United States offered no answer to the "race" question.[45]

In this situation, might not the imminent freedom of the African-American lead to a peopling of the United States by a primarily African-European blend?[46] The Spanish and the Portuguese had blended with "not-whites" in their areas of American settlement without losing their Spanish or Portuguese identity. Among the population of the British West Indies the descendants of Englishmen were overwhelmingly persons of African descent, whose very struggle for equal rights was largely predicated upon their British identity.[47]

Jordan ascribes the West Indies blending to "race" and sex ratios such as were unachievable in the continental colonies.[48] But the "attitudes of ["white"] Americans", which is his proclaimed concern, did not show much of Jordan's faith in the demographic ratios as the controlling factor. The belief that such a blending with African-Americans was sure to happen was the major argument of the advocates of forced shipping of freed Negroes to the West Indies, Latin America, Africa or the periphery of the United States.[49]

They had known "who they were" in the seventeenth century and during most of the eighteenth century: they were Englishmen. But then something happened to their "need to know" that they were Englishmen, and they found a new identity, as "white" Americans. Might not the same obsolescence swallow up the "need to know" they were "white", just as their previous "need to know" that they were "Englishmen" had been superseded? They had been Englishmen far longer than they had been "white". Might they not have experienced "a new birth of freedom", and a new identity, American still, but simply human instead of "white"?

But there is more here than a mere lapse of professionalism. Jordan takes as his subject "attitudes ... thoughts and feelings (as opposed to actions)," regarding them as "discrete entities susceptible of historical analysis." He proclaims his philosophic adherence to the ultimate primacy of "attitudes" in delimiting "the categories of possibilities within which for the time being we are born to live."[50] Was it possible that because of his personal conviction that nothing much can be done by remedial social action to end the curse of racism, Jordan was far from careful about the extent to which this attitude might lower his guard against his own "white" bias in his presentation of the picture of American society up to 1812?[51] Bad as this was in itself, it caused Jordan's analysis of "attitudes" to parody more than it explained of the "actions", the causal course of events, to which they stand opposed.[52]

As the root of "white attitudes" toward the African-American, Jordan staked all on what he saw as the ineluctable need of the English psycho-cultural heritage to preserve its identity in the New World. But how could the same heritage produce the "social accommodation of mixed offspring" in the British West Indies and the contrasting refusal to allow for any such special status for "mulattos" in the continental plantation colonies? Faced by this problem (which the Handlins had suggested and Degler had ignored), Jordan was compelled to acknowledge that the variance could not derive from "the English cultural heritage."[53] But in so doing Jordan punctured his basic assumption. He was saying that the gene-pool factor, the "need to know they were 'white'", etcetera were not, after all, timeless absolutes in the English psyche; rather, they were only relative, alterable by sudden circumstance.

Jordan began his repair work with a sly reference to "the push and pull of an irreconcilable conflict between desire and aversion for interracial sexual union," with desire proving the stronger in the British West Indies.[54] "No one thought intermixture [of African and Anglo] was a good thing," Jordan asserted.[55] But it is just as true to say that no one in England thought that the "intermixture" by seduction and rape of poor women by propertied men was "a good thing", and the law and the pulpit were as productive of the appropriate expressions of disapproval there as they were in the corresponding case in the Anglo-American plantation colonies. Jordan's belief in "aversion" as a special operative factor in "biracial" America is unsupported by contrasting evidence involving dependent-class women in England and Ireland. (J. H. Plumb makes a similar criticism in his review of Jordan's book.) It seems doubtful that Jordan fairly conveys the feelings of English colonists in Jamaica in this regard. They disdained to account for their "interracial liaisons" as a result of a scarcity of European women. Quite the contrary; they proclaimed the moral superiority of their conduct as compared with that of the master class in England, contrasting the "relatively permanent" relationships in Jamaican society with the "prostitution, infanticide and unnatural neglect of illegitimate children in England."[56]

As for the Caribbean versus continental differences, since the push of desire under continental elms is no less fundamental than it is under insular palms,[57] Jordan turned a metaphor of his own: "The West Indian planters were lost . . . in a sea of blacks."[58] That men of the owning leisure classes impose their desires on women of the non-owning laboring classes is as old and as general as the division of society into such classes, although those men are never thought of as being "lost in a sea of laborers."

Still, demographic facts are appropriate to demographic studies. In colonial Anglo-America, the higher the proportion of African-American laboring women among the non-owning classes in an area, the higher we could expect to be the incidence of sexual unions of Anglo men with African-American women. The varying degrees of "acceptance" of the relationship among Anglos in the plantation colonies was basically a function of its practice, with a tendency to vary toward "desire" rather than "aversion." If we can accept the testimony of two of the most cited chroniclers of Jamaican affairs prior to emancipation, we must conclude that the proportion of English men there involved in child-producing unions with non-European women was greater than might be expected from the demographic ratios.[59] That fact testifies to the racist operation of ruling-class male domination, but not to the "aversion" thesis posited by Jordan. Discounting the differences in opportunity as determined by demographic variations, the sexual exploitation of African-American women by European-American men (the main, though not the only social form of "interracial" sex) does not appear to have been less practiced on the continent than in the British West Indies.[60]

The difference in the status won by the Anglo-African in the West Indies, on the one hand, and in the continental plantation colonies, on the other, was, Jordan said, due to differences of "self-identification" by the fathers in the two different settings.[61] And how the Anglo fathers identified themselves was determined by demographics, the "race" and sex ratios. Whereas the Caribbean Anglos, he argued, were "lost in a sea of blacks," the continental colonist felt "the weight of the Negroes on his community heavy enough to be a burden, yet not so heavy as to make him abandon all hope of maintaining his own identity."[62] This conclusion is tautological since the maintenance of "white" identity was equivalent to rejection of the "mulatto."

We turn now to what Jordan calls the "single exception" to the pattern of non-acceptance of "mulatto" status in the Anglo-American continental colonies. Georgia colony originated in 1732 as a buffer against Spanish Florida. It was set up especially to stop African-American bond-laborers from fleeing to freedom in Florida, either to the Spanish or to friendly Indians. For this reason, the new colony was founded on the exclusion of "Negroes," in order to seal South Carolina against the outflow of fugitive bond-laborers. But in less than twenty years the expansive power of the South Carolina plantation bourgeoisie made hash of the no-slavery principle and quickly brought Georgia into the system.

The consequent rise in the proportion of African-American bond-laborers in the total population of the new colony largely negated the territorial buffer function, despite the English takeover of Florida in 1763 at the end of the Seven Years War. Faced with this crisis, the Georgia authorities acted to erect a new *social* buffer to reinforce, restore, replace the territorial one. In 1765, the Georgia Commons House of Assembly enacted that free "mulatto" immigrants be "naturalized" and accorded "all the Rights, Priviledges, Powers and Immunities whatsoever which [belong to] any person born of British parents."[63]

In the shadow world of "attitudes," this Georgia law may seem merely an exception to the general policy of rejection of the "mulatto" as it was practiced in the continental Anglo-American colonies. But, in its own person it appears not as an exception, but as a perfectly consistent element of a general policy of social control, a *sine qua non* of all government, at all times, in all places. The Georgia case was exceptional only in the brevity of its duration. Every plantation colony faced the same social control problem; each required a buffer social control stratum to stand between the mass of slaves and the numerically tiny class of slaveholders. In the Americas there was no such historically developed middle stratum, and therefore it had to be invented.

The records richly attest to the deliberate pursuit of this fundamental principle of colonial policy in the English colonies. Repeatedly, the theory and the practice of promoting the "free colored" to an intermediate social status in the British West Indies was proposed in order that they "would ... attach themselves to the White race ... and so become a barrier against the designs of the Black."[64] This essential social control function was operative in Jamaica in the 1730s. The European militia there was found altogether inadequate to the task of combating the African-Jamaican runaway maroons, who from mountain bases encouraged plantation workers to join them. In 1739, when a military campaign was waged against the maroons, the British forces were composed of two hundred British sailors and two hundred Moskito Indians, free Negroes and "mulattoes."[65] In Barbados, in order to control the bond-laborers the plantation bourgeoisie "created" and promoted the "mulatto" group, which then "functioned as 'whites' *vis à vis* the slaves."[66] In Georgia the 1765 "mulatto" policy was designed, as Jordan himself put it, "to attract men who might be *counted as white* and who would thereby strengthen the colony's defenses against her foreign and domestic enemies," the powerful Indian tribes on its frontiers and the rising proportion of Negro bond-laborers.[67] Whatever reasons Jordan had for ignoring the obvious parallel of the Georgia case, a fair inference is that he found it incompatible with his approach to the question of the origin and function of racial slavery. The parallel argues that everywhere in Anglo-America, not just in Georgia, the "white attitude" was, in the final analysis, shaped by the exigencies of the relationship of contending social forces. In the dynamic tension of ideas and experience, ideas were the bowstring, experience was the bow. The "mulatto" distinction was a functional one; being necessarily and above all concerned with maintaining their ascendancy, members of the plantation bourgeoisie sometimes made accommodations in their thinking in the interest of having a "mulatto" buffer between themselves and the plantation bond-laborers.[68]

Sometimes, but not always. Why was this not the practice, except to the possible extent of the Georgia case, in continental Anglo-America, in either its colonial or its regenerate United States form? Jordan, from other premises, argues that unlike the English in the Caribbean, "lost in a sea of blacks," those on the continent were able to beat back the challenge to their ancestral "white" identity.[69] But as Jordan himself points out, the continental slaveholders no less than those in the West Indies were constantly concerned with dealing with the various forms of resistance on the part of those whom they held in bondage.[70] The Georgia case shows that they were prepared, in certain circumstances, to resort to the "mulatto" option. If the "mulatto" on the continent were not generally, however, to be accorded the West Indies style social promotion, nevertheless for the slaveholders – outnumbered sometimes twenty or more times by their African-American bond-laborers – the "mulatto" *function* was as necessary as it was in the West Indies. If, there, "mulattos" could "function as whites," then on the continent laboring-class, largely propertyless and poor European-Americans could function as "mulattos". In the West Indies the "mulatto" was compensated by emancipation and promotion to some sort of petit bourgeois status.[71] Since the poor European-Americans were or, after a term of servitude, would be free, and since they typically had already lost upward social mobility, they were promoted to the "white race" and endowed with unprecedented civil and social privileges *vis-à-vis* the African-American, privileges that, furthermore, were made to appear to be conditional on keeping "not-whites" down and out. This entailed the exclusion of "free Negroes" from participation in the buffer role in the continental colonies, because their inclusion would have undermined the racial privileges upon which depended the loyalty of the laboring-class "whites" to the plantation bourgeoisie.[72] Whatever might have been the case with literate members of the ruling class, the record indicates that laboring-class European-Americans in the continental plantation colonies showed little interest in "white identity" before the institution of the system of "race" privileges at the end of the seventeenth century.[73]

The Socio-economic Argument

Despite the more or less obvious inadequacies and fallacies of the Jordan–Degler psycho-cultural analysis, efforts by the opposition to emphasize the primacy of socio-economic causes have often betrayed a critical ambiguity toward the origin of anti-Negro prejudice. In other cases an "economic" thesis was weakened by oversimplification. In still others, economic facts were tendentiously attenuated to the point where they could not bear the weight of their argument. In one instance, the embryo of a complete and consistent socio-economic interpretation was formulated, but remained undeveloped.

Although the Handlins were aware of the uncongenial inferences they were inviting, they nevertheless explained the rise of anti-Negro discrimination as "simply the reaction of [English and other European] immigrants ... isolated in an immense wilderness ... [who] longed in the strangeness for the company of those who were most like themselves."[74] This was pure intuition on the part of the Handlins, devoid of any reference to the colonial records. They had thus adopted so much of the Degler natural racism principle, that Degler could say, "Actually our two positions are not as far apart as the Handlins would lead one to believe."[75]

Eric Williams, at the very outset of post-1945 discussion of the origin of Anglo-American slavery, provided a corrective for a fundamental historiographical blindspot. Referring specifically to the political crisis in Britain that more than a century earlier had led to the emancipation of bond-laborers in the West Indies, he made a point of fundamental importance not only for the Anglo-Caribbean but for the Americas generally, including the Anglo-American continental plantation colonies:

> Contrary to popular and even learned belief, ... the most dynamic and powerful social force in the colonies was the slave himself. This aspect of the ... problem has been studiously ignored. ... The planter looked upon slavery as eternal, ordained by God. ... There was no reason [however] why the slave should think the same.[76]

The bond-laborer accordingly made the counter-argument of resistance by "indolence, sabotage and revolt."

After Williams made this point, European-American historians showed a greater awareness of the need to include the African-American bond-laborers as self-activating participants in historic events. But generally they continued the old tendency of ignoring an equally crucial matter, namely, the question of social control. Unfortunately Williams, by an oversimplification of the particular reason for the employment of Africans as plantation bond-laborers, may have contributed to a perpetuation of this problem.

In the course of his refutation of the various "racial" explanations for the unique enslavement of the African (climatic adaptability, skin color, race prejudice, etcetera), Williams argued from "a simple economic fact: that the colonies needed labor and resorted to Negro labor because it was cheapest and best."[77] There is no evidence, however, to show that the cost of the acquisition and delivery of African laborers to Anglo-America, even the Caribbean, was lower than the corresponding costs for laborers brought from England, Scotland and Ireland.[78] The significant relationship between cheapness and enslavement was this: the African laborers were cheaper because they were enslaved, before they were enslaved because they were cheaper. To assume the cheapness is to assume the enslavement. That is an error against which, as has been noted above, Williams himself argued most forcefully, in pointing out that the desire of the plantation bourgeoisie for cheap labor was matched by the African laborer's desire not to be enslaved. Clearly, then, their enslavement was not simply the result of the plantation bourgeoisie's perception of an economic advantage to be gained by it. Such a perception meant nothing without its other half, the successful construction of a system of social control whereby the normal process of peaceful day-to-day exploitation of bond-labor could be conducted.[79]

A number of other historians seeking an economic interpretation of the origin of racial slavery in continental Anglo-America have leaned heavily on the "cheaper labor" rationale.[80] They have then proceeded as if the ability of the plantation bourgeoisie to control the African-American bond-laborer could be taken for granted. That assumption is especially harmful for the study of the continental colonies, because it was there that the operation of social control was obscured by its "white race" form.

Edmund S. Morgan authored several journal articles in 1971 and 1972 bearing on the establishment of racial slavery in colonial Virginia. The publication in 1975 of his full 500-page treatment of the subject, *American Slavery/American Freedom: The Ordeal of Colonial Virginia*, provided the most substantial contribution so far to a socio-economic interpretation of the origin of racial slavery. Morgan was recognized by reviewers as the socio-economic party's counterpoise to Jordan.[81]

Making use of the Virginia Colony and County Records (to an extent exceeded only by Philip Alexander Bruce more than seventy-five years earlier) Morgan drew a picture of seventeenth-century Virginia as "the Volatile Society," in which the ruling elite was faced with critical problems of social control. Racism was not a significant factor. African-American bond-laborers were increasing in number, but they still made up only one-fourth or one-fifth of the bond-labor force until the 1690s. The threat to social order, Morgan said, came from propertyless, discontented, poverty-ridden European-Americans, mainly former limited-term bond-laborers.

Social order was achieved, according to Morgan, through two policies. First, motivated by simple profit considerations, the plantation bourgeoisie gained, incidentally and unconsciously, a more docile laboring class by shifting its primary reliance from limited-term to lifetime bond-labor. "Slaves," Morgan said, "[were] less dangerous than free or semi-free [limited-term-bond-] laborers," because slaves "had none of the rising expectations that have so often prompted rebellion in human history."[82] Morgan dismissed the frequently encountered ruling-class fears of servile rebellion as unfounded in reality. In explaining why only Africans were enslaved, Morgan differed sharply with the Jordan–Degler thesis. Morgan showed that the bourgeoisie was quite willing to consider proposals for the enslavement of Englishmen and Scots. But whereas the Africans arrived already enslaved, Morgan argued, "the transformation of free men [from England, for example] into slaves would have been a tricky business."[83] Welcome as his rejection of the "innate racism" explanation of racial slavery may be, Morgan's "non-rebellious slave" belongs with the mythical "friendly master" in the analysis of the dynamics of slavery in the Americas.[84] If the extent of rebellion by African-American bond-laborers in continental Anglo-America did not reach the levels witnessed in such countries as Santo Domingo, Jamaica, Guiana and Brazil, it was not because of any difference in their status upon their arrival in America.

The second policy was deliberately calculated as a social control measure. It was in this connection that Morgan made his most valuable contribution to the socio-economic analysis of the origin of racial slavery. The plantation bourgeoisie did not hold Morgan's low opinion of the bond-laborers as potential rebels; their ultimate fear was that "freemen with disappointed hopes should make common cause with slaves of desperate hope ..." and jointly re-enact their part in Bacon's Rebellion of 1676, in which African-American and Anglo bond-laborers together had demanded an end to bond-servitude.[85] Against this danger, "the answer ... obvious if unspoken and only gradually recognized, was racism, to separate free whites from dangerous slave blacks by a screen of racial contempt."[86] Morgan then proceeded to catalogue and analyze "a series of acts" passed by the Virginia Assembly over a period of some thirty-five years, culminating with the revisal of the laws in 1705, whereby "the assembly deliberately did what it could to foster the contempt of whites for blacks and Indians."[87] He argued that European-Americans of the laboring classes, since they were not slaveowners, did not derive any "direct economic benefits" from the establishment of slavery. But, according to Morgan, the "small men," the old rebellious types, "were ... allowed to prosper" and were accorded "social, psychological, and political advantages." The deliberately calculated result was to turn "the thrust of exploitation" away from the European-American petty bourgeoisie and "[align] them on the side of the exploiters," that is, the slaveholders.[88] Morgan also noted that, as "Christian whites," even the unpropertied European-Americans (including bond-laborers) were offered a number of benefits previously denied them, in order to alienate them from their African-American fellow bondmen and bondwomen.[89]

Thus Morgan carried the argument against the "unthinking decision" explanation of racial slavery to its logical conclusion: deliberate ruling-class choice. The resort of the plantation bourgeoisie to slave labor might have been a matter of mere profit-seeking instinct, he said, but racial slavery and racism were a calculated form, designed to cope with problems of social control.[90]

Bold and cogent, and full of promise as it was at the start, Morgan's argument involved false premises that would vitiate its full development. With the turn to African and African-American lifetime bond-labor as the basis of the economy, coupled with the simultaneous expansion of opportunities for European-American freedmen, the social control problem, according to Morgan, evaporated in a cloud of upward mobility until "the remaining free laborers and tenant farmers were too few in number to be a serious threat."[91]

Morgan had documented most convincingly the non-racist character of the volatile society of seventeenth-century Virginia, and the deliberateness of the development of the racist policy of social control. But now (without, however, his customarily scrupulous documentation), he presented a denouement that not only rendered redundant the theme of "racism as the answer" to social discontent, but spared the life of the "innate racism" idea that he had so trenchantly attacked as an explanation of racial slavery.

In proceeding on the assumption that there were now "too few free poor on hand to matter,"[92] Morgan was wrong on the facts and wrong on the theory. The proportion of landless European-Americans did not shrink to insignificance as a social category in the plantation colonies in the century between Bacon's Rebellion and the American Revolution. In 1676, the overwhelming proportion of the population of Virginia was in the Tidewater region. Of its economically active (tithable) European-American population, half were bond-laborers and another one-eighth were propertyless freemen.[93] A century later this proletarian proportion of the European-American population of that same area was still more than 40 per cent. This marked the limit of proletarian promotion to the owning classes. Furthermore, relative to the conditions prevailing in the northern, non-plantation colonies, those of the European-Americans were worse in general in the plantation colonies.[94]

Consider now the theory of it. If the European-American laboring classes "aligned themselves with the exploiters" because they, the "white" poor, benefited indirectly in the slave-labor-based monocultural plantation economy by becoming property-holders during the so-called golden age of the Chesapeake (that is, the colonies of Virginia and Maryland bordering the Chesapeake Bay) in the middle quarters of the eighteenth century, then why did that collaboration not diminish as the contrary tendency set in, as it evidently did, and "racial" competition for employment became one of the well-known features of American society? Or again, if the operation of slave economics was such as to make free people generally into property-holders, why were the free African-Americans excluded from a fair share of the bounty? Would not their participation have strengthened the front against the threat of slave revolt, which strengthening, as we well know, was calculated to be the effect elsewhere in the plantation Americas? The exclusion of the free African-American from such participation is prima facie proof that the mass of the "whites" was not composed of property-owners but of proletarians and semi-proletarians, whose social status thus depended not upon their property but upon their "race."[95]

In contrast with the British West Indies, the social control problem in the continental plantation colonies was not that there were too few European-American laborers, but that there were too many. It was this circumstance that accounted for the decisive role of "race" which came to characterize the system of social control in the continental colonies. Primary emphasis upon "race" became the pattern only where the bourgeoisie could not form its social control apparatus without the inclusion of propertyless European-Americans. If, in the plantation colonies, there had really been "too few free poor to matter", as Morgan argued, then those few would have been relegated to social irrelevance, as indeed happened in the West Indies, and the "white race" would never have become the essence of the social control policy of the Anglo-American continental plantation bourgeoisie. By conceptually erasing the European-American proletarian, Morgan was inviting back the psycho-cultural theory of the origin of racism, the theory he had done so much to refute by his scholarly study of seventeenth-century Virginia. Propertied classes do not need special motivation to unite around their interests *vis-à-vis* the propertyless and exploited. Racism among the propertied classes alone would be evidence for the psycho-cultural belief in "natural" racism. But Morgan's theory that practically all European-Americans benefited, directly or indirectly, from keeping African-Americans out and down has more specific and dire implications favorable to the psycho-cultural view with respect to "modern tensions." For, whether racism be "natural-born" in European-Americans, or whether it be the function of actual (as against illusory) benefits for all "whites" as a result of racial oppression, the implications for ridding our society of the curse of racism are equally unfavorable.

In seeking to understand this trend of Morgan's argument, it may be helpful to note that he shares with Jordan the "paradox" theory of American history.[96] "In committing themselves to a slavery whose logic rested, in the final analysis, on racial differences," Jordan wrote, "the colonists may in fact have enhanced the fluidity of the American social structure above the racial line."[97] A paraphrase of Jordan accurately expresses Morgan: in committing themselves to a political order whose logic rested, in the final analysis, on racial distinctions, Virginians such as Jefferson and Madison had assured equality and justice for all "above the racial line." There is no place in this scenario for a growth of proletarian misery on the "white" side of the line. But even in Jefferson's time, the ugly fact was evident.[98]

Plowing furrows through the records side by side with Morgan, Timothy H.

Breen produced strong reinforcement for the socio-economic explanation of the emergence of racial slavery in colonial Virginia. In his 1973 article "A Changing Labor Force and Race Relations in Virginia 1660–1710,"[99] Breen drew attention to the extent and significance of actual rebellion involving African-American and European-American bond-laborers, and poor freedmen. Breen, furthermore, regarded the African-American bond-laborers as a constant potential for rebellion against the plantocracy.[100]

On the other hand, in this article, and as co-author with Stephen Innes of a book published in 1980,[101] Breen ascribes the cancellation of laboring-class solidarity by the counterfeit of "white race" identification to exclusively objective factors. Of these, said Breen, "none was more important than the rise of tobacco prices after 1684 ... [which] raised white laborers out of poverty."[102] But there does not seem to have been any significant rise in tobacco prices and production in the critical period chosen by Breen. Allan Kulikoff in a later study found that, "From 1680 to 1715, except for a short boom between 1697 and 1702, the real [tobacco] price level was almost always low or declining." Although the status of poor whites was elevated relative to African-Americans by the new system of racial privileges, they faced a decline of opportunity for social mobility in the decades after 1680.[103] According to economic historian Jacob M. Price, "It was precisely in the 1680s and 1690s that slaves were first introduced into the Chesapeake in large numbers, yet we can observe no effect on production before the 1720s."[104]

The second of the factors listed by Breen was the increasing proportion of laborers arriving in Virginia direct from Africa, lacking previous Christian "seasoning." "No white servant," said Breen, "... could identify with these frightened Africans."[105] The concomitant "language barrier," he added, further inhibited the development of labor solidarity. On this point, in the absence of documentation Breen resorted to intuition, as first Degler and then others on both sides of the aisle had taken to doing. He made no attempt, however, to learn by a comparison with the at least somewhat parallel situation elsewhere in the Americas, where new laborers were constantly arriving direct from Africa in far larger proportions, and where language differences not only occurred naturally, but were deliberately manipulated by the capitalist employers hoping thereby to frustrate bond-labor solidarity. To reject out of hand, or not even think of, such a possible light on the question seems justifiable only on the assumption of the existence in the European-American bond-laborers of an overriding sense of "white" identity with their owners, contrary to the tenor of the well-documented presentation that Breen had made up to that point.

Finally, among these objective factors Breen included improved wage scales for a relatively diminished number of free laborers, and improved opportunities for freedmen to become landholders (a point whose limited importance has been indicated above in connection with Morgan, and which is further to be inferred from Breen's comment that "If landless freemen could not afford acreage in Virginia, they could move to Carolina or Pennsylvania ..."[106]) Whatever those expanded opportunities, and whatever the increase in the number of African-American bond-laborers might be, such objective factors could not explain the exclusion of the free African-American from their benefits.

Despite the obvious limitations of such mechanical reliance upon objective factors to explain white racism among European-Americans of the laboring classes, Breen gives no scope at all to deliberate ruling-class policy in the displacement of European-American proletarian class consciousness by the incubus of a "white" identity with the employing classes, which has presided over our history for three centuries.

Of all the historians of the "social" side of the question, only the African-American historian Lerone Bennett Jr. succeeds in placing the argument on the three essential bearing points from which it cannot be toppled. First, that racial slavery constituted a ruling-class response to a problem of labor solidarity. Second, that a system of racial privileges for the propertyless "whites" was deliberately instituted in order to align them on the side of the plantation bourgeoisie against the African-American bond-laborers. Third, that the consequence was not only ruinous to the interests of the African-Americans, but was "disastrous" for the propertyless "whites" as well.[107]

Bennett's aim was to look at three and a half centuries of African-American history. Understandably, he was limited in the scope he could give in his book to his treatment of the origin of racial slavery, a development of the first century of that history. Whether or not he might otherwise have devoted attention to Bacon's Rebellion and compared the various systems of social control in the colonial period we do not know. In any case, when primary attention is directed to the origin of racial slavery, these matters need to be taken into consideration.

On the Misleading Term "Race"

In an avowed attempt to make clear the meaning of the terms "race" and "racial" as he used them in *White over Black*, Winthrop D. Jordan appended a "Note on the Concept of Race," which he had composed as editor of an earlier book. He also devoted a section of his "Essay on Sources" to works by anthropologists and biologists, particularly geneticists, which he had consulted on the question of "race."

Two geneticists whose works obviously influenced the formulation of that note were Stanley M. Garn and Theodosius Dobzhansky.[108] Garn's book *Human Races* was said by Jordan to be "the best single book on race." Of Dobzhansky's well-known writings, Jordan particularly mentioned *Mankind*

Evolving as "an absorbing treatment" of the subject. But a study of these two sources does not help one understand why Jordan thought that their concept of "race" was important to him as a historian.

Garn concludes his discussion of "The Contemporary Approach to Race" by explicitly separating genetics from the social sciences with regard to "race" and "racism." His book, he says:

> has nothing to do with racism, which is simply the attempt to deny some people de-served opportunities simply because of their origin, or to accord other people certain undeserved opportunities, only because of their origins. The history of our species is far too long (and periods of national glory far too short) to direct attention away from race as an evolutionary phenomenon to futile arguments about superiority, inferiority, or moral supremacy, which become two-edged and detrimental to all who wield them. (pp. v–vi)

In *Mankind Evolving*, Dobzhansky insists on the cultural significance of "race differences," but condemns any and all attempts to find in the human genetic make-up any justification for racism; there is no gene for a "white" attitude. "The mighty vision of human equality," he says, "belongs to the realm of ethics and politics, not to that of biology" (p. 13).

Jordan's search among arcana of genetic evolution to better understand "white men's attitudes," was, at best, an exercise in irrelevancy. For when an emigrant population from "multiracial" Europe goes to North America or South Africa and there, by constitutional fiat, incorporates itself as the "white race," that is no part of genetic evolution. It is rather a political act: the invention of "the white race." It lies within the proper sphere of study of social scientists, and it is an appropriate objective for alteration by social activists. Leave genetics to the geneticists; as Garn and Dobzhansky say, genetics has nothing but disclaimers to contribute to the study of racism as a historical phenomenon.

The Irish Mirror

Just as instruments of observation operating above the earth's enveloping atmosphere reveal significant meteorological phenomena with a clarity unachievable from the earth's lowly surface, so does the reflector of Irish history afford insights into American racial oppression and white supremacy – the overriding jetstream that has governed the flow of United States history down to this very day – free of the "White Blindspot" that Dr DuBois warned us about in *Black Reconstruction*.[109] Irish history presents a case of *racial oppression without reference to alleged skin color or, as the jargon goes, "phenotype."*

That is why *Racial Oppression and Social Control*, Volume One of this study of the origin of the paramount issue in American history, begins with a long look into an Irish mirror.

From that vantage point I will: (1) substantiate a definition of racial slavery as a sociogenic rather than a phylogenic phenomenon; (2) show racial oppression introduced as a deliberate ruling-class policy where it was not originally intended; (3) present an example of the casting-off of racial oppression to be superseded by "non-racial," natural human affinity (though in the contexts of a normally class-differentiated society); (4) show how, at a critical moment, when racial oppression might have been displaced, it was renewed by deliberate ruling-class decision; (5) demonstrate historically that racial oppression can be maintained only by a military establishment, except where the oppressor group is in a majority; (6) show how, even after centuries of racial oppression, where the oppressed group is the majority a ruling class can be forced to abandon racial oppression (or face civil war), even though, as in the Irish case, racial oppression may be replaced by national oppression under the same ruling class; (7) supply, incidentally, a definition of the difference between national and racial oppression, in terms of the recruitment of the intermediate buffer social control stratum; (8) show by examples how propertyless classes are recruited into the intermediate stratum, through anomalous "racial" privileges not involving escape from propertylessness; (9) present analogies, relating to the question of racial oppression, between features of continental Anglo-American and United States history and the history of Ireland; and, finally, (10) show the relativity of race by describing how persons, actually the same individuals, or at least persons of the same "gene pool," were first transformed from Irish haters of racial oppression into white-supremacists in America.

The Invention of the White Race

With the conceptual groundwork laid, free of the "White Blindspot," *The Invention of the White Race* turns its attention in Volume Two to the plantation colonies of Anglo-America during the period from the founding of Jamestown in 1607 to the cancellation of the original ban on slavery in the colony of Georgia in 1750. The pivotal events are seen to be Bacon's Rebellion in 1676 and the 1705 revision of the Virginia laws, in particular, the "Act concerning Servants and Slaves." Topics to be considered in Volume Two include: the English background, the origin and peculiarities of England's original colonial labor supply and their implications for the evolution of the bond-labor system in Anglo-America; why the Spanish example could not be followed in regard to the labor force; the consequence of the economic addiction to tobacco – the plantation system, foreclosing the emergence of an intermediate buffer social control stratum; the chattelization of labor; the oppression and resistance of the

bond-laborers – African-Americans and Euro-Americans – together; the
growing interest on the part of the Anglo-American continental plantation
bourgeoisie in reducing African-Americans to lifetime hereditary bond-
servitude; the divided mind of the English law on the enslavability of
Christians; the sharpening class struggle – in the absence of a system of racial
oppression – between the plantation elite on the one hand and on the other the
debt-burdened small planters and the majority of the economically productive
population, the bond-laborers, three-fourths Anglo-, one-fourth African-
American; the dispute over "Indian policy" between "frontier" planters and the
ruling elite; the eruption of the social contradictions in Bacon's Rebellion, in
which the main rebel force came to be made up of Anglo- and African-
American bond-laborers together demanding an end to bond-servitude; the
defeat of the rebels, followed by a period of continued instability of social
control; apprehension of a recurrence of rebellion; the social control problem
in attempting to exploit the newly gained African source of labor by reducing
African-Americans to lifetime hereditary bondage, especially considering the
refuge available for escaping bond-laborers in the mountains at the back of the
colonies, and in a continent beyond; the problem of social control recon-
sidered; the invention of the "white race" – the truly Peculiar Institution – as
the solution to the problem of social control, its failure in the West Indies, its
establishment in the continental plantation colonies, signaled by the enactment
of the "Act concerning Servants and Slaves," which formally instituted the
system of privileges for European-Americans, of even the lowest social status,
vis-à-vis any person of any degree of African ancestry, not only bond-laborers
but free Negroes as well, however possessed of property they might be; the
remolding of male supremacy as white male supremacy, the peculiar American
form of male supremacy, as an essential element of the system of white-skin
privileges; the creation of white male privileges with regard to African-
American women – white male supremacy. Volume Two will take note of the
fact that the revision of the laws in Virginia to codify racial oppression
coincided with the codification of racial oppression in Ireland by the enactment
of the Penal Laws. It will also contain my observations on how the "Ordeal of
Colonial Virginia" gave birth to the Ordeal of America.

VOLUME ONE
Racial Oppression and Social Control

1

The Anatomy of Racial Oppression

However one may choose to define the term "racial", it concerns the historian only as it relates to a pattern of oppression (subordination, subjugation, exploitation) of one set of human beings by another. Orlando Patterson, in his *Slavery and Social Death*, takes "the racial factor to mean the assumption of innate differences based on real or imagined physical or other differences."[1] But, as I have pointed out in the Introduction, such an assumption does not an oppressor make; presumably the objects of racial oppression (however the term is defined) are capable of the same sorts of assumptions. David Brion Davis, explaining slavery in the United States, says, "racial dissimilarity [was] offered as an excuse" for it.[2] That is true enough and consistent with Patterson's definition of "the racial factor." But again, excuses are not an automatic promotion to oppressor; before racial oppression is excused, it must first be imposed and sustained. That is what needs to be explained.

Unfortunately, "racial dissimilarity" in the conventional phenotypical sense proves to be more banana peel than stepping stone. Historically, "racial dissimilarities" have not only been artificially used, they are themselves artificial. In colonial Hispanic America, it was possible for a person, regardless of phenotype (physical appearance), to become "white" by purchasing a royal certificate of "whiteness."[3] With less formality, but equal success, one may move from one "racial category" to another in today's Brazil where, it is said, "money whitens."[4] On the other hand, in the United States the organizing principle of society is that no such "whitening" be recognized – whether "whitening" by genetic variation or by simple wealth. In 1890, a Portuguese emigrant settling in Guyana (British Guiana) would learn that he/she was not "white." But a sibling of that same person arriving in the United States in that same year would learn that by a sea-change he/she had become "white."[5] In the last Spanish census of Cuba, Mexican Indians and Chinese were classified as "white", but in 1907 the first United States census there classed these groups as "colored."[6] According to Virginia law in 1860, a person with but three "white" grandparents was a Negro; in 1907, having no more than fifteen out of sixteen "white" great-great-grandparents entitled one to the same classification; in 1910, the limit was asymptotic: "every person in whom there is ascertainable any Negro blood . . . [was to] be deemed a colored person."[7] As of 1983, the National Center for Health Statistics was effectively following the 1910 Virginia principle by classifying any person as black if either of the parents was black. At the same time, in Texas the "race" classification was determined by the "race" of the father.[8] Prior to 1970, a set of Louisiana court decisions dating back to the late 1700s had upheld the legal concept that "any traceable amount" of African ancestry defined a "Negro." In 1970, "racial" classification became the subject of hard bargaining in the Louisiana state legislature. The Conservatives held out for 1/64, but the "more enlightened" opposition forced a compromise at 1/32 as the requisite proportion of Negro forebears, a principle that was upheld by the state's Supreme Court in 1974.[9]

By considering the notion of "racial oppression" in terms of the substantive, the operative element, namely "oppression," it is possible to avoid the contradictions and howling absurdities that result from attempts to splice genetics and sociology.[10] By examining racial oppression as a particular system of oppression – like gender oppression or class oppression or national oppression – we find firmer footing for analyzing racial slavery and the invention and peculiar function of the "white race," and for confronting the theory that racial oppression can be explained in terms of "phenotype" – the old ace-in-the-hole of racist apologetics. This approach also preserves the basis for a consistent theory of the organic interconnection of racial, class, national, and gender oppression.[11]

The Irish Analogy

To our conditioned minds, the attitude and behavior of Anglo-Americans toward African-Americans and American Indians have the readily recognizable character of racial oppression. But when racial oppression is defined in terms of its operational principles, the exclusion of the Irish case is seen to be wholly arbitrary. The exclusion is especially deplorable when practiced by European-American scholars, because it ignores a case where "white" consciousness on the part of the observer is least likely to affect the drawing of conclusions. A "need to know they were white"[12] cannot possibly serve to explain the attitude of the English toward the Irish. The history of English rule in Ireland, and of the Irish in America, presents instructive parallels and divergences for the understanding of "race" as a sociogenic rather than a phylogenic category; and of racial slavery as a system of social control.

Historians and the Analogy

Even as the nineteenth-century imperialist "scramble for Africa" was unfolding, resonances of English abolitionism and Chartism, and of the great Civil War and Emancipation in America, still thrilled somewhere in the collective consciousness of historians toiling to interpret the past to the present. One such, the distinguished English historian and abolitionist Henry Hallam (1777–1859), pointed out the racist affinity of the Spanish genocide of the Christian Moors and the English oppression of the Irish.[13]

The pre-eminent Anglo-Irish historian William Edward Hartpole Lecky (1838–1903) noted how the people of the English Pale in Ireland came to "look upon the Irish as later colonists looked upon the Red Indians."[14] Or consider the remarkable insight of W. K. Sullivan, Irish historian and President of Queen's College, Cork, who analogized the social role of the non-gentry Protestants in Ireland and the "poor whites" in America.[15] Karl Marx applied the analogy in pursuit of the unity of working people of all countries:

> The ordinary English worker hates the Irish worker . . . [and] in relation to the Irish worker he feels himself a member of the *ruling* nation. . . . His attitude is much the same as that of the "poor whites" to the "niggers".[16]

The most depraved derivation of the analogy was voiced by the English historian Edward A. Freeman (1823–92) during a visit to America in 1881. The United States, he said, "would be a grand land if only every Irishman would kill a negro, and be hanged for it."[17]

World War Two had an obvious effect on consciousness of the analogy among historians concerned with the problem of slavery and racism. They have devoted considerable attention to the attitudes of the English in the Tudor and Stuart periods toward the Irish, as homologues of the general European attitude toward the Indians of the Americas.[18] In his richly documented exposition of the close relation of the images of the Irish and the American Indians and Africans, David Beers Quinn claims that this closeness revealed "what some Englishmen thought about some Irishmen and about Irish society."[19] Historians such as Quinn, Jones, Canny and Muldoon argue effectively that racism among Europeans is not limited to their relations with non-Europeans, but that it can exist in the most extreme form between one European nation, such as England, and another, such as Ireland. To that extent they make a worthy contribution to the analysis of the societies based on lifetime bond-labor in the Americas, and of the Anglo-American continental plantation colonies in particular.

Since their studies center mainly on Elizabethan times, they give no particular attention to the white-supremacism directed particularly against African-Americans that is of central importance for the study of American history. The same circumstance forecloses any close examination and analysis of the parallels between white supremacy in Anglo-America and the religio-racial oppression of the Irish resulting from the Cromwellian English conquest in 1652 and the Penal Laws of the eighteenth-century Protestant Ascendancy. Finally, this limitation of perspective leaves unconsidered the case of the Irish immigrant who, however poor, Catholic and racially oppressed he/she might have been in Ireland, could emerge in Anglo-America as an ordained member of the "white race" along with Anglo- and other European-Americans, with all the privileges, rights and immunities appertaining thereto. This peculiar social transition is instructive in the principle of the relativity of "race." It certainly was a thing not dreamt of in the philosophy of the English planters of Munster.

Some historians accept the parallels so far as the American Indians are concerned, but do so in such a way as to deny their relevance to the white-supremacist oppression of African-Americans. They cite the opinion of certain seventeenth-century Englishmen to the effect that Indians are born "white" and only become "tawny" by prolonged exposure to the elements.[20] Muldoon, for example, taking note of the English way of lumping the Irish and the Indians together as "savages", asserts, "Crucial to this comparison was the belief that Indians were white men . . ."[21]

George M. Frederickson defines "racism" in such a way as to exclude extension of the parallel between Irish and Indians to the African-American. While noting that the English justified their genocidal treatment of the Irish and the American Indians by classing them as "savages," he maintains that this did not involve "a 'racial' concept in the modern sense" because it was "not yet associated with pigmentation."[22]

Nicholas P. Canny, developing the lead provided by David Beers Quinn, documented and analyzed significant parallels in the attitudes taken by the Elizabethan English ruling classes toward the Irish and the American Indians. English executors of American colonial projects, Professor Canny writes, brought "the same indictments against the Indians and later the blacks in the New World that had been brought against the Irish." It was his specific aim "to show how the justification for colonization influenced or reflected English attitudes toward the Gaelic Irish and, by extension, toward the imported slave and the indigenous populations in North America."[23] While Canny does not undertake a treatment of the parallel between the Irish and African-Americans, it is not because he considers it irrelevant. Quite the contrary; he writes: "We find the same indictments being brought against the Indians, and later the blacks, in the New World that had been brought against the Irish."[24]

Michael Hechter makes a special contribution by explicitly challenging, in the context of the same parallel, the dominance of the "phenotype" fixation.

Anglo-Saxons and Celts cannot be differentiated by *color*. Despite this, however, racism came to flower [in Ireland] as well. I think that Americans have come to realize how this is possible by following the recent events in Northern Ireland.[25]

The Analogy as Practice

The chronology of English colonial exploits being what it was, Professor Quinn found that the Irish became the "standard of savage or outlandish" social behavior for interpreting African and American Indian societies.[26] In its sameness with respect to the Irish and to American Indians and African-Americans, this ideology and practice was not concerned with "phenotype," color, etcetera, but rather with the "uncivilized ways" of the victims.[27] Once categorized as "uncivilized," they were regarded by the ruling class as doubtful prospects, at best, for admittance to the "Christian" establishment. Resistance to conquest and the ways of colonial exploitation was interpreted in terms of an incapacity for civilization, and this exclusion from "Christian civilization" served to excuse further oppression.[28]

Walter Devereux (1541–76), the first Earl of Essex, who unsuccessfully attempted to plant an English colony in Ulster in 1573, envisaged Ireland as England's Indies, and he predicted that the English government would soon be forced to restrict emigration to Ireland just as the Spanish imposed restraints "for going to the Indies."[29] Another early English conquistador was Robert Dudley (1532–88), first Earl of Leicester. The Irish were "a barbarous people," said Leicester, and the English should deal with them as other Christian colonizers did with barbarians elsewhere in the world.[30] This theme, repeated with variations, supplied a continuing rationale for English oppression of the Irish.

At the time of the plantation of Ulster launched in 1609, the English appealed to Christian fellowship in urging the Spanish government not to give aid and comfort to the Irish resistance. Addressing the Spanish Lords of Council in Madrid, the English ambassador, Sir Charles Cornwallis, asserted that the Irish were "so savage a people" that they long ago deserved the same treatment "used by the Kings of Spain in the Indies, or those employed with the Moors ... scattering them in other parts."[31]

Nearly two centuries later Dublin-born Edmund Burke, then the pre-eminent British statesman, observed that the English Protestant Ascendancy regarded the Irish "as enemies to God and Man, and indeed, as a race of savages who were a disgrace to human nature."[32]

English practice in Ireland included elements that are counterposed in the experiences of the Indians and of the African-Americans: namely the expropriation of the lands of the former, and the super-exploitation of the labor and the incorporation-without-integration of the latter. In the one case, "Irish land might be confiscated without much more scruple than the land over which the Red Indian roves."[33] In the other, "The poor people of Ireland [in the eighteenth century] are used worse than negroes by their lords and masters, and their deputies of deputies of deputies."[34]

In 1814, the great Irish leader Daniel O'Connell, himself a staunch abolitionist, wishing to express his disappointment with his English Whig friends for lapsing into chauvinism toward the Irish people, chose to base his comment on the same analogy. "I did imagine," he said, "we [Catholic Irish] had ceased to be whitewashed negroes, and had thrown off for them [the Whigs] all traces of the colour of servitude."[35]

The Whig baron Henry Brougham, for all of his avowed abolitionism, found reason to protest in the House of Lords when Robert Tyler and then his father, United States President John Tyler of Virginia, spoke out in favor of repeal of the Union of Britain and Ireland. It was, Brougham said:

> ... as if the Queen of this country, like the President, were to say she had her heart and soul in the cause of the Carolina and Virginia negroes, and that she hoped ere long to see a white republic in the north, and a black republic in the south.[36]

The Hallmark of Racial Oppression

The assault upon the tribal affinities, customs, laws and institutions of the Africans, the American Indians and the Irish by English/British and Anglo-American colonialism reduced all members of the oppressed group to one undifferentiated social status, a status beneath that of any member of any social class within the colonizing population. *This is the hallmark of racial oppression* in its colonial origins, and as it has persisted in subsequent historical contexts.

The African-Americans

Of the bond-laborers who escaped to become leaders of maroon settlements before 1700, four had been kings in Africa. Toussaint L'Ouverture was the son of an African chieftain, as was his general, Henri Christophe, a subsequent ruler of Haiti, who died in 1820.[37] It is notable that the names of these representatives of African chieftaincy have endured only because they successfully revolted and threw off the social death of racial oppression that the European colonizers intended for them. One "Moorish chief," Abdul Rahamah, was sold into bondage in Mississippi early in the nineteenth century.[38] Abou Bekir Sadliki endured thirty years of bondage in Jamaica before being freed from post-Emancipation "apprenticeship" in Jamaica. The daughter of an "Ebo" (Ibo?) king and her daughter Christiana Gibbons were living in Philadelphia in 1833, having been freed from chattel bondage some time earlier by their Georgia mistress.[39] We can never know how many more Africans were stripped of all vestiges of the social distinction they had known in their homelands by a social order predicated upon "the subordination of the servile class to every free white person," however base.[40]

In taking note of the plight of Africans shipped as bond-laborers to Anglo-American plantations and deprived of their very names, Adam Smith in 1759 touched the essence of the matter of racial oppression. "Fortune never exerted more cruelly her empire over mankind," he wrote, "than when she subjected those nations of heroes to the refuse of Europe."[41] A century later the United States Supreme Court affirmed the constitutional principle that any "white" man, however degraded, was the social superior of any African-American, however cultured and independent in means.[42]

This hallmark of racial oppression in the United States was no less tragically apparent even after the abolition of chattel bond-servitude. In 1867, the newly freed African-Americans bespoke the tragic indignation of generations yet to come: "The virtuous aspirations of our children must be continually checked by the knowledge that no matter how upright their conduct, they will be looked upon as less worthy of respect than the lowest wretch on earth who wears a white skin."[43]

The American Indians

In 1831 a delegation of the Cherokee nation went to Washington to appeal first to the Supreme Court and then to President Andrew Jackson to halt the treaty-breaking "Indian Removal" policy, designed to drive them from their ancestral homes. The delegation included men who were not only chosen chiefs of their tribe but had succeeded in farming and commerce to become "Cherokee planter-merchants."[44] Their appeals were rebuffed; President Jackson was well pleased with the decision of the Supreme Court denying the Cherokees legitimacy as an independent tribal entity in relation to the United States.[45]

This was a culmination, as well as a beginning. Proposals made over a period of two decades by church groups and by the Secretary of War for the assimilation of the Indians by intermarriage had been rejected.[46] At the same time, the independent tribal rights of the Indians were challenged by United States "frontier" aggression. As a consequence of this rejection on the one hand and the disallowance of tribal self-existence on the other, the individual American Indian, or whatever degree of social distinction, was increasingly exposed to personal degradation by any "white" person. In 1823, the Cherokee leader John Ridge (son of Major Ridge), a man of considerable wealth, supplied out of his own experience this scornful definition of racial oppression of the Indian:

An Indian ... is frowned upon by the meanest peasant, and the scum of the earth are considered sacred in comparison to the son of nature. If an Indian is educated in the sciences, has a good knowledge of the classics, astronomy, mathematics, moral and natural philosophy, and his conduct equally modest and polite, yet he is an Indian, and the most stupid and illiterate white man will disdain and triumph over this worthy individual. It is disgusting to enter the house of a white man and be stared at full face in inquisitive ignorance.[47]

The Irish

From early in the thirteenth century until their power entered a two-and-a-half-century eclipse in 1315,[48] the English dealt with the contradictions between English law and Irish tribal Brehon law by refusing to recognize the latter, at the same time denying the Irish admittance to the writs and rights of English law.[49]

In 1277, high Irish churchmen, having secured support among powerful tribal chieftains, submitted a petition to the English king Edward I, offering to pay him 8,000 marks in gold over a five-year period for the general enfranchisement of free Irishmen under English law. The king was not himself unwilling to make this grant of English law. But he thought he ought to get more money for it, and so the Irish three years later raised the offer to 10,000 marks.[50]

What was being asked was not the revolutionary reconstitution of society but merely the abandonment of a "racial" distinction among freemen ruled by English law in Ireland. In the end the king left the decision to the Anglo-Norman magnates of Ireland, and they declined to give their assent. Referring to a replay of this issue which occurred some years later, Sir John Davies concluded, "The great [English] Lordes of Ireland had informed the king that the Irishry might not be naturalized, without damage and prejudice either to themselves, or to the Crowne."[51]

Irish resentment and anger found full voice in the wake of the Scots invasion effected in 1315 at the invitation of some Irish tribes. In 1317, Irish chieftains led by Donal O'Neill, king of Tyrone, joined in a Remonstrance to John XXII, Pope to both English and Irish. In that manifesto the Irish charged that the kings of England and the Anglo-Norman "middle nation" had practiced genocide against the Irish, "enacting for the extermination of our race most pernicious laws."[52] The manifesto presented a four-count indictment: (1) Any Englishman could bring an Irishman into court on complaint or charge, but "every Irishman, except prelates, is refused all recourse to the law by the very fact [of being Irish]"; (2) "When . . . some Englishman kills an Irishman . . . no punishment or correction is inflicted;" (3) Irish widows of English men were denied their proper portion of inheritance; and (4) Irish men were denied the right to bequeath property.

Whatever exactly the remonstrants meant by their word "race," their grievances, like those of the African-Americans and the American Indians I have cited, bore the hallmark of racial oppression. From the Petition of 1277 to the Remonstrance of 1317, it was specifically the legal status of the free Irish men, rather than the unfree, which was at issue.

> The really peculiar feature about the situation in Ireland is that the free Irishman who had not been admitted to English law was, as far as the royal courts were concerned, in much the same position as the betagh [the Irish laborer bound to the land].[53]

From Analogy to Analysis: Colony versus Tribe

In each of these historical instances, a society organized on the basis of the segmentation of land and other natural resources under private, heritable individual titles, and having a corresponding set of laws and customs, acting under the direction of its ruling class brings under its colonial authority people of societies organized on principles of collective, tribal tenure of land and other natural resources, and having their respective corresponding sets of laws and customs.[54] In each of these confrontations of incompatible principles, the colonizing power institutes a system of rule of a special character: designed to deny, disregard and delegitimate the hierarchical social – tribal, kinship – distinctions previously existing among the people brought under colonial rule. The members of the subjugated group, stripped of their tribal and kinship identity, are rendered institutionally naked to their enemies, completely deprived of the shield of social identity and the corresponding self-protective forms of the tribal and kinship associations that were formerly theirs. Although not all are to be made slaves of the colonizing power, the object is social death for the subjugated group as a whole, whether individually and in groups they are forcibly torn from their home country to serve abroad among strangers, or they are made strangers in their own native land.[55] They are "desocialized by the brutal rupture of the relations which characterize the social person," the tribal, kinship and even the unit family relationships that constituted their social identity. They are to be allowed only one social tie, that which "attache[s] them unilaterally to" the colonizing power.[56]

Once the conquest is complete, the "clash of cultures" takes on the flesh-and-blood form of a host of colonists with newly acquired property claims.[57] These interests, and their concomitant social and legal attributes, once more bar the subject people from admittance to the common law of the colonizing power, although tribal and kinship-group law and custom have been over-thrown.

The social death of the subjugated people is followed by social resurrection in new forms from which they take up the task of overthrowing racial oppression. In some cases, the ruling power is able to maintain its dominance only by co-opting a stratum of the subject population into the system of social control. In thus officially establishing a social distinction among the oppressed, the colonial power transforms its system of social control from racial oppression to national oppression. In the nineteenth century, the Haitian Revolution represented the failure of this colonial policy of co-optation; British policy in the West Indies, and the policy of Union with Britain and Catholic Emancipation in Ireland, represented its success. On the other hand, in continental Anglo-America and in the Union of South Africa, the colonial power succeeded in stabilizing its rule on the foundation of racial oppression.

The assault on tribal relations among Africans

The English and other Europeans, and in time European-Americans, first came to Africa as traders and raiders, not as colonists. The colonial option was not theirs, since the people of subequatorial Africa, universally organized as tribal societies made up of kinship groups, were then too strong and independent to allow the seaborne Europeans any other course.[58] For that reason the inherent contradiction of the tribal relations of the African peoples and the European relations based on individual ownership of land and other natural resources remained a latent factor offering no serious obstacle to the development of the enterprises characteristic of that period of the history of that region.[59]

But upon those millions, mainly from West Africa and Angola, who were transported as captive bondmen and bondwomen to the plantation Americas, the clash of cultures was visited with the abruptness of a thunderclap, undiminished by time, and with the harsh and stifling cruelty of exile in chains. In America the colonial employers made "detribalization" a deliberate part of the "seasoning" process undergone by all newly arriving bond-laborers.[60] Colonial authorities made it a matter of policy to frustrate bond-labor rebelliousness by segregating laborers of the same language or other affinity groups from each other. The Coromantees and the Ashanti were particularly feared, it was said.[61]

The acquisition of African bond-laborers for American plantation colonies was made exclusively by capture and abduction. The consequent destruction of their family ties was unaccompanied by the gloss of Christian preachments on the "heathenism" of kinship group and marriage customs, such as were directed at the Irish and the American Indians.

The assault on American Indian tribal relationships

Whilst United States policy very early showed a disregard for the rights of Indian tribes, the avowed determination to destroy Indian tribal relations did not become the dominant theme until after the Civil War. Prior to that time, "Indian policy" moved in a three-phase cycle – massive treaty-breaking incursions by Americans on Indian lands; war; and then another "treaty" involving "cessions" of Indian lands – systematically repeated, until finally the Indians had been "ceded" into the confines of "reservations."[62]

The direct assault on tribal relations had been anticipated by half a century; in 1830 the Georgia state legislature nullified Indian tribal laws within the state's boundaries. This legislation was condemned by its critics as an attack against "the entire social existence of the [Cherokee] tribe." The exiling of thousands of the Cherokee people over the Trail of Tears in 1838 was justified on the grounds that "Common property and civilization cannot coexist."[63] In 1854 (the year of the passage of the Kansas–Nebraska "squatter sovereignty" law) the Omaha Indians "ceded" 10,000,000 acres of land to the United States in a "treaty" which, for the first time, provided for the breaking up of the tribe's remaining lands into individual allotments.[64] The treaty was hailed as giving hope that soon all Indian lands would be "thrown open to the Anglo-Saxon plough."[65]

To the extent that they were consulted in the matter, the Indians over-whelmingly rejected the "severalty" (individual ownership) option for cancel-ling tribal land rights. If, in the end, their wishes were ignored, it was not because the Indian point of view was not understood. As the ethnologist J. W. Powell of the Smithsonian Institution informed the United States Congress:

> In Indian tribes individual or personal rights and clan rights are very carefully differentiated. The right to the soil, with many other rights, inheres in the clan. Indian morality consists chiefly in the recognition of clan rights; and crime in Indian society chiefly consists in the violation of these clan rights. In Indian society the greatest crime is the claim of an individual to land, and it is also a heinous sin against religion.[66]

"Citizenship," he concluded, "is incompatible with kinship society."

By 1859, a general assault on tribal ownership of land was under way, which would become the central feature of United States "Indian policy" and its "civilizing mission." The legislative culmination of that assault came with Congressional passage in 1887 of the Dawes General Allotment Act. Its purpose and rationale were articulated with drumfire consistency and remark-able clarity. In his 1859 annual report to Congress, US Indian Affairs Commissioner Charles E. Mix advocated converting reservation lands to individual allotments. Indian "possession of large bodies of land in common" was the root of what Mix saw as "habits of indolence and profligacy."[67] A Congressman cited Mix's report in arguing that "the first step to be taken" in the execution of Indian policy was in "uprooting the community of property system [and] . . . extinguishing or modifying the tribal relation."[68] In the course of the 1866 debate on relations with the Sioux, Representative Burleigh of Dakota recalled that, as United States Indian Agent there in 1862, he "did advocate the removal of the [Sioux] women and children with a view to wiping out the tribe."[69]

While the Paris Commune was yet within living memory, in the era of Haymarket and the robber barons,[70] the destruction of tribal relations was polemically associated with the threat of socialism and communism. In the year the Second Socialist International was formed, Indian Commissioner T. J. Morgan showed, more than most socialists did, an instinctual grasp of the vital link between white supremacy and anti-socialism. "The Indians," Morgan said, "must conform to 'the white man's ways,' peaceably if they will, forcibly if they must. The tribal relations should be broken up, socialism destroyed and the family and the autonomy of the individual substituted." The year before, Commissioner Oberly had pointed out the great moral gulf fixed between the two societies. He condemned "the degrading communism" of Indian tribal ownership, where "neither can say of all the acres of the tribe, 'This is mine.'" With the allotment to individuals of Indian tribal lands, he theorized, the Indian would be able to emulate "the exalting egotism of American civilization, so that he will say 'I' instead of 'We,' and 'This is mine,' instead of 'This is ours.'" If the Indians rejected this tutelage, he concluded, it should be forced on them, as it were, for their own good.[71]

The assault on Irish tribal relationships

The conflict between colonizing powers, on the one hand, and African and American Indian societies, on the other, is a familiar story (however distorted); indeed, it is still not completely played out. Not so with Irish tribal society, which was finally and completely destroyed even as the first English settlers were setting foot outside Europe. For that reason, and because everything that is "white" in our historiography instinctively rejects the notion of an affinity of non-European and Irish tribal societies, it seems necessary to treat the Irish case in somewhat greater detail.[72]

In ancient Ireland, that is, up to the invasion of the Norsemen in the middle of the ninth century, "The legal and political unit ... was the *tuath*, ruled by the tribal king," writes D. A. Binchy, "and though the number of tribes tended to vary with the vicissitudes of Irish and political history, it never fell below one hundred."[73] The *tuath*, though tribal,[74] that is, a kinship society, was characterized by a highly developed class differentiation, originating perhaps in the differential disposition of spoils from inter-tribal raids and wars, and in adventitious turns of fortune. However class differentiation began, it represented a contradiction within tribal society. The general evolutionary course of Irish tribal life, as it was at the time of the Anglo-Norman invasion in 1169, appears to have been shaped by this internal contradiction along the following lines: (1) there was a predominant tendency toward downward social mobility;[75] (2) although only a small proportion of the land was held as private property by generations of individual chieftain families,[76] a much larger proportion of the cattle, the main form of wealth, was owned by these nobles (*flaiths*) and by cattle-lords (*boaires*);[77] (3) these chiefs were able to "leverage" (as we might say today) certain factors, such as relative over-population[78] and the recruitment of laborers and tenants (*fuidirs*) from "kin-wrecked" remnants of broken tribes, in a way that enhanced the social power of the chieftain class relative to the generality of tribe members;[79] (4) increasing numbers of tribe members, from the lower category of tenant and share-herder (the *daer-chele*) on down were very poor and dependent,[80] and increasingly reduced to the serflike status of the *sen-cleithe*, who made up the common labor class known to the Anglo-Normans as the *betagh*.[81]

This process of class differentiation took place within the matrix of tribal kinship relationships, the basic social unit of which was the *fine*, more particularly the *derbfine*.[82] Each *derbfine* was made up of all the males patrilineally descended from the same great-grandfather. The *derbfine* was the most basic form of the *fine*; although the latter term is given a wide-ranging application, it always signifies "kinship group." The *fine*, more particularly the *derbfine*, was the radial center of the obligations and loyalties of the individual tribe members, and the sanctuary of that member's rights.

Each *derbfine* occupied its land by assignment from the tribal authority. Upon the death of the great-grandfather there would be, let us say, four surviving grandfathers (his sons). Each of these, then, would be the peak of a new *derbfine*, and usually its chosen chief. Or, at the other extreme, the appearance of a new generation, being a fresh set of great-grandsons, would create, let us say, four new or immanent *derbfines*. Consequently, at regular intervals a redistribution of the lands of the old *fine* was necessary, according to the prescribed schedule of apportionment. (The same schedule governed the distribution of the *derbfine*'s share of booty from cattle raids, and of the lands and property of any deceased member of the *derbfine*.)

The tribal form circumscribed and inhibited the process of class differentiation. For instance, since the *derbfine* was collectively responsible for default by any of its members, no member could become a "free" client of a lord belonging to another *derbfine*, without the collective consent of the *derbfine* as a whole. Likewise, the chief of the *derbfine* could not enter into any external contract without the consent of the entire *derbfine*. Or again, in the exceptional case of the individual acquisition of land by means other than through *derbfine* distribution, the land could not be sold by its acquirer without the consent of the full membership of the *derbfine* – an unlikely prospect. Nor could an individual member of the *derbfine* dispose of his inherited land without the consent of the full membership of the *derbfine*. In general, to the maximum possible extent trade or contract relations were to be entered into only with fellow *derbfine* members. In a society in which the members of the noble (chieftain) class derived their main support from the contracted services of share-herders, such tribal principles obviously would present barriers to class differentiation.[83]

A small proportion of the land was possessed and passed down from generation to generation by chieftains and by certain professional families (families of historians, poets, judges, artisans, physicians). But the vast majority of the land belonged to the tribe as a whole, and not to any individual.

Out of the tribal lands, arable land was assigned by the tribal council to the respective kinship groups as their own, to be used and periodically redistributed among their members as described above. The largest part of the land (which later appeared in the records as "waste, woods, bog, and mountain land") was common land, open without artificial or legal barrier for the free use of all members of the tribe, according to established practices, for grazing cattle, finding fuel, hunting, and whatever other advantages it might offer.[84]

The general tendency of the development of the contradiction between the tribal principles and class differentiation, along the lines noted above, culminated in the emergence of a handful of chieftains, who not only dominated their respective *tuaths* but also subordinated weaker tribes simply by *force majeure*. The eleventh and twelfth centuries, up to the coming of the Anglo-Normans, were consumed by this internecine struggle of these over-kings, some of whom aspired to the eminence of high king (*ard-ri*) over all Ireland.

To what extent – if any – did the emergence of provincial tribal powers and their struggles for dominance affect the basic tribal constitution of Irish society? Was history working its purpose out and "a race evolving its monarchy" so far toward a European-style Irish feudal order that "[t]ribes had ceased to exist ... the Brehon law did not check kings; the tribal control had ceased; old rules and customs were inapplicable to the new order of things"?[85] Was this century and a half of ceaseless war and destruction preparing Ireland to "join Europe" under Anglo-Norman and papal sponsorship?[86] Or did "The structure of [Irish] society ... [retain] a recognizable identity throughout the first half of Irish history, up to the coming of the Normans,"[87] despite this bloody epoch of "centralization" by battle-axe? Was Otway-Ruthren's verdict still correct?

> ... the structure of Celtic society differed far more widely from the general continental pattern than had that of Anglo-Saxon England [at the time of the Norman Conquest], while by the later twelfth century the new Anglo-Norman society was setting on lines which had been so marked a feature of the Norman conquest of Wales and Italy.[88]

If we are to grant political economy its dominion, at the root of the question lies the fact that whereas the English economy was based mainly on land cultivation, the Irish economy was primarily based on cattle-herding.

England's Domesday Book, compiled about 1086 to estimate the national wealth for royal tax purposes, was essentially a survey of cultivable landholdings and resources for their cultivation. A century later in Gaelic Ireland, hides, wool and meat were still the essentials of commerce, and animals and animal products supplied the staples of everyday existence.[89] The main demands of the English Peasant Revolt of 1381 were for an end to the serf's bondage to the land, and for the limiting of rent to four pence per acre. (See Volume Two.) The main problem of the Irish tenant (client) family (along with just surviving the perils of the depopulating random wars) was that of keeping up with the annual rent on the cattle advanced on loan by the chief, which was to be paid back out of the increase and produce of their cattle.[90]

The difference between herding and tillage produced a corresponding variation in the manner of holding and distributing land. Herds vary in extent within very elastic limits, according to their rate of natural increase. They are not fixed in one place, except by the daily care of the herders. Otherwise they rove over the land, no respecters of plot markers, guided by their own feeding and sheltering instincts, their scope limited only by seasonal changes, natural variations of terrain, and grass yield. The net product is measured in terms of the natural increase and produce of the herd. Land, by contrast, is a limited, specific, fixed portion of the earth's surface. For cultivation purposes, it lends itself to parcelling on virtually permanent lines, and to the exclusive use of the parcels by individual production units, where some enforceable advantage is seen in it, according to the differential rent – the marginal yield per unit of labor per measured unit of land.

In Gaelic Ireland, whatever the form of landholding, an individual could not own a large tract of land "in the same sense that he might own a knife or a spade ... [L]ordship of the land belonged to the political rather than the economic order of ideas. It implied authority rather than ownership."[91] Under English (Anglo-Norman) law every inch of land was either held directly by the king or held in fee from the king by private individuals.[92] The colonizers coming from England

> ... believed that they were acquiring a rigid, complete and perpetual ownership of the "land" from the zenith to the uttermost depths – an ownership more complete than that of any chattel – an ownership which they imagined to be self-existing even when the person in whom it should be "vested" was unknown or unascertained. They called this sort of ownership an "estate," i.e., a status, something that stood of its own virtue.[93]

Out of this basic divergence arose a set of superstructural dissonances with regard to principles of marriage and family, post-mortem reversion of property, succession as chief or king, and the conduct of war, to say nothing of other lifestyle and cultural values.[94] There were two conflicting rules of inheritance: gavelkind (an English word adapted for a much different Irish custom) and English primogeniture; two laws of succession: the Irish "tanistry" and the English royal primogeniture; two marriage forms: polygyny for men of the Irish noble classes, and the formally strict but strictly formal monogamy of the English man; two concepts of criminal justice: the adjudication of compensatory liability for particular individual damages, as determined by Irish judges, known as Brehons; and the English public law of offenses against "the king's peace"; and two styles of war: Irish cattle-raiding and tribal political alliances, but non-interference in internal affairs,[95] in contrast to the English territorial conquest and possession under new, presumably permanent sovereignty and land title.

Under the custom of Irish gavelkind, a deceased man's partible wealth – most notably his cattle and assigned cultivable land – was distributed among the surviving men of his particular kinship group, numbering perhaps four to the fourth power,[96] according to a prescribed order of apportionment up and down the generation ladder. Brotherless daughters had restricted rights of inheritance.[97] By English feudal, and later bourgeois, law, the firstborn son was the sole heir, and in the case of "a failure in the male line" the inheritance belonged to the widow, or to the daughters equally. Upon the subsequent marriage of such a female heir, her "estate" became the husband's.

Upon the death of an Irish king or tribal chief, his wealth was disposed of by gavelkind in the same way as that of any other man so summoned. His successor in office was chosen from the ranks of the most influential kinship group, by election of all the enfranchised members of the tribe. This man also succeeded to the perquisites of office, including free entertainment as he travelled the territory, and the use of mesne land cultivated by "base clients" or bond-laborers. In England, at least from the thirteenth century onward, whenever succession to the throne was orderly it was by the rule of primogeniture, and carried with it, of course, private ownership of royal property.

A man of an Irish tribe typically sought to have a large number of sons to add to the strength of his *fine* as a part of his tribe.[98] To that end, the man of sufficient wealth might have a plurality of wives. "Irish law, even in the Christian period," Binchy writes, "extends a limited recognition to other types of union [other than the one with the *cetmuinter*, the "head wife"] of varying degrees of social standing (*lanamnas*), which are neither permanent nor monogamous."[99] The sons of each wife enjoyed equal social standing. The exception was the son of a slave woman, who was barred from inheriting not because the union was any less legitimate than any other, but because the slave was not a member of the kinship group.[100]

The feudal order that the Anglo-Normans brought to Ireland was conceived of as a pyramid of authority and obligation radiating from the king down through various grades of lordship and vassalage, and based on the principle that every rood of ground was privately owned, whether the owner be the king himself or a holder "in fee" from the king. Great lords then let out their lands to lesser lords, and ultimately to the laboring people of various degrees. Given this pyramid of power, the benefits (then as now) were apt to be greater as one rose in the scale of power. Under the terms of the "fee," the land was held "in perpetuity," to be passed undiminished from generation to generation and, more particularly, from eldest son to eldest son. This principle was intended to promote and preserve the stability of the pyramid of authority, which it was thought would be weakened by the division of the land among several heirs. And when a father or other male guardian was negotiating an alliance by the marriage of a prospective heir, a son or a brotherless daughter, there was advantage in brokering for a whole inheritance rather than by fractions of it. Thus entrenched, the principle of primogeniture produced by logical extension the extreme feudal cult of bridal virginity, the chastity-belt mentality, and the illegitimizing of "bastards" in order to assure the integrity of the inheritance.

The contrasting English and Irish laws of inheritance appear to be at the root of one of the most remarkable of the ineluctable contradictions between the two social systems. Under English law, children of wealthy fathers were hostages to their inheritances.[101] The eldest son was the heir; a younger son might move into that position by the death of an elder brother; daughters were to be assigned "marriage portions." Orphan children of the wealthy classes were assigned as "wards" of male "guardians" who exercised the legal authority of parents over them, including the privilege of disposing in marriage of the orphans along with their inheritances or "portions." Where estates of the greatest extent were involved, the marriage engagement of orphans became a source of enrichment for monarchs, at first, and then of the members of a Court of Wards. Whatever the circumstance, it was an essential principle of estate management to preserve a male heir and the virginity of daughters. Consequently, the closest supervision over the children was enforced by the father or the guardian who had the disposal of the estate and the marriage portions. It would have been unthinkable for an English lord to give complete custody of his children to another lord, to be reared and educated from the age of seven until the girls reached the age of fourteen and the boys seventeen.

But in Ireland just such a system of fosterage (called by the English "gossipred") was practiced.[102] For all its formal resemblance to hostage-giving,[103] it was something quite different; it bound rich families to each other in strong fraternal relations. The foster children were cared for with such affection and concern that the foster family ties became as close as those within their own respective families. But whatever might by accident befall the foster child, the disposition of the inheritance among the father's kinship group would not otherwise be affected.

Except for high political offenses such as treason, crimes under the laws of Celtic Ireland were treated as private, personal grievances, indeed like civil suits. The aim was to provide satisfaction for the aggrieved party, and thereby to prevent resort to vengeance. What was denied to the victims, the state did not arrogate to itself. There was, therefore, no capital punishment,[104] no jail, no sheriff, no special instrument of punishment touching life or limb. Complaints originated exclusively with the suit of the aggrieved party, who if successful was awarded reparations assessed by the Brehon. If the guilty party defaulted, his kinship group was liable. English law, by contrast, was aimed at maintaining "the king's peace." Crimes against individuals were breaches of that peace, and subject to public prosecution under public law. Having assumed the role of aggrieved party, the English state, "the crown," substituted public vengeance for private vengeance, and imposed it by means of chains, stocks and prisons, but most commonly the gibbet. In appropriate cases the estate of the guilty party was also subject to heavy fines or escheat to the crown.

Four and a half centuries of coexistence of Gaels with the foreigners, from Henry II to Henry VIII, added force to the transforming effect on the tribal system of the internal contradiction of developing class differentiation. Yet there remained at the end a residue of deep-rooted conflicts between the constitutional principles of the Gaelic and English systems: (1) corporate ownership of land by agnatic descent groups (the *derbfines*) as against individual ownership with testamentary rights; (2) tanistry and election against primogeniture in choosing kings; (3) crimes as torts, and collective liability, in contrast to private liability, the concept of "crown" against the individual for breach of "the king's peace"; (4) inheritance by gavelkind as against primogeniture.

There can be no doubt that the constitutional differences of the Celtic Irish and the English social orders were regarded by the English as a fundamental barrier to colonization. The need for English colonialism to destroy Irish tribal forms and ways was analyzed by Sir John Davies (1569–1626) in his *A Discovery of the True Causes why Ireland was never entirely Subdued ...*, written in 1612.[105] Davies's career uniquely qualified him to observe the course of English interests in Ireland, as he had already served King James I there as Solicitor-General for three years (1603–1606), and then as Attorney-General. He made a thorough research of the records of all reigns from the Anglo-Norman invasion of Ireland in 1169 to the Plantation of Ulster in 1609. In the course of his study he presented the case against the laws and customs of the Irish tribes, which in the English fashion he called "septs."

Tribal customs, Davies said, necessarily tended to cause the Irish to be "Rebelles to all good Government," to "destroy the commonwealth wherein they live, and bring Barbarisme and desolation upon the richest and most fruitfull Land of the world."[106] Unlike "well-governed Kingdomes and Commonweals," Ireland lacked the death penalty, and consequently the strong might freely prey upon the weak.[107] Tanistry made for unstable government because chieftaincy was not a hereditary estate, and election was to the "strong hand."[108] Gavelkind, made more ruinous by the equal standing of "bastards," was the root cause of the "barbarous and desolate" condition of the country. It fragmented estates and made titles transitory, impoverishing the nobility, who nevertheless would not engage in trade or mechanical arts.[109] It was all of a piece with the Irish family form, with its "common repudiation of their wives," the "promiscuous generation of children," and the "neglect of lawful matrimony."[110] The solidarity of the kinship groups, doubly reinforced by the close-as-blood affinities of fosterage, had made it impossible, Davies said, for English authorities to prosecute Irish malefactors.[111]

But as experience in Scotland and Wales would show, and as Davies himself pointed out, such a clash of systems did not make racial oppression the only option. The papal assignment of "lordship" over Ireland to the English in about 1155 did not envisage any such a socio-political monstrosity as racial oppression, but merely the imposition of conformity in Christian practices.[112] For their part, the Anglo-Normans under kings Henry II and John were prepared to proceed in Ireland as they had in Scotland. There they had supplanted tribal organization with feudal power vested in the Scottish chieftains Malcolm Canmore and David I in the late eleventh and the early twelfth centuries.[113] In such proceedings, intermarriage linking families of the respective upper classes was a normal, indeed essential, part of the process. So it began in Ireland. The first of the Anglo-Norman arrivers, Richard Fitzgilbert (Strongbow) de Clare, agreed in 1169 to assist an Irish king, Diarmuit Macmurchada, to regain the domains from which he had been driven by rival Irish chieftains, but only on condition that Strongbow take Macmurchada's daughter in marriage. In 1180 Hugh de Lacy, then chief bearer of King Henry's authority in Ireland, married the daughter of another Irish king, Ruaidri Ua Conchobair. In both cases King Henry reacted with suspicion, sensing a threat to his authority in Strongbow and de Lacy thus independently becoming heirs to Irish lands.[114] Both the marriages and the king's suspicions were rooted in recognition of the legitimacy, in Anglo-Norman terms, of class distinctions among the Gaelic Irish. For the first fifty years of the Anglo-Norman incursion, the English government under three successive kings held to this policy of "assimilating [Gaelic] Irish local government to the system prevailing in England," even though, as I have suggested, it seemed to be learning that this clash of social orders was perhaps more profound than that which the Normans had faced when they invaded England a century before.[115]

Why then was the tested Scottish policy of overlordship abandoned in favor of an attempt to rule in Ireland by racial oppression? Sir John Davies, looking back, ascribed the decision to power jealousy on the part of the Anglo-Norman lords toward any rivalry for royal favor that might evolve among native Irish.[116] A recent study suggests a more particular, that is, economic, basis for the case against the Anglo-Norman lords, along the following lines.[117]

The change of policy began with the death of the English king, John, in 1216, followed by the installation of the Anglo-Norman triumvirate – William Marshal, Geoffrey de Marisco and Archbishop Henry "of London" – in charge of Irish affairs. By that time European grain prices had been rising sharply for fifty years to a level which remained high throughout the thirteenth century.[118] The merchant-connected palatinate Anglo-Norman lords, headed by the aggressive triumvirate, reacted to the prospects for profit to be made by a change from herding to tillage by becoming impatient with the slow-moving, more civil policy of converting the Irish to European ways. William Marshal himself was one of those who profited by switching the land he seized from herding to tillage, and his labor supply from Irish herders to English tillers.[119] We may well believe that such motives were a sharp spur to the abandonment of the policy of assimilation and to the turn to the abortive but historically instructive first attempt to impose racial oppression in Ireland.

How well, if at all, this economic determinist thesis will stand the test of focused research must be left to Irish scholars to decide. That the change was being made with regard to priests was evident by 1220. In June of that year, Pope Honorius III replaced his papal legate in Ireland, Henry of London, for complicity in an English decree "that no Irish cleric, no matter how educated or reputable, is to be admitted to any ecclesiastical dignity."[120] Whatever the explanation – Anglo-Norman power jealousy or high grain prices or a combination of these, and/or possibly still other factors – a pope is our witness that this turn to racial oppression was made by deliberate ruling-class decree, rather than by compulsive fulfillment of some gene-ordained "need to know they were English."

Compelling Parallels

Given the common constitutional principles of the three cases – the Irish, the American Indian, and the African-American – the abundant parallels they present are more than suggestive; they constitute a compelling argument for the sociogenic theory of racial oppression.[121]

If from the beginning of the eighteenth century in Anglo-America the term "negro" meant slave, except when explicitly modified by the word "free,"[122] so under English law the term "hibernicus," Latin for "Irishman," was the legal term for "unfree."[123] If African-Americans were obliged to guard closely any document they might have attesting their freedom, so in Ireland, at the beginning of the fourteenth century, letters patent, attesting to a person's Englishness, were cherished by those who might fall under suspicion of trying to "pass."[124] If under Anglo-American slavery "the rape of a female slave was not a crime, but a mere trespass on the master's property,"[125] so in 1278 two Anglo-Normans brought into court and charged with raping Margaret O'Rorke were found not guilty because "the said Margaret is an Irishwoman."[126] If a law enacted in Virginia in 1723 provided that "manslaughter of a slave is not punishable,"[127] so under Anglo-Norman law it sufficed for acquittal to show that the victim in a killing was Irish.[128] Anglo-Norman priests granted absolution on the grounds that it was "no more sin to kill an Irishman than a dog or any other brute."[129] If the Georgia Supreme Court ruled in 1851 that "the killing of a negro" was not a felony, but upheld an award of damages to the owner of an African-American bond-laborer murdered by another "white" man,[130] so an English court freed Robert Walsh, an Anglo-Norman charged with killing John Mac Gilmore, because the victim was "a mere Irishman and not of free blood," it being stipulated that "when the master of the said John shall ask damages for the slaying, he [Walsh] will be ready to answer him as the law may require."[131] If in 1884 the United States Supreme Court, citing much precedent authority, including the Dred Scott decision, declared that Indians were legally like immigrants, and therefore not citizens except by process of individual naturalization,[132] so for more than four centuries, until 1613, the Irish were regarded by English law as foreigners in their own land. If the testimony of even free African-Americans was inadmissible,[133] so in Anglo-Norman Ireland native Irish of the free classes were deprived of legal defense against English abuse because they were not "admitted to English law," and hence had no rights that an Englishman was bound to respect.

A minor proportion of the Irish were enfranchised in that two-thirds to three-fourths of Ireland where English law prevailed at the height of the Anglo-Norman era.[134] Members of five noble Irish families were granted procedural standing in English courts. Designated the "Five Bloods," they were the O'Neills of Ulster, the O'Connors of Connaught, the O'Melaglins of Meath, the O'Briens of Munster and the M'Murroughs of Leinster.[135] The inclusion of the M'Murroughs and the O'Connors in this list suggests that these exceptions were made, in part at least, to protect land titles and ancillary rights deriving from some of the previously mentioned early intermarriages between Irish and English. Just as in Jamaica centuries later individual free "persons of color" might be enfranchised by "private bills" approved by the colonial authorities, just as prospering individuals of African or Indian descent in colonial Spanish-America could buy royal certificates of "whiteness,"[136] so in the thirteenth century individual free Irishmen might occasionally purchase admission to English law. However, in the three years when this form of enfranchisement was most used, only twenty-six Irish were enrolled. Whilst the number enfranchised is said to have been greater than the number formally enrolled in that status, the generality of the free Irish remained outside its protection.[137] However, unlike the Jamaica and Spanish-America instances, events in Ireland aborted the initial possibility of the emergence of an Irish buffer social control stratum for the English.

The Persistence of Racial Oppression – by Policy Decision

The renewal of English efforts to reduce Ireland to its control in the latter part of the sixteenth century coincided with the full and final commitment of England to the Reformation.[138] Since the twelfth century the English had operated in Ireland under papal authorization; now that benign relationship came quickly to an end, emphasized by continual English Crown expropriations of Church property in Ireland. Not only was Ireland made the object of a more aggressive English colonial expansionism, it became a particular focus of the rivalry between Protestant England and Catholic Spain, then England's chief colonial competitor. In this historical context the Protestant Reformation worked its purpose out by recasting anti-Irish racism in a deeper and more enduring mold. What had fed primarily on simple xenophobia now, as religio-racism, drank at eternal springs of private feelings about "man and God." The historian and member of the British House of Commons Thomas Babington Macaulay would say that the Reformation "brought new divisions to embitter the old ... a new line of demarcation was drawn; theological antipathies were added to the previous differences, and revived the dying animosities of race."[139]

For more than two centuries, Anglo-Irish and native Irish over almost all of Ireland had coexisted in a "nonracial" symbiosis. But now increasing English colonial expansionism and desperate Irish resistance culminated in the nine-year Tyrone War, 1594–1603, over the issue of the very existence of Celtic society. The spiral of history had come full circle. "The issue in the Nine Years War," writes Sean O'Domhnaill, "was knit as never before in any war in Ireland since the days of Edward Bruce." It was not merely a matter of the English "breaking the great lords"; in so doing they had "to subjugate the Irish people."[140] "Neither the Irish nobles nor their followers," writes O'Domhnaill, "wanted innovations in religion, or laws which were not of their own making, or a centralised system of government based on a kingship which had its origin and being in another country."[141] This supreme historic effort of Celtic Ireland by its forces alone to throw off English colonialism ended in defeat.

Before, Irish chieftains had retained sufficient initiative to strengthen their tribal authority by the opportune exploitation of relationships with the English (or with the Spanish). But their social base remained the tribe, with its basic principles of landholding, inheritance and succession.[142] In the decades of "the king's peace" that followed the Tyrone War, however, the English social order in Ireland demonstrated the advantages it held for economic survival and advancement in the context of the emergent modern capitalist commodity production system. The English landlord system was more profitable for the exploitation of Irish tenants and laborers than the Irish tribal system. It was a period of economic undermining of the Celtic system, marked by steady English pressure in the form of "plantation" projects, and by a degree of assimilation of the Irish chieftains into the English system through leasing and mortgaging.[143] It would seem that such erosive factors account in part for the fact that when Irish rebellion was renewed in 1641, rather than being an independent Gaelic struggle it became a subordinate component of the Royalist side in the War of the Three Kingdoms, which grew out of the English Civil War of Crown and Parliament.

Besides the Celtic Catholic Irish, there were the "Old English" Catholics, descended mainly from pre-seventeenth-century settlers. Although they used Gaelic extensively, rather than English, as their everyday language, they sought to assure Protestant English authorities of their loyalty to the mother country and their abhorrence of the ways of the native Irish.[144] Even so, they were stigmatized and penalized as "recusants" for refusing to abandon the faith of their fathers. In 1628 Charles I, hard pressed by the sea of troubles that would eventually topple his throne, sought to raise money by selling certain concessions, called Graces, to the Catholic Anglo-Irish. These dispensations were to include: security of the land titles of Catholics in possession for sixty years or more; permission for Catholic lawyers to represent clients before the courts; and an easing of the pressure to conform to Protestant forms of worship. In return, Anglo-Irish Catholics fulfilled an undertaking to provide the king with £120,000 sterling in three annual installments. But within a few years the king, having spent the money, lost all interest in giving the Graces the promised force of law.

The royal repudiation of the Graces was the culmination of a long train of slights, disabilities and confiscations endured by the Catholic Old English under Protestant English monarchs and the Church of England. Yet despite Charles's bad faith, when the choice was to be made between an Anglican king and Establishment and various kinds of no-bishop Puritans, the Catholic Anglo-Irish became involved for some period and to some extent on the losing royal side in alliance with the native Irish.

The Irish phase of the War of the Three Kingdoms ended in 1652 with complete English Parliamentary victory and conquest. The terms of the English Act of Settlement of 1652 and the Act of Satisfaction of the following year[145] resounded in Celtic Ireland like clods on a coffin lid. Irish rebellion having become fatally involved in the English Civil War, the complete extirpation of Celtic society was made an integral part of the settlement imposed by the Parliamentary Party even though its members might engage in the most bitter polemics over aspects of its implementation. In 1655 a pamphlet by Vincent Gookin, a Cromwellian adviser and functionary in Ireland, called for a tempering of the wholesale uprooting of the Irish under the English "transplantation" policy as set down in the 1652 Act of Settlement.[146] Colonel Richard Lawrence, a member of the parliamentary commission charged with carrying out the transplantation policy, was a Cromwellian settler in Ireland and a leading spokesman for the military party in regard to Irish affairs. Apparently offended by what he considered Gookin's unwarranted interference with his execution of his duties, Lawrence charged Gookin with launching "poisoned arrows against authority ... intended to wound and weaken the English government [in Ireland]."[147] But on the matter of completing the destruction of the Irish tribes, he and Gookin were as one. The Irish, Gookin said, must above all be prevented from "knitting again like

Worms, their divided septs and amities." Lawrence declared that the first requirement of a successful Irish policy was to:

> break or (at le[a]st) much weaken and limit that great spreading interest of the Irish, (viz.) their spreading Septs, which have been hetherto the very seed spots and nurseries of all factions and Rebellions, and (withal) the preservers of all their old Heathenish, wicked Customs and Habits, which are like the Humane, Jewish and Popish Traditions (though generally of a more wicked nature and tendentie) recommended from father to son, and so rivited into them by the reputation of Antiquity that there is little hope of reclaiming them while those Septs continue.[148]

Not only were previous social distinctions among the Irish to be ignored by English colonial law; now the English proceeded unrelentingly to decimate the Irish tribal lords by exile. Within a space of some twenty-four months, 35,000 to 40,000 Irish men – that is to say, one out of every six men over the age of about twenty-five – were sold in groups to serve as soldiers in foreign armies, chiefly the Spanish.[149] Vincent Gookin noted with satisfaction that "the chiefest and eminentest of the nobility and many of the Gentry" had been driven into exile.[150] As for those that remained, one colonial administrator was overheard to say, they "must . . . turn into common peasants or die if they don't."[151]

A Classic Case of Racial Oppression

Before the outbreak of the rebellion in 1641, the Celtic, "native" Irish Catholics, the Old English Catholics and the Protestant "New English" shared possession of Irish lands in roughly equal proportions.[152] Under the Act of Settlement all persons, except such as could prove they had maintained "constant good affection" toward the English Parliamentary government between 1642 and 1652, were to be totally expropriated and evicted from their holdings. Such of the "ill-affected" as were not under sentence of death or banishment, were nevertheless also to be expropriated of their lands. They, however, were to be assigned some fractional equivalent of their original acreage in Connaught and County Clare. Catholics, according to their degree of "guilt," were to receive from one-half to one-third portions. "Ill-affected" Protestants were to forfeit only one-fifth of their estates, and were allowed to relocate outside of Connaught.[153] More than half the land in Ireland fell under this attainder; of Catholic landlords, only twenty-six out of a total of around ten thousand were excepted.[154] As for the native Irish, whatever distribution of their lands might subsequently be made, it would be done according to English law. This expropriation meant, therefore, the destruction of Celtic tribal landholding, and of Celtic society, even in its last stronghold west of the Shannon. Except for the Royalist Protestants,[155] those of the attainted class who were not hanged or exiled or otherwise debarred were – much like American Indians of the nineteenth century – assigned to live on some fractional equivalent of their former holdings in Connaught and in Clare where they found "not wood enough to hang a man, water enough to drown him, nor earth enough to bury him."[156] Of the ten thousand Catholic landholders of 1641, no more than four thousand qualified for any such land assignment at all; only one in five of the original ten thousand was actually assigned land west of the Shannon; and of these about six hundred were in possession twenty years later.[157]

About five out of every eight acres of profitable land were held by Catholics in 1641; by 1654 that share was reduced to one out of twelve.[158] The restoration of Charles II to the English throne in 1660 was followed by some restitution of Catholic lands, to a total of two out of every nine acres.[159] The defeat of Ireland's last great trial at arms, 1689–91, under the banner of the deposed English Catholic king, James II,[160] was made the occasion for the final swamping wave of expropriations, until in 1703 Catholics, who were fifteen out of every twenty in the population, held no more than one acre in nine of the profitable land; within another fifty years the Penal Laws operated to reduce the share to one out of every sixteen acres.[161] Four centuries before, the Anglo-Normans had refused to share English law with the Irish; now the English refused to share Irish land with the Irish. There was to be no new ascendance of assimilation and equality such as the amities of the fourteenth and fifteenth centuries might have promised. From 1652 onward, racial oppression, written into every new title deed, was anchored in the very bedrock of the Irish colonial economy. It was "The Act [of Settlement] by which most of us hold our Estates," said Chancellor John Fitzgibbon with painful candor. ". . . [E]very acre of land which pays quitrent to the Crown is held by title derived under the Act of Settlement."[162]

The native or, as they were termed, the "mere" Irish had been "admitted to" English law in 1613 (11 James I c. 5 [Irish Statutes]), only to be outlawed as "Papists," the common English epithet for Roman Catholics, in 1641. In December of that year the English Parliament in a joint declaration of both Houses had vowed unalterable determination to prevent the practice of the "Popish" religion in Ireland.[163] Now, in the aftermath of the rebellion, the Catholic Anglo-Irish landlords – no less "Popish" than the native Irish – were to suffer under the same religio-racist interdictions as did the Irish chiefs and lords, tenants and laborers.[164] The ancient amities of Anglo-Irish and native Irish survived only in the common fate of Catholics.

When the historian W. F. T. Butler concluded that "A common misfortune had welded all these [Catholics – Old English and native Irish] into one race,"[165] he was not referring to a genetic "merger" of Old English and Irish Catholics, nor to the appearance of some new Irish phenotype. He was affirming, rather, that that which in Ireland took the form of anti-Popery, and in time would be officially known as the Protestant Ascendancy, was a classic system of racial oppression.

2

Social Control and the
Intermediate Strata: Ireland

From the standpoint of the ruling classes generally, the imposition on a colony of racial oppression afforded a dual advantage. It relieved the colonial regime of encumbering social forms unsuited to its purposes. Free of such impediments, it could exploit the wealth and the labor of the country with a minimum of interference or embarrassment. The employer could resort to compulsion, by corporal "correction" of a bond-laborer in one case or the threat of eviction of a tenant-at-will in another, in order to secure greater exertion from the laborer, who was denied protection of the law.[1] Normally protected rights or customs could be disregarded in the case of the racially oppressed. A married woman could be denied "coverture," that is, exemption from service to any except her own personal "lord and master," thus affording the master class the opportunity to exploit her labor directly.[2] Labor costs could be reduced by the disregard of religious customs. In Ireland Catholic holidays were disallowed, being not only "heretical" but, more important from a profit-and-loss perspective, more numerous than those provided in the Protestant calendar.[3] American Indian religious observances, such as the Sun Dance, the Ghost Dance and the Messiah phenomenon, were suppressed by United States military force at the end of the nineteenth century in pursuit of white America's "Manifest Destiny" and the capitalist exploitation of the "public" lands and their natural resources.[4]

On the other hand, racial oppression produced an extreme degree of alienation of the laboring people of the oppressed group, and at the same time deprived the colonial ruling class of the services of an indigenous intermediate social control stratum as an instrument for profitable operations.[5] It was a system that limited the possibilities of resort to the normal bourgeois methods for raising of the rate of return by exploitation of labor. In Anglo-America large plantations worked under the system of racial slavery had a higher rate of labor productivity than smaller farms engaged in the same lines of production employing free labor.[6] But the chief means of raising the productivity of plantation labor (given the same input of constant capital on land of the same natural fertility) was the intensification of labor, which necessitated increased supervisory investment, and was absolutely limited by the physical constitution of the laborers.[7] The alternative method, the chief one under "normal" capitalist operations, the revolutionizing of the instruments of production, was inhibited under racial slavery by the employers' reluctance "to trust delicate and costly implements to the carelessness of slaves,"[8] for whom they promised nothing but an intensification of labor. In Ireland under the eighteenth-century Penal Laws, the ban on the Catholic acquisition of land, even on long-term leases – a ban which lay at the very core of British rule there – foreclosed all possibility of significantly raising the productivity of labor by resort to incentives for the Catholics of the laboring classes. In Ireland and in the continental Anglo-American plantation colonies, the criminalization of literacy among the laboring classes made impossible the achievement of even that minimum degree of general elementary literacy required for the use of increasingly complex implements and techniques of production.

The successful conduct of colonial policy required that neither of the negative tendencies reach its fullest development. Exploitation without check led to the genocidal destruction of labor resources; unrelieved alienation led to the revolutionary overthrow of the colonial regime. The history of Hispaniola at the beginning of the sixteenth century and again at the end of the eighteenth century presents examples of both these extreme denouements.[9] Where the option was for racial oppression, the art and science of colonial rule lay in seeking the golden mean to maximize the return on capital investment from a social order based on racial oppression, while assuring its perpetuation through an efficient system of social control.

The history of England in Ireland for more than four centuries from early in the thirteenth century to the initiation of the plantation of Ulster in 1609 is a history of the failure of three strategies of social control: the Anglo-Norman "middle nation"; the policy of "surrender-and-regrant"; and the policy of "plantation".

The First Strategy – the Anglo-Norman "Middle Nation"

The English (Anglo-Norman) invaders found it impossible to establish an adequate social base in Ireland by the permanent settlement of English tenants and laborers, whose situations would be dependent on keeping the natives down and out. "Above all," writes the Irish historian J. C. Beckett, "the number of settlers was too small ... there was no solid body of English or Anglo-Norman middle-class population."[10] This fact was destined to be perpetuated as the historic Achilles heel of English social control policy in Ireland.[11]

On the other hand, the English would not broaden their base of power by admitting the Irish free classes to English law, and for this they lost the power to rule Ireland.[12] Such was the considered judgment of Sir John Davies:

> For as long as they [the Irish] were out of the protection of the Lawe; so as every English-man might oppress, spoyle, and kill them without controulment, Howe was it possible they should bee other than Out-lawes? ... In a word ... the English would neither in peace govern them by the Lawe nor could in war root them out by the sword ... and so the Conquest [could] never be brought to completion.[13]

It was the Scots invasion in 1315–18, under Edward and Robert Bruce, in support of an Irish resistance already begun, that sounded the knell of the medieval English attempt to rule Ireland through an intermediate stratum of colonial settlers.[14] The Scots went home, but in the decade that followed Irish resistance proved stronger than the English conquest and by 1400, "English lordship in Ireland in any real sense [had] ceased to exist."[15] Thereafter, the range of actual English control in Ireland was reduced to a few towns and shires; before the end of the fifteenth century it had dwindled to an even smaller area around Dublin, called the English Pale. Elsewhere in Ireland, English control was only nominal at best, being represented by the formal acknowledgement of English suzerainty by the Anglo-Irish feudal lords, and when opportune by occasional native Irish chieftains.

The initial, thirteenth-century attempt to impose racial oppression on the Irish had thus contributed decisively to the defeat of its perpetrators. Speaking specifically of the Anglo-Norman feudal lords, to whom the Anglicization of Ireland had been entrusted, Orpen concludes: "above all, their lack of sympathy with the Irish, whom they regarded as an inferior race, prevented them from establishing their power on the firm basis of a contented people."[16]

While in absolute terms the overall strength of the English side became weaker *vis-à-vis* the native Irish, the strength of the Anglo-Irish[17] *vis-à-vis* the English became greater. It became a matter of concern to the Anglo-Irish lords to make accommodation with the native Irish chieftains. Concomitantly, the old fears of a dilution of their authority with the Crown as a result of the enfranchisement of the native Irish free classes became doubly inappropriate. First, the authority of the Crown itself was reduced nearly to vanishing point in Ireland; second, the English had lost the power to arbitrate Irish rights. Before, the sharing of power with "an inferior race" had seemed impossible. Now it had suddenly become possible, so that "a Gaelic and Norman aristocracy divided the land."[18] Basic questions of landholding and inheritance, formerly so insoluble, were seen in a new light. As previously noted, the Celtic rules of inheritance found favor among the resident Anglo-Irish concerned with the difficulties attendant upon the growth of absentee ownership. And, in a longer process, the Gaelic chieftains came to see possible advantages in the transition from tribal to individual, hereditary forms of landholding, succession and revenue-raising.[19]

More remarkable still, perhaps, the "inferior race" now became the object of the sincerest form of Anglo-Irish flattery. The Anglo-Irish, who had given a social definition to a nationality by synonymizing "hibernicus" with "unfree," now saw the value of themselves becoming "hibernicized." Normal tendencies of social assimilation derived added force from the attraction exerted on the Anglo-Irish by the Gaelic society, its language, family forms and general social customs; and by the native interpreters of the country's culture, its poets, bards, storytellers, and singers.[20]

The English government was understandably alarmed. As Edmund Curtis has noted, "Without the consent and aid of this [Anglo-Irish] 'middle nation' Ireland could not be reconquered. But ... this great class, the race of 'the first Conquest,' which held a third of Ireland, was becoming with every generation more and more Irish in habit, speech, custom, and sympathy."[21] In 1367, the English government convoked an Anglo-Irish Parliament at Kilkenny to cope with the "degenerate English" phenomenon, which was described in the following terms:

> ... now many of the English of the said land, forsaking the English language, fashion, mode of riding, laws and usages, live and govern themselves according to the manners, fashion and language of the Irish enemies, and have also made divers marriages and alliances between themselves and the Irish enemies aforesaid; whereby the said land and the liege people thereof, the English language, and the allegiance due to our lord the King, and the English laws there, are put in subjection and decayed.[22]

One of the most deplored forms of "alliance" was the custom of "fostering," or "gossipred," the giving over of the child of one family into the care and rearing of another, as a way of strengthening class ties (see page 43). The Statute of Kilkenny enacted by this Anglo-Irish Parliament established harsh penalties aimed at stamping out such practices. Any Englishman who thereafter entered into the relationship of "fostering" with any native Irish family, or who married any Irish person, was to be judged guilty of treason and made subject to the full penalty thereof. Other provisions forbade any Englishman to assume an Irish name, use the Irish language or adopt the Irish mode of dress or riding, under penalty of forfeiture of all his lands and tenements.[23]

Seeking to emphasize the distinction to be enforced between all English (native-born or Ireland-born) on the one hand and the native Irish ("the Irish enemy") on the other, the Statute of Kilkenny prohibited Irish tenants, laborers, and tradespeople from speaking their own language while engaged in their occupations within English-held territory. The ban against the Irish grazing their herds within lands claimed by the English suggests a level of economic interpenetration of borderline Gaelic and Anglo-Norman sectors. Members of the Gaelic upper classes were barred from becoming priests or lawyers. All "minstrels, tympanours, pipers, story-tellers, rimers, and harpers" were forbidden to come among the English, on pain of fine or imprisonment and forfeiture of their pipes, percussive instruments, harps, and other weapons.[24]

All in vain. Before it ended in 1534, this phase of Irish history had produced the "all-but-kingship" of Gerald Fitzgerald, the Anglo-Irish eighth Earl of Kildare (1477–1513).[25] Known by the Gaelic name of Garret More (the Great Earl), Kildare formally professed allegiance to the English Crown while presiding, after his fashion, over a grand cohabitation of Anglo-Irish lords and Irish chieftains that was much fortified by intermarriage and fostering, or gossipred, and much disturbed by a constant round of warring over cattle, land, and power.[26]

The political economy of this transformation seems to have brought a net gain for Ireland. The basic factor was the relative weakness of the English colony, the most dramatic demonstration of which was the regular payment of "black rents," or protection money, by the English colonists to the Irish tribes, from the early fourteenth to the early sixteenth century. Viewed macro-economically, as we might say today, these assessments are seen as a form of redistribution of wealth. Following the death of King Edward III in 1377, an Irish Parliament called by the Viceroy was interrupted by Irish, come to demand their "black rent." The Irish agreed to settle for 100 marks, but there were only nine in the exchequer. The balance was made up by individual donations. The O'Connors of Offaly at the end of the fifteenth century "were paid a black rent of £40 a year from the exchequer." By that time, the historians tell us, the English king, Henry VII, had learned that the cheapest way to protect the border of the Pale against the Irish was by payment of "black rents" to the O'Conchobhairs and the O'Neills. Payments were made almost routinely by towns and by counties – Clonmel, Carlow, Wexford, Cork, Waterford. When the English Lord Deputy in Ireland, Richard Nugent Lord Delvin decided not to continue the payments to O'Neill and O'Conchobhair, he was seized and held hostage until the arrangements were made for resumption of the payments.[27] At the same time the disruption of former ruling-class arrangements, coupled with the direct and indirect effects of the plague, tended to improve the conditions of those laborers who survived and for whose services landlords and cattle-lords were forced into extraordinary competition.[28] Although English control of Ireland was eclipsed and the racist mode of rule was supplanted by the workings of "hibernization," ruling-class control in both colonial and Gaelic Ireland remained effective. The Irish laboring classes had probably benefited from the Peasant Revolt in England which, by increasing labor income in England, reduced the incentive for emigrating to or staying in Ireland. But there was to be no replay of that social upheaval in Ireland.

The English identity of the Anglo-Normans proved to be no serious barrier to the emergence of the intimate partnership of the "degenerate English" with the Irish chieftains in ruling Ireland from the fourteenth to the sixteenth century. This fact of medieval Irish history refutes the most fundamental assumption of the Jordan/Degler thesis, namely that, given a choice, persons of a given "gene pool" will naturally choose to maintain that "identity."

The Second Strategy – Surrender-and-Regrant

What the Anglo-Irish palatinate lords could not or would not do, Henry VIII, having taken direct charge of Irish affairs in 1534, would attempt by a strategy of coopting Irish tribal chieftains through a policy of surrender-and-regrant.[29] Under this plan, Gaelic chiefs who surrendered their land claims and pledged their allegiance to the English Crown were in turn regranted English titles to the lands that they already held. (The plan was also designed to cover the cases of "degenerate English" whose land titles might have emerged tainted in the wake of the War of the Roses.)[30] To facilitate and regularize matters, Henry caused the Anglo-Irish Parliament to enact two laws, in 1536 and 1541 respectively. The first (28 Henry VIII, c. 5, *Irish Statutes*) proclaimed Henry VIII to be the spiritual head of the Church of Ireland and obliged all government officers to swear an oath of support of that Church (the Oath of Supremacy); non-compliance was to be punished as treason. The second (33 Henry VIII, c. 2, *Irish Statutes*) established that any king of England was, *ex officio*, king of Ireland.

To the English government the arrangement implied the displacement of Gaelic tribal and customary law regarding landholding, inheritance, marriage and family, and civil and criminal justice generally, and its replacement with English statutory and common law, together with its corresponding administrative forms. For the Irish chieftains, there was a definite appeal in the prospect that – in the Scottish and Welsh way – they might, by a mere formality, secure personal hereditary title to authority and wealth, in place of the Celtic-style elected leadership and tribal ownership. The attitude of the O'Neills of Ulster was typical. "They were not unwilling to be English earls, provided they might retain their sovereignty as O'Neills."[31]

But the Irish chieftains were not disposed to trade Irish land and power for mere English parchment and wax. By way of emphasizing the point, and bringing home to the English government a proper sense of reality, the Irish continued occasionally to collect "black rents" – from English landlords in Ireland. In short, surrender-and-regrant bespoke a parity of weakness in which momentary advantage was decisive. The English government, for its part, was unable or unwilling to pay the cost of a decisive military conquest and occupation of Ireland, and the quartering of troops on the Anglo-Irish proved often more burdensome than the terms that the Anglo-Irish could arrange with the Gaelic lords. The Irish chieftains, on the other hand, could not or would not achieve sufficient unity of will to remove the English thorn from their country's side. In the main, only on those limited occasions when the English could, with their improved military technical means, obtain the advantage was the surrender-and-regrant ritual performed. In sum, for the English, land was "easier won than kept ... if it be gotten one day it [was] lost the next."[32] As for the Anglo-Irish, the complaint of "degeneracy" raised at Kilkenny was being heard a hundred and fifty years later: except in the walled towns, they were still adherents "of Irish habits, [and] of Irish language."[33]

If the Irish chieftains might sometimes be tempted, the tribes of which they were the elected leaders were not; they rejected surrender-and-regrant as a recipe for Celtic suicide. They took their stand on constitutional principles: a tribal chief "had no more than a lifetime tenure of the territory to be ruled and ... in accepting feudal tenure of the territory he was disposing of what did not belong to him."[34] In 1585, the English-educated Hugh O'Neill asked to be given the title Earl of Tyrone, which his grandfather had borne, and agreed to forswear the title "the O'Neill." Elizabeth and her councillors eagerly granted the request, believing that in the greatest Ulster chieftain they had found, as Hill puts it, "an apostle worthy of his great mission, to wit, the introduction of English manners and customs – and even costumes – in Ulster." But, he continues, "they had evidently calculated 'without their host,' or at least had overlooked the fact that, even were the earl thoroughly disposed to carry out his friends' ideas, he had not the power to impress this new policy, at least not very promptly, on the native population."[35]

Such promptness was not to be expected, however, for the completion of a process in Ireland such as had required a century (mid-eleventh to mid-twelfth) in Scotland and, after nearly four centuries, was completed in Wales only in 1534. Furthermore, events in Ireland were overtaken by rapid developments on the wider stage of European history that doomed this second social control strategy after a trial period of less than twenty-five years.

The Third Strategy – Protestant Plantation

The failure of the surrender-and-regrant policy became apparent at the very time the split with Rome resulting from the English Protestant Reformation was bringing new complications and greater urgency to the "Irish problem." Here began the redefinition of the struggle between England and Ireland as one of Protestant against Catholic, a process which took more than a century to reach its fullest development. Encouraged by Rome and Spain, Irish Catholics, Anglo and Gaelic, began to show occasional readiness to unite not just for a change of English government, but for the end of English rule in Ireland.

In the face of this challenge, the English had recourse to a third plan, that of "plantation," begun, interestingly, during the last two years of the Catholic

Mary Tudor's reign (1553–58).[36] Just as the eclipse of the feudal barons and the rise of the bourgeois monarchy in England had necessitated the development of a new buffer social control group of gentry and yeomen (see Chapter 2 of Volume Two), so now with the "removal of the Old English as a buffer" in Ireland "a colonizing gentry and yeomanry were desired instead."[37]

Under this new plan the English capitalists were to finance the settlement of English tenants in Ireland in numbers sufficient to provide a self-supporting militia to guarantee the eventual subjugation of the entire country. Title to the lands to be settled would be transferred from Gaelic Irish and Old English to New English, by confiscation of Church lands, by challenge to defective titles, and especially by the escheat of lands of Irish and Anglo-Irish resisters. The English tenants would supplant Irish tenants for the most part, although laborers were to be mainly native Irish; for the rest, the Irish would to some considerable degree be displaced and transplanted beyond the advancing areas of English settlement. Under the rules laid down for the ill-starred first Ulster plantation (1572–73), for instance, no member of the Celtic Irish owning or learned classes was to be admitted. Within the plantation boundaries, to be Irish was to be a "churl," a laborer "that will plow the ground and bear no kind of weapon."[38] It was even proposed by some of these early English colonialists that the Irish be enslaved *en masse*.[39] In any case, it was ordered that, "no Irishman, born of Irish race and brought up Irish, shall purchase land, beare office, be chosen of any jury or admitted witness in any real or personal action, nor be bound apprentice to any science or art that may damage the Queen's Majesty's subjects."[40]

Designed as a "specific response to rebellion,"[41] plantations were undertaken with varying degrees of success in Leix and Offaly (1556), Ulster (first attempt 1572) and Munster (1585).[42] Yet, none of the basic barriers to the establishment of an English peace in Ireland was cleared away. Gaelic resistance proved incurably resilient, and the ambivalent Catholic Anglo-Irish (the English by "blood") were increasingly put on the defensive and alienated by the government-fostered Protestant New English (the English by "birth"). The effort continued to be hampered throughout the period by the fiscal priorities and limitations of an English exchequer burdened with the charges incident to England's increased role in world affairs, while military and administrative costs in Ireland generally exceeded Irish Crown revenues.[43]

As a program for establishing social control, the plantation concept was a negation of surrender-and-regrant. The latter presumed the cooptation of the Irish chieftains as the social buffer; "plantation" was based on their degradation and exclusion. That did not, however, prevent a cynical use of the vestige of surrender-and-regrant as a mask for a two-step expropriation of tribal lands into the hands of Protestant English "planters." In such instances, the English first went through the form of granting a chieftain title as owner of the tribal lands. Then charges were trumped up against him, he was tried by a corrupt

and/or coerced jury, and executed. The chieftain having been convicted of a
crime against English law, "his" – that is, the tribe's – lands were escheated
by the English crown for distribution to English planters, often the same
officials who had themselves managed the matter.[44]

The anger, revulsion and trepidation that the Irish chiefs and tribes felt on
witnessing such a treacherous assault on Celtic rights precipitated the most
dramatic demonstration of the ineffectualness of the plantation policy, the
great Celtic war of liberation, the Tyrone War, 1594–1603. Hugh O'Neill and
Red Hugh O'Donnell had been "ennobled" as the earls of Tyrone and
Tyrconnell respectively under the surrender-and-regrant arrangement. Under
their leadership, the Irish defeated the English forces in a series of field
engagements in the north, climaxed by the great victory at Yellow Ford (called
"the defeat of Blackwater" by the English) on 14 August 1598.[45] The
contagion of the rebellion swept southward and "shaked the English government in this kingdom [of Ireland], till it tottered, and wanted little of fatal
ruine." By November the Irish had obliterated the Plantation of Munster,
which the English had boasted was theirs by right of fire, sword, and famine.
"Neither did these gentle Undertakers make any resistance to the Rebels,"
wrote an English chronicler, "but left their dwellings and fled to walled
Townes,"[46] and thereby supplied the epitaph for three failed English strategies
for establishing an intermediate social control stratum in Ireland.

Within the walls of the port city of Cork, Edmund Spenser, the promised
Sheriff of Cork, "mused full sadly in his sullen mind"[47] upon the ruin of the
English plantation, and of his own personal estate there.[48] As poet, Spenser had
written his masterpiece *The Faerie Queene* with Queen Elizabeth as his model.
Now, "out of the desolation and wastedness of this ... wretched Realm of
Ireland," Spenser addressed to her "A Breife Note of Ireland." The policy of
conquest by piecemeal plantation was a demonstrated failure, he told her, nor
would England ever win the submission of the Irish by negotiated terms. He
proffered his judgment that only by complete conquest with overwhelming
force, and by a strategy of famine, could a lasting English peace be achieved
in Ireland.[49]

Celtic Ireland in a New World Context

To equate "the king's peace" in Ireland with the complete conquest of the
entire island was by no means a timeless truism. The Anglo-Normans, even at
the height of their power at the beginning of the fourteenth century, were
reconciled to the fact that one-fourth to one-third of Ireland was outside the
range of English authority.[50] From that time, English power in Ireland waned
and wasted for more than two centuries, during which English policy did not
equate "the king's peace" with complete conquest, but merely with the defense

and control of the area of the English Pale. While the English government condemned the "Irish enemy" in extreme terms, its operational object for "conquest" was not the "wild Irish" but the "degenerate English" throughout most of the island. Even as the tide was beginning to turn in England's favor, England felt obliged at least to pretend that the surrender-and-regrant policy was intended only as a formal rather than as a substantive alteration of the power equation in Ireland.

As late as 1600, the English position in relation to Ireland was much like that of the European powers as it was and would remain until well into the nineteenth century with respect to sub-Saharan Africa. In neither case could the invaders accomplish the first essential step in colonization, the establishment of their commanding authority over the prospective colonial territory.[51] "If the Europeans were masters on the water," writes Basil Davidson, "the Africans were masters on the land; and they made sure they remained so."[52] Consequently, instead of conquering and occupying African territory as they were able to do in the nineteenth and twentieth centuries, the Europeans, as Kenneth G. Davies puts it, could only be "drawn into quarrels which they had not sufficient force to conclude."[53] In a review of Irish history made in 1800, Lord Clare, the Chancellor of Ireland, commented on the parallel. "The first English settlements here," he said, "[were] ... such as has [sic] been made by the different nations of Europe on the coast of Asia, Africa, or America."[54]

The frustration of the English was all the more galling as they watched the Iberians establish successful colonies on newly discovered territories, not merely to raid or trade, but to exploit directly the labor of the native peoples and transported Africans. The ruin of the English plantation of Munster lent emphasis to Sir Edwin Sandy's comment on the apparent inability of "Northern people" to compete with Iberia in the matter of "durable and grounded settlement."[55]

A turning point came, however, with the close of the sixteenth century. On a surging tide of economic development, and of a corresponding social and political transformation, England emerged as an aggressive competitor in the new-fledged world market that had been opened up by the Portuguese as navigators and colonists and the Spanish as colonialists and gold-grabbing conquistadors. In this new role England entered into an historic confrontation with Spain (with whom Portugal was united in a single kingdom from 1580 to 1640). This challenge was signalled most dramatically by Sir Francis Drake's 1577–80 circumnavigation of the globe, from which he returned to England laden with Spanish treasure worth half a million English pounds sterling,[56] and by the defeat of the Spanish Armada in the English Channel eight years later. In addition to its simple exploitative colonialist ambitions regarding Ireland, the English government was preoccupied with the potential Spanish threat from that quarter. If the proximity of Ireland to England was an advantage for the purposes of English expansionism, that very proximity made it a potentially deadly staging point for the invasion of England. It was already an "old Prophesie" in 1600, that "He that will England winne / Must with Ireland first beginne."[57] Now England was poised at the threshold of its career as a world colonial power, with Ireland as its first objective. Such was the wider context out of which, at the very moment marked by the ruin of the Munster plantation, England's new "complete conquest" perspective arose.[58]

Conquest by Famine

For nearly a year and a half after the Battle of Yellow Ford, the cause of Irish independence remained in the ascendant. The largest English army ever assembled in Ireland until that time, twenty thousand men under Robert Devereux, second Earl of Essex, marched and counter-marched, dwindled, and (some said) dawdled through the spring and summer of 1599, but to no other end than an empty truce with O'Neill. The English were fain to acknowledge that "Tyrone [is] now master of the field."[59] But under Queen Elizabeth's Great Warrant of Ireland of January 1600, the English created a new military establishment in Ireland of twelve thousand foot and three hundred horse, which was increased to sixteen thousand foot and twelve hundred horse by November 1601.[60] The newly constituted army was commanded by a new Lord Deputy, Charles Blount, Lord Mountjoy.[61] In the four and a half years between the Battle of Yellow Ford and Tyrone's submission on 31 March 1603, the English government expended 1.3 million pounds sterling for the conduct of the war in Ireland, not counting charges for munitions, employment of spies, bribe money and military construction, or the costs of transporting personnel, equipment, and supplies.[62]

England's "early industrial revolution" (with assistance, of course, from piratical depredations like Drake's) provided the money capital needed to support massive military expenditures in Ireland; it made particular technological contributions vital to English victory in the Tyrone War. By this period English cast iron cannon were of such excellent quality and yet so low in price that they were being exported to countries throughout Europe.[63] It is not surprising, then, that the English made telling use of their artillery advantage in Ireland.[64] Thanks to England's rapidly expanding cloth industry, the English army's appeals for warm clothing were on the whole adequately met. Of the total charges of 283,674 pounds sterling for the English army in Ireland for the fiscal year 1601–2, almost one-fourth went for soldiers' apparel made in England.[65]

The new and rapidly expanding gunpowder mills in England gave the English army in Ireland a very substantial advantage.[66] Moryson explained the disparity in the respective numbers of battle casualties of the English and the Irish thus:

". . . we had plentie of powder, and sparing not to shoot at random, might well kill many more of them, than they ill furnished of powder, and commanded to spare it, could kill of ours."[67] The advantage was limited by the fact that fewer than six out of every ten of the English foot soldiers were armed with muskets. The bulk of the remainder were pikemen,[68] a category in which the Irish were a match for the English.

Although Spain's rate of industrial progress was by now slower than England's, Spanish industrial production, except in the output of cheap cloth, was at that time on the whole equal to the English.[69] Still, aside from whatever merit there was in Irish complaints regarding Spain's commitment to the Irish cause, the Spanish unquestionably were at a disadvantage by virtue of the fact that men and materials sent to Ireland from Spain had to travel six times as far as those sent from England.

Great as England's resources were with respect to Ireland's, and more favorable as was its geographic position than Spain's for purposes of intervention in Irish affairs, the advantages were not all on the English side. The Irish were fighting on their own ground for their own way of life; and they were leagued with Rome. When it came to enduring the rigors of campaigning, especially in cold weather, the English believed that the Irish soldiers were "harder" than the English.[70] England's enormous war expenditures could not be sustained indefinitely, draining one-third more every year than was invested in joint stock overseas ventures. This problem increasingly preoccupied the English government, as the correspondence of Queen Elizabeth and Robert Cecil with Mountjoy reveals. Lord Cecil, a chief minister, wrote to Mountjoy about the end of June 1602 to say that the army could not continue to be maintained at its present size, "without extreme prejudice to [the English] state." For that reason he was, he said, trying to persuade the queen to propose terms to the Irish for ending the war, for "in short time the sword cannot end the warre, and long time the State of England cannot wel indure it." Four months later the queen expressed her alarm that the cost of the war "consumes Our treasure, which is the sinewes of our Crowne."[71] The English had to win clearly and decisively; the Irish had only not to lose.

Edmund Spenser in his "Breife Note" to the queen had coined an English maxim: "Until Ireland can be famished, it cannot be subdued."[72] As secretary to the Lord Deputy of Ireland, Spenser had seen this method practiced during the second Desmond War (1578–83).[73] Although Essex had been unable to carry his mission through to success, he had based his early hopes on "burning and spoiling the Country in all places ... [thus to] starve the Rebell." When Mountjoy arrived, he resolved unhesitatingly to base his strategy on that same principle, the war being "no way so likely to be brought to an end, as by general famine."[74] The denial of all sense of human fellowship, even to the most eminent Irish chieftain,[75] implicit in this policy was given a gloss of Christian religiosity and English patriotism. At one point, as he surveyed the

death and desolation he had brought to Tyrone's country, Mountjoy confessed
a feeling of "humane commiseration," especially because the souls of the dead
starved Irish had "never had the meanes to know God," nor to acknowledge
a divinely anointed sovereign like England's, but only a tribal Irish chieftain.[76]

Under Mountjoy, the starvation strategy was prosecuted without remission
for three and a half years throughout three-fourths of the country, most
significantly in Ulster, the main stronghold of Celtic tribal power. The strategy
was pressed in harvest and in seedtime; by winter warfare, driving the Irish
naked into the woods; and in all seasons cutting down crops in the field,
preventing planting, and confiscating stored grain.[77]

In Ulster, it appears, the English strategy involved not merely reducing the
natives to submission, but at the same time clearing the territory for English
plantation. Writing to the government in August of 1601, Mountjoy said, "We
doe not omit anything of our purposes, but ... every day cut downe his
[Tyrone's] Woods or his Corne." Mountjoy went on to express the hope that
before the end of the winter he could depopulate Tyrone's country and thus
prepare the way "to make Ulster one of the most quiet, assured, and profitable
Provinces."[78] Although he was unable to keep to his original schedule,
Mountjoy remained firm in his resolve. In September he directed Sir Arthur
Chichester to proceed with "clearing the Country of Tyrone of all inhabitants,
and to spoil all the Corne which he could not preserve for the Garrisons."[79]

None the less, it seems likely that the English might again have failed of
complete conquest if they had not been able to procure the collaboration of a
number of the native chieftain class by promises of support in securing tribal
leadership.[80]

Throughout the war the English recruited surrendering Irish units who
pledged their allegiance to the queen. At times more than half of the English
fighting force was made up of such recruits, and Mountjoy was provided with
a special allowance of 1,000 pounds sterling per month for their employment.[81] Whatever expedient arrangements were made with members of the
Irish chieftain class, however, the English government did not find it
appropriate to make any promises of future favor for the rank-and-file Irish
soldier. Indeed, a deliberate policy was followed most likely to foreclose his
future altogether. While such Irish units remained in English service,
Mountjoy was resolved to "so employ them ... as they shall not be idle, but
shall be exposed to endure the brunt of service upon all occasions." These Irish
submitters, Mountjoy said, "were kept in pay, rather to prevent their fighting
against us, than for confidence in their fighting for us."[82] In the same cynical
vein, Moryson wrote: "the death of these peaceable swordsmen, though falling
on our [English] side, was yet [regarded as] rather a gain than a loss."[83]
Clearly, such new-won Irish adherents were not looked upon as harbingers of
a peacetime reconciliation in a "king's peace" of fraternal English subjects all;

they were not presumed to be prototypes of an emergent Irish middle class.[84]

Plantation – Once More

In the wake of Mountjoy's victory over the Irish, the English Solicitor-General for Ireland, Sir John Davies, was duly sanguine about English colonial prospects in Ireland under the "happier reign" of his new sovereign, James I, whose succession to the throne of England upon Elizabeth's death near the end of March 1603 coincided with the formal surrender of the Celtic forces. By Davies's own definition, however, the English were still a long way from having achieved an English peace in Ireland. "For, though the Prince both beare the Title of Soveraigne Lord of an entire Country," said Davies, the conquest cannot be regarded as complete "if the jurisdiction of his ordinary Courts of justice doth not extend" to all parts of the territory, and if "he cannot punish Treasons, Murders, or Thefts, unlesse he send an Army to do it."[85]

For nearly a decade the English had warred against O'Neill, invariably termed by them "the arch traitor." But instead of rooting him out and hanging him (as they had done with many lesser "rebels"), they granted him personally generous terms. O'Neill was to retain the title Earl of Tyrone and was allowed to keep the greater part of his lands, long since legally transmuted from tribal to individual chieftain property by surrender-and-regrant. Indeed the title was allowed as a specific quid pro quo for O'Neill's disavowal of the tribal title of "the O'Neill."[86]

Celtic Ireland was defeated but not uprooted; its Ulster bastion was overthrown, but tribal affinities remained strong in Connaught, and in refugee bogs and woods in Ulster and other parts of the country. English armies had dispersed the Irish military forces, but in Connaught and most of the rest of Ireland "the jurisdiction of ... ordinary courts of justice" did not prevail. At the same time, for urgent state reasons, financial and otherwise, the English army in Ireland had to be reduced from over twelve thousand to nine thousand by April 1604.[87] Despite the devastation and conquest that Mountjoy had achieved, Moryson said, "Yet hee left this great worke unperfect."[88] Indeed it was the ancient imperfection: the lack of a system of social control "without sending an army to do it"; and the essence of that problem was still the lack of an intermediate social control stratum.

Opting for Racial Oppression

So long as the English colonialists had lacked the force to impose and stabilize their commanding authority in Ireland, all schemes for English social control had been foredoomed. English victory in the Tyrone War, however, presented a realistic prospect for reducing Ireland to an English colony. At that point the English might have opted for the establishment of social control by the cooptation method, as Portugal and Spain did in appropriate circumstances, or along the lines that the English themselves had employed with respect to Scotland and Wales. But the very process that produced English military dominance over Ireland had made Ireland a major focus of the struggle between Catholic Spain and Protestant England. As a consequence, just when cooptation of the Irish upper classes might have supplied a basis for a viable system of social control in the Irish colony, the option was foreclosed by a redefinition of racial oppression in Ireland as *religio-racial* oppression. For the same reason, the English ruling class could not recruit an intermediate stratum by promotion of a portion of the Irish laboring classes to the yeoman status, on the English model. Such being the limitations, there was no alternative for the English colonialists but a return to the policy of plantation, in the hope that Mountjoy had finally cleared the way for the installation of a Protestant middle-class buffer and social control stratum throughout Ireland.

But military conquest, however complete, could not free English policy from the fundamental contradiction inherent in its option for racial oppression in Ireland. The heart of the matter was that the fundamental purpose was to accumulate capital at the highest possible annual rate by the exploitation of labor, primarily, at the time, the labor of high-rent-paying Irish tenants-at-will. As Sir John Davies said in his *Discovery of the True Causes why Ireland was never Entirely Subdued*, considered from the standpoint of the colonial bourgeoisie as a whole, this objective required for its most profitable development the establishment of a "civil" regime, free of heavy deductions necessary for military occupation. But he had already concluded, as English Attorney-General in Ireland, that a civil regime could not be achieved until the majority of the population were settlers, not native Irish. Since this result could not be accomplished by converting the Irish to Protestantism nor by genocidal depopulation, a massive infusion of Protestant settlers was needed. Aside from the Scots and Ulster, and the "Ulster custom", which will be discussed in Chapter 5, this meant almost complete reliance on bringing in English tenants. But as noted in Chapter 3, and more fully in Chapter 5, the English tenant's prospects in Ireland were unattractive because the rents that the Irish were required to pay to the landlords were so much higher than they were at home in England that it would not pay the English tenant to emigrate to Ireland. For their part, the English landlords throughout plantation Ireland had long since proclaimed their preference for Irish tenants on account of the high rents they paid. The English Privy Council, at the beginning of the seventeenth century, laid down rules against employing the natives in the new Plantation of Ulster, on the premiss that: "As long as the British undertakers may receive their rents from the natives, they will never remove them."[89]

"Here," concluded historian George Hill, "was the grand dilemma . . . for the undertakers [the capitalist landlord investors] . . . naturally held out their hands for help to those who could most readily and efficiently render it. In fact they actually clung to the Irish . . . although to do so was risking more or less the overthrow of the whole [plantation] movement."[90]

Because the English were unable to escape that dilemma, plantation as a strategy of social control would fail finally and forever in three-fourths of the country. Ulster was of course the exception. There, plantation did ultimately achieve an historic success, due to special circumstances that made it possible to avoid the paralysis of the grand dilemma. The Ulster plantation is reserved for a later point of our discussion (see Chapter 5).

It is to be noted in proceeding to the implementation of the plantation policy, the first step toward "the king's peace" was invariably a military one: the mass exiling of tens of thousands of Irish men – in the wake of the Tyrone War; again, after the peace of 1652; and at the end of the Jacobite war of 1689–91.

In 1634, after thirty years of "complete conquest," England's Irish Council was fain to confess to King Charles I that dependence upon the treasury-draining, "rebel"-infested (that is, made up mainly of native Irish Catholics) army was "of absolute necessity" as "the great Preserver of public Peace, and the most effectual Minister in the Execution of your Majesty's Justice amongst us."[91] Between 1616 and 1641, plantation was tried in Longford, Leitrim, Wexford, southern Offaly and Galway. Despite some limited success, the effort ultimately ground to a halt, its basic purpose as unrealized as ever.[92] Thus, eighty years and nine plantations after that strategy was first undertaken, the Gaelic Irish still held one-third of all the profitable land in Ireland, the same proportion that they had held at the beginning.[93] The greatest of all Irish wars of resistance was in the offing.

The exiling of the defeated Irish soldiers by the victorious English under the terms of the Cromwellian Act of Settlement of 1652 did improve the prospects for reducing the English government's prohibitively high military costs in Ireland. By January 1653, thirteen thousand Irish soldiers had gone to "foreign parts," and some time later that year the English army of occupation was reduced by ten thousand to a level of twenty-four thousand. By the spring of 1654, the remaining twenty-some thousand Irish soldiers had been sold away. In August of the following year, the English forces were reduced again, to nineteen thousand on a budget of £336,000 per year. Officials in England were trying to convince those in Ireland that the number should be still further reduced to fifteen thousand.[94] Yet in 1658, annual military expenditure was still £246,000, far exceeding total English revenue from the colony.[95] Nevertheless, Lord Deputy Henry Cromwell had already concluded that no further reductions should be made "until an efficient Protestant militia could be provided."[96]

The first specific aim of the Cromwellian expropriation policy provided for in the Act of Settlement and the Act of Satisfaction was to reward the capitalists (called "Adventurers") who had lent the Parliament war money, and to pay off the veteran officers and soldiers who had served in Ireland. But it was to be done in a form designed to provide Ireland with enough yeomen and resident gentry to make a self-sustaining, well-officered, horse-and-foot, Protestant English settler militia.

As a capital fund for discharging English government obligations and pledges,[97] Irish land served its purpose. By May 1656 all soldier claims had been settled.[98] But settling claims against the English government was one thing; settling Protestant English on Irish soil was another. By 1670, 7,500 disbanded English soldiers out of 35,000, and 500 out of 15,000 Adventurers, had received confirmed titles to Irish land.[99] Yet, of those, only a fraction actually settled there, far too few to provide the hoped-for militia. In 1662, Sir William Petty expressed the opinion that even if every last one of the 50,000 Adventurers and soldiers settled in Ireland, military government would still be necessary. "Government [in Ireland] can never be safe without chargeable Armies," said Petty, "until the major part of the Inhabitants be English."[100] He was thus stating a general principle of social control by regimes based on racial oppression.

Added emphasis was lent to the impossibility of achieving any such requisite proportions of English emigration when the flow of migration was actually reversed during the brief reign of the Catholic James II (1685–88). Protestant settlers fled Ireland in large numbers, and almost no Protestants remained in the nominally English army there, all as a result of the pressure of the Irish Catholic cause, reinvigorated by the expectation of imminent repeal of the Act of Settlement.[101] At that point, in the summer of 1687, Petty was led to propose a final solution to the Irish question, one intended to eliminate the need to develop an intermediate social control stratum, and at the same time to reduce the requisite military administration there to fiscally manageable proportions.

Displaying his professional penchant for quantification, Petty estimated the adult Catholic population of Ireland at somewhat over 1,200,000. The maintenance of social control by military administration, he said, required somewhat more than one English soldier to every ten Irish men.[102] At such a ratio, the English would need to maintain an Irish military establishment of more than 60,000 men, a fiscal impossibility.

Citing supposed historic precedents, Petty proposed a way out: a mass transplantation to end all transplantations, to be achieved not by force but by the appeal of universal benefit to be derived by English and Irish, Protestant and Catholic.[103] Protestants and Catholics in proportional numbers would be transplanted to England, reducing the total population of Ireland from 1,300,000 to 300,000,[104] eight-ninths Catholic, one-ninth Protestant. Though the Irish Catholics to be transplanted to England would number nearly 900,000, they could, he argued, be safely controlled by the Protestant majority there only slightly diluted from its existing eight-to-one majority. The 300,000 Catholics remaining in Ireland would be kept exclusively to animal husbandry, half as "herdsmen" and half as "dairy women" (a division of labor by gender). According to Petty, this arrangement would prosper both England and Ireland.[105] In this way the problem of social control in the colony was to be reduced to manageable proportions. The proper one-to-ten ratio of military forces to subject population could be maintained, the 150,000 Irish herdsmen being matched by 15,000 English foot soldiers. Some 2,000 horse soldiers and 4,000 men at sea would make assurance doubly secure.[106]

Petty's proposal, though courteously received by the king, did not get lengthy consideration because at that moment the Jacobite–Catholic cause was riding high. However wildly implausible this plan may seem in retrospect, we should not believe it was so regarded by Petty's English contemporaries.[107] But no practical implementation of the idea was ever attempted; within a couple of years, James II was defeated and deposed, Petty had died, and the plan became no more than a footnote.

Fantastic and unrealizable as it was, nevertheless it is a very illuminating footnote for the subject of social control. For it proceeded with flawless logic from the ineluctable problem of the establishment of a civil regime in Ireland.

Ireland and General Principles of Colonial Social Control

The English efforts to establish social control in Ireland that are noted in this chapter present a variation on the general principles of the social control problems and policies of colonizing powers, and their relationship to the option for racial oppression. After first establishing commanding authority, colonizers pursued one of two general lines of policy according to circumstances as they found them.[108] Where they found a developed and well-defined hierarchical system of classes, the new rulers sought to adapt the pre-existing social structure to their own needs, coopting amenable elements of the old order into their colonial administration as a buffer and social control stratum over and against the masses of the superexploited wealth-producing laboring classes. Such was the case of the Spanish in Peru and Mexico;[109] of the Portuguese in India[110] and the East Indies; of the English in India; and of the Dutch in the East Indies.

Where, on the other hand, the conquerors encountered a society with no previously developed significant class differentiation, and therefore with no available social handle to serve their rule, they employed a policy tending to the complete elimination of the indigenous population by slaughter and expulsion. The Spanish in the Caribbean, the Portuguese in Brazil, the English in St Vincent, and the English and Anglo-Americans in North America demonstrated this approach. In such cases, the colonizers found themselves obliged to seek foreign supplies of commodity-producing labor,[111] and were obliged to invent and establish an intermediate social control stratum for each colony by promoting elements of the imported laboring class.

With regard to the extermination option, English military and economic policies from the sixteenth to the eighteenth century produced in Ireland episodes of mass extermination, as we have noted, which in absolute numerical terms and ferocity were possibly a match for those chronicled by Las Casas in the West Indies. But it would have been impossible for the English to have perpetrated such complete extermination of the Irish people as that executed upon the Caribs and Arawaks by the Spanish in the Caribbean in the sixteenth century. Unlike the situation of the Spanish in the Caribbean, there was in Ireland a much more substantial general English hostage population subject to retaliation for any such attempt. Although the English achieved an overwhelming military advantage over the Irish, still they at no time enjoyed the degree of practical invulnerability possessed by the Spanish *vis-à-vis* the indigenous peoples of the Americas. Moreover, but one Las Casas arose to deplore genocide in the Caribbean, and then only after the deed was done. But the Catholic Irish and Anglo-Irish had as allies popes, potentates and powers, sworn antagonists all of the English Protestant "heretics." In the struggle against their English rivals, the hopes of these powers depended, militarily and morally, on the preservation of the Irish resistance to the English, though not necessarily upon Irish independence. Finally, even if the English colonialists could have safely undertaken a Caribbean-style extermination of the Irish, it would have been detrimental to their own interest. Unlike the Spanish, the English were sixty years away from sure access to African sources of labor. And England could not supply English agricultural laborers for Ireland at a cost matching that of Irish labor already in place.[112]

On the other hand, the English option for religio-racial oppression in Ireland at the end of the sixteenth century eliminated the possibility of recruiting an indigenous intermediate social control stratum. This would remain the central problem of British rule in Ireland for more than two centuries. To the partial extent, namely in Ulster, that they succeeded in establishing an intermediate stratum, they were able to maintain racial oppression "without sending an army to do it." Outside Ulster, they would in time be forced to abandon rule by racial oppression. These developments and their Anglo-American parallels will be the subject of other chapters.

3

Protestant Ascendancy and White Supremacy

Following the defeat of the Irish–Jacobite cause in the brief war of 1689–91, the Protestant Parliament of Ireland embarked on a seventy-year program of Penal Law enactments to rivet the Protestant Ascendancy in place.[1] In due historical course, Edmund Burke analyzed and arraigned Protestant Ascendancy as a "contrivance," an invention unexcelled in the history of statecraft "for the oppression, impoverishment, and degradation of a people." But it is the less frequently cited analytical portion of his argument that exposes the hallmark of racial oppression characteristic of Protestant Ascendancy, and which is equally applicable to white supremacy. Burke compared various forms of the normal principles of social hierarchy characteristic of class societies, as exampled by the Venetian oligarchy, on the one hand, and the British constitutional combination of aristocracy and democracy, on the other. In the former, the members of the subject population are excluded from all participation in "the State." But they are "indemnified" by the untrammeled freedom to find places in the "subordinate employments," according to their individual competitiveness and their mutual accommodation. "The nobles" in such a society, said Burke, "have the monopoly of honor; the plebeians a monopoly of all the means of acquiring wealth." The British state, on the other hand, has a plebeian component; yet the aristocrats and plebeians do not compete with each other, and social rank among the non-aristocrats is arranged, again, by the normal process of free competition. But, "A plebeian aristocracy is a monster," said Burke, and such was the system of Protestant Ascendancy in Ireland. There, he said, Roman Catholics are obliged to submit to "[Protestant] plebeians like themselves, and many of them tradesmen, servants, and otherwise inferior to some of them [yet] ... exercising upon them, daily and hourly, an insulting and vexatious superiority."[2]

A full century of Irish history – between the overshadowing English Glorious Revolution of 1688 and the French Revolution of 1789 – was entirely dominated by the Protestant Ascendancy and its Penal Laws. Down to the present day, the spirit of Protestant Ascendancy has continued to inform British rule in Ireland.[3] Students of Irish history have therefore necessarily devoted much attention to the nature and operation of the Ascendancy and the Penal Laws. Students of American history, however, have almost completely neglected this field of investigation for insights into the system of racial oppression which, more than any other force or factor, has controlled the flow of United States history.[4]

This neglect is due, no doubt, to the fact that they mistake the chattel form of labor, along with perceived variations in physical appearance, for the essential substance of racial oppression. This shallow view has remained an unchallenged assumption. But if asked to defend the exclusion of the Protestant Ascendancy from the category of racial oppression, our historians might seek to rest their case on two arguments. First, they might say, however relentlessly destructive the intentions of the English ruling class might have been, they did not try to impose a system of chattel bond-servitude on the Irish in Ireland, as they did on African-Americans. They might further argue that the Irish could escape from the penalties of the Penal Laws simply by becoming Protestant, whereas the African-Americans had no such simple way out of their bondage. A fairly long digression is required here to confront these two issues. Readers who wish to avoid the detour may go directly to the subheading, "Penal Laws and 'Race' Laws" (page 81).

Why Not Chattel Bond-servitude?

If the English conquistadors did not formally enslave the Irish, it was not because they were economically and militarily weaker in relation to the Irish than they were *vis-à-vis* the chattel bond-laborers in the distant American plantations. In 1654 Ireland's armies had been defeated and exiled; the only horses to be seen bore English soldiery. To the English ruling class Ireland was a *tabula rasa* on which it could inscribe what it would.[5]

Nor was it because the slavery idea was unthinkable among the British ruling classes. In the period 1571–75 the English government sponsored two unsuccessful private enterprise efforts to colonize Ulster, the northern province of Ireland. At least some of the organizers of these projects proposed to reduce the natives of the area to slavery, as their role models had done in "the Indies."[6] In 1662 Sir William Petty proposed that slavery be instituted in England itself for "insolvent Thieves," as a profitable alternative to the customary hanging. "As slaves," he said, "they may be forced to as much labour and as cheap fare as nature will endure."[7]

Indeed, in Scotland, whence so many Presbyterian lowlanders came to Ireland as junior partners in the English colonization, that very prescription had been established practice since the sixteenth century.[8] Then, in 1606, not only thieves and vagrants but free coalminers and salt-pan workers were made bond-slaves by law. Out of consideration of the "great prejudice" to the owners of coal and salt enterprises resulting from workers leaving their jobs "upon hope of greater gain" in some other employment, the Privy Council legally bound those workers to their masters, for life, unless they were sold along with the mine or saltworks, or were otherwise disposed of by their owners.[9] Their servitude was not only perpetual but in practice hereditary. This chattel slavery lasted until after it had ceased to be economically advantageous to the employers at the end of the eighteenth century.[10] In the second half of the seventeenth century, the expansion of Anglo-American colonial enterprises opened a wider field for employment of "vagrants" and convicts as chattel bond-laborers, although for terms somewhat shorter than those commonly imposed in Scotland. Bond-laborers, said the *Edinburgh Review*, "were a leading export of the country, and it was the regular custom, when a ship was sailing for the plantations, for the master, or owner, or charterer to petition the Privy Council for a certain number of vagrants."[11] These unfortunates would then be provided as if they were so many bushels of oats, or tubs of coal. In the period between the Restoration and the Act of Union of England and Scotland in 1707, when the English Trade and Navigation Laws were effective in reducing Scottish trade with the colonies, "a cargo of Scottish servants ... was probably the most profitable cargo a merchant could take to the colonies."[12]

In Ireland, the resumption of the bond-labor trade after a lapse of some five hundred years began as an English – primarily political – policy. The English embarked on the plantation of Ulster in 1609, aiming to establish a colony of English and Scots in six counties[13] in the north of Ireland, the land there having been expropriated from Irish "rebels" defeated in the Tyrone War.[14] There were in Ulster still four thousand "idle men ... who have neither house, lands, trade nor other means,"[15] and whose heads were full of "treasonous" designs against the English occupiers of their lands. At this point the English found a way of promoting the colony's tranquility and improving the balance of trade at the same time. In the autumn of 1610, one thousand Irish men, nine hundred of them from Ulster, were shipped under a contract of sale to the King of Sweden to serve his royal Protestant will, presumably as soldiers. An English officer was to go along and look after the exporters' interests in the completion of the transaction.[16]

After the victory over the Irish in the 1641–52 rebellion and war, the English renewed this policy on a scale which proved to have fateful historic consequences. As mentioned on page 249, note 149, some 35,000 to 40,000 defeated Irish soldiers were sold to foreign states,[17] again presumably to serve as soldiers, although some number, thought to have been less than a thousand, were shipped to the West Indies as plantation laborers.[18] At some point in the process, these Irish soldiers would fall into the power of "drovers and sellers ... who now find the miserable Irishman to be the best commodity in trade."[19] Petty says that six thousand priests, women and boys were shipped along with

the soldiers, although it does not appear that they were separately entered in
the accounts.[20] In this case, the primary concern of the English was again
political; so much so that when the Spanish Crown or some other customer was
slow in paying, the English government would underwrite the process.[21] But
for those alert to opportunity and favorably situated socially, it offered a
profitable field of private enterprise.[22]

In the forced transportation of Irish women, children and men to bond-
servitude in the Anglo-American colonies between 1652 and 1657, mercenary
motives were predominant. On 20 April 1652, the English House of Commons
empowered the Council of State "to give away to the Transporting out of
Ireland, into foreign parts such of the Irish as they shall think fit, for the
Advantage of the Commonwealth."[23] Upon application to the English
authorities, merchants were issued licenses to take cargoes of Irish to America
for sale as bond-laborers. The terms were such as to assure the merchant's
profit. At first, it seems, the licenses were issued upon application to the
English Council of State. In a period of less than one year, April 1653 to
January 1654, six merchants were thus authorized to take nearly 2,000 Irish,
including 400 children and 310 women, to be sold as bond-laborers in Anglo-
America. Among the transport ships to be used under these licenses were two
specifically designed for this beginning of "the Irish slave trade," a characterization made by contemporary observers and adopted by a number of Irish
historians.[24] Subsequently the common practice was direct negotiation
between the slave trader and the magistrates, jail-keepers and overseers of the
poor in specific Irish localities. The procedure was conducted under color of
the English vagrancy act of 1597 (39 Eliz. c. 4), an English domestic law
transposed unceremoniously to another country for a purpose for which it had
never been contemplated. It was a legal fiction, of course. The people taken up
were not, for the most part, "rogues, vagabonds or sturdy beggars," as defined
in the English Poor Law of 1601 (43 Eliz. I c. 2). Furthermore, these measures
were taken under color of an English statute; it had never been enacted by the
Irish Parliament. Nevertheless, it served just as well for capturing, selling and
transporting non-vagrants, as actual vagrants. There ensued, says Abbot E.
Smith, "a period of licensed kidnapping on a large scale, with the magistrates
and officers of the law actively conniving at it under some pretense of statutory
sanction."[25] When this slave trade was ended in 1657, the Council of State, all
in seeming innocence, declared that "for the money's sake" the system had
"enticed and forced women from their children and husbands, and children
from their parents, who maintained them at school."[26] The execution of this
policy, writes Prendergast, "must have exhibited scenes in every part like the
slave hunts in Africa."[27] Again, following the defeat of the Irish–Jacobite
struggle of 1689–91, Irish soldiers were shipped by the thousands into
perpetual exile, mainly to France.[28]

If the English did not establish their regime in Ireland on a system of chattel bond-labor as they did in the plantation colonies in America, it was simply a matter of relative "cost/benefit" ratios. A comparative study of the living standards of laborers in Ireland and bond-laborers in continental Anglo-America is yet to be made. But there is much evidence to suggest that the cost of labor per unit of output in Ireland would not have been reduced by the substitution of chattel bond-labor for the common Irish condition of tenancy-at-will.[29]

In 1652, at the end of eleven years of war, the land of Ireland was "void as a wilderness," so that, as the records found by Prendergast told, people were driven by desperate hunger to eat carrion and even human flesh.[30] Over the next two decades, a remarkable economic recovery occurred, but only the merchants and landlords benefited by it; six-sevenths of the population of Ireland were still living at mere subsistence level.[31] It was during that period that William Petty wrote his *Political Anatomy of Ireland* for the edification of the restored Stuart monarch, Charles II, in the course of which he estimated the financial losses suffered in Ireland as a result of the 1641–52 war. The cost of the population loss he put at £10,355,000 sterling, on the assumption that "you value the people who have been destroyed in Ireland as Slaves and Negroes are usually rated, viz., at about £15 one with another; Men being sold for £25 and Children £5 each."[32]

During the eighteenth century, normal economic conditions prevailed generally in Ireland. Yet despite the fame of Irish livestock products, Ireland's tenants were obliged to "live on potatoes and buttermilk, and yield all other profitable produce as rent."[33]

A weekly newspaper in 1721 described the cottiers of Ireland (a category closely corresponding to the United States sharecropper of the post-Reconstruction period, except that the cottiers were share-laborers, paying their rent by laboring on the landlord's land) as "Poor wretches who think themselves blessed if they can obtain a hut worse than the squire's dog kennel, and an acre of ground for potato plantation, on condition of being as very slaves as any in America."[34] An Englishman who traveled in Ireland in 1764 observed that their condition was "little better than slavery." That same year Lord Chesterfield, who had served as Lord Lieutenant of Ireland twenty years before, declared: "The poor people of Ireland are used worse than the negroes."[35] Yet according to Lecky the unemployed agricultural laborers, without a "cabbin and garden" were even worse off than the cottiers. The mass of the Irish laboring people were cottiers, he says, "because in most parts of Ireland it was impossible to gain a livelihood as agricultural labourers or in mechanical pursuits."[36] The great majority of the Irish Catholic cottier families were forced to eke out a subsistence on plots of less than an English acre.[37] Yet they were by law forbidden to surrender less than two-thirds of the crop yield to the landlord, or less than one-tenth to the Anglican Church of Ireland.[38] An indication of how much the Irish laborer's conditions had deteriorated may perhaps be inferred from the fact that in 1589 English landlords in Ireland preferred Irish to English as tenants because, it was said, Irish tenants, paying one-fourth the yield as rent, were a much more profitable labor force.[39]

Being too impoverished to put by any store, the people were famished when crops failed. Untold thousands of people died in famines between 1721 and 1741.[40] At such times the cost of labor might sink beneath the absolute limit required to sustain it. During one such dearth, in 1729, a keen observer of Irish life estimated that only 15 percent of "breeding couples" in the country were able to maintain their own children. The workers were generally unemployed, but their deprivation was such, he said, that "if at any time they are accidentally hired to common labour, they have not strength to perform it."[41] During the worst of these eighteenth-century famines, in 1740–41, a country gentleman in Munster wrote of its horror in a letter to Primate Boulter:

> I have seen the labourer endeavouring to work at his spade, but fainting for want of food, and forced to quit it. I have seen the aged father eating grass like a beast and in the anguish of his soul wishing for his dissolution. I have seen the helpless orphan exposed on the dunghill, and none to take him in for fear of infection; and I have seen the hungry infant sucking at the breast of the already expired parent.[42]

In that famine, according to one historian, nearly 400,000 people died,[43] nearly one out of every five of the total population. Then might people driven to beggary seek a competitive edge by blinding their children, to make them more appealing objects for charity.[44]

In the non-famine year of 1787, the Attorney-General of Ireland declared in a speech to the Irish House of Commons:

> It was impossible for the peasantry of Munster any longer to exist in the extreme wretchedness, under which they laboured. A poor man was to pay £6 for an acre of potato ground, which £6 he was obliged to work out with his landlord at 5d. per day.[45]

The impossibility of the peasant's position was a mathematical certainty. At 5d. a day, in order to pay the rent for his potato ground the peasant would have to devote 288 days a year exclusively to working for the landlord.

If the eighteenth-century Anglo-Irish Establishment ever wondered whether, from the standpoint of political economy, they had chosen wisely in the matter of labor relations, they could have found comfort in the following fact. Taking English and American current money wage rates as the respective bases, the relative cost differential between English and Irish common labor was more than two and a half times the cost differential between wage-labor and bond-labor in continental Anglo-America. In real terms, the England/Ireland differential was still greater than the American free/bond differential.[46]

Why not Conversion to Protestantism?

The consensus of authorities is that the population of Ireland doubled, rising from around 2 million to 4 million over the course of the eighteenth century,[47] of whom between 75 and 80 percent were Catholics.[48] Beginning in 1703 an official record was kept of all Irish Catholics converted to Protestantism; by the end of 1800, about 5,800 names had been enrolled.[49] Let it be assumed for purposes of statistical convenience that the incidence of conversion was constant from year to year, and remained so for the entire eighteenth century, and that the rate of natural increase among the convert population was the same as it was for the general population.[50] The indicated convert population at the end of the century would then be less than 8,000, representing a ratio of less than three converts to 1,000 nonconverts.

Since conversion was the only road to emancipation for the Irish Catholics ground down by the Penal Laws, it is interesting to compare these Irish statistics with those regarding the achievement of emancipation from the slave laws in the Americas by persons of African descent. In the African-American population at the end of the eighteenth century, the ratio of free to bond persons appears to have been not less than ten times the convert-to-nonconvert ratio in Ireland. In the United States the overall proportion of free African-Americans to those in bondage was thirty-five times the corresponding Irish ratio.[51]

Where conversion did take place, it occurred mainly among the propertied and professional strata (and with varying degrees of religious conviction).[52] By becoming Protestants – and only by becoming Protestants – they were enabled to enjoy social recognition and the privileges normal and essential to members of their class: the rights to purchase land, hold office, serve on grand juries, hold army commissions, have their sons educated in schools and universities, bear arms, exercise the rights of patriarchy (including that of bequeathing their property), etcetera.

For the rank-and-file of Catholic laboring people there was little prospect of bourgeois enrichment; yet even for them, as Butler puts it, "there was always the possibility of escape from all disabilities, and of a rise into the dominant caste provided only that they embraced the dominant religion."[53] Within that "dominant caste," even those of the laboring classes had their Protestant privileges: the right to long-term leases and security against eviction; the right to become trades apprentices, and to that end to be taught to read and write; the right to marry without the landlord's permission, and exemption from systematized degradation at the hands of the Protestant landlords, "middle-men," etcetera. "A Protestant boy," writes J. C. Beckett, "however humble his origin, might hope to rise, by some combination of ability, good luck and patronage, to a position of influence from which a Roman Catholic, however well-born or wealthy, would be utterly excluded."[54]

Why then was the Protestant harvest of souls so meagre? There was certainly an aversion to surrendering this last main institutional vestige of Celtic Irish selfhood, an aversion daily reinforced by the indefatigable labors of a thousand Catholic priests, working illegally, and the equally energetic efforts of the Protestant tithe-proctors. But, if there had been not one Catholic priest in Ireland, if the Irish people could have amnestied the Protestant conquistadors and their descendants for their arrogant rapacity, if 997 out of 1,000 of the Catholic Irish had signified a desire to become "born-again" as Anglican Protestants, it is doubtful whether so much as a page would thereby have been added to the roll of converts.

The reason is not hard to see. Ireland, as a British colonial enterprise, was founded on the original expropriation of Catholic-owned lands and the continuing exclusion of Catholics from acquiring new land titles or even long-term leases. From this flowed the disfranchisement of Irish people of the entrepreneurial and professional classes, as well as the superexploitation of the laboring people, mainly tenants-at-will.[55] Speaking of the motives for the enactment of the Penal Laws, Lecky writes:

> ... behind all this lay the great fact that most of the land of the country was held by the title of recent confiscation, and that the old possessors or their children were still living, still remembered, still honoured by the people. It was the dread of a change of property springing from this fact that was the real cause of most of the enactments of the penal code.... It was this which gave the landlord class most of their arrogance.... It was this above all that made them implacably hostile to every project for ameliorating the condition of the Catholics. In 1709, the [Irish] House of Commons presented an address to the Queen [reminding her that] "the titles of more than half the estates now belonging to Protestants depend on the forfeitures in the two last rebellions."[56]

To impede and frustrate the efforts of Catholics to get legal redress for the loss of lands and rights in the wake of the 1689–91 war, the Irish Parliament enacted a law, effective 1 March 1698, barring any Catholic from acting as "solicitor, agent, or manager in any cause or sute ... in this kingdom [Ireland]."[57] When, in time, conforming former Catholics began to enter law practice, the Protestant Ascendancy, instead of rejoicing at the growth of their flock and the betokened defeat of the "Papist enemy," slammed the gate against further entry. A law was enacted requiring conformists to undergo years of closely supervised probation of the sincerity of their conversion. Only when, after that period, they merited the Protestant seal of approval, might they practice their profession.[58] Between 1703 and 1760 a dozen laws were enacted "To prevent the growth of Popery," but not even one "To promote the growth of Protestantism."

"There are too many amongst us," said Archbishop Synge, "who had rather keep the Papists in an almost slavish subjection, than have them made Protestants, and thereby entitled to the same liberties and privileges with the rest of their fellow-subjects."[59] The historian W. K. Sullivan concurred. "If the whole body of the Catholics had become Protestant," he wrote, "the Ascendancy would lose their advantages." The unwillingness of the Protestant Ascendancy to promote the conversion of Catholics to Protestantism was, he declared, "one of the great central facts of Irish history."[60] The findings of the late Maureen Wall led her to concur with those opinions, and to advert to an analogy: "The religious bar operated to exclude the Catholic majority from all positions of importance . . . in the same way as the colour bar has operated to ensure white ascendancy in African countries."[61]

There was another set of reasons for the ruling-class opposition to conversion, reasons having to do with the problem of social control. Although the ruling party was the Anglican Church of Ireland Establishment, two-thirds of the Protestants were Dissenters, primarily the Presbyterian Scots-Irish of Ulster. From the very first year of his assumption of the role of manager of Irish affairs in 1724, Primate Hugh Boulter understood that the maintenance of British rule in Ireland required the prevention of any tendency toward coalescence of a potential opposition majority.[62] Above all, that meant preventing the aggrieved middle-class yeomanry-type Presbyterian and other Dissenters from making common "nationalist" cause with the mass of the peasantry. The time-tested key to that strategy was the inveterate prejudice of the Dissenters against the Catholic peasantry. In 1798, the rebellion of the United Irishmen was defeated, and with it the last best hope (until 1922) for a republican and independent Ireland. In the aftermath of that defeat, John Beresford, one of the most powerful figures in the Anglo-Irish establishment, pointed to this anti-Catholic prejudice as the key to the government's victorious policy:

> The lower order of Roman Catholics of this country are totally inimical to the English Government. . . . Again, the Dissenters are another set of enemies to British Government. They are greatly under the influence of their clergy also, and are taught from their cradles to be republicans; but their religion, which is as fierce as their politics, forbids them to unite with the Catholics; and to that, in a great measure, is owing that we were not all destroyed in this rebellion.[63]

Obviously, any serious effort to convert Irish Catholics to Protestantism would have been potentially ruinous for Anglo-Irish statecraft. On both primary and secondary grounds, therefore, if the English colonial system of racial oppression in Ireland was to be perpetuated, it was essential that the people not be converted, but remain Catholic.[64]

Anglo-America: Parallels and Divergence

In Anglo-America, no less than in Ireland, spiritual rebirth by conversion to Protestant Christianity presented a contradiction to social death by racial oppression. It had been received doctrine in England, at least since before the publication of Thomas Smith's *De Republica Anglorum* in 1583, that Christians could not hold Christians in bondage.[65]

In the early 1630s, the directors in England of the ill-fated English colony on Providence Island rebuked the resident official, Samuel Rishworth, in this regard. Rishworth, they said, had been in error in saying that African laborers who had not yet been converted to Christianity, could not legally be held in bondage.[66] The Englishman Richard Ligon lived in Barbados from 1647 to 1650. In those years the island was beginning its transition from a primarily tobacco-based economy to one of sugar planting, with the help of fellow Protestant Dutch sugar planters retreating from Brazil.[67] At that time the majority of the workers were English, Irish and Scots limited-term bond-laborers, although African workers, serving unlimited terms, were present in an increasing proportion; by 1655, they would outnumber the Europeans in the labor force.[68] At one plantation an African-Barbadian asked Ligon to help him become a convert to the English religion. Ligon promised "to do my best endeavours," it being understood that the worker's owner had the final say. But when approached, the owner rejected the suggestion as bad business practice. "The people of that Island were governed by the Lawes of England," he said, "and by those Lawes, we could not make a Christian a slave." Ligon then advanced the argument which, half a century later, would be the staple of plantation missionaries. He was not requesting that a Christian be made a slave, said Ligon, but merely that a slave be made a Christian. The owner rejected this as mere prevarication. Once the man was converted to the English religion, he said, "he could no more account him a slave," and "all the planters in the Island would curse him" for having opened "such a gap" whereby these laborers could escape from their bondage.[69]

In Virginia in 1656, an African-American woman successfully sued for her freedom, citing among other grounds the fact that she was a Christian.[70] The implications of the decision in this case caused considerable concern among Virginia employers of bond-labor. In 1667, the Virginia Assembly cut the knot wherein freedom was tangled with conversion; they enacted a law providing that "the conferring of baptisme doth not alter the condition of the person as to his bondage or freedome."[71] Thus the Anglo-American plantation bourgeoisie had found a way to have the best of both the sacred and the profane spheres. The best of the sacred was gained in a new gospel that reconciled "English liberties" to slavery; the best of the profane by insuring against legal challenges made on religious grounds against holding lifetime hereditary bond-laborers.

Despite the assurance of this Virginia precedent, South Carolina owners were still wary of the conversion of Africans and African-Americans to the English religion. By 1710, the Society for the Propagation of the Gospel, whose business was converting "heathens," had learned that it was "to do nothing without the Master's good testimony" as to the reliability of the prospective convert.[72]

The very language of conversion became an issue both in Ireland and in the English beginnings in the West Indies. In the first flush of Reformationism, the Anglo-Irish Parliament excluded the use of Gaelic in the conduct of church services.[73] Despite an Elizabethan mood swing on the matter of Gaelic, and despite occasional evangelical gambits, official policy continued to be guided by the warning that Edmund Spenser took from history and taught to his fellow English colonizers: "The speech being Irish, the heart must need be."[74]

In Anglo-America, plantation owners at first viewed the diversity of languages among the bond-laborers as a major factor in effective social control. In 1680 the Gentlemen Planters of Barbados in London argued that they had "no greater security than the diversity of our negroe's languages [,] which would be destroyed by conversion, in that it would be necessary to teach them in English."[75] For reasons already discussed, avoidance of conversion of the Irish to the English religion was essential to the system of religio-racial oppression. On the other hand, the Anglo-American plantation bourgeoisie, whose land claims and social control did not rest on religious distinctions, learned – with the help of the new exegesis – to reconcile their class interests with the conversion of Africans to the English religion.

Penal Laws and "Race" Laws

The parallels to be noted here are the more forceful, perhaps, because they originate in contemporary aspects of British colonialism.[76] At the threshold of the eighteenth century, it was Virginia that led the way among Anglo-American continental colonies in codifying the concept that, "race, not class ... [is] the great distinction in society."[77] It was then, too, that the Protestant Ascendancy instituted its system of Penal Laws, designed to "put an end to all other distinctions in Ireland, but that of Protestant and Papist."[78]

Professor Maureen Wall extended the parallel with racial oppression. The Penal Laws, she wrote:

> operated to exclude the Catholic majority from all positions of importance in the country – from the professions, from parliament, and from the ownership of property – in the same way as the colour bar has operated to ensure white ascendancy in African countries in recent times.[79]

The essential elements of discrimination against the Irish in Ireland, and

*against the African-Americans, which gave these respective regimes the
character of racial oppression, were those that destroyed the original forms
of social identity, and then excluded the oppressed groups from admittance
into the forms of social identity normal to the colonizing power.* Take away
these elements, and racial oppression would cease to exist. The codification of
this system in the Penal Laws of the Protestant Ascendancy in Ireland and in
the slave codes of white supremacy in continental Anglo-America have been
frequently abstracted and analyzed in the works cited here. The discussion that
follows considers them according to the defining characteristics of racial
oppression: (1) declassing legislation, directed at property-holding members of
the oppressed group; (2) deprivation of civil rights; (3) illegalization of
literacy; and (4) displacement of family rights and authorities.

Declassing legislation

The English had destroyed the Celtic tribal form of individual social identity.
With the Penal Laws they proceeded to bar the Irish from the system of social
class identification normal to the bourgeois social order. The process began
with laws designed to declass the members of the Catholic Irish freehold
classes of all degrees from life tenants upward. The aim was, as Sigerson put
it, "to thrust them down into the slough of despond with the racked under-
tenantry."[80] This non-recognition of social distinction among the oppressed
population was made explicit by the highest judicial authorities in Ireland, the
Chancellor and Chief Justice, who laid down the principle that except for
repression and punishment "the law does not suppose any such person to exist
as an Irish Roman Catholic."[81]

Even in the wake of the last great sweeping confiscations, there were still
a few Catholic landholders in Ireland with undisputed titles to their estates.
Normally, though reduced in means these freeholders, gentry and noblemen,
would enter into the fortune-building activities appropriate to persons of their
economic status. But the Anglo-Irish government proceeded with speedy
deliberation to frustrate such hopes.[82] Though garbed as a holy war against
popery, this policy was governed mainly by considerations of capital
accumulation.[83]

The cornerstone of the legislative prisonhouse that was the Penal Law
system was "The Act to Prevent the Growth of Popery," passed in 1704
(2 Anne c. 6).[84] Under this law, as amended in 1709 (8 Anne c. 3), and enforced
by confiscatorial penalties:

1. Catholic tenants could not acquire land from a Protestant, neither by
purchase, gift or inheritance, or have benefit of annuities on any land held by
a Protestant.

2.   Catholic tenants could not lease land for more than thirty-one years. They were thus barred from becoming freeholders and, as such, voters. Social class degradation was made especially effective by the requirement that they pay rent of not less than two-thirds of the yield on the land they rented. In this respect all Catholic Irish tenants were reduced to the status of the lowest-ranking tenant of ancient Celtic custom, that of the marginal free *fuidir* class, reserved for the wandering stranger. (The likeness to the free *fuidir* was soon made more complete as the workings of the Penal Laws reduced the overwhelming majority of the Irish to one-year tenants-at-will.)[85]

3.   A Catholic landholder was deprived of all rights of testament over his estate. Here, the gavelkind principle, which the British had once so abominated, was put to use as a deliberate means to fragment Catholic landholdings (2 Anne c. 6). An amendment provided that any Protestant, regardless of social rank, had standing to "discover" Catholic evasions of the land restriction laws, the title to the land to be awarded to the discoverer (8 Anne 27).

4.   Catholic men were barred from acquiring property from Protestants by dowry, under terms of a law of 1697 (9 Will. III c. 3) forbidding the marriage of a Catholic to a Protestant. The language of the law's preamble seems worth sampling: "Many protestant maidens and women," it says, "... have been seduced ... to take to husband, papists or popish persons ... [thus] corrupting and perverting such protestants ... [as they] become papists to the great dishonour of Almighty God".

   In order to compete in the world of the colonial bourgeoisie in Ireland, or in Anglo-America, two things were necessary: land and labor. In Ireland, Catholics who might have succeeded in bourgeois terms had ready access to labor, but they were by law forbidden to acquire land (except as short-term tenants). In Virginia (the pattern-setting colony), the African-Americans who might have succeeded in bourgeois terms could, by virtue of the headright system, have had access to land, but by a law enacted in 1670 they were forbidden to acquire any bond-laborers except those of African ancestry.[86] Being necessarily persons of small means, African-Americans were thus put at an almost insurmountable competitive disadvantage, since the capital outlay for each African or African-American bond-laborer was about two or three times as high as that required for each bond-laborer from Europe.[87] After 1691, African-Americans who sought to enter the competitive struggle as newly emancipated persons were not (except by express official leave) allowed to remain in Virginia. And, like the Catholic Irish by law forbidden to marry Protestants, the African-Americans were by a 1691 law barred from acquiring property by marriage with Europeans or European-Americans.[88] Unlike the Catholic Irish, however, African-American property-holders seem to have retained their testamentary rights intact.[89]

Deprivation of civil rights

In trying to defend such property as did remain to them, or in any effort at social mobility, the Catholic Irish labored under the burden of a general denial of civil rights. A series of a dozen laws forbade "Papists" to possess arms or gunpowder; or practice law, publicly or privately; or serve on grand juries; or hold any position of authority or trust above subordinate constable; or have the freedom of cities and towns corporate; or serve in the army or navy; or own a horse worth more than £5; or serve in Parliament; or vote in any election for public office.[90]

All the disabilities imposed on the Catholic Irish in Ireland in regard to civil rights were sooner or later imposed against African-Americans. In Ireland, the Protestant Ascendancy and the Penal Laws were based on the legal fiction that, as Scully put it, "All the effective inhabitants of Ireland are presumed to be Protestants – and therefore . . . the Catholics . . . are not to be supposed to exist – save for reprehension and penalty."[91] That would be a fair representation, *mutatis mutandis*, of the situation of the African-American in Anglo-America, as Chief Justice Taney characterized it in the Dred Scott decision, saying, "there are no rights which negroes have that white men are bound to respect."[92]

The kinship of spirit between the Protestant Ascendancy and white supremacy was put on record at the outset of the "white race" era in a 1705 Virginia law reconstituting the Virginia Court system: "popish recusants convict, negroes, mulattoes and Indian servants, and others not being christians, shall be deemed and taken to be persons incapable in law, to be witnesses in any case whatsoever."[93] Under the slave codes in continental Anglo-America, beginning with a Virginia law of 1705, African-American bond-laborers were excluded from the right to trial by jury; and in 1832, in the wake of Nat Turner's Rebellion,[94] even free African-Americans were denied jury trials, except in capital cases.[95] In Ireland the jury form of trial was not canceled, but the jury could be limited to Protestants only in any case in which the defendant was a Catholic.[96]

The absolute disfranchisement of the Catholic Irish in Ireland and the disfranchisement of African-Americans in Virginia occurred about the same time. In 1727 an act passed by the Irish Parliament provided that "[n]o papist, though not convict, shall be entitled or admitted to vote at the election of any member to serve in Parliament as knight, citizen, or burgess, or at the election of any magistrate for any city or other town-corporate."[97]

Prior to 1723, all freeholders in Virginia, African-American and European-American, were permitted to vote, with the exception of women, persons under twenty-one years of age, and non-conforming Catholics. These categories had been excluded from the franchise by laws passed in 1699 and again in 1705.[98] But in 1723, an act concerned with "the better government of Negroes,

Mulattos, and Indians, bond or free," for the first time deprived African-Americans of the vote.[99]

The illegalization of literacy

A more general barrier to maintaining or achieving propertied status was the illegalization of literacy. Even before the formal inauguration of the Penal Laws system, a 1692 law (4 W & M c. 2) made it a crime for a Catholic to go abroad to be educated. Then the first of the Penal Laws (7 Will. III c. 4, *Irish Statutes*), passed in 1695, made it a criminal offense for any person (except within one's immediate family) to teach "Papists" to read or write, or otherwise school them. "No person whatsoever of the popish religion," it said, "shall publickly or in private houses teach school or instruct youth in learning within this realm." In its final version (8 Anne c. 3 [1709]), the penalty for Catholics who ventured to teach the youth was increased, from three months in jail and a £20 fine, to perpetual imprisonment and complete forfeiture of property, that being the punishment prescribed for unlicensed Catholic clergy.[100] Protestants who employed Catholics as even assistant teachers were subject to a £10 fine for each offense.

In like spirit, Catholics were by law strictly excluded from some apprenticeships (7 Will. III c. 4, sec. 8); even Catholic masters were discriminated against as to the number and terms of the apprentices they could employ (8 Anne c. 3, sec. 37).[101] The most prevalent form of discrimination was by local custom and regulation. "At present," said an observer writing in 1724, "there is not one freeman or master of any corporation ... of the Roman Catholic religion in all the kingdom [Ireland]."[102] Lecky adds the comment, "In the most Catholic parts of Ireland many of the most lucrative.trades were long a strict monopoly of the Protestants, who refused to admit any Catholic as an apprentice."[103] In the last quarter of the eighteenth century, Arthur Young found the Catholic Irish "under such discouragements that they cannot engage in any trade which requires both capital and industry.... [E]very means is taken to reduce and keep them in a state of poverty."[104]

Sooner or later laws were enacted in the Anglo-American South to forbid the teaching of reading and writing to African-American bond-laborers,[105] on the grounds that it unsuited them for slavery.[106] In Virginia in 1832, after Nat Turner's Rebellion, it was made a crime to teach a free African-American to read and write.[107] The same law forbade the return to Virginia of African-Americans who went north to be educated. The Protestant Ascendancy had acted in a similar vein in Ireland by passing a law taking away all civil rights from any Catholic Irish person who went abroad for an education (7 Will. III c. 4 [1695]).

With regard to the trades, African-Americans were confronted with the same sort of exclusion by law and customary discrimination as was faced by the

Catholics in Ireland. In the 1690s Protestant porters in Dublin and "white" porters in New York City were petitioning the authorities against allowing the employment of "Papists" and "Negroes" respectively in that trade.[108] Under the heading "Concerted Action by White Workmen Against Negro Artisans," Professor Morris cited from the record of the eighteenth and early nineteenth centuries more than a dozen such instances involving white racist appeals for legislative prohibitions against free or bond African-American workers in non-agricultural labor.[109] A study made in Philadelphia in 1821 found that on account of racial discrimination, free African-Americans were "excluded from most of the respectable and profitable employments of life, confined to the humblest and least gainful occupations."[110] Frederick Douglass relates his personal experience with this sort of "white" exclusionism both as a bondman in Baltimore and as a free person in New Bedford.[111]

Assault on the family

The Protestant Ascendancy being a system of racial oppression, even the family was no refuge of social identity for the Irish Catholics under the Penal Laws. In the social displacement of the Irish propertied classes, the prerogatives of the husband and father were set aside. As already noted, a Catholic Irish male could not add to his estate by marrying a Protestant. If he married a Catholic woman who subsequently became a Protestant, the very basis of his status of lord and master over her was drastically impaired, unless he too became a Protestant. Ordinarily, a widow was not entitled to any share of her deceased husband's real estate (lands, houses, etcetera), unless under the terms of her marriage contract some particular and explicit contrary provision were required to be included in the husband's last will and testament. Under the Penal Laws (8 Anne 3, sections 14 and 15 [1709]), a wife who became a convert to Protestantism was automatically entitled to inherit one-third of her husband's lands, as well as retaining her right to the customary one-third "widow's portion" of his personal estate (silver, money, movables, etcetera).

The Catholic father's authority over his children was similarly undermined if they chose to desert the faith of their fathers by becoming Protestants (2 Anne 6, section 3). The father, regardless of his own wishes, could be compelled to provide for such convert children "fitting maintenance" and to guarantee "future provision" for them appropriate to his material means. If that convert happened to be the eldest son, the father was automatically rendered a mere tenant-for-life; the son became the landlord with all the vested rights of that title, as if the father were dead. Given the cunning pressure thus exerted on propertied Catholics, more than a few of them understandably became at least formally Protestants.

In all this disallowance of the legitimacy of the Catholic Irish family, of course, nothing was intended against the patriarchy or male supremacy as such. It was another variation of the attack on Catholic property-holding, and another way of delegitimating whatever degree of social eminence that the Catholic property-holder might still retain. It was at the same time the continuation of expropriation by other means. But as far as male privileges were concerned, the modifications were limited and specific, and by no means represented any equalitarian impulse.

With regard to the propertyless masses, the tenants-at-will, the male privileges of the Protestant landlord had precedence over those of the tenant with respect to the women members of the tenant's family. More than one landlord boasted to Arthur Young that "Many of their cotters would think themselves honoured by having their wives and daughters sent for to the bed of their masters."[112] A peasant might not appreciate such lordly condescension, but he knew that he "would have his bones broken if he offered to raise his hand" against the landlord. The custom, says Young, was "a mark of slavery." If the cottier appealed to the Justice of the Peace for redress, the Justice would not even venture to issue a summons to the landlord for fear of affronting the landlord's honor. Incredible as it is, Sigerson assures us that even in the early nineteenth century there were cases in which this ultimate form of negation of the Catholic Irish family was stipulated in the lease as a privilege of the landlord.[113]

The Protestant Ascendancy gave special attention to breaking the tie of parent to child in Catholic Irish families of the poorer classes. In so doing the Ascendancy produced a living irony to match that of Jonathan Swift's *Modest Proposal*. Swift's essay provides the most widely known testimony regarding the devastation of the Irish family by the effects of the recurring "dearths" and famines in eighteenth-century Ireland. Writing in 1729, a third successive year of famine, Swift noted that on every hand one found hungry Irish mothers begging for food, accompanied by their starving children. Swift's proposal to make food *of* the children, rather than *for* them, remains the classic of English literary irony.

The same starving time that inspired Swift's essay gave rise to the notion of a system of schools "to teach the children of the papists ... the principles of the Christian religion," as Primate Boulter put it. (Boulter had despaired of making headway with the adults.)[114] That proposal took on material form as the "Charter Society of Protestant Schools" in 1733.[115] Just as Swift's *Modest Proposal* included aspects designed to appeal to the interests of Irish parents, the Charter Schools administration promised to care for and educate young children. It was supposed to make the boys apprentices in farming, and to train the girls in housekeeping duties, and provide them with a small marriage portion when the time should arrive.[116]

It was here that the racist refusal to recognize the legitimacy of the Irish family took on its cruelest – and most ironic – aspect.[117] Under the Charter Schools scheme, in the name of religion children were taken from their families. To prevent risk of their further exposure to "papist idolatry," all further contact between parents and children was forbidden. Driven by hunger, parents were obliged to accept this condition. But it was found that as soon as their circumstances had sufficiently mended, the parents would take their children back again. The law countered by requiring that, once lodged in one of the institutions, the inmates were never to be released from Protestant custody while they remained children. By way of guaranteeing the effect of this rule, the children "were transplanted to the districts most remote from their parents." There, "they were brought up in profound ignorance of their names, situation and very existence."[118] Enrollment lagged and was supplemented by facilities for taking in foundlings. At the same time, the Charter Schools were given the authority to take into their permanent custody, with or without parental consent, any child between the ages of five and twelve who might be found begging.[119]

The families paid the price, willingly or not, but in return their children were cheated of the most elementary instruction in literacy, and instead were exploited as field laborers for the profit of their masters. In 1788 the Irish Inspector-General and the prison reformer John Howard reported to the Irish House of Commons that the inmates of the Charter Schools "generally speaking, are unhealthy; half starved; in rags; *totally uneducated*; too much worked; and, in all respects, shamefully neglected."[120]

An alternative educational track was established by a law passed in 1716 directing "That the Parsons and churchwardens in every parish should together with a Justice of the Peace, bind any child found begging, or any other child (with consent of the Parent) to a Protestant master, until his age of 21, or to a Protestant tradesman until his age of 24 years."[121] Again, it is to be noted that parental consent was not necessary in the case of children found begging. A child who fled such bondage was subject to punishment by being put in the stocks and ten days' hard-labor imprisonment. Any person, even his own parents, who sheltered the runaway was subject to a crushing penalty of £40, payable to the master.

Corporations were established, first in Dublin and then in Cork, whose business it was to take up all children of five years of age or older found begging and keep them in their service until the children were sixteen, and then apprentice them to serve Protestant masters, the boys until they were twenty-four, the girls until twenty-one. When it was found that "Popish" mothers were clandestinely securing employment as parish nurses in order to be near their own kidnapped children, arrangements were made to exchange the inmate populations between the two cities, the 170-mile separation being calculated to foil such connivance.[122]

Nothing so became the Charter Schools as their general failure. They represented the one major concerted effort to convert Catholics to Protestants, and yet their average "enrollment" for the entire country averaged less than

2,000. It was the regretful judgment of John Howard, after his investigation of the Charter Schools, that they were "so deplorable as to disgrace Protestantism and to encourage Popery in Ireland, rather than the contrary."[123] Lecky probed more harshly, calling them "a system which in the supposed interests of religion, made it a first object to break the tie of affection between the parent and the child."[124] What then was this but an assault upon the family as a form of social identification for members of the racially oppressed population?

A few years before Arthur Young recorded the Protestant landlords' boasts of their sexual privileges with regard to women of "their" cottier families, the Maryland Provincial Court proclaimed similar white-male privileges as constitutional Anglo-American law. Lifetime hereditary bond-laborers "are incapable of marriage," the court said; therefore, it continued, "we do not consider them as objects of such laws as relate to the commerce between the sexes. A slave [has no legal recourse], against the violator of his bed."[125] As far as the law was concerned, the most intimate and sacred attachments could be unceremoniously broken at any time by any of a number of forms of intrusion by the "white race," including separation by purchase and sale. As for the normal course of everyday life: "The slave woman was first a full-time worker for her owner . . . she was not usually nurse to her husband or children during illness . . . children soon learned that their parents were . . . [not] the seat of authority. . . . The husband was not the head of the family."[126]

Even free African-Americans were restricted in regard to the civil right of marriage. In 1691, Virginia law for the first time instituted penalties for marriages between European-Americans on the one hand and African-Americans and Indians, bond or free.[127] The pattern became general: free African-Americans might marry, but only if the spouse was not a European-American. In Ireland the bar to the intermarriage of English and Irish had precedent as far back as the fourteenth century. The Anglo-Irish Parliament, as I have noted, re-enacted that principle in law as a part of the Penal Laws in 1697.[128] In Virginia the cry was "abominable mixture"; in Ireland it was "corruption and perversion" and "dishonour to Almighty God."

Mention has been made earlier in this work of the United States Indian Agent in the Dakotas who forcefully removed Sioux women and children in order to "wipe out" that tribe.[129] In the general effort made by the United States government to break up Indian tribal society, the program of individuation of Indian land ownership involved a conscious challenge to the Indian family. Just as the Anglo-Irish Penal Laws presented the irony of resort to "gavelkind" in order to reduce the size of Catholic Irish landholdings, so the United States attempted to make use of empowerment of the husband as the "head of the family" as a part of the destruction of the power of the tribe. The process of expropriating the Indian lands did not, however, depend upon this legal fiction. As late as 1905, the United States Supreme Court decided a case in favor of an Indian woman, "the head of a family, consisting of herself, her husband, and children," even when (as in this particular case) her husband was a "white" man.[130]

The difference of these two American cases is not that the Indians were any less the object of racial oppression, but that the form of the Indian family was not a decisive obstacle to the expropriation of their lands and the extirpation of their people, while the African-American family represented a fundamental barrier to the system of chattel bondage. A Maryland Provincial Court decision made the point in 1767:

> No one has ever imagined that the property of the master can be affected by the contract of a slave, whether of marriage, or any other occasion, utility being the parent of right and justice.[131]

4

Social Control: From Racial to National Oppression

The English Parliament in 1689 established as a constitutional principle that no standing army be maintained in that country in time of peace; for the future, when England was at peace the militia was to guarantee the safety of the country.[1] But in Ireland, where a funereal conqueror's peace would descend for a century following the Jacobite War of 1689–90, the English military establishment was to be maintained at an "invariable 12,000."[2] Some historians believe that keeping such a large regular army in Ireland was more of an English convenience than an Irish necessity. They point out that the cost was borne altogether by exactions on the people in Ireland, even though the forces were from time to time drawn upon for duty elsewhere. The fact remains, however, that English rule in Ireland continued to be dependent on regular military forces for ordinary police duty.[3] The military role was supplemented by that of Protestant civil officers, magistrates, sheriffs, and constables, and Protestant petit juries and grand juries. There were places, such as parts of Ulster and some cities and towns, where the Protestant proportion of the population was kept large enough to make possible some normal degree of local civil administration, but the garrisons were there anyway. For the greater part of Ireland, however, the Catholic Irish so far outnumbered the Protestant English – sometimes by more than thirty to one – that there the writ of Protestant civil law could not run.[4]

But before the end of the eighteenth century a cloud of doubt formed over even the traditional resort to the military option – the tradition of Mountjoy and Cromwell – for maintaining racial oppression in Ireland.

Two centuries before, Ireland had been drawn, thrust, dragged into the context of international colonial power rivalry. Now that new world context erupted in a storm of revolution: Anglo-American continental colonies, 1776 to 1782; France, 1789 to 1794; Haiti (St Domingue), 1791 to 1804; and the English government's military forces were everywhere engaged in counter-revolution. In Ireland, Protestant nationalists raised their sails to catch the winds for independence from English trade restrictions, and for a time looked favorably on the connection of independence with the cause of Catholic "emancipation". At the same time, a large part of the Irish military establishment was being shipped for war in America, in St Domingue, Guadeloupe, Martinique, and other eastern Caribbean islands;[5] and around the world against the Napoleonic genie loosed by the French Revolution, a round of wars that would last for forty years, 1775–1815. In 1798 the armed revolt of the United Irishmen broke out, on such a scale that a military force of 76,000 was needed to suppress it,[6] and the politicization of the Catholic masses had just begun.

The crisis of British rule in Ireland – with its threat of revolution and French invasion – brought to maturation a process of rapprochement between the British king, Parliament and the Protestant Ascendancy, on the one hand, and the emergent Catholic bourgeoisie, on the other. "The professed object [of the Penal Laws]," said Edmund Burke, had been "to deprive the few [Catholic] men who, in spite of those laws, might hold or retain any property amongst them, of all sort of influence or authority over the rest."[7] That was a luxury that the British ruling class could no longer afford. *The resolution of the crisis, therefore, would mean nothing less, and nothing more, than a change in the system of British colonial rule in Ireland from racial oppression to national oppression, by the incorporation of the Irish bourgeoisie into the intermediate buffer social control stratum.* The process – from the first exchange of glances to the disestablishment of the Church of Ireland in 1869 – occupied a century of vicissitudes. But by 1793 the decision was irrevocable, by 1829 it was affirmed in law, and by 1843 it was defined in practice.

Facing a heavy demand for cannon-fodder in the Seven Years War (1757–63) for colonial empire against France, the British government had decided to abandon the Penal Law against recruiting Irish Catholics for military service.[8] This decision meant that a vital interest of the British empire was made dependent upon the Irish Catholic clergy, without whose assent Irishmen – however needy their families might be – would not join the British army. From then on, Thomas Bartlett writes, "war would mean opportunity rather than danger for Irish Catholics . . . [and therefore it] was no coincidence that the major catholic relief acts of the late eighteenth century were put through in time of war."[9]

Penal Laws that effectively denied Catholics the right to acquire or retain land ownership had been inspired by the ghost of confiscations past.[10] The first and most comprehensive of these, the "Act to Prevent the Growth of Popery," passed in 1704, set a limit of thirty-one acres on the amount of land a Catholic might lease, and allowed that much only on the condition that the rent be no less than two-thirds of the net yield.[11] But after half a dozen generations had been buried, and with them prospects for a restoration of those confiscated lands to Catholic claimants, other motives came to bear upon policy decisions of the English and Anglo-Irish Establishment.[12] As revolutionary sentiment for an independent republican Ireland began to grow, inspired by events in France and America, the prospect of such a change of policy in respect to the propertied Irish Catholics appeared increasingly opportune for the British colonialists.

The Protestant Irish Parliament itself proclaimed the strategic reorientation. The anti-Popery laws of 1704 and 1709, which had made "Roman Catholics of Ireland ... subject to several disabilities and incapacities," they said, had become obsolete and indeed counter-productive. Finding that the Catholics had exhibited "uniform peaceable behavior for a long series of years," Parliament declared that it was:

> reasonable and expedient to relax the [laws], and [that] it must tend not only to the cultivation and improvement of this kingdom, but to the prosperity and strength of all his Majesty's dominions, that his subjects of all denominations should enjoy the blessings of our free constitution, and should be bound by mutual interest and mutual affection.[13]

Parliament accordingly began to enact substantial land reforms. In 1772, the law was amended in order to encourage the reclamation of bogland and other wastelands for agriculture and, at the same time, to promote the detente with the Catholic hierarchy and bourgeoisie that was sprouting between the cracks of Protestant Ascendancy.[14] The new law provided that Catholics were to be permitted to take leases on such worthless lands tax free for seven years, although a Catholic tenant still could lease no more than fifty acres, and that much for not more than sixty-one years. In 1778, Parliament eliminated all the formal legal disabilities of Catholics with respect to leasing; finally, in 1782, the ban on Catholic purchase and inheritance of lands was ended.[15] After a century and more of enforced tenancy-at-will, such reforms could have little effect on the proportion of land held by the Catholic rank and file. What good was the right to own land, or even to sustain the entry fees on long-term leases, for rack-rented, tithe-extorted tenants-at-will, or for laborers living in semi-beggary?[16] But for the emergent Catholic bourgeoisie, with access to capital or credit, the leasehold reforms proved to be of substantial significance.[17]

America and France, and the Spectre of Republicanism

In 1778, when the regular garrisons had been depleted for service in America, there arose in Ireland the (overwhelmingly Protestant) Volunteers movement, ostensibly to defend the country from foreign invasion. Soon the Volunteers began to alarm the government by their obvious republican and independentist tendency and, above all, by their declarations of support for equal rights for Catholics. In December 1791, the British government proposed that the Irish Parliament allow the elective franchise to sufficiently propertied Catholics.[18] The calculated effect was that the Catholics of "the most consequence and property" would become "sharers in" the system of social control.[19] Within little over a year, the government and the authoritative negotiating team, known as the Catholic Committee, reached an agreement that in effect ended Catholic collaboration with the Volunteers in exchange for the passage of a law in 1793 (33 Geo. III, c. 21 [*Irish Statutes*]), giving Catholic forty-shilling freeholders the right to vote in elections of members of the exclusively Protestant Irish Parliament.[20] A companion act (33 Geo. III, c. 22 [*Irish Statutes*]) established an Irish militia of about fifteen thousand (increased to nearly twenty-two thousand two years later) which, although officered by Protestants, had a predominantly Catholic rank and file.[21]

Thrown on the political defensive by the cumulative effect of this shift in the strategic orientation of the British government, the forces of Protestant Ascendancy rallied behind the racist tradition symbolized by the Dutch William of Orange (of "glorious . . . and immortal memory") who, as King William III of England, had defeated the Irish and Catholic cause in 1689 and ushered in the long night of the Penal Laws.

The first to rally were laboring-class Protestants in 1795, who sensed a creeping Catholic Emancipationism threatening their racial privileges – such as their preferential tenant status and the right to keep and bear arms.[22] The surge of Protestant bigotry took organized form with the establishment of the Orange Order, following an armed clash between Protestant and Catholic tenants in County Armagh in September 1795. This event was immediately followed by a terror campaign which drove hundreds of Catholic families from their Ulster homes into stony Connaught.[23] Viewed at first with a considerable degree of upper-class suspicion for its lowly origins, Orangeism gained in respectability, especially among the diehard Protestant Ascendancy elements of the ruling class who had not yet got the message that it was time for a change. In the Rebellion of 1798, the Orange Order, now formally constituted in Ireland and Britain, played a key role in splitting Protestants from the equalitarian stand of the United Irishmen, and in the form of the armed and mounted yeomanry units served also as auxiliaries in the repressive operations of the military.[24]

The Act of Union – a Role for the Catholic Bourgeoisie

Faced with this formidable Orangeist opposition on the one hand and the ominous implications of the 1793 voting rights and militia acts in a country with an overwhelmingly Catholic population on the other,[25] and with the French threat undiminished, the British government, headed by William Pitt, resorted to the tactic of legislative union of Great Britain and Ireland. It was a sort of symbolic adaptation of the notion that William Petty had suggested to James II in 1672 (see pages 68–69). The majority principle would be preserved, but in a 658-member Parliament in which only 100 members would be from Ireland. In this setting, any Irish Home Rule or less radical nationalist minority could be easily controlled. It was a prototype of the pattern to be followed by the British colonialists of embedding a hook in each concession as an essential component at every juncture of the process, to ensure that the transition to a new system of social control in Ireland would not get out of hand. In this case, the newly enfranchised Irish forty-shilling freeholders were safely "landed" by the dilution of their representation in the British Parliament.

The opponents to union expressed a variety of political interests, even directly contradictory ones; they included republican independentist United Irishmen (and the young Daniel O'Connell, destined to be the dominant leader of the Irish national liberation struggle), and on the other hand some Protestant Ascendancy types fearful that the new United Kingdom Parliament would be heavily infiltrated with liberals and abolitionists soft on Catholicism. In addition, there was the resistance of the placemen in the Irish church and state Establishment, worried about their careers, which were dependent upon the maintenance of the separate kingdom.

In the political pulling and hauling on the issue, the "support of the catholic hierarchy was decisive".[26] It was not to be expected that the Irish Catholics, riding a tide of "great and sanguine expectations," would go quietly into parliamentary union, with a Parliament from which not merely were Catholics excluded, but in which the Irish were to be in a permanent minority.[27] In January 1799, Pitt and the Irish Catholic hierarchy (four archbishops and six of the bishops) came to an agreement in which the hierarchy agreed to support the Union Bill and to grant British Protestant monarchs a veto over the naming of Catholic bishops in Ireland. In return the British government was to pay the salaries of Catholic priests.[28] The government further led the Catholics to expect favorable consideration of "reform" of the tithe system (the compulsory exaction of payments for the support of the Church of Ireland), and a "catholic relief" bill, removing the ban on Catholic membership in Parliament.[29] Pitt's immediate purpose was achieved: the Act of Union was passed in 1800. But in Ireland and England the Orange and Tory forces of Protestant Ascendancy, staunchly backed by three successive British monarchs, were able to postpone the consummation of the bargain for thirty years.

From a far-sighted post-Union British ruling-class point of view, this Ascendancy element in Ireland might conceivably have been seen as a historical anachronism, like the pre-European peoples of Canada or Australia, where the parliaments would represent the invested colonist-descended majority. But Ireland was different.[30] In Ireland the British Protestants were a minority, yet strategically a very significant minority, the historic trustee of English rule and now anchor of the Empire, the embodiment of Protestant Ascendancy, socially dominant throughout Ireland. It was a very substantial, deep-rooted interest, as it had demonstrated in frustrating the promise of Catholic Emancipation in the understanding reached between Pitt and the Catholic episcopate on parliamentary union. Most significant of all in the present context, it was constituted in the main of members of the laboring classes. In order to carry through the transition to Union national oppression, not only the Protestant exploiting classes but the laboring-class Protestants as well had to be given reassurances on their privileges *vis-à-vis* laboring-class Catholics, at least in Ulster, the main stronghold of Protestant Ascendancy.[31] Historians and others agree that Catholic Emancipation – the admission of Catholics to civil rights, to membership in Parliament, to the professions and to positions of public trust, military or civilian – was an historical inevitability.[32] In the British Parliament "the Catholics could count on the general support of the whole body of the English Whigs, of a considerable section of the English Tories, including ... most of the rising men of ability, and also of a large and perhaps preponderating section of the English press."[33] But, for twenty-five of the twenty-eight years from Union to Emancipation, the House of Commons was controlled by the Tory Party, the main political bastion of Protestant Ascendancy. The Ascendancy was even more strongly entrenched in the House of Lords, and, as noted, the Hanoverian English kings of the time were last-ditch, hard-loser Ascendancy men.

Here was a new version of the Grand Dilemma: how could the Catholic bourgeoisie be incorporated into the colonial buffer social control stratum without sparking a movement for Irish national independence, or, alternatively, alienating the Irish Protestants by threats to their dominance in ownership, and preference in tenancy and employment, thereby risking the re-emergence of the United Irishmen phenomenon, republican and independentist? This dilemma would govern the course of Irish history from 1801 (the Union as law), to 1843 (the Union as settled fact).

Defining Issues

In the second half of that period the overlapping issues of "Catholic Emancipation" so-called,[34] agrarian grievances, and repeal of the Union erupted in three acute crises of British social control in Ireland, in 1828–29, 1832–35 and 1843.

For the Catholic bourgeoisie the strategic issues were Catholic Emancipation and repeal of the Union. Within limits, each reinforced the other, yet they were fundamentally contradictory. Catholic Emancipation meant the ending of the Penal Law exclusion of propertied Catholics from Parliament and other offices, jobs, emoluments and perquisites, as well as entry into trades and professions on an equal basis with non-Catholics of those classes; in short, the formal admittance of propertied Catholics, although on a necessarily subordinate basis, into the buffer social control stratum.[35] As William Grenville, one of the principal advocates of Catholic Emancipation, put it to the House of Lords, what concerned the Irish Catholic propertied classes was "not their situation as subjects, but their claim to political power." The idea was clearly stated by the Irish Catholic aristocracy and gentry themselves, in their emancipation petition to Parliament in 1805. The trouble with Protestant Ascendancy, they said, was that "it detach[ed] from property its proportion of political power under a [British] constitution whose vital principle is the union of one with the other . . . the best constitution that has ever been established."[36] It was the same demand that the free classes of Ireland had made in 1277 for admittance to English law, but with the difference wrought by nearly six hundred years of invasion, resistance, conquest and racial oppression. In the thirteenth century the Gaelic tribal chieftains, in undislodgeable control of at least one-third of the island, were confronting a tentative and insecure invader. Modern Emancipationism, on the other hand, was conditioned on the acknowledgement of the indefeasibility of British Protestant landlordism, of the British domination of the Irish national economy, and of the permanent subordination of Ireland to the authority of a British Parliament, in which Catholics were forever a minority. In short, what was called Catholic Emancipation involved the acceptance of the national subordination of Ireland to Britain.[37]

Repeal of the Union, on the other hand, was a demand for national independence: not necessarily separation, as in the case of the United States, but nothing less than a proto-dominion status, like that granted to Canada in 1840, and practiced in Australia in its various parts. But, again, Ireland was not Australia or Canada. The demand for repeal of the Union not only went far beyond Catholic Emancipation; its proposed independent Irish Parliament was a dagger pointed at British Protestant landlordism, at the automatic priority of British economic interests, and at the whole legacy of two centuries of preferential treatment of Protestants.[38] It was seen as a threat to the British Empire as a whole.[39] Repeal of the Union promised to remove the very question of British social control in Ireland from history's agenda.

For the British colonial bourgeoisie, the categorical imperative was maintenance of the legislative union. If forced to it, they would be ready to abandon rule by religio-racial oppression in favor of admitting the Irish Catholic bourgeoisie into a role in the system of social control. But the British government made manifest its resolve to go to war to prevent the establishment of a separate Irish parliament, whether of an independent country or of a British dominion. For the Irish Catholic bourgeoisie the categorical imperative was that there must be no return to the Penal Laws regime with its denial of their class status. If forced to it, they (including O'Connell) were ready to accept the role of being the major component in the system of British colonial control in Ireland; in short, to content themselves with the transition from racial oppression to national oppression, instead of Irish self-rule.[40]

Enter the Irish Peasant

In the end it was neither the British nor the Irish bourgeoisie that drove the issue to crisis and resolution, but rather the laboring classes of the countryside with *their* strategic joint issue of tithes and tenant rights. The poor tenants and laborers who made up the great majority of the Irish population had little practical interest in either Emancipation or repeal.[41] They were more particularly concerned with the oppressive landlord system, the fall of agricultural prices after the defeat of Napoleon, the ravages of famine in a number of these years, and the predations of the tithe proctor, who was empowered to seize the crops and stock of those delinquent in their payments for the support of the Protestant Church of Ireland.[42] They were not going to run for Parliament, few laboring people were even voters,[43] and tradition's chains bound those few to vote for the landlord's candidate, or face retribution. Nor were they going to be candidates for admittance to trades or professions. They, "the poverty of the country," as O'Connell called them, were more disposed to translate Emancipation and repeal in their own terms. They expected the Catholic "'rent' to be used for the purchase of arms, and that after emancipation ... the land would be redivided."[44] Maintaining a direct-action tradition that had begun in the 1760s with the White Boys, they organized as Threshers, as White Feet, and as Ribbon Men to prosecute their grievances by various means. They maimed cattle, prevented foreclosure sales and forcible tithe collections; they intimidated Catholic or Protestant landlords and their witnesses, and fought with what arms they had against law-enforcing police and yeomanry;[45] and they enforced "exclusive dealing," a practice later to be eponymously known as "boycotting." From 1815 until the Great Famine struck in 1845, agrarian unrest was a constant reminder of the unresolved state of the social control problem. As evidence for this we have the successive pronouncements of one of the dominant figures in British politics throughout this period, the Irish-born arch-Tory Duke of Wellington (1769–1852). In December 1828, as the campaign for Catholic Emancipation was approaching culmination, Wellington, then Prime Minister, declared that the situation in Ireland could not be worse, short of actual civil war. During the tithe war of the early 1830s, Wellington, then in the parliamentary Opposition, was uncontradicted when he told the House of Lords that all former "disturbances in Ireland ... were trifling compared to the scenes" currently to be witnessed in that country. In 1843, when the struggle for repeal of the Union approached its climax and he was once more a member of the government, Wellington's cold eye judged Ireland to be "in truth no longer in a civil state."[46] In each case, it was the involvement of the masses of the peasantry and rural proletariat that made the situation critical.

The leaders of the Catholic bourgeoisie could not have ignored the surging agrarian unrest if they had wanted to do so. By class instinct they were mistrustful of spontaneity and independence among the laboring classes; they were painfully aware of the sentiments current among the rural poor majority favoring revolutionary land redistribution. At the same time, the tithe system was a grievance that the Catholic bourgeoisie shared with their co-religionists of other classes.[47] It was symbol and substance of the very exclusion from "official society" for which they were seeking remedy in Emancipation and repeal; and, of more practical importance, it was the ideal link to the power of agrarian anger. In moving to exploit the power of laboring-class discontent, the Catholic Irish bourgeoisie was following standard operating procedure for the national bourgeoisie, wherever that class was still aspiring to power or to a share in it.[48]

The Campaign for Catholic Emancipation

The quest for empowerment began with the campaign for Catholic Emancipation, so-called, organized by the Catholic Association, formed in 1823 by Daniel O'Connell (The Great Emancipator), Richard Lalor Sheil (who would emerge as O'Connell's co-leader) and Thomas Wyse.[49] Under the leadership of O'Connell and his co-workers, starting with only forty-seven members the association produced a non-revolutionary liberationist movement of a scope and depth probably unmatched except by that led by Gandhi in another English colony a century later. The key to their success lay in enlisting the priesthood as "lashers up" of the rural masses, as dues collection supervisors, and as grassroots agitators and mobilizers.[50] The chief tactic of the movement consisted of mass mobilizations, peaceful indeed in the assemblies but, more than that, disciplined in coming and going in mass contingents.[51] On 13 January 1828, Emancipation rallies were held in some 1,600 of Ireland's 2,500 parishes.[52] Besides the meetings, there were the "processions," marches done in military form but without arms. In the summer and fall of 1828 – on local initiative, rather than by central direction – processions of two or three thousand men drilled and marched in the southwest of Ireland wearing green insignia of various sorts, and organized "like regular troops."[53]

Since 1792, the British had become practiced in responding to threats in the Irish quarter with both repression and concessions. In part this reflected differences of policy within the British ruling class, but perhaps more often it merely represented dual aspects of a single strategy.[54] Habeas corpus, the most fundamental British constitutional right, was suspended in Ireland during twelve of the twenty-five years from the passage of the Act of Union to the founding of the Catholic Association in 1823.[55] As the campaign for Catholic Emancipation approached its peak of intensity, overwhelming military force was arrayed against it. Between 1823 and 1828, the British garrison in Ireland was increased from 28,000 to 35,000, when five out of every six members of the regular infantry were either in Ireland or on the west coast of England ready to go there.[56]

The use of concessions to maintain control began with the granting of the forty-shilling freehold franchise in 1793. Although the passage of the Act of Union of 1800 was not accompanied by the promised "Catholic relief," there were always those, aside from the "Catholic sympathizers," in the British Parliament who advocated Catholic Emancipation as a means of tying the Catholic bourgeoisie to the cause of the Empire.[57] The British government had established an Irish Catholic seminary at Maynooth in 1795 to provide training for Irish students for the priesthood without their having to risk contamination with republican ideas by the traditional sojourn in France.[58] In 1807, Parliament raised the annual grant to Maynooth from £8,000 to £9,200.[59] The idea of state payment of Catholic clergy salaries, linked to one form or another of the royal veto on nominations of Irish Catholic bishops (see note 29), gained support in Parliament until Catholic lay opposition in Ireland forced the Irish Catholic hierarchy to repudiate the proposal in 1808, and forced its temporary abandonment in Parliament.[60] Slowly, and with many checks and challenges, the conviction grew that conciliation of the Irish Catholics was not merely (if at all) a matter of justice, nor of countering the threat of foreign invasion (after the battle of Trafalgar in 1805), but rather a requirement for keeping "the king's peace" in the face of the democratic force of the Catholic liberation movement. The conciliationist tendency was expressed in ongoing contacts with the Vatican, and in the Tory proposal of the "two-wings" bill in 1825, coupling state payment of priests' salaries with repeal of the franchise of the forty-shilling freeholders.[61] But by the end of 1826 the initiative had passed to the Irish national liberation movement.[62]

Finally, even the Tory Wellington government with Peel as Home Secretary (1828–30) adopted the Emancipation Bill as its own, convinced as it was that the only alternative was a war of incalculable financial, military, diplomatic, and political costs.[63] Even as the Tories swallowed hard, the concession was fashioned with the invariable hook or, as Peel phrased it, "the securities and restrictions by which it is fitting that this measure of relief should be accompanied." In this case, it was the cancellation of the franchise of the forty-shilling freeholder. In this way, Peel argued, as "the avenues to honour, and power, and distinction" were being opened to the Irish Catholic upper crust, the "disfranchisement of poverty and ignorance" would "restore the Protestants to [their] just weight in the [Parliamentary] representation;" it was to be hoped that finally "a respectable [English-style] class of yeomanry would be created."[64] Still, for all the long reluctance in coming to it, the passage of what was known as the Catholic Emancipation Act on 13 April 1829 was the crossing of the Rubicon from the era of racial oppression: "the State was no longer committed to Protestant Ascendancy."[65]

Although passage of the Emancipation Act did make it possible for

O'Connell and a number of other Catholic Irishmen to enter upon the "honour, and power, and distinction" of membership in the British Parliament,[66] it was too little and too late to pacify the country. First of all, the Catholic bourgeoisie had surrendered the forty-shilling freehold vote – the very ram that had forced open the doors of Parliament to them – and thus seriously impaired their electoral range of action.[67] By raising the property-yield requirement for voting from forty shillings to ten pounds (200 shillings), Parliament had succeeded in its intention to "limit the practical implications of the admission of Catholics to full civil rights."[68] The higher property qualification reduced the electoral rolls in Ireland from a hundred thousand to sixteen thousand.[69] As far as the small tenant was concerned, this meant not only a loss of political rights; it deprived him of that degree of protection from eviction, or access to perquisites, that being a landlord's constituent might provide. The Tory government had said "A" by passing Catholic Emancipation, but from congenital defect appeared incapable of saying "B"; they were resistant to clearing away the debris of the old regime of social control, still highly operative in Ireland in the form of the Orange Order, composed of tens of thousands of armed and militant Protestants,[70] and the official local agencies of social control, the Orange magistrates and yeomanry. This obsolescent Establishment in effect denied the Catholic bourgeoisie the *normal* access to their proper political base, the Catholic masses. Accordingly, the "avenues to honour, and power, and distinction" that Peel had promised to the Catholic propertied, professional and commercial classes were still closed. Above all, the begrudged Emancipation was too late because the movement had been lastingly imbued with a passion for relief from Protestant tithes, for agrarian reform, and for repeal of the Union.

The Tithe War of the Irish Peasantry

The mass organized protest of the angry and impoverished peasants against payment of the tithe to the Church of Ireland began in November 1830, at Graiguenamanach in County Carlow, when an attempt was made to seize cattle belonging to a Catholic priest.[71] The scope and intensity of the protest were unprecedented in Irish history.[72] It went on for more than five years, and even after that the substantive issue continued unresolved so far as leaseholders were concerned. Besides the Catholics, the Dissenters, mainly Ulster Presbyterians, being peasants, also resisted payment of tithes to the Established Church of Ireland, even though as anti-Catholics they were wary of the predominant anti-Protestant tone of the campaign as a whole.

According to official claims, in the year 1832 nine thousand crimes, including 196 homicides, were attributable to the tithe protesters. The peasants and laborers were charged with "agrarian outrages;" but when the police and the yeomanry killed thirteen unarmed protesters and wounded twenty others at Newtonbarry or carried off a poor widow's cow for tithes at Rathcormack, that was a matter of keeping "the king's peace." At any rate, the attempt to collect the tithes arrears was a failure; after spending £15,000 in the effort, the authorities had collected only £12,000 of the £104,000 owed for the year 1831.[73]

In 1833, Parliament enacted a Coercion Bill (3 & 4 William IV c. 4), providing that any county in Ireland could be placed under martial law, with a sun-down to sun-up curfew, violators to be transported to penal colonies in Australia.[74] Nevertheless, the government was fought to a standstill in the tithe war, and was forced to resort to concessions and political maneuvers. The government itself undertook to compensate the Church of Ireland for uncollected tithes due for 1831 and 1832, in effect admitting defeat in the effort to collect them by the use of magistrates, constables and yeomanry; attempts to collect the arrears for 1832, 1833, and 1834 were abandoned. Legislatively, the matter was concluded in August 1838 with passage of 1 & 2 Victoria c. 109. All tithes arrears for 1834 through 1837 were written off. The great mass of the peasantry, the tenants-at-will, were exempted from the tithe. For all other tenants, the tithe was folded into the rent, the landlords being allowed a 25 percent rebate for making the collection. Parliament was convinced that the landlord, wielding his powers of eviction, was a more reliable agent than the tithe proctor.[75]

The Repeal Campaign – Bidding for a Form of Independence

As O'Connell and others had warned, by turning landlords into tithe proctors the commutation of tithes into rents for leaseholders had the simultaneous effect of merging the struggle against tithes into the general agrarian struggle directed against rents and, indeed, "property rights" in general.[76] O'Connell moved to turn this dreaded result to advantage. Intending to replicate the Emancipation victory of 1829, he sought to direct the wrath of the peasants into a revival of the repeal campaign, organized under the Loyal National Repeal Association (the name it took a year after its founding in 1840). The association proclaimed 1843 Repeal Year. Again, and despite ever-stronger rescripts from the Vatican, which was fearful of imperiling its increasingly promising negotiations with the British government, the priesthood with a few high-ranked exceptions supported quite strongly the repeal campaign.[77] The government was guided by its own police reports, which called the priesthood "the very spring and essence" of the campaign.[78] When the Irish administration dismissed seven Catholic magistrates who had attended repeal meetings, the effect was to bring wider bourgeois support to the movement, particularly among persons in the legal profession. The masses who rallied to the cause, however, continued to be the peasants and proletarians,[79] as is self-evident from the estimates (even discounted for friendly exaggeration) of the attendance at the "monster meetings." These mass mobilizations were the main tactic of the repeal movement, as they had been in the Emancipation campaign. Beginning at Carrickmacross, in Ulster, on the first Sunday after Easter with 150,000 in attendance, in the months until the first day of October, a score of "monster meetings" were held, attended by an estimated average of over 300,000 persons,[80] including 150,000 people at Donnybrook, 300,000 at Tuam, half a million at Cork in May and 1 million at Tara in August,[81] despite the intimidating deployment of 35,000 British troops.[82] Before the campaign was over, almost the entire adult population of Ireland (outside of Ulster) had been in attendance at repeal meetings, on the parish or some grander scale.[83]

The Decommissioning of the Protestant Yeomanry

The decision of the British government in about 1835 to abandon attempts at forcible collection of tithes was a defining moment in the fundamental change being made in the system of social control in Ireland. The controversy within the British ruling class between the defenders of the Protestant Ascendancy status quo and those who favored conciliation of the Catholics was to be seen in ambivalence toward the Protestant yeomanry. From its origin as an opposition to the republican and pro-Emancipation United Irishmen, and its notoriously cruel participation in the suppression of the rebellion of 1798, the yeomanry remained for twenty-five years the principal instrument for policing the Catholic peasantry. At that time it had come to number nearly twenty-five thousand, more indeed than the total combined yeomanry of England, Scotland, and Wales.[84] Its main base of strength was in the Protestant areas of Ulster, but its local units were the staple of law and order throughout the country.[85] Obviously, the yeomanry's "croppy-lie-down" credo was fundamentally contradictory to the trend toward conciliation of the Catholic bourgeoisie. The yeomanry was supplanted in 1822 as the primary police force by an all-Ireland constabulary, composed roughly half and half of Catholics and Protestants, and thus guarded against domination by Protestant bigotry.[86] Nevertheless, Protestant response to the intensifying conflict increased the yeomanry to some thirty thousand men by the time of the tithe war.[87] The British government re-equipped them in 1830 with modern weapons, on the recommendation of the Whig Prime Minister who privately avowed that, in a pinch, "there is no body in Ireland like the Protestant yeomanry in the North."[88] The "croppies," however, were less and less disposed to "lie down"; instead, in the struggle against the Protestant tithes, they were openly defying the yeomanry with a fierce determination and on a scale that alarmed not only the British ruling class but also the Irish bourgeoisie, fearful of the logic: tithes today, rents tomorrow.[89] Rather suddenly, the English ruling class, heeding arguments of the Irish bourgeoisie, found that there was more risk than security to be found in resort to the yeomanry. The Orange Order, which was the directing force of the yeomanry, was dissolved in 1836, and a new all-Ireland, "professionalized," non-sectarian police force was established.[90] The new police force, which superseded the county and peace preservation forces (except in Dublin, Belfast and Derry), was distinguished, writes historian Oliver MacDonagh, by "their complete centralisation and coordination, their professionalism and mobility, and their quasi-military organisation and discipline." It was "integrated," and by the time it took the name Royal Irish Constabulary in 1867, its ranks were in great majority Catholic. All in all, it represented a great change from the regime of the yeomanry, and represented an essential aspect of the change in the system of social control from one of racial oppression to one of national oppression. Outside Ulster, the last hurrah of the yeomanry was a lament for the Protestant intermediate social control stratum.[91]

Nor could the problem any longer be solved by resort to the British army. The reason was not simply fiscal, as it had been in the days of Sir John Davies or Sir William Petty – nor, indeed, as it was in the view of Sir Robert Peel in 1829, when he said, "reliance can be placed on the army," though he, in his historic turn, doubted that the British people would be willing to "bear the enormous expense" of such an effort. Now he said, "We cannot replace the Roman Catholics in the position in which we found them, when the system of relaxation and indulgence began."[92] By 1845 Peel would publicly admit, referring to the Irish independence movement, "you can not break it up by force."[93] *Outside Ulster, therefore, the British had abandoned rule by racial oppression, that is, rule by Protestant Ascendancy, in return for the Catholic bourgeoisie's abandonment of national independence and land reform.* In terms of social control this meant that, outside Ulster, the Catholic bourgeoisie, in its new capacity of intermediate buffer social control stratum, would be the first guarantor of "the king's peace."

The Apprenticeship of the Catholic Bourgeoisie

The British concession-cum-hook strategy for dividing and/or appeasing the Irish Catholic bourgeoisie would not have succeeded unless the latter had actually been able to prove its ability to function as a buffer social control stratum *vis-à-vis* the Irish peasantry. Time and again the British were in a state of great anxiety concerning the need for the O'Connellite leaders to play along with peasant militancy in order to control it; time and again, the government expected the buffer would not hold. For their part, O'Connell and his party were fully aware of the role they were playing; indeed, at times they reveled in it for the leverage it gave them in winning concessions from the British colonial bourgeoisie without violence.[94]

In December 1824, British Home Secretary Robert Peel regarded the situation in Ireland as so turbulent and the role of the Catholic Association as so critical that only "the prudence and discretion" of the leadership of the association stood between the government and imminent rebellion in Ireland.[95] Indeed, in the next five years the situation at times became touch and go.[96] Would the Catholic Association be able to turn the peasant movement aside before it became a general assault on rents and tithes? Priests trying to rein in the movement were spurned by their congregations. The Association leadership, most notably O'Connell and Sheil, threw all their energies into the effort to keep the masses quiet. O'Connell issued an address to the peasants of Munster commanding them to stop their meetings; hundreds of posters were distributed bearing the same urgent appeal. Even within the Association, O'Connell had to exert himself to stop an endorsement of the resort to "exclusive dealing," which was already being practiced widely by the peasants against their enemies and all who trafficked with them. Within the Protestant establishment, private letters and official reports expressed a general apprehension that some slight incident might set off a general rebellion. O'Connell and Sheil were determined to keep the lid on "predial agitation," that is, land agitation, even as they were turning up the rhetorical fires of "political agitation" to secure their more narrow goal of achieving the legitimacy of their class in the British system.[97] Indeed, they were successful, although not by repudiating agrarian demands but rather by persuading the peasants that Catholic so-called Emancipation was the way to go. Expressing a sense of gratitude to the British government for Emancipation, the Catholic bishops of Ireland on 9 February 1830 aimed a blow at the solar plexus of the Irish national liberation movement by directing all priests to avoid political controversy.[98]

By these efforts, the Catholic bourgeoisie gave the first great demonstration of its fitness for the buffer social control function. Its members' acquiescence in the disfranchisement of the forty-shilling freeholders was an earnest of their acceptance of the status of subordinates to an alien upper class.[99] In passing the Catholic Emancipation Act of 1829 the British Parliament certified the end of religio-racial oppression of Ireland, and the inauguration of the Catholic Irish bourgeoisie in its new role in the British system of social control in Ireland.

Out of the experience of this Emancipation crisis, O'Connell propounded a general theoretical proposition regarding social control for Ireland in those times: "The fact is," he said, "that political agitation is calculated to stop predial agitation."[100] He made the point in the course of an eloquent but vain effort to dissuade the British Parliament from enacting the Coercion Bill of 1833 (3 William IV c. 4), directed at suppressing the tithe war of the early

1830s. The danger to the social order posed by the tithe war, he argued, would be more wisely handled by working with the Irish Catholic bourgeois leadership than by adding another hateful round of military repression and penal transportation to the shameful history of British rule in Ireland.

In their dismay over the increasingly militant development of the tithe war, the O'Connellites were motivated by general bourgeois class interests, British and Irish, Protestant and Catholic, as well as by the new role of the Irish bourgeoisie in the British system. In 1833, the Catholic clergy withdrew support from the anti-tithe movement, and a year later the bishops secretly ordered priests to abstain from political activity and forbade the further use of chapels for political meetings. In these pronouncements, the bishops were expressing the attitude of O'Connell and the Catholic bourgeoisie in general, who had "abandoned full-scale opposition to the tithe."[101] In January, at the height of the tithe war, O'Connell, in Dublin, wrote to British Lord Chancellor Duncannon, "the only person connected with power" to whom he felt he could write who might "appreciate the exact state of this country." There was in Ireland at that moment, he said, "so general a disposition for ... insurrectionary outrage" as he had never seen before. O'Connell warned, however, against any attempt to use the hated Protestant yeomanry against the Catholic peasants; they would "prove to be weakness not strength." Military repression should be left to the British army, he thought, and "the more troops sent over here the better." For his part, he promised, "I will use all my influence to stop the career of those who are engaged in urging on the people."[102] The earnestness of that pledge is to be read in the public warning to the rebellious peasantry that was posted in market towns of O'Connell's home county, Clare, over the name of one of his close friends: "Unless you desist," it said, "I denounce you as traitors to the cause of the liberty of Ireland.... I leave you to the Government and the fire and bayonet of the military. Your blood be upon your own souls."[103]

James Warren Doyle (1796–1834), Catholic Bishop of Kildare and Leighlin, having made a record for "repressing all disorders" in his diocese before becoming the first bishop to join the Repeal Association, was the pre-eminent spokesman among the Catholic hierarchy with respect to political questions. Doctor Doyle regretted the British resort to the 1833 Coercion Bill, but, when the chips were down he put his trust in – gentlemen. "If we are to be subjected to a despotism," he said, "let it be the despotism of gentlemen ... not of the brutal *canaille* composing the Trades Union and Black Feet confederacies."[104] Doyle's comment captured the essence of the choice the Irish Catholic bourgeoisie was making in order to enter upon its new role in the governing of Ireland.

The same class affinity governed the repeal campaign when it reached its most critical juncture. Historians have all pointed out the ambiguity of the term "repeal" as O'Connell defined it in his public and his private pronouncements.

This ambiguity would in time take the objective form of a split between the O'Connellite old guard and the nationalist New Ireland tendency. But "repeal" meant at least a dominion status like that of Canada, or, like Jamaica, a colony under the authority of the "home" country government, but with a legislature with authority in insular matters.[105] However, even so limited a degree of Irish legislative autonomy carried unacceptable risks to real British economic interests, and to the real or fancied geopolitical interests of empire.[106] The government of Robert Peel therefore threw down the gauntlet in the form of a decree banning the climactic "monster meeting" planned for 8 October 1843 at Clontarf. The challenge could hardly have been more flagrant, as the order was promulgated in Dublin less than twenty-four hours before the time set for the meeting. O'Connell capitulated. The Repeal Association looked at the alternatives – rule by a Parliament forever dominated by their ancient English enemy, or the specter of the French Revolution being re-embodied in an Irish *jacquerie* – and chose the first.[107] The desperate haste with which the Repeal Association reacted to the government's ultimatum was nothing less than a caricature of itself as a buffer social control agency. O'Connell immediately proclaimed the cancellation of the Clontarf meeting, saw to the dismantling of the speakers' platform, and sent swift riders out in all directions to intercept people already *en route* to Clontarf and turn them back. Although it proved to be an act of political self-immolation for O'Connell personally, it was the ultimate proof of the readiness of the Catholic Irish bourgeoisie for its indispensable role in the British national domination of Ireland.

The decade and a half following the passage of the Catholic Emancipation Act of 1829 witnessed the maturation of a process begun in 1793 with the enfranchisement of the Catholic forty-shilling freeholder in exchange for the disavowal by the Catholic bourgeoisie of the Volunteer movement and the cause of Irish national independence. True to its congenital nature, the phenomenon in its full development presents itself to history in a dual aspect.[108] The Catholic bourgeoisie, which under the Penal Laws system of racial oppression had been denied recognition as a class, effectively exploited the opportunity presented by the exigencies of British government policy to achieve social legitimacy, with officially sanctioned hegemony over the Catholic population, in exchange for its enlistment as the main buffer social control stratum in the British system of rule in Catholic Ireland.

Historian Oliver MacDonagh speaks of this fifteen-year period as one of "very substantial change in approach to the government of Ireland," which set a new and long-enduring "pattern for Anglo-Irish relations."[109] The essentials of this change were three: (1) the ending of reliance on Protestant Ascendancy for social control in Ireland, and simultaneous "moves toward religious parity"; (2) a greater degree of parity between Catholics and Protestants with respect to courts, political patronage and favors, government employment, etcetera; (3) integration of Catholics in the British parliamentary and party system.

The most dramatic demonstration of the inauguration of the O'Connellite contingent into the British parliamentary and party system was the so-called Lichfield House Compact, an agreement arrived at in a series of meetings of Parliamentary Whigs, O'Connellites, and English Radicals in February, March and April 1835.[110] The technical parliamentary basis of the arrangement was that the Irish Repealers and Liberals as well as the English Radicals preferred the more liberal Whigs to Robert Peel, Wellington and the Tories; second, the elections of December–January 1834–35 had so reduced the Whig fraction in Parliament that the party could form a government only with the support of O'Connell and the "Irish Party."[111] The fundamental socio-economic basis for the O'Connellite–Whig alliance was, first, agrarian rebellion as manifested in the struggle against the tithes and, second, the fact that since the final repeal of the Penal Law prohibitions against Catholic landholding in 1782, the proportion of Irish land owned by Catholics had increased, according to a contemporary estimate, from around 5 percent to around 20 percent. Nearly half the land in Ireland was held on long-term lease by Catholics.[112]

Just two years before, in 1833, the Whig government had secured the passage of the Coercion Bill to put down peasant resistance to the tithes. Now an altered Whig Party made a number of concessions to support the efforts of its O'Connellite partners to defuse the explosive situation in the Irish countryside.[113] But the relationship became a general one, in which the O'Connellites soft-pedaled repeal and worked as an auxiliary of the Whig government in exchange for the promise of the Whigs "to do something for" Ireland.[114] The representatives of the Catholic Irish bourgeoisie in Parliament did not hesitate long over the alternative policy of greater independence from the Whigs and closer alliance with the English Radicals and Chartists. The English Radicals and Chartists were generally supportive of equal rights of Catholics in Ireland within the Union. When the Radicals and Chartists pressed their demand that Parliament go beyond the mere abolition of rotten boroughs and the extremely limited extension of the suffrage in the Whig Reform Bill of 1832, and instead enact "universal" (male) suffrage, the Irish Party took the side of the Whig party leaders. The O'Connell party likewise opposed the Ten-hour Day Bill that was being demanded by the English workers but was opposed by the English bourgeoisie.[115]

In the execution of this bore-from-within tactic, O'Connell did not always succeed in placing his choices in government posts in Ireland, but he did have a veto on appointments he opposed.[116] The social promotion of the Catholic bourgeoisie as a class was personified in the careers of Catholic Irishmen – repealers, Liberals and others. Of the original thirty-nine members of the Repeal Party in the House of Commons in 1832, twenty-six were Catholics; of the Catholics, nine were given offices, places or titles; they included junior cabinet ministers, one of whom was made an hereditary baronet; another of the group was knighted.[117] Richard Lalor Sheil became Commissioner of

Greenwich Hospital and progressed to ever more exalted office; he was Master of the Mint (1846–50) before ending his career as British Minister at the Court of Tuscany.

The Whig three-member executive put in place in Ireland, especially Thomas Drummond (British Under-Secretary for Ireland, 1835–40), aggressively promoted a policy of fairness to Catholics and opposition to Orangeism in the appointment of judges, magistrates, commissioners and army officers, and in the reorganization of the police force.[118] At a time when a "liberal" Protestant was one who opposed Orangeism and favored an end to anti-Catholic discrimination, half the judges, salaried magistrates and police inspectors appointed in Ireland were Protestant liberals and half were Catholics.[119] Simultaneously, a traditional phalanx of Protestant Ascendancy, the unpaid squireen magistracy, was purged of one-third of its members. But the most important single blow to the Protestant Ascendancy was the establishment of a centralized professional police force, recruited and organized with an unprecedented degree of religious impartiality.[120]

This Whig government was voted down in 1841, despite O'Connell's loyalty. Basically, its demise resulted not from its differences with the Conservative (Tory) opposition, but rather because it shared the same fundamental class interests. Thus limited, it fell, a victim of the intractability of the agrarian-rooted "Irish Question," Conservative obstructionism in the House of Commons, constant badgering by the Tory-dominated House of Lords, and attrition at the polls, deliberately exacerbated by Conservative appeals to British "no popery" sentiments.

But the eventual course taken by Peel's new Conservative government would show that the new departure with regard to the Catholic Irish bourgeoisie was not merely a coalition-building Whig maneuver; a shift of the political center of gravity had occurred within the British ruling class.[121] Having said "A" by passage of Catholic Emancipation in 1829, the British bourgeoisie as a whole was finally ready to say "B," to accept the practical consequences of the fact that it could not govern Ireland without the enlistment of the Catholic bourgeoisie in the system of social control. Peel was determined to adhere to the ancient principle of English statecraft of withholding necessary concessions until a point is reached at which the concessions can appear as royal largesse rather than as a surrender to popular pressure.[122] It was obvious that the course of excessive delay followed by panicky surrender to popular clamor for Catholic Emancipation in 1829 had weakened the government's authority rather than strengthening it. It was therefore only after he had successfully challenged the "monster meeting" strategy and the plan to make 1843 the "Repeal Year" that Peel found it opportune to advance reforms that he had for some time understood would be necessary. He then proceeded, guided by two general principles: first, "sever the clergy from the agitators and the agitation must cease";[123] second, open up patronage for Catholics.

Under the Penal Laws, as I have noted, priests had been outlaws, to be run down by bounty-hunters. The British government now resolved on a course aimed at making the Catholic clergy independent of Irish democracy and dependent upon the British Exchequer, on an equal legal basis with the Protestant clergy, and thus installing them as the most pervasive agency of social control in Catholic Ireland. This matter would not be fully settled until the disestablishment of the Protestant Church of Ireland by the passage of the Irish Church Act (32 & 33 Vict. c. 42) in 1869. But the course was irrevocably set by laws enacted in 1844 and 1845.[124] A major source of funds, blocked under the Penal Laws, was opened to the Catholic Church and its institutions by passage of the Charitable Donations and Bequests Act (7 & 8 Vict. c. 97). The administrative board of thirteen established under this act included five Catholics. The following year, Maynooth College was given a capital grant of £30,000, and its annual grant was tripled and made permanent (8 & 9 Vict. c. 25). More significant in terms of a direct social control function was the inclusion of priests as ex-officio members of the government's famine relief committees in 1846, as priests in general were "increasingly accepted as a legitimate part of local power and influence."[125]

Although the British government attached great importance to measures designed to detach the bourgeois Irish Catholic priesthood from democratic movements, that policy would have been utterly ineffective except for measures taken to detach the Catholic bourgeoisie from the discontents of the masses of the Irish peasants, cottiers and laborers.[126] Without that, the priesthood as an instrument of social control would have broken in the government's hands, a fact clearly implicit in the experience with both the Emancipation and the Repeal struggles.

Affirmative Action to Implement the New Arrangement

The social promotion of the Irish Catholic bourgeoisie made necessary an historic program of affirmative action to install Catholics in posts and fields of activity previously reserved for Protestants. "We must look out for respectable Roman Catholics for office," Peel told his Home Secretary, stressing the necessity to reject as a "specious principle" the idea that "if Protestants are better qualified for appointments that fall vacant, Protestants ought [therefore] to be preferred to Catholics." Peel urged Earl De Grey, the Lord Lieutenant in Ireland, to get on with the promotion to office of a certain well-regarded Catholic barrister. When De Grey argued that he did "not feel that it is either wise or expedient to appoint an unfit man to an office merely because he is a Catholic," Peel patiently explained the alphabetical logic of their situation: "What motive can we hold out to the well-affected Roman Catholic to abjure agitation . . . if the avenue to . . . legitimate distinction be in point of fact closed to him ..." It was folly, he continued, to open up for the Catholic bourgeoisie access to "popular favour" by passage of the Catholic Emancipation Act, while at the same time, "every avenue to Royal favour be closed" to them. To combine Emancipation with such persistent anti-Catholic exclusionism, he concluded, would simply have been to "organize a force of mischievous demagogues" to pour oil on the fire of Irish insurrectionism.[127] In 1845 a number of senior offices in the Irish government were given to Catholics, while a county deputy lieutenant and a magistrate were dismissed from office for participation in protests against what they called the government's "surrender to popery."[128]

Under the racial oppression of the Penal Laws period, Catholic tradesmen, before they could practice their trades, were made to pay extortionate fees every quarter to the "masters" of their respective trades, the alternative being to swear an oath abjuring the Catholic religion; and in the 1776–80 period, Arthur Young found that Irish Catholics were effectively barred from trades requiring capital.[129] From 1835 onward, despite reflexive Orangeist obstructionism and partisan jockeying by the Conservative Party when it was the parliamentary opposition, there occurred an historic degree of "progressive dismantling of Protestant privilege."[130]

The transformation was made the basis for urging the elevation of Archbishop Paul Cullen to the College of Cardinals as a manifestation of the enhanced status of the Irish Catholic bourgeoisie in general. "We are ... a population growing every day in wealth and social importance," wrote one advocate of the archbishop's elevation. "Out of *three* Chief Justices of the Supreme Counts the Catholics have *two*. Of nine Judges of the same Courts we have *three* – with minor judgeships too numerous to reckon." The writer also asserted: "*Commercially* we have almost one half of the administrative power in all the great undertakings," of which he specifically mentions banks and railways. Though Protestants still outnumbered Catholics in the higher levels of public office, increasing numbers of Catholics were appointed in the 1850s and 1860s, whilst the prospects were increasingly favorable for lower-order positions, for which qualification was by competitive examination.[131] These appointees were not mere window-dressing, tokens to ward off evil social spirits for a season; they gained position by virtue of their base, which was made up not only of the peasants and farm laborers who were the majority of the total population, but also of the Catholic half or more of the skilled and semi-skilled workers in trades and industries and public service employees in such key social control sectors as the police (70 percent Catholics), school-teachers (61 percent), and civil servants (50 percent).[132]

At the same time the national subordination of Ireland to Britain was apparent in the gross under-representation of Catholics in the professions, notably medicine and the law. It was most substantial in the major field of economic activity, agriculture. Of the total number of landowners, 38 percent were Catholics, but they received only 15 percent of the land rent; this probably reflected their share of the total agricultural land area.[133] The peasants of Catholic Ireland, reduced in number by famine and emigration, and still mainly dependants of Protestant landlords, were still fighting to win the tenant rights that the Protestant peasants in Ulster had enjoyed for two and a half centuries.

Making the Besiegers Part of the Garrison

Sir John Davies could finally rest in peace: the English sovereign could at last govern Ireland through "Ordinary Lawes and Magistrates" without the necessity of "sending an army to do it." By 1850, Ireland had a police force of 14,000, half of them Catholics, a force equal to one policeman for every 425 people (as compared to a ratio of only one to about 1,060 in Scotland, and one to about 840 in England and Wales).[134] At the same time, the continued presence of a standing British army of twenty to thirty thousand in Ireland was the most blatant symbol of the country's national oppression. However, since the British constitution forbade a standing army in the home country, the military establishment in Ireland provided a ready reserve for both empire and home country service. It was the proud boast of O'Connell and his English Whig colleagues that the social control services of the Catholic bourgeoisie had enabled the government to supply from its Irish garrisons one force to put down the English workers fighting for the right to vote, and another to fight the French Catholic and English rebels in Canada in 1837.[135]

A realist ahead of his time, the famous Whig politician Charles James Fox had said in 1805: "The Protestant Ascendancy has been compared to a garrison in Ireland; it is not in our power to add to the strength of this garrison, but I would make the besiegers themselves part of the garrison."[136]

The "garrison," an intermediate buffer social control stratum adequate to the needs of British rule in Ireland, could not be had without scrapping racial oppression; the "besiegers," the Catholic bourgeoisie lay and clerical, would now be the main part of the garrison of a system of national oppression.

Of Divergence and Parallels

In Ireland, the British ruling class found it necessary to draw the Irish Catholic bourgeoisie into the intermediate social control stratum and thus to end racial oppression, except in Ulster. Whilst the history of the United States presents no parallel of this phenomenon, a parallel is seen in the history of the British West Indies. Both the British West Indies and Ireland demonstrate the general principle of "relativity of race" as a function of ruling-class social control. In both cases the colonial ruling power, faced with a combination of insurrectionary pressures and external threats, over a period of time (much the same period of time, indeed) resolved the situation by the decision to recruit elements of the oppressed group – Catholics in one case and persons of African descent in the other – into the intermediate buffer social control stratum. (The British West Indies parallel will be further considered in Volume Two of the present study. See p. 144 for the brief United States parallel.)

Aside from whatever light this fact has for the study of West Indies history, it helps us to understand better the testimony and studies regarding the integration of West Indian immigrants into United States society as African-Americans. Such works serve to underscore the contrast in the systems of bourgeois social control – national oppression in the West Indies, racial oppression in the United States.

These immigrants experienced the "cultural shock" of the transition from the class-based "tri-partite social order"[137] with its African-Caribbean "colored" intermediate stratum,[138] to the white-supremacist social order in the United States that subordinates class distinction to an all-pervading "race" distinction. In the West Indies these immigrants had "had access to all skilled trades and professions," but in the United States they were barred from the trades by "white" unions and employers, and from participation in the "mainstream" of professional life. Marcus Garvey, leader of the United Negro Improvement Association, was trained in the printing trade by his godfather in Jamaica, but he came to "acknowledge the difference";[139] in the United States he would have been barred from the "whites"-only union of his trade. In Danish St Croix in the Virgin Islands the free "colored" were a middle-class category – in 1834, thirteen years before the abolition of slavery was decreed there.[140] The "culture shock" in this instance was brought to the island from the United States, in the form of the regime instituted there under the administration of the United States navy after the United States purchase of the island in 1917. The official policy of disregard of class distinctions among persons of African ancestry was combined with the strict racial segregation policies of the United States. The new white-supremacist order, such as had never been known on St Croix, was "violently thrust upon the islanders," according to Hubert H. Harrison, a Crucian immigrant in the United States who kept in close touch with his homeland.[141]

Writing of the period between 1900 and 1937, scholar Ira De A. Reid said the West Indian immigrant did not understand "the synonymous use of 'Negro' and 'colored' in the United States" – a distinction which was critical in the tripartite social order in the West Indies, but which was to be strictly ignored in the racial oppression system in the United States. Reid observed: "Many Negro immigrants had to go into a mental reverse to accept such stratification."[142] For that same reason, says Wilfred Samuels, African-Caribbean immigrants resisted "being cast in the same mold as their Afro-American kinsmen."[143] Perhaps we should find that the experience of these West Indian immigrants to the United States was like that of landless and unemployed Catholic Irish migrating to Belfast. The difference was, of course, that the starved-out Irish peasant and weaver could escape submission to racial oppression by emigrating and becoming a part of the system of "white" supremacy in the United States, where being Catholic was a forgivable offense, but being not-"white" was not.

5

Ulster

Catholic Emancipation in 1829 led within a decade and a half to the replacement of racial oppression by national oppression as the main form of British colonial rule in Ireland, and to the concomitant incorporation of the Catholic Irish bourgeoisie into the British system of social control over that country. "Negro Emancipation," proclaimed in 1863, did not lead to the end of racial oppression in the United States, nor to any fundamental change in the system of bourgeois social control. Why the difference?[1] Within the context of this study of racial oppression, social control and the invention of the white race, the Ulster analogy, to which the next two chapters are devoted, best illuminates that problem of United States history and its ongoing development.[2]

The Plantation of Ulster

When the plantation of Ulster was launched in 1609 – two years after the founding of Jamestown – King James's Lord Deputy for Ireland, Sir Arthur Chichester, did not envision it as a more successful Munster or Leinster. Rather, he said, it was "as if His Majesty were to begin a new plantation in America, from which it does not greatly differ."[3] There was, sadly, more prophecy in his remark than he could know. Thus far, however, he could see: it would begin with the extirpation of the native social order, and a massive displacement of the native population by laboring-class immigrant settlers.

Victory in the Tyrone War (1594–1603) had convinced the British colonialists that the conditions were finally ripe for the success of the plantation policy, provided the lessons of past experience were kept in mind. They had learned that a civil regime of racial oppression would be destroyed by rebelling Irish or by the "degeneracy" of the English colonists "within a few years, if the number of civil persons who are planted do not exceed the number of the natives."[4] But in those days Ulster was the most Irish of the four Irish provinces. "The entire mass of the population was Irish," said Sir John Davies, "following Irish customs and obeying only Irish law."[5]

The English began by taking advantage of the opportunity provided by the Flight of the Earls in 1607 and the defeat of O'Doherty's revolt in 1608, events famous to Irish history. In order to bring to an end the prohibitively expensive war in Ireland, in 1603 the English government had granted O'Neill and O'Donnell generous terms of submission, pardoning them and restoring their lands and titles as English earls, of Tyrone and Tyrconnell respectively.[6] It soon became apparent, however, that this was merely a tactical maneuver, designed to gain time for the putting into place of the administrative and legal apparatus for dismantling the old Gaelic social order completely. By portentous land surveys, by legal challenges to the chieftains' land titles and authority, and by deliberate insults, this prospect was borne in upon O'Neill and O'Donnell, with adumbrations of a tragic fate by English treachery. Finally, in fear for their very lives, or of perpetual imprisonment, Tyrone and Tyrconnell fled into exile, sailing secretly out of Lough Swilly at midnight on 4 September 1607.[7]

Cahir O'Doherty, on the other hand, had been an ally of the English. Upon failing to win election to succeed his father as head of his tribe, he had deserted to the English side at a critical moment of the Tyrone War. The arrangement involved an English pledge to support Sir Cahir in gaining the chieftaincy, and the grant of the O'Doherty tribal lands and fisheries of Inishowen to Sir Cahir as his private estate.[8] But when the war was won, the English conveniently displaced the commander, Sir Henry Docwra, who had made the wartime agreement. Even though O'Doherty had served as the foreman of the jury that had indicted O'Neill and O'Donnell for treason,[9] the English government proceeded piecemeal to cancel their promise to O'Doherty, all the while adding the meanest sort of personal insult to the injury they were doing him. In May 1608, provoked beyond endurance by the faithless English for whom he had been faithless to the Irish cause, O'Doherty rose in a brief but fiery revolt, which ended with his death in battle in the following July. Two years later O'Doherty's vast domain in Inishowen was granted to the Lord Deputy, Sir Arthur Chichester.[10] Before the outbreak of the rebellion, King James had sent an order to make O'Doherty whole, but it was fatally "delayed in transmission," according to its addressee, Chichester. But, in a historical sense, it was already too late when it was written.[11]

Under color of "punishing" these three "rebels," the English government confiscated ("escheated") six entire northern Irish counties, the lands of Irish tribes from time immemorial.[12] In seeking the economic, political and social degradation of its conquered enemies, the government was merely honoring a long tradition in English statecraft: reward your friends and punish your enemies. But in Ulster it was to be punish your enemies and punish your friends. Few if any British civil or military servitors in Ireland had contributed more to the English cause than did such Irish of the chieftain class as O'Doherty, Nial Garve O'Donnell, Ballagh O'Cahan, Mulmorie Og O'Reilly,

Oghie O'Hanlon and Connor Roe Maguire ("the English Maguire"). These friends of the English had made possible the opening of the second front on the northern shore of Ireland, whereby Mountjoy was at last able to overwhelm Ulster, the bastion of Celtic power. For their treachery each of these Irish chieftains was promised possession of vast tribal lands. And, for their part, these chieftains were ready, even eager, to be integrated into the English-style social order, as the Scots and the Welsh chieftains had been in an earlier time.[13]

But the option for racial oppression left no room in the ranks of the colonial upper class for Catholic Irish chieftains, for all that some of them might wear the title "Sir." The English therefore proceeded systematically with the repudiation of their promises to their Irish wartime allies.[14] Whether they had been enemies (like O'Neill and O'Donnell) or allies (like O'Doherty) in the Tyrone War, whether they flew to arms or merely protested at court, the Irish of chieftain class were to be demoted socially to the status of no more than small landlords, politically excluded from posts of authority, and placed socially beyond the pale of British respectability. Tanistry and gavelkind, the Celtic forms of succession and inheritance, were outlawed.[15] Irish chieftains might be expropriated and put to death for making an appeal based on Celtic law, and the practice of the Catholic religion was outlawed. "Britons" were forbidden to acquire land from "Britons," that is, English or Scots;[16] they were to get it from the Irish. In the six escheated Ulster counties, only a score of the "deserving Irish" were allowed to keep as much as one thousand acres of land.[17] Some 280 others were granted an average of 180 acres each.[18] "Few of the favored Irish received grants of land which they actually occupied"; writes Aidan Clarke, "none received as much as they believed themselves entitled to."[19] Whatever their former standing or their service to the English, the natives, being Celts and Catholics, were to be excluded from any role in the English colonial social control system. Throughout the six escheated counties, they were to be beset by social and legal disabilities that steadily eroded their economic status.[20]

Nor was this wholesale demotion of the native chieftain class to be balanced by a Tudor-style social promotion of select members of the lower orders to the yeoman farmer and small gentry classes. The great majority of the Ulster natives were to be left to find places as they might as tenants-at-will of British settlers, or were forced to take up a more precarious existence on wastelands.[21]

Many of these displaced natives formed themselves into bands of "wood-kernes" who "stood upon their keeping," living off the land in the fastnesses of woods and mountains, issuing forth on occasion to impose upon the British settlers the payment of the equivalent of the old "black rents." By official estimates, in October 1609, there were 12,000 of these "loose and idle swordsmen" in Ireland, one-third of them in Ulster.[22]

The English authorities decided to round up these men and sell them to the Protestant King of Sweden as soldiers.[23] The only actual mass shipment of which there is a record occurred in the autumn of 1610. The treacherous deceit with which the authorities conducted the round-up, and the frenzied resistance of the intended victims are reminiscent of accounts of the capture and shipment of Africans into bond-servitude in the Americas.[24] Precaution was taken to keep the Irish unaware of the fact that they were destined for sale "into a country so remote, and of no good fame" as far as the Irish were concerned. In order to prevent an explosive reaction when the men intended for shipment should suddenly "perceive that an alteration of their state and course of life [was] intended," Lord Deputy Chichester ordered that they not be assembled until all was in order for prompt embarkation. Even so, the shock of recognition of the fate intended for them set off a revolt among the intended transportees. Three shiploads sailed from Derry. But the men on the fourth ship, at Carlingford, rose in mutiny, with the intention of beaching the vessel a short way from its mooring and thus escaping into the countryside. Unfortunately, a contrary wind fatally delayed them, and after twenty-four hours they were subdued by English forces, although a number of them did manage to escape. The Lord Deputy ordered "exemplary punishment of three, four, five, or six" of the leaders of the mutiny; the rest were finally shipped.[25] Although perils of the sea forced all four of the vessels into harbors in England, most of the original transportees were ultimately delivered in Sweden.[26]

Despite such draconian measures, the discontent of the majority of the native population, who had received nothing, became merged with the alarm of remnants of the old Irish chieftain class, to generate a hostility that endangered the success of the British colonial project. In 1615 the colony was in a state of high tension because of a revolt conspiracy led by declassed and persecuted members of the native chieftain class.[27] The conspirators were undone by disdaining to conceal their aims. But a quarter of a century later in Ulster a like-purposed revolt would begin the War of the Three Kingdoms.

The first social control measure proposed for the plantation of Ulster was aimed at establishing a special category of planters, composed of veterans of military service in Ireland and accordingly called "servitors." The intention was to reward past service, but to do so in such a way as to recruit a corps of men qualified in repressing Irish resistance. This being the main consideration, most of the servitors were not expected to supply significant investment capital. With the exception of a few high officials of the colony, servitors were in the main to be "captains and officers who have served in those parts, and are yet so poor as not to be able to manure [that is, work] any great quantity of land."[28] So critical was their role conceived to be for keeping the Irish natives under control that in May 1609 the bishop of Armagh successfully urged that installation of the other category of planters, the "undertakers" (so called because they undertook to supply the investment capital for the plantation) be delayed until a sufficient complement of servitors could be installed. "Except the servitors defend the borders and fastnesses and suppress the Irishry," the bishop said, "the new planters who neither know the country nor the wars nor the qualities of that people can never prosper."[29] Besides those posted to protect against the woodkernes at the borders of settlement, other servitors were to be posted to keep watch over such of the native Irish as were allowed grants within the area of plantation.[30]

Special inducements were provided to attract servitors. Whilst those who had managed to prosper by their years of military duty had the most promising prospects, others, being men "of least ability of purse," were to be assigned the most perilous locations. These latter were to be encouraged by allowances of military perquisites sufficient to enable them to "help themselves" to succeed and possibly to move up to the undertaker rank.[31]

Although the prospects of such social mobility were limited, servitors were accorded certain unique privileges. For example, they did not have to build and maintain two-story fortifications at their own expense, as undertakers were obliged to do. The most substantial of their privileges, however, concerned the terms of engagement of tenants. Whereas undertakers were to be permitted to let their land only to non-Irish settler tenants, and only on long-term leases, the servitors were allowed the option of retaining tenants-at-will from the ranks of the great mass of displaced natives. Although the servitors had to pay a 50 percent premium in quit-rent to the Crown for the privilege, the benefit of the higher rents obtainable from the hard-pressed native Irish made this a very profitable option.[32]

The servitors embodied the essential characteristics of a system of racial oppression: their social status was predicated upon the exclusion of Catholics from social mobility, and, second, their civic function was to maintain and enforce that exclusion. The number of servitor planters was so limited, however (fewer than sixty in 1610, fewer than seventy in 1618),[33] that they could be no more than a small-gentry embryo of an artificial middle-class implant adequate to the social control needs of the Ulster plantation. The requisite adequate body of substantial Protestant yeomanry was yet to be formed.

The Scottish Factor

With the succession of James VI of Scotland as James I of England in 1603, two sixteenth-century developments of Scottish national life suddenly assumed a historical relevance for English policy in Ireland.[34] The first of these was the triumph of Protestantism, although in the unepiscopal Presbyterian form. The other was the mass impoverishment that resulted from the reduction of the mass of the agricultural population from the effective status of "kindly tenants" to that of tenants-at-will.[35]

The turn to Protestantism brought Scotland and England into basic anti-Catholic alignment. National doctrinal differences between the Scottish Kirk and the Anglican Church (including its eventual Anglo-Irish Church of Ireland form) were the occasion for major political conflicts that lasted in Britain until the Glorious Revolution, and in Ireland a century longer.[36] If the British occupiers treated the Catholic Irish like aliens in their own country, it was also true that the Scots-Irish junior partners of the English were slighted as second-class citizens for their nonconformist Presbyterian, "Dissenter," religious beliefs. Nevertheless, when put to the test the anti-Catholic accord between Presbyterians and Anglicans has so far proved stronger than their sectarian differences.[37]

The second factor, mass impoverishment, reduced the laboring people of Scotland to an even more extreme condition of destitution than was visited upon the English peasantry by the Agrarian Revolution. In the Lowlands of Scotland, "life was generally harder and rougher than in England," wrote the late Professor Moody. The Scots migrant was therefore more likely to persevere as an Ulster "pioneer" than many of the English colonists, who were so disappointed by Ulster conditions that "they sold out and returned home."[38] The land was less fertile and the tenant was in a less favorable relationship to the landlord in Scotland than in England.[39]

At the end of the sixteenth century, when Scotland's population was less than 1 million,[40] every tenth person was a vagrant.[41] Scotland had no Early Industrial Revolution such as that which to a degree had afforded alternative opportunities for the displaced peasantry in England; nor did Scotland experience in the seventeenth century the overall economic expansion such as developed in England following the beginning of the English Revolution in 1640.[42] At the end of the seventeenth century, when the Scots numbered somewhat over 1 million,[43] there were among them 200,000 vagrants, according to Andrew Fletcher of Saltoun. While noting that a recent run of bad harvests had swollen the ranks of the homeless, Fletcher asserted that even in good times they numbered one hundred thousand.[44]

Fletcher ascribed this impoverishment mainly to exorbitant rents, which made "the tenant poorer even than his servant whose wages he cannot pay."[45] It was these "surplussed" Scots tenants and cottagers who chiefly supplied the migration to Ulster.[46] To the extent that this displacement was the product of the workings of the expansion of commodity production and a money economy, the pool of potential emigrants was supplied mainly from the more anglicized Lowland Presbyterian areas.[47] To the degree that the emigrants had delayed their evictions by credit, they were debtors on the run. To the extent that they were forced into vagrancy but proved unsuited to the competition of beggary, they were thieves. In so far as the ruling class saw no hope for their reabsorption into normal economic life, they were a surplus population of which Scotland was "constrained to disburthen herself."[48]

A Scottish minister, the Reverend Andrew Stewart, who settled in the port town of Donaghadee in County Down, would achieve a kind of immortality by his ever-quoted description of the Ulster immigrants passing by his door:

> From Scotland came many, and from England not a few, yet all of them generally the scum of both nations, who, for debts, or breaking and fleeing from justice, or seeking shelter, came hither, hoping to be without fear of man's justice in a land where there was nothing or but little, as yet, of the fear of God. . . . Going for Ireland was looked upon as the miserable mark of a deplorable person.[49]

It was such as these who were to make up the majority of Scots immigrant leaseholders and cottagers in Ulster.[50] They were to be the main bulwark of social control over the dispossessed native Irish chiefs and lords and their tribes. These Scots, writes Perceval-Maxwell, "were ideal material for populating a frontier." He cites a settlement scheme for County Monaghan put forward in 1622, in which it was recommended that Scots be planted in the northern part of that county, bordering Tyrone and Armagh, where English tenants could not be readily induced to settle. In this way, it was said, "the difficulties of the plantation [would be] ended[,] for the English then wilt gladly sitt down upon the other when *the Scots shall be as a walt [wall] betwixt them and the Irish* [emphasis added]".[51]

The Ulster Custom

Whatever their station in life may have been in Scotland, Scots emigrated to Ulster as a way to a substantial improvement of their lot. Early emigrants of the gentry class could double their wealth as capitalist planters in Ireland, and most of them became richer than the nobility in Scotland. As much money could be made in trade in Ulster in four years as could be made in England in ten. In the building trades, wages in Ulster were 20 percent above the level at which they were set in Scotland. The great hopeful expectation was increased wealth, and for a chance at a rise in social status.[52]

If the mass of Protestants who were to make up the "wall between" were to be expected to emigrate from their native lands, to serve in the posts of greatest danger, to bear the day-to-day burden of controlling the Ulster natives, and to cultivate the land and make it fruitful, they would obviously have to be assured a status other than that of tenants-at-will, even though they too would sweat at the plow and ache from their labors even as the natives did.

The solution was to be the establishment of a system of Protestant privilege specifically designed for the laboring-class British (mainly Scots) immigrants and their descendants. No promise was made or could be made that they would become "gentlemen"; the colony depended upon their remaining productive laborers. This privilege system did not, strictly speaking, mean automatic social mobility out of the laboring class; but it was a leg up, and a scrambling chance. And most important of all, it was made conditional upon the guarantee of preferential consideration *vis-à-vis* all Catholics under all circumstances.

These laboring-class settlers received guarantees of most favorable treatment in the beginning not only because they were Protestants, but also because Protestants were scarce. In effect, the Scots majority of them regained in Ulster the status of "kindly tenants" of which they had been divested in Scotland.[53] This was the beginning of the "Ulster custom," although it came to be known by that name only in the early eighteenth century, when it was tested by the emergence of a relative surplus of tenants and consequently significant antagonisms between landlords and tenants.[54]

The core of the Ulster Custom, the Protestant "tenant-right," was the privilege of heritable leases (leases "for lives") and of a full equity claim for any and all improvements made by the tenant. Appearing before the Devon Commission in 1844, the land agent to Lord Lurgan, a magistrate of the counties of Armagh and Down, gave a description of the Ulster Custom, the tenant-right, which deserves quotation at length for its combination of historical, economic and sociological aspects.

> Tenant right ... [is] the claim of the tenant and his heirs to continue in undisturbed possession of the farm, so long as the rent is paid; and in case of an ejectment, or in the event of a change of occupancy, whether at the wish of the landlord or the tenant, it is the sum of money which the new occupier must pay to the old one, for the peaceable enjoyment of his holding. It is a system which has more or less prevailed since the settlement of Ulster by James I when the ancestors of many of the present landlords got grants, on condition of bringing over a certain number of sturdy yeomen and their families as settlers.... [T]he early settlers built their own houses, and made their improvements at their own expense, contrary to English practice. This, together with the fact of their being Protestants, with arms in their hands, gave them strong claims on their landlord and leader, and it is probable ... the tenant-right may have first originated ... [by] the Protestant settler obtaining it in this way.[55]

There were never any restrictions on the time for which a Protestant tenant could take a leasehold. But by a royal decree promulgated in 1628, the longest term for a Catholic tenant's lease was twenty-one years or "three lives" (meaning as long as the tenant, his wife, or his oldest son lived). But even this right was rendered practically meaningless by the requirement that the tenant's children be brought up in the Protestant religion. It was still further limited by the provision that the total area leased to Catholics not exceed one-fourth of the landlord's leased land. The remaining three-fourths had to be reserved for Protestants.[56] The plantation scheme called for the physical removal of natives from lands allotted to the undertakers, who were to be allowed to take only Scots or English tenants (non-"papists," of course). But, since the dispossessed

Irish were available at the lowest cost of all, the undertakers often evaded these restrictions, preferring to engage as tenants-at-will the natives who were willing to accept that social degradation in order to wait for fairer times on their ancestral ground.[57] As already noted, the servitors were legally permitted to engage native Irish as tenants. Servitor Thomas Dutton, for example, "wisely let his lands to Irish tenants who could be cleared off at very short notice, but who, whilst permitted to remain, paid higher rents than British settlers would consent to pay."[58] Whether employed legally by individual servitors or illegally by individual undertakers, the Irish tenant was excluded from the tenant-right; the whole point of the tenant-right was that it be maintained as a Protestant privilege of laboring-class British immigrants.

The Protestant tenant's long-term lease privilege came to carry with it certain ancillary aspects which further exalted the Protestant tenants' social standing over the Catholic natives. Since Catholic tenants were limited generally to the status of tenant-at-will, any improvements made by them could be claimed by the landlord as his own property. This early discrimination marked the system of racial oppression that would come to be called Protestant Ascendancy. By making doubly certain that the Catholic tenants could not accumulate savings wherewith to expand their enterprises it implemented the cardinal feature of racial oppression, the refusal to acknowledge the legitimacy of class differentiation and normal social mobility within and by members of the oppressed group.[59] If in rare cases the natives did manage, by whatever means, to secure a store of capital, they were by law forbidden to purchase land from any Protestant, and their testamentary rights were hedged about with legal disqualifications, noted in Chapter 2.[60] Protestant laboring-class tenants, on the other hand, by virtue of their long hereditary leases were able to secure a vested interest in any improvements they made to the land, its buildings, fencing, ditching hedges, orchards, etcetera. Upon expiry of the lease the Protestant tenant had the right to renew it. If he was unwilling or unable to pay the rent demanded for renewal of the lease, he was practically immovable unless he received full satisfaction for the improvements that the family had made over a period of perhaps decades. And, being Protestant, whatever he died possessed of, including his lease rights, was inherited by his surviving family in accordance with English law.[61]

The effective range of this immigration scheme for providing a "potential army at practically no cost"[62] would be limited to Ulster. In Ireland's other three provinces – Leinster, Munster, and Connaught – English land claims had priority, whether they stemmed from ancient Old English desmesnes, or from New English post-Reformation encroachments, or from bounties to Cromwellian adventurers and English officers and soldiers, or from gifts to royal favorites in the wake of the Williamite confiscations. The prospect for laboring-class Presbyterian Scots settling in those remote quarters under a Dutch-English king and exclusively English landlords at the end of the seventeenth century was far less promising than that presented to those who settled in Ulster at the start of the century under a Scots-English king where, by legal quota, half the undertakers were Scots.[63]

Eighty years and several immigrant surges after the plantation of Ulster was begun, the full and final establishment of this Protestant social control force was celebrated on the walls of Derry and the banks of the Boyne.[64] Then, between 1689 and 1698, a great wave of some 50,000 to 80,000 Scots settled in Ireland, chiefly in Ulster.[65]

The irrepressible rebelliousness of the Catholic peasant revolt that made possible the repeal crisis of 1840–43 (see Chapter 4), forced British official society to take a critical look at the land tenure system in Ireland. The Devon Commission, which Parliament established for that purpose, observed that the Ulster Custom was "a most striking peculiarity." It was, they said, indeed "anomalous ... if considered with reference to all ordinary notions of property." Yet the commission "foresaw some danger to the just rights of property" in any attempt to legislate it for Catholics (the commission's words were "unlimited allowance of this 'tenant-right'").[66] The British government would rely on the Catholic lay and clerical bourgeoisie, newly installed in the social control system, to maintain the understanding that had been established with the cancellation of the monster meeting at Clontarf. (Concern along that line was soon to be greatly eased by the demoralizing effect of the massive depopulation of Catholic Ireland by the Great Famine of 1845–49, and the consequent mass emigration.) On the other hand, the commission was "sure that evils more immediate, and of still greater magnitude, would result from any hasty or general disallowance of it." In other words, the interests of the British ruling class in Ireland required that the Protestant privilege of tenant-right, the Ulster Custom, for all its "anomaly" and contravention of "the just rights" of the landlords of Protestant tenants, must not be interfered with. For the employing class, it afforded the optimal settlement of the competing claims of security and maximum profit. Individual landlords and employers might risk the penalties for disregarding the principle in the interest of private profit. But it was generally understood that – whatever the inconveniences and expense – the privileges of the Protestant laboring classes could not be disregarded without endangering the entire structure of social control upon which all operations depended.[67]

Intramural Tensions in Protestant Ulster

Despite the class collaboration that was the political heart of Protestant Ascendancy,[68] the arrangement was subject to strain and stress resulting from the vicissitudes of capitalist economy and from episcopal establishmentarianism. Furthermore, intramural conflicts were inevitably affected by pressure from the Irish Catholic struggle against racial oppression, by occasional devastating crop failures, by unfavorable turns in the terms of trade with Britain and the rest of Europe, and ultimately by the nationalist and republican influence of the American and the French revolutions. At the same time, the Protestant tenants' position was being undermined both by the subdivision of holdings generation after generation and by the consequent development of a new and potentially unsettling class differentiation between the over-tenant and his sub-tenants, the latter reduced, at least formally, to tenants-at-will.[69]

Ensconced in their indefeasible tenant-right, Protestant laboring-class tenant families during the greater part of the eighteenth century were able to earn additional income by the sale of linen cloth woven on their three or four looms, from yarn they spun from flax they grew.[70] A time would come when tenants' income from the sale of cloth exceeded their income from primary agricultural products. The typical small-plot, single-loom sub-tenants were dependent on weaving to pay their rent.[71]

The Ulster Scots, the Scots-Irish, were second-class citizens in Ireland as "dissenters" from the doctrines of the established Anglican state church. True, they were not subject to the economic exclusionism enforced against Catholics; indeed, the Presbyterian Kirk in Ulster was allotted an annual stipend for its support under Charles II, which was later increased under William of Orange. But from the Act of Uniformity of 1666 (17 & 18 Chas. II c. 6) until the Toleration Act of 1719 (6 Geo. I c. 2, 5), Dissenters were required to attend Anglican church services. Unlike their brethren in Scotland in the eighteenth century, the Presbyterian clergy in Ulster were even denied legitimacy in their normal pastoral functions. Marriages performed by them, for example, were not legal, and children of such marriages were "illegit-imate." Presbyterian ministers were forbidden to conduct schools. Although Dissenters were eligible to be elected to the Irish Parliament, this right was hedged about by the Religious Test Oath (2 Anne c. 6, sec. 17), which barred them from holding any salaried office, civil or military, and which was not repealed until 1780 (19 & 20 Geo. III c. 6).

The Anglo-Irish bourgeoisie itself had grievances against British domina-tion. Until 1782, the Anglo-Irish Parliament was denied the power to enact laws for Ireland unless and until those laws were first proposed by the English government.[72] At the same time, the development of trade was subject to such restrictions as the English Parliament was disposed to enact. A 1663 law (15 Chas II c. 7) banned Irish exports, except chattel bond-laborers, horses and provisions. Four years later, a ban that would last ninety-two years was imposed on the import of Irish cattle into England (18 Chas II c. 2). For a period of ten years beginning in 1671, Ireland was forbidden to import directly from the colonies. The ban was reinstituted in 1685 (1 Jas II c. 17), and remained in effect until 1731. In 1699 import duties that would last for nearly half a century were imposed on English imports of Irish woollens (10 Will. III

c. 5); in the same year the export of Irish woollens to any country but England was forbidden (10 & 11 Will. III c. 10).[73]

Protestant revolutionaries versus the Orange strategy

Large-scale emigration served as a safety valve for relieving social tensions in Protestant Ulster. Between 1715 and 1775, America alone was the destination of some quarter-million Ulster emigrants. The emigration came in waves, each from three to five years' duration, corresponding to periods of severe economic difficulty in Ulster.[74] But the worsening lot of the tenant weavers gave rise to secret direct-action societies of Protestant peasants in Ulster (Oakboys and Hearts of Steel) to resist the general weakening of their position *vis-à-vis* the landlords, just as the Catholic Whiteboys in the other provinces had first resisted capitalist-landlord exploitation intensified by racial oppression.

Among the Anglo-Irish bourgeoisie, a faction emerged favoring some form of national independence and Catholic Emancipation. The examples of the American Revolution and the French Revolution had an irresistible appeal. "In those years," writes A. T. Q. Stewart, referring to the last quarter of the eighteenth century, "the Protestant north produced the most ambitious attempt yet made in Ireland to separate religion from politics, and to unite all Irishmen in a purpose at once liberal and patriotic."[75] Rebellion, when it came in 1798, was plotted and launched by members of this bourgeoisie, first organized as United Irishmen in 1791, with Ulster Protestants in the front rank. Their 1794 Parliamentary Reform manifesto was like a combined Declaration of Independence and Emancipation Proclamation. "We have no National Government," they declared, "we are ruled by Englishmen and the Servants of Englishmen." There was revolutionary republicanism in their demand for "equal representation of all the People," as "the Great measure essential to the Prosperity and Freedom of Ireland." Most important of all, they understood and avowed "That no Reform is practicable, efficacious or just, which shall not include Irishmen of every religious Persuasion."[76]

This bold bid for Irish independence, or at least coequal dominion status within the British empire, which came within the context of the developing tendency toward a new entente between the British colonial power and the Irish Catholic bourgeoisie, was countered, as we have seen, by what modern-day apologists of racial oppression might call a Protestant backlash. It was formally established as the Orange Order in 1795, but Orangeism had emerged in Ulster a decade before as an anti-Catholic movement dedicated to preserving the racial privileges of the laboring-class Protestant tenants. Anger at increasing rents for ever-smaller holdings[77] was translated in anti-popery terms against Protestant landlords, in those parts of the province between the respectively Protestant and Catholic majority areas, who let their lands to Catholic tenants. But the movement reserved its greatest fury for Catholic tenants, burning their homes, driving them out and searching for violators of the Penal Laws that forbade Catholics to keep arms.

"The fate of Ulster," writes Liam de Paor, "now turned on the decisions . . . of Protestant democrats and radicals, whether to opt for orange or green."[78] By way of influencing that decision, the government brought to bear its legal and extralegal forces to intimidate and suppress the United Irishmen, by the use of informants, arrests, destruction of printing facilities, martial law and the disarming of United Irishmen. British success depended ultimately, however, on the support of the Orange rank-and-file, laboring-class Protestants, on their choosing to regard equality with Catholics as the equivalent of treason, that is, as an attack on the privileges they were accorded by the system of racial oppression. The concept was explained in the frequently cited report of a British general at Dungannon in County Tyrone:

> I have arranged . . . to increase the animosity between the Orange men and the United Irish. Upon that animosity depends the safety of the centre counties of the North. Were the orangemen disarmed or put down, or were they coalesced with the other party, the whole of Ulster would be as bad as Antrim and Down.[79]

What to the British military commanders at Dungannon was a local tactic would become an essential of British overall political strategy in Ireland. In coming to grips with the problem of social control, the British colonial bourgeoisie was opting for the admission of the Catholic bourgeoisie into the intermediate buffer social control stratum. But if social control was to be maintained in the Catholic provinces of Leinster, Munster and Connaught by the abandonment of the system of racial oppression, it was equally imperative that racial oppression – Protestant Ascendancy – remain in place in Ulster. Anything other than that would invite a resurrection of the equalitarian notions of the United Irishmen, with all their uncongenial implications for the British bourgeoisie. The maintenance of the racial privileges of the Protestant tenants in Ulster therefore was the necessary complement of the strategic admission of the Catholic lay and clerical bourgeoisie in the rest of Ireland into the system of social control.

Industrialization Governed by Ascendancy Principles

So far as British capital was concerned, industrialization when it came to Ireland was to be cast in the mold of Protestant Ascendancy. In 1825 James Cropper, Esquire, Liverpool merchant, abolitionist and supporter of Catholic Emancipation, testified before the Parliamentary Inquiry on the State of Ireland. Cropper had personally toured almost a dozen Irish cities and towns to investigate the prospects for profitable investment in industrial enterprise. If "political and moral" factors were the same in Ireland as they were in

England, he said, flax, cotton, woolen, and silk manufacture would thrive in Catholic Ireland. The great obstacle, he asserted, lay in the "feelings that are generated by the Catholic question, by the disabilities of the Catholics." He expressed his full agreement with the proposition stated by the presider over the inquiry: "... so long as the statute law of the country treats four-fifths of the country as persons who are dangerous to the State ... there will exist a distrust on the part of English capitalists which will keep them from investing in the country."[80] Four years after this hearing, the Catholic Emancipation Bill became law; but the policy of "red-lining" (to use a modern American term describing discriminatory lending by banks in favour of "whites" and "white" areas) continued in effect to bar British investment in industrializing the Catholic provinces.

In the post-Emancipation period, considerations of social control continued to produce a pro-Protestant policy with respect to industrial investment. The emergence of Belfast, and Belfast alone of Irish towns and cities, as a major industrial center was based on the Protestants' heritage of two centuries of racial privileges. *The Formation of the Irish Economy*, edited by the eminent Irish economic historian L. M. Cullen (Cork, 1969), presents a number of articles, including the concluding article by the editor himself, "Irish Economic History: Fact and Myth," which argue "that Irish economic development is more independent of non-economic factors than has been generally believed" (p. 113). According to this view, "The real determinants of Irish economic retardation, although political resentment obscured the issue ... were the technological and organizational advances of the Industrial Revolution and the radical improvement in transport wrought by the railroads ... [and] the growth of the population" (p. 114). Cullen contends that after a fairly prosperous eighteenth century, Ireland went into decline in the nineteenth century. He rejects earlier writers, such as Hely Hutchinson (member of the Irish Parliament and author in 1779 of *The commercial restraints on Ireland*) and W. E. H. Lecky, who attributed Ireland's difficulties to the British mode of rule, trade restriction, and Penal Laws against Catholics. Those arguments, says Cullen, have merely served to fuel "nationalist" obfuscation of economic questions. He concludes that "this [eighteenth–nineteenth-century] decline was inevitable." The explanation is not easy, he says, but, "Lack of capital was not a cause" (p. 123). Contributor Michael Drake ("Population Growth and the Irish Economy") believes that "even with a much more favourable political and social climate" the Industrial Revolution was an impossible dream for Ireland because it lacked coal and iron resources (p. 74). Another writer, J. M. Goldstrom, deals specifically with "The Industrialisation of the North-East." The key to Ulster's prosperity, he claims, "was its dependence on foreign markets." He notes, without further comment, that Belfast was able to rely on coal imports from Britain. The reason that Ulster's prosperity did not spread to the rest of Ireland was the lack of "a thriving agricultural sector," he suggests (p. 110), as if that were just a fact of life, unrelated to the heritage of religio-racial oppression.[81]

The reader will see by my footnotes that I have relied on authorities who effectively resist the anti-nationalist revision of Irish economic history represented by the Cullen school. I am led to do so by a desire to see objective economic circumstances in the context of the great all-pervasive effect of the racial oppression wrought in the name of Protestant Ascendancy; Cullen et al. seem to dismiss the latter as irrelevant. I have been more influenced, therefore, by such historians as Joel Mokyr, author of *Why Ireland Starved: A Quantitative and Analytical History of the Irish Economy, 1800–1850* (1983), and R. F. Foster, whose *Modern Ireland, 1600–1972* was first published in 1988. The Ulster Custom, a Protestant privilege, made possible the accumulation of capital in the hands of successful tenants, capital that was readily moved into the linen industry in that northern province.[82] By 1820, it was said that Protestants owned nearly forty times as much of Belfast's merchant and industrial capital as did Catholics.[83] One "objective" factor did favor Belfast; being only a hundred miles from the Scottish shipyards on the Clyde, Belfast shipbuilding got its start as a convenient extension of those Scottish enterprises. It was the infusion of large amounts of British capital, however, that was decisive. The Belfast Harbour Commission was established and subsidized by Parliament to encourage British investment. Under its supervision extensive improvements were undertaken, including the making of the Belfast docks accessible to ships in low tide. This cleared the way for Belfast to become a major shipbuilding and ship repair center.[84] Except for the policy of deliberate exclusion of Catholic Munster, Leinster and Connaught from investment of industrial capital, there is no reason to believe that centers of industry would not have appeared in those areas just as Belfast did in Ulster.[85]

The Ulster Custom preserved as a proletarian privilege

Protestant tenants had rallied successfully against the extension of Catholic Emancipation to Ulster. At the same time, however, their most precious racial privilege, the Ulster tenant-right, was being drained of much of its material substance by normal processes of capital accumulation. When the lease expired, the tenant who had profited by sub-tenants lost the tenant-right with respect to those sublet portions of his holding. The sub-tenants, for their part, were glad to be promoted to direct lessees of the landlord. Soon, however, they would find themselves reduced to tenants-at-will, as a result of the refusal of the landlords to grant leases on the ever-smaller subdivisions of their lands, whereon the sole economically significant activity was weaving,[86] and which were too small to provide a forty-shilling freeholder voter for the landlord's candidate at election time. Still, even the smallest of these cottier-weavers invoked the Ulster Custom to maintain his right of tenure. The Ulster tenant-at-will was thus brought within political hailing distance of the Catholic peasant, so that far-sighted reformers could hope for an all-Ireland tenant movement that would guarantee the Ulster Custom to Catholics as well as Protestants. A number of Protestant leaders, including Presbyterian clergymen, took the initiative, organizing the Tenant Right Association in 1847. Within three years they joined with southern Catholics to form the League of North and South, and a "cross-cultural" exchange was practiced, with Catholic priests invited to address Ulster Protestant tenants, and Presbyterian ministers responding to similar invitations to Catholic parishes in the other provinces.[87] But in the end, the bogey of "Catholic domination" and Irish nationalism worked to prevent Protestant tenants in Ulster from consummating the engagement.[88]

The very basis of the issue facing the hard-pressed Protestant cottier-weavers – to accept or reject common cause with Catholic cottier-weavers – was washed away by the Industrial Revolution, which spelled the doom of cottage weaving in Ireland as it did in Britain. The process would take place over some four decades, beginning with spinning about 1825. Weaving, while still done in the individual tenant's home, underwent some dislocation because of the weavers' dependence upon proximity to the factory-supplied yarn. As a result, the incomes of the weavers were severely undermined by the re-entry of surplussed spinners into the labor market as weavers. Twenty-five years later, hand-weaving quickly lost out to the textile mill.

Tenant families by the thousands abandoned the unequal struggle against the machine and flocked into Belfast, looking for work in the last city of the Industrial Revolution.[89] The process was speeded by the Famine, 1845–49, although predominantly Protestant Ulster counties were among the areas least affected by that scourge of nature and British policy.[90] After 1850 came a period of rapid development not only in textiles, where weaving as well as spinning was now done by machine, but in shipbuilding and civil and mechanical engineering, until the typical Ulster laboring-class Protestant was socially transmuted from smallholder rural tenant to slum-dwelling proletarian.[91]

In Daniel O'Connell's judgment, the Protestants of Ireland were only "political protestants, that is, Protestants by reason of their participation in political power"; once they were put on an equal plane with Catholics, he thought, the bigotry represented by Orangeism would wither away.[92] As a result of the economic changes that have been described, the Protestant tenant-right, which for more than two hundred years had been the main social bulwark of British rule in Ireland, was now deprived of that significance.

Laboring-class Catholics emigrated from Ireland by the millions in the nineteenth century. In the single decade that began with the famine year of 1846, the United States alone received nearly 1,300,000 Irish *émigrés*, the overwhelming majority being laboring-class Catholics. Others took the road, within their own country, to Belfast, where the Catholic proportion of the population grew from less than 10 percent in a town of 20,000 in 1800, to more than one-third in a city of more than 120,000 in 1861.[93] Would sectarian conflict be dissolved in the pool of "abstract labour" to be replaced by "the strongest bond of human sympathy, outside of the family relation ... one uniting laboring people of all nations, and tongues, and kindreds"?[94] Would, then, racial oppression finally be left behind, even in Protestant-majority Ulster? Would "Protestant politics" die out with the eclipse of the Protestant tenantry and be superseded by working-class solidarity, under the "pressure of a common exploitation"?[95]

Just as it had been arranged in the case of the tenants three hundred years before, again it was arranged by the British ruling class, with all necessary deliberation, that the "pressure of exploitation" of Protestant and Catholic workers would not be a "common" one. In doing so, the British ruling class was able to draw upon the superstructural elements – "anti-popery," the habituation to Protestant preferment, the "croppies lie down" arrogance – anchored in a history of more than two centuries of religio-racial oppression. "The widespread practice of keeping jobs for one's own co-religionists"[96] in a situation in which almost all the industrial jobs were in the keeping of Protestant employers defined the most elemental form of Protestant racial privilege. The Catholic workers came, but found that "networks of family and friends reinforced the hold which the protestant community had obtained over the engineering trades," and barred Catholics from apprenticeships, the only path to skilled jobs. Catholic workers were obliged to serve as laborers, making less than half the wage of the Protestant tradesmen under whom they worked; in general, they worked longer hours under the pressure of a high rate of unemployment.[97] Workers in general would have to live in slums, but if there was an extra room, if there was running water, the Protestant worker customarily had the preference in housing. By the 1860s, housing in Belfast was almost completely segregated, a factor that facilitates racial discrimination in housing conditions,[98] as it has in Anglo-America ever since the institution of separate "quarters" for African-Americans in the late seventeenth century. Still, the Catholic workers came; more women than men. Though forced to submit to the gender discrimination that barred all women from apprentice-ships and thus doubly excluded them from the better-paid jobs, Catholic women in large numbers found work, mainly in textile mills in classifications reserved for women. By 1901, at a time when the divorce rate was practically zero, one-third of all Catholic households in Belfast were headed by women, as compared with one-fourth of Protestant households. The statistical differ-ence was in the figures for "single heads, unmarried."[99]

In short, in place of the tenant-right system, the religio-racial privileges of the Ulster Protestants were translated into a proletarian mode.[100] Although the wages of the Protestant workers of Belfast were not especially high as compared with workers in the same trades in Britain, the differential between skilled and unskilled workers was far greater in Belfast than it was in any area in Britain.[101] The British skilled tradesmen would have had to receive more than a 40 percent wage increase to achieve the same wage position relative to that of the unskilled British laborer as that enjoyed by the skilled Protestant worker in Belfast *vis-à-vis* the Catholic laborer. This is characteristic of systems of racial oppression, where workers of the oppressed group are generally confined to the lowest-paid occupations, as in the United States and South Africa.[102]

If the Protestant privilege of job preference replaced tenant-right as the economic link between the Protestant worker and the British ruling class, the oppressive role of the Protestant yeomen was taken up by Protestant workers; eventually, in a perversion of class struggle, the role was cast in the form of an "Orange" labor movement.[103] Rallying to the slogan "Home Rule is Rome Rule," these workers became champions of union with Britain, which they saw clearly as the ultimate guarantee of their Protestant privileges. Arrogance was the customary bearing of the Protestant worker toward Catholics. This supremacist behavior led to deadly full-scale riots in 1857, 1864, 1872, 1886 and 1893.[104] The Protestants appear to have been even less inhibited than usual about escalating the violence on these occasions. A presumably Protestant justice of the peace, testifying before the commission investigating the Belfast riot(s) of 1886, denied that Catholics had provoked the riot; "The endurance and patience of the Roman Catholics was, in my opinion, simply wonderful," he said.[105] "Patience" was a term not found in testimony with regard to the general conduct of Protestants in such situations. The advantages were with them – the mayor and town council were all Protestants, as were the employers (who could punish absenteeism), the police were Protestants, and, if matters got to that stage, verdicts would be made by Protestant-majority juries, in Protestant magistrates' courts. The outbreaks were often set off by provocative marches celebrating Protestant victories of nearly two hundred summers before. The riot or, more accurately, series of riots during June, July and August 1886 was one of the worst, if not the worst, in terms of injuries, fatal or otherwise, and destruction of dwellings and other structures.[106] It began when Protestant shipyard workers took the occasion of a fight between a Catholic and a Protestant at work on a nearby dock to launch a general assault on Catholic workers, in the true yeoman tradition. A constant element in all these outbreaks was the driving of Catholic men from the workplace. The largest single employer in Belfast was the Harland and Wolff shipyard, which employed 3,000 workers at the time. Sir Edward Harland, senior partner in the firm and also Lord Mayor of Belfast, testified before the commission investigating the riots. "Are these men of mixed religion?" he was asked. "Mixed," said Harland, "but they are almost all, or chiefly Protestants," and he gave the figures. There had been about 225 Catholic workers employed by his firm before the riot; 190 were driven off the job, of whom 77 returned after the situation had calmed down.[107] It was the hateful pressure to which Catholic men were subjected, reaching its most flagrant forms in the riots, that mainly accounts for the fact that Catholics, who were more than one in three of the population in Belfast in 1861, were fewer than one in four in 1901.[108]

Partition – the Salvation of Racial Oppression

The preservation of the Ulster Protestant bastion proved to be an overriding principle of British ruling-class policy, despite Catholic Emancipation. The British were not prepared to grant Ireland separate nationhood or, as events would prove, even Home Rule. The Liberal Party, faced with a Conservative-backed threat of armed insurrection by Ulster Protestants, opted to "compromise" its way to defeat on the issue.[109] There were also Empire interests: Ireland must be kept from any involvement in foreign affairs that might be inimical to British overseas interests. There were also the traditional links between the militaristic English Conservatives and Protestant Ascendancy in Ireland, which were the prevailing interest in the veto-holding (until 1911) House of Lords. The abandonment of Protestant racial domination in Ulster would render irresistible the demand for Irish national independence (in one form or another). The Ireland that would emerge, "a nation once again," containing a population one-fourth Protestant, could never be a sectarian state, giving a special place and special influence to the Catholic Church; the social control function of the clerical section of the Irish bourgeoisie (which the British had worked so earnestly to put in place) would be rendered ineffective. It would mean the second coming of the United Irishmen, with dreadful democratic implications for Britain itself. Consider the comments made by George Bernard Shaw, writing as a "Protestant Irishman" his "Preface for Politicians" for his 1904 play *John Bull's Other Island*. "[T]he Irish coast is for the invasion-scaremonger the heel of Achilles," he said, and that fixation was made to justify the denial of Irish Home Rule. But that belief could not justify rule by the "Protestant 'Loyalist' garrison." The sectarian conflict between Catholics and Protestants, in which that fear was rooted, would be resolved if England would only "take its thumb away" and grant Ireland Home Rule, for then "the unnaturally combined elements in Irish politics would fly asunder and recombine, according to their proper nature with results entirely satisfactory to real Protestantism ... [and] the Catholic laity will make as short work of sacerdotal tyranny in Ireland as it has done in France and Italy."[110] In the play, Father Keegan, chief exponent for this Shavian concept of a better Ireland, is made to call it "the dream of a madman."[111] Prime Minister Balfour is said to have been so delighted by the play that he went to see it four times. At the command performance King Edward laughed so hard that his exertions broke the chair beneath him.[112]

On General Principles

With "perfectly devilish ingenuity," as James Connolly put it in 1913, "the master class" had contrived to turn the Protestant Ulster workers into allies not of the Catholic workers, but of the exploiting class itself. He sadly concluded that the obligatory Marxist optimism with which three years before he had ended his *Labour in Irish History* – that common proletarian experience could "make enthusiastic rebels out of a Protestant working class" – had "missed the mark by several million miles." He seemed to say that the Protestant workers had been corrupted beyond socialist and nationalist redemption by "having been reared up among a people whose conditions of servitude were more slavish than their own."[113] Liam de Paor's work *Divided Ulster*, which has been much relied upon in the writing of this chapter, was published in 1970. Twenty years later, he published further reflections in his *Unfinished Business*. As Connolly seemed to despair of the Protestant worker, de Paor seems to have finally despaired of a united Ireland, placing his hopes on "a large section of the Catholic population and a large section of the Protestant population in which there is a desire for mutual agreement to make a new Northern Ireland work." Success, he stresses, would require "ensuring equality under law … [and] personal and civil rights of all citizens."[114] It is not for this foreigner to attempt to make a judgment on de Paor's new thesis. But for the analogy of Protestant Ascendancy and white supremacy, one comment seems in order. Just as Connolly saw the religio-racial privileges of the Protestant workers as the ultimate frustration of Irish socialism and nationalism, de Paor's solution, however widely different from that first envisaged by Connolly, still requires confronting the issue of Protestant racial privileges.

This episodic review of Ulster history provides positive evidence[115] of four essential operative principles of social control in a stable civil society constituted on the basis of racial oppression:

1.   The oppressor group must be in the majority. This might be called the Sir William Petty principle, after the person who first formulated it. This principle may incidentally serve to give racial oppression a "democratic" gloss.

2.   From this "majority principle," and from the pyramidal structure of class society, it follows that the majority of the oppressor group is necessarily composed not of members of the exploiting classes, but of an intermediate social control stratum of laboring classes, non-capitalist tenants, and wage-laborers.

3. These laboring-class members of the oppressor group are to be shielded against the competition of the members of the oppressed group by the establishment of economically artificial, "anomalous" privileges – artificial because they subordinate short-term private individual profits to considerations of social control.

4. Just as the system of capitalist production presents cyclical crises and regeneration, so the system of racial privileges of the laboring classes of the oppressor group is adapted and preserved, come what may of economic crisis, impoverishment, famine, intramural conflict, natural calamity or war, in order to maintain the function of the intermediate buffer social control stratum.

6

Anglo-America: Ulster Writ Large

In continental Anglo-America the most fundamental obstacle facing the English colonizers was that the undifferentiated social structure typical of the Indian tribes in North America did not present a serviceable indigenous ruling class that could be co-opted as supplier and controller of a labor force. Indeed, it would be some time before the English would achieve sufficient relative strength *vis-à-vis* the native peoples even to be able to think in terms of social control over them.[1] Well before that time, the English in continental Anglo-America had chosen the course of plantation monoculture and the combination of racial oppression with the chattel labor form, both of which ruled out the use of Indian labor (although thousands of Indian "war captives" were shipped to perpetual bond-servitude in the Caribbean before the end of the seventeenth century). The fateful option for tobacco monoculture required the continual expansion of the "frontier" and the displacement of the Indians from their ancestral lands, a fact not calculated to promote mutual goodwill and peaceful cohabitation. The option for chattel bond-servitude rendered counter-productive the enslavement of Indians, which would have deprived Anglo-American employers of essential assistance in combating the problem of runaway bond-laborers.[2]

The Extirpation of the Native Social Order

Every aspect of the Ulster Plantation policy aimed at destroying the tribal leadership and dispersing the tribe is matched by typical examples from Anglo-American colonial and United States policy toward the indigenous population, the "American Indians" – a policy we clearly recognize as racial oppression of "the red man." In the Creek War of 1813–14 of the United States against the Red Stick Creek Indians, White Stick Creeks and Cherokees fought on the victorious "American" side under the command of General Andrew Jackson. In the decisive battle of that war forty-nine of Jackson's men were killed; of these, twenty-three were Indians, eighteen Cherokees and five Creeks.[3] Under

136

the terms of the peace treaty subsequently dictated by Jackson,[4] two-thirds of the Creek territories were confiscated by the United States at one stroke, aimed at allies no less than enemies: White Sticks and the Red Sticks, all were driven from their tribal lands.[5] Might not the White Sticks have felt a kindred fury to that which drove O'Doherty in 1608 into revolt against the English false-promisers for whom he and his kin had risked and sacrificed so much?

Note has been made of the Cherokee tribal leaders who successfully adapted to Anglo-American ways of commercial agriculture and were prepared to relate to the settlers on that basis, just as some of the Ulster Irish chieftains appeared prepared, even eager, to do in 1609. As one of the Cherokee leaders, John Ridge, pleaded so eloquently before a New York City rally against President Jackson's Indian Removal policy in 1832:

> You asked us to throw off the hunter and the warrior state: We did so – you asked us to form a republican government: We did so – adopting your own as a model. You asked us to cultivate the earth, and learn the mechanic arts: We did so. You asked us to learn to read: We did so. You asked us to cast away our idols, and worship your God: We did so.[6]

Yet like the thousands of Irish woodkernes whom Lord Deputy Chichester shipped by force to Sweden, at a stroke thousands of Cherokee families were uprooted in 1837 and 1838 from their ancestral lands in northern Georgia and Alabama, western North Carolina and eastern Tennessee, and force-marched over the Trail of Tears[7] a thousand miles to a country that was, as Sweden to the Irish, "remote and of no good fame to them." The protesting Cherokees invoked United States government treaty promises; but as it had been with the king's mislaid reassurance to O'Doherty, it was "already too late," gold having been discovered within Cherokee lands in northern Georgia ten years before.[8]

The Social Control "Anomalies" in America

As in Ulster, the ruling class saw that it was necessary to support the privileges of the laboring class of the oppressor group as an investment in social control made at the expense of immediate profits.[9] Ulrich Bonnell Phillips, an eminent white historian of American slavery, concluded, "In the divergence of economic interest and social needs it became increasingly clear that social needs were paramount."[10] The records are replete with precept and example showing the general prevalence of this principle of governance in Anglo-American plantation colonies.[11] It was expressed, for example, in "deficiency laws" to provide quotas, as they might be termed today, according to which the plantation owners were required, under penalty of the law, to employ at least one "white" male for every so many "Negroes," the proportion varying from colony to colony and time to time, from one-to-twenty (Nevis, 1701) to one-to-four (Georgia, 1750).[12] While the Nevis "white" quota law stressed the importance of measures "for the Importation of white Servants," it specified "the Irish Papist excepted." This provision was related to actual incidents of liberationist solidarity of Irish and African bond-laborers and the widely expressed official fears on this score.[13] Just as the Penal Laws excluded Catholics generally from apprenticeships to trades, Anglo-American plantation colonies (Barbados, 1670; South Carolina, 1742; Georgia, 1750) were urged to exclude Negroes from trades in order to preserve the trades for "white" artisans.[14] Tenancy did not take on the great significance in the Anglo-America plantation colonies that it did in Ireland, but its relation to social control was not completely ignored. Just as promises of restored fortune were used to entice laboring-class Scots to Ulster to serve as "the wall betwixt" the landlords and the Irish natives, so were "Swiss" immigrants solicited for the American Piedmont with promises of prosperous tenancies and a ten-year exemption from taxes, on the assumption that they would prevent runaway African-Americans from passing through to establish maroon settlements in the mountains beyond, like those in Jamaica.[15] On a grander scale, at the same time, the exclusively Protestant Anglo-American colony of Georgia was being founded as a buffer to prevent African-American bond-laborers from escaping to freedom in Spanish Florida.[16]

The Ulster custom found its most complete parallel in the United States homestead right, which reached its perfected form in the Homestead Act of 1862, after decades of controversial evolution. The heart of the policy was to make land available in small parcels at little or very modest cost to European-American laboring-class settlers (160 acres free, according to the 1862 act). The land to be distributed was "public land," the Indians' rights thereto having been punctiliously "extinguished." The mass campaign for this policy took the form of Free Soil – first the movement and then the party. Its rallying standard was the Wilmot Proviso which, in the words of its author, Representative David Wilmot of Pennsylvania, was intended to "preserve to free white labor a fair country, a rich inheritance, where the sons of toil of my own race and own color can live without the disgrace which association with Negro slavery brings upon free labor."[17] Accordingly, the 1854 Graduation Act, designed to make unsold "public" lands available to "squatters" and others at prices graduated from $1.25 to as low as $12\frac{1}{2}$ cents an acre, limited its benefits to "white" persons.[18]

Six years earlier the historic Women's Rights Convention, held in Seneca Falls, New York, included in its resolutions the demand for the right of women to own property.[19] It was gratifying for the supporters of equal rights for women, therefore, that the Graduation Act of 1854 did make women eligible to be homesteaders "in their own right."[20] But African-Americans of either sex, including strong advocates of equal rights for women such as Sojourner Truth and Frederick Douglass, himself an active participant in the Seneca Falls meeting, were denied the right to become homesteaders.

In the same year in which Congress passed the Graduation Act, it also passed the "squatter sovereignty" Kansas–Nebraska Act, leaving it to the citizens of these territories to decide whether their respective states-to-be should be "free" or "slave." As far as Kansas was concerned, the issue would in the end be merged with the greater struggle to determine whether any state could exclude slavery.[21] Before that time a tense, prolonged and sometimes deadly struggle in that territory between the supporters of Free Soil and the pro-slavery "Missouri ruffians" earned it the name of "Bleeding Kansas." Early in the struggle, Frederick Douglass proposed a "Plan for Making Kansas a Free State," which called for the settling of a thousand free Negroes on homesteads in that territory as a means of greatly strengthening the hand of those who wanted to keep Kansas out of the grasp of the slave power.[22] The outcome of the struggle in Kansas, which was critical for the cause of Free Soil, hung in the balance; indeed for a time the territory had a dual government. Such a reinforcement as Douglass was suggesting would have decisively strengthened the Free Soil cause. But the Free Soil "Free State" convention held in Topeka in the fall of 1855 proposed a constitution that would have barred African-Americans altogether from the proposed state, preferring to risk everything in order to keep the homestead right as a "race" privilege.

The historic Homestead Act of 1862 maintained the exclusion, by limiting the homestead right to citizens or those immigrants who intended to become citizens of the United States, a status which the Constitution denied to African-Americans.

Reconstruction: Racial Oppression Challenged and Defended

Racial slavery, the Fugitive Slave Laws, and Taney's notorious phrase (see Chapter 1, note 132) were smashed by the Union armies and navies, whose ranks included more than 200,000 African-Americans and at least 48,000 European-Americans, representing every state of the Confederacy, among them a full brigade of Irish laborers from Louisiana.[23] Among the European-Americans of the defeated Confederate states, there were manifestations of a readiness to share with the freemen in the confiscation and redistribution of plantation lands.[24] Such factors, and the general implications of their victory, confronted the victorious Northern bourgeoisie with a fundamental question of social control: whether to continue the system of racial oppression or to undertake to institute a new system of social control – as the British ruling class had been obliged to do in respect to Ireland a few decades before.

Just as in Ulster there were urban bourgeois republican-minded Protestants who favored equal rights for Catholics, there were in the United States in the 1860s elements – and, for a time, very powerful elements – of the industrial bourgeoisie who believed in fulfilling the logic of Emancipation by the redistribution of land in the South, transforming the economy there into one of small independent farmers in place of an economy dominated by large plantations and plantation owners. Senator Charles Sumner of Massachusetts, for instance, became convinced of the correctness of this path.

> We must see that the freedmen are established on the soil, and that they may become proprietors.... The great plantations, which have been so many nurseries of rebellion, must be broken up, and the freedmen must have the pieces.[25]

His colleague Thaddeus Stevens of Pennsylvania proposed a detailed plan for implementing this revolutionary confiscation and redistribution of the lands of the former slaveholders. Stevens's proposal called for the giving to every male former bond-laborer of forty acres of this land, and for further opportunity for other African-Americans – discharged Union soldiers, and the more prosperous of the 400,000 African-Americans who were already free at the time of Emancipation – who might have sufficient money or credit to join the bidding for moderate-sized plots at ten dollars per acre.[26]

Finding the opposition to confiscation of plantation lands insurmountable, the Radical Republicans succeeded in passing the Southern Homestead Law in June 1866, providing for 47 million acres of public lands to be opened for eighty-acre homesteading. But the author of the bill, Representative George W. Julian of Indiana, understood that it "could only prove a very partial measure without an enactment reaching the fee of the slaveholders."[27] Nevertheless, land historian Paul Wallace Gates writes that, "between 1867 and 1876, there was more homesteading in [the South] in proportion to the land available than there was elsewhere in the public land states."[28] Some 40,000 original entries were made under this act, although an indeterminate large number of them were "dummy" claims managed by land and timber companies.[29] Within sixteen months of its enactment 2,012 homesteads, totaling 168,960 acres, were taken up.[30] Even this token measure was repealed in 1876, as part of the repudiation of Reconstruction, most specifically because "Southerners wanted to have all restrictions upon [access to timber and mineral lands] removed so that extensive areas could be acquired by capitalist groups which might utilize their resources."[31]

The momentous significance of the program for redistribution of plantation lands was that it meant the abandonment of the principle that made slavery in the United States a special form of a general racial oppression and likewise made Protestant Ascendancy and the Penal Laws system racial oppression in Ireland: the refusal to give legitimacy to social class differentiation among the oppressed group. The creation of a class of one million African-American freeholders by decree of the national legislature was necessarily predicated upon the presumption that African-Americans were to be accorded social status according to the norms of any society based on capitalist commodity production.

Still, despite the fact that the class to be expropriated had been responsible for a war that cost one million lives for the right to buy and sell babies by the pound,[32] the Sumner and Stevens proposals failed to be enacted because of their unacceptable implications for the capitalist class in general.[33] "Expropriate the expropriators" had, since 1848, become a slogan intended for general application, and the United States bourgeoisie was ready to perceive "the specter of communism" in the expropriation of the plantation lands. But the implications for the American system of social control were more immediate and critical. The entire United States, not just a sector of it, was a society wherein the heedless, heartless, headlong, pell-mell push for capital accumulation could proceed with "the consent of the governed" only by virtue of the "white" racial privileges of the European-American laboring-class population. That population, particularly in the cities, was increasingly wretched[34] and, at the same time, was constitutionally guaranteed the citizen's right to bear arms. Yet the social control system worked, *mutatis mutandis*, as it did in Ulster where the Protestant worker "however wretched he might be, could still be persuaded" to tolerate it all, "so long as he could keep his Catholic neighbour in a still more wretched state."[35]

Working-class European-Americans were well aware that they had the homestead right as a "white" racial privilege, although in fact few of them had any real prospects of actualizing it.[36] Now it was proposed to extend a variation of that right to African-Americans, but on the very land they had worked as bond-laborers. The transcendent significance of the proposal was that it necessarily implied the end of racial oppression, of social control by means of racial privileges for laboring-class "whites"; it posed "a new birth of freedom" versus "a white man's country."

Just as the Ulster Protestants had had a choice between Green and Orange, between the United Irishmen and the Protestant Ascendancy in 1798, the European-Americans of the wage-laboring class faced a fateful choice in the late 1860s. For at least several decades, the "white labor" rationale for opposing the abolition of slavery was the competition argument, namely, that Negroes, if freed, would become part of the wage-labor supply and would lower wages and reduce opportunities for "white" workers. This same basic argument, as we have noted, was made more respectable by the Free Soilers preachments against competition between "free" and slave labor. But now the land distribution program of the Radical Republicans presented an historically unique practical opportunity to reduce the impoverishing effect of the competition of an oversupply of wage labor.

The land question in the United States at that time presented itself in two aspects, the Western, "free land" aspect and the Southern, rebel land aspect. In actual practice, the former was primarily the interest of the petty bourgeoisie, and not of the masses of wage workers (which is not to deny that the emigration of petit bourgeois families to the West may have made the over-supply of labor less than it would have become if they had stayed on the Atlantic seaboard where they first landed). The most realistic hope that ever existed for proletarians, European-American and African-American, to become successful homesteaders lay in the appropriation of the rebel plantations, along the lines put forward by the Radical Republicans.

By deed, as well as in words, the African-American freedmen expressed their dedication to that proposition. Before the guns of war were still, African-American families were making crops as independent farmers on lands where they had been chattel slaves on the Sea Islands and other South Carolina, Georgia and Florida lands set aside for them under General Sherman's Field Order No. 15 of 16 January 1865.[37] In the face of fierce opposition from the old plantation owners and ambivalence within the government, South Carolina freedmen demanded that "no impediments be put in the way of our acquiring homesteads."[38] In the South as a whole, 800,000 acres of confiscated rebel land were worked by freedmen families as renters under the administration of the Freedmen's Bureau of the federal government. After the issues of the franchise and public education, which were addressed by the Reconstruction Conventions of the various states, "none was more critical than the question of the land," writes John Hope Franklin.[39] In Alabama they spoke of confiscation of land "forfeited by the treason of its owners."[40] The Negro National Labor Union at its first convention in Washington, DC, in 1869, speaking of the dreadful dimensions of the problem of oversupply of wage labor in the Southern states, urged the United States Congress to understand that, "The true and immediate practicable remedy lies in making a fair proportion of the laborers themselves land-owners."[41]

Meanwhile, the white National Labor Union (NLU) at its founding convention in 1866 put the land question first in its "Address to the Workingmen of the United States" but limited it to consideration of "the Public Lands."[42] The following year, citing the jobs lost in New England mills because of a shortage of cotton, the NLU called for "the speedy restoration of the Southern states" to the Union, meaning a speedy end to Reconstruction with its promise of expropriation of rebels' plantations for distribution to the landless.[43] William H. Sylvis, the most famous of the leaders of the NLU, speaking as its president in 1868, stridently denounced Reconstruction. Instead of financing the Freedmen's Bureau, he said, "it would have been much better to loan the planters a few millions of dollars."[44] In an attack on the "Land Monopoly" in the United States, Sylvis pointed to Ireland where the land was economically and politically dominated by large plantation owners. He regarded the Irish case as an instructive parallel for the United States, and urged the English government to "divide the land equitably."[45] He chose to ignore the fact that such a reform in Ireland involved taking land not from the "public domain" but from plantation owners – the very policy which he and the NLU refused to support in the United States.

By making freedom a *human right*, Negro Emancipation had destroyed it as *racial privilege*, and thereby threatened to dissolve on the instant the mortar holding together the system of bourgeois social control, the system of "white"-labor privileges based on the presumption of African-American chattel bond-servitude. Writing to President Lincoln on behalf of the International Working-men's Association, Karl Marx was hopeful:

> While the working men, the true political power of the North, allowed slavery to defile their own republic, while before the Negro, mastered and sold without his concurrence, they boasted it the highest prerogative of the white-skinned labourer to sell himself and choose his own master, they were unable to attain the true freedom of labour ... but this barrier to progress has been swept off by the red sea of civil war.

Emancipation, said Marx, therefore heralded "a new era ... of ascendancy of the working classes."[46] Radical Republican congressman William Darrah Kelley of Pennsylvania was a vigorous promoter of American industrial capitalism. He appreciated the opportunities for the development of natural resources in the South with the aid of Northern capital, but under Republican leadership based on the suffrage of, and equal rights and opportunity for, African-Americans. At about the time that Marx's letter was being delivered to Lincoln, Kelley was making his point in a speech in the House of Representatives.

> Shall he [the Negro], though black as ebony his skin, who by patient industry, obedience to the laws, and unvarying good habits, has accumulated property on which he cheerfully pays taxes be denied the right of a choice in the government ... while the idle reckless, thriftless men of fairer complexion shall vote away his earnings and trifle with his life or interests as a juror?[47]

Kelley regarded it as intolerable that the African-American soldier who had endured the perils of battle in defense of the Constitution should be denied its protection, while "traitors in the conquest of whom he assisted enjoy those rights, and use them as instruments for his oppression and degradation."

Today it is apparent that Marx's vision was falsely heralded; but the record left by bourgeois Radical Republicans like William D. Kelley reminds us that it was not an impossible dream for the United States to have ended the curse of racial oppression; given that, all else might have been added unto us. With more proper detachment, a modern historian writes: "... the race question [as it stood at the end of the Civil War] raised new problems for the South. Slavery was gone.... The status of both white and colored men remained to be defined."[48]

In the end, the status question was resolved when the bourgeoisie as a whole,[49] drawing upon practices that had ante-bellum roots, opted for what we may term White Reconstruction, that is, the re-establishment of the social control system of racial oppression, based on racial privileges for laboring-class "whites" with regard to "free" land, immigration, and industrial employment. In that process, the Negro Exodus of 1879 and the Cotton Mill Campaign, dated from the following year, were to be defining moments.

The Material Basis for the Abandonment of Reconstruction

Just as the British ruling class had come to accept the necessity of involving the Catholic bourgeoisie in Ireland in the maintenance of social control, so the Northern bourgeoisie, though only for a limited period of time as it turned out, "made him [the Negro] a part of the state," as the investigative journalist Charles Nordhoff wrote. "If the North had not given the negroes suffrage," a Southern Democrat confided to him, "it would have had to hold our states under an exclusively military government for ten years."[50] John Pool, a Republican Senator from North Carolina, said he "accepted the necessity of Negro suffrage only reluctantly," as the only means by which the country could be "nationalized."[51] The country was in fact in a material sense "nationalized" by other agencies. In 1867 Abilene, Kansas, became the railroad loading point for cattle driven up the Chisholm Trail from Texas, intended for northern and eastern markets. Two years later, the Union Pacific and the Central Pacific railroads met at Promontory Point in Utah, completing the transcontinental steel spine of United States industrial capitalism. Thus were doomed the hopes of the slave bourgeoisie beyond all appeals to ink or blood. The Northern bourgeoisie, its hegemony in national affairs thus undergirded, signified its acceptance of post-Emancipation racial oppression by abandoning Reconstruction. The subsequent white-supremacist system in the South was established not by civil means, but by nightrider terror and one-sided "riots" in order to deprive African-Americans of their constitutional rights,[52] reducing them again, by debt peonage and prisoner-leasing, to a status that was slavery in all but name.[53]

That still left the basic problem, however – the problem that concerned Sir John Davies and Sir William Petty in Ireland – how to achieve stability and civil order in a system based on racial oppression. Even from the ruling-class point of view, there is a limit to profitability in the maintenance of social control by unconstitutional methods ("sending an army to do it"); that manifests a deficiency in the intermediate, buffer social control stratum, a situation that discourages venture capital.[54]

The Negro Exodus of 1879

A hundred thousand laboring-class African-Americans in the South had a different sense of the limits, and they determined to make a withdrawal of variable capital, that is, their own labor power, from the plantation system. They ventured for the dream deferred, of homes and homesteads, by making an exodus like that of ancient example.[55] They persevered, despite objections voiced by Frederick Douglass and some other leaders, local as well as national, who argued that the tide could still be reversed in the South, and that the Exodus was a sort of desertion of the cause.[56] The best-known leaders of the Exodus, such as Benjamin "Pap" Singleton of Tennessee and Henry Adams of Louisiana, were former bond-laborers. Singleton had escaped to points north, and Adams had served as a sergeant in the Union army.[57] They were not likely to be deterred by advice belied by their experience.

Groundwork, and underground work, had been under way for some years before. Indeed over the decade many African-Americans had gone into Kansas from Tennessee, Kentucky and Missouri. In Texas, Louisiana, Mississippi and Alabama, the organizers of the Exodus had since 1874 enrolled 98,000 persons for the enterprise.[58] The destination was "free ground";[59] for some that meant Indiana or Ohio, but the most favored place was Kansas – the Kansas of old John Brown – and thousands got there. Between 1870 and 1880, the number of African-Americans living in Kansas but not born there increased by more than two and a half times, from about 12,000 to about 33,000; a major contribution was made by the arrival of around 6,000 from Louisiana, Mississippi and Texas in that dramatic spring of 1879. Thousands more arrived at the transfer point of Saint Louis, who migrated then to other states.[60] Most of the migrants had little or no financial resources; sympathizers, locally and throughout the country ("a few incurable fanatics," as a spiteful New York journal called them),[61] organized to defend the right of migration, to assist the Exodusters in finding gainful employment, and in general to help them surmount their difficulties.[62] Only a handful of the Exodusters gave up and returned to the South; most of the others, with or without further assistance, found places for themselves in the local economy, although they were not financially able to start out as homesteaders.[63] Many of those from Texas, however, three or four thousand of whom arrived between November 1879 and March 1880, came in their own wagons with their own furniture and were financially able to fend for themselves from the beginning.[64]

One fairly prominent Republican, Benjamin H. Bristow of Kentucky, was optimistic; he saw the Exodus as "Perhaps . . . the final settlement of the 'Negro question.'"[65] Whatever the particulars as Bristow conceived them, there is no doubt that the migration of African-Americans from the South had profound implications for the course of United States history. If African-Americans had become completely free to escape from the South, the white-supremacists would have been unable to institute and maintain the white reign of terror by which they overthrew Reconstruction. Then, paradoxically, those who stayed might indeed have prospered in freedom in the South, in the way that Douglass envisioned.

But just as Home Rule for Ireland proved to be unacceptable to the British ruling class as a whole because of its threatening democratic implications for England itself, so the United States ruling class in the end rejected this, or any, "settlement of the Negro question," sensing the potential emergence of an unwelcome array of popular forces against the course of unchecked capitalist greed, an array freed of the paralyzing incubus of "white" racial privileges. Just as the British played the Orange card against Home Rule,[66] so did the bourgeoisie in the United States play the "White card" to destroy the Exodus. Before the Exodusters could even set foot on the Exodus Road, they were subjected to threats and violence by whites for expressing the intention of leaving. "[Y]ou will get your head shot away," a Louisiana landlord told one of his black tenants who said he wanted to leave the state. A white mob hanged a woman, although she was in an advanced stage of pregnancy, for intending to go to Kansas to join her husband; her child was born as she was being murdered.[67] There was the threatening publication by a white-owned Mississippi newspaper of the names of those active in enrolling people for the Exodus. A group of white men "killed [a Mississippi man] because he wanted to go to Kansas," one Exoduster testified. Most common was the threatened or actual imprisonment of would-be Exodusters on the charge of attempting to escape the systemic indebtedness to the landlord.[68]

The main strategy was directed at the most vulnerable point, the Mississippi river landings. The river being the lifeline of escape, the effort to stop it centered on depriving the migrants of riverboat transportation. Armed and mounted gangs of white men, known as "bulldozers," ranged both sides of the river, not only to intimidate the Exodusters but also to prevent boats from even stopping where Exodusters were congregated. Direct terrorism was supplemented by non-terroristic measures, such as the pressure brought by St Louis businessmen to force ship operators to raise ticket prices to levels that would be prohibitive for the Exodusters.[69]

The strategy proved effective.[70] Many hundreds of Exodusters were actually stranded at the landings; others, who had not yet reached the river, were likely to be deterred by the prospect. They had the money (about four dollars) for the fare on the riverboat, but only if their embarkation was prompt and if the price of the tickets was not raised. But they were not prepared to withstand the pressures entailed by delay. If they spent their money for food, their ticket money was gone. If, as it often happened, white merchants refused to sell to them, hunger forced them to stop where they were and hire themselves out locally. They were subjected to constant efforts to get them to turn back, an activity in which some African-Americans engaged as agents of the plantation owners. The Exodusters were strong in spirit and faith, but the movement was structurally weak. What the bulldozers and the ship companies were doing was eventually stopped by threats of court action and of providing alternative shipping facilities. But by that time the back of the Exodus had been broken.[71]

The Exodus and the white immigration privilege

Some Kansas whites reacted negatively to the spectacular proportions of the Exodus. At Leavenworth, white authorities refused to allow boats carrying Exodusters to land. Others saw in the Exodus a threat of tax-draining pauperism. In one area aspiring to countyhood, it was suggested that only "whites" be counted toward the minimum population requirement. On the outskirts of Topeka, a gang of whites destroyed a temporary shelter provided by friends of the Exodusters.[72] By contrast, the increasing hundreds of North Carolina whites migrating to the West at that time seem not to have been bulldozed or otherwise intimidated into returning to the plantation country, nor driven away by residents of the states of their destination.[73]

The rationale that whites were being crowded out by an excessive influx of black people should scarcely have satisfied even those disposed to think in such bigoted terms. The decennial census figures indicate that the rate of influx of white people was slightly greater than that of black people. For every 10 African-Americans in Kansas in 1870, there were 204 Euro-Americans; in 1880 there were 210.[74] The white-skin privilege of immigration was apparent in the fact that for every 10 African-Americans in Kansas at the end of that decade who were not born in Kansas, there were 14 foreign-born persons. Yet there is no record of boats being interfered with for bringing the foreigners to Kansas; they, of course, had been baptized "white" when they first set foot in the country, and thus endowed with the inalienable right of immigration. Some of these came by riverboat from New Orleans, a fact that will be further noted below (pp. 155–7).

A Mutual Understanding Regarding Social Control

"Northern commercial interests," writes Hirshson, "espousing views which they consistently advocated since 1877, strongly opposed the exodus." A typical instance was given by the New York *Commercial Bulletin*: "Can the South or the North be benefited by encouraging the migration of that labor upon which our chief commercial crop is dependent?" it asked. Another business organ, the New York *Journal of Commerce*, was eager to "assure the Southerners, once for all, that . . . the people of the North feel no desire to break up the Southern labor system."[75]

The African-Americans were not objecting to making cotton – that was a specialty of many of them. All they asked was put simply by John Solomon Lewis of Tensas parish, Louisiana: to be allowed "to make headway like white workingmen,"[76] and not to be terrorized out of the constitutional rights that they had fought for in the Union army, cheated of their pay, or forced into peonage; and that a black woman not have to live in fear of being made the victim of sexual molestation by any white man who encountered her.[77] That was "the Southern labor system" to those who did the labor. When the dominant sections of the bourgeoisie called for its preservation, they were opting for the post-Emancipation reinstitution of racial oppression. And again, as in the days of the Fugitive Slave Laws, the preservation of "the southern labor system" required the maintenance of the system of racial privileges of laboring-class Euro-Americans, the "whites," vis-à-vis African-Americans not just in the South, but throughout the country. On this a mutual North–South bourgeois understanding was attained, as can be gleaned from a US senator's questioning of a typical representative of the plantation bourgeoisie, John C. Calhoun, grandson and namesake of the South Carolina statesman. The testimony, given in September 1883 before the Senate Education and Labor Committee on the Relations between Labor and Capital,[78] seems the more interesting since it was the elder Calhoun who first defied the authority of the United States over his own state in the famous Nullification controversy in the 1830s.

The grandson left South Carolina at the height of Reconstruction in 1869, for reasons which we may in part infer were not altogether limited to matters of soil exhaustion, to take up a large plantation on the Arkansas side of the Mississippi river.[79] In 1879, some one hundred and fifty of his African-American laborers and/or tenants set out on the Exodus to Kansas, a move he claimed to have had some success in discouraging by intercepting them at the banks of the Mississippi.[80] Times had changed since his grandfather's day, and the South, Calhoun told the committee, was now "strongly for the Union," for which he gave the following reason:

> ... the negro population of the South, compared with the white population of the South, might be a dangerous element, but the negro population, compared with the whole white population of the United States as an integral body, sinks into insignificance.

Calhoun endorsed the view expressed by committee chairman Senator Blair of New Hampshire, who was questioning him, that it was to the advantage of "the South" that

> ... the negro should be dealt with by the forty or fifty millions of whites, that the races should be balanced in that proportion rather than in the proportion that exists between them and the white population of the South.[81]

Sir William Petty would have been pleased by this grand realization of the principle of his proposal to James II for a merger of the Irish and English populations to achieve the proportions necessary for social control in a society based on racial oppression.

Calhoun felt that in the light of all that had happened, "There is really very little conflict between labor and capital. The conflict in my section, if any should come in the future, will not assume the form of labor against capital, but of race against race."[82]

The Organized White Workers

But did the motivations and plans of the white workers, especially as organized in the National Labor Union between 1866 and 1872, justify such ruling-class self-assurance as that voiced by Calhoun? The NLU had entered into fraternal relations with the International Workingmen's Association, which had high expectations of labor in the United States as the trailblazer toward "the ascendancy of the working class." The record of the NLU's deliberations on "negro labor," and of its relations with the Black National Labor Union, needs to be studied closely, with the heightened consciousness that is one legacy of the civil rights struggles of the 1960s. It is too extensive for treatment in the present context, but the tone of it, beneath occasional rhetorical flourishes, seems more likely to anticipate Calhoun's expectations than to affirm those of the First International.

At its inaugural convention in Baltimore in 1866, the NLU urged the inculcation of the idea that:

> ... the interests of labor are one; that there should be no distinction of race or nationality; no classification of Jew or Gentile, Christian or Infidel; that there is but one dividing line – that which separates mankind into two great classes, the class that labors and the class that lives by others' labor.[83]

But then and thereafter, as the documents show, the NLU was determined to interpret that idea in the same narrow "white labor" sense as before the war, namely, the desire to avoid competition by black workers. Obviously, the International had not sent the NLU a copy of Marx's letter to Lincoln, with its injunction to throw off the incubus of "white" labor's privileges over black labor. I have already noted the disparagement of black Reconstruction by the NLU and its President William Sylvis. The NLU went out of existence after 1872, but the "white labor" principles by which it was bound unfortunately did not. Solidarity with the Exodusters was left to the remnants of Radical Republicanism; there is no record of a labor component in it.

It is to the credit of Frederick A. Sorge, Marx's friend and correspondent and NLU activist, that he came later to understand this much about his adopted country: "The race prejudice of the Caucasians against the Negro prevents the rise of labor organizations in many southern states, and the beginning of a healthy labor movement."[84] By way of remedy, however, Sorge merely offered the suggestion that the mass of black workers on the cotton and sugar plantations of the South "will arise by their own strength and must put an end to the misery under which they suffer." He was silent on what to do about the white workers' "prejudice," and put his faith in the "rise of industry in the New South," which he believed would "pull the Negro population into the movement – [and] ... revolutionize *them*"[85] (emphasis added). But what was to revolutionize the Euro-American workers by ridding them of "race" prejudice? The absurdity of putting faith in "objective" factors such as the industrialization of the South will appear in the discussion of the Cotton Mill Campaign below.

At the very moment, in December 1879, when thousands of Exodusters were making their way overland from Texas to Kansas, the Socialist Labor Party, of which Sorge was a chief founder, held its national convention in Pittsburgh, Pennsylvania. Albert Parsons, himself a Texan driven out for his equalitarian views, introduced a resolution "concerning land grants." The whole country by that time was aware of the Exodus, but the records do not show whether Parsons made any mention of it in his talk and resolution. In any case, the convention as a whole ignored it; the resolution was referred to the Committee on Platforms and is not heard of again.[86]

The South Revisits the Problem of Social Control

I have noted how the Protestant tenants, their exclusive Ulster Custom tenant-right eroded by structural economic changes and drained by reduction of the size of their holdings, indicated for a brief period a readiness to make common cause with the Catholic peasants to secure the legal enactment of a tenant-right law for all Ireland. Radical Reconstruction had likewise shown that there were some Southern whites who were ready to make common cause with the black population to establish a society there based on racial equality of constitutional rights.[87]

They dared, and some died as John Brown had done, struggling side by side with African-American freedom fighters for their common cause, the end of racial oppression. They are not so well known as they should be; here is a selected list of ten of them:

- A. P. Dostie, described by one historian as "animated by a fanatical ambition to subdue rebels and elevate slaves" (Shugg, *Class Struggle in Louisiana*, p. 217), killed in a mob attack on the New Orleans Black and White Convention in July 1866; his dying words: "Let the good fight go on!" (*Proceedings of the Southern Loyalist Convention*, September 1866, printed in the *Reporter*, no. 33, Washington, DC, 17 September 1866).

- Calvin Pepper of Virginia, the only white person on the delegation which Frederick Douglass led to present a petition to the President on behalf of Negro suffrage (Black, *Home-made Yankees*, p. 189. John Richard Dennett, *The South As It Is, 1865–1866* [New York, 1866], pp. 6–7).

- James W. Hunnicutt of Virginia, who "campaigned vigorously against the vagrancy laws, for racial equality, and against voting and office-holding by 'rebels'" (Black, p. 250, citing Union League Club of New York, *Aid for Virginia* [New York, 1867]).

- George W. Ashburn of Georgia, murdered "for consorting with Negroes" (Black, p. 30).

- J. W. Smith, of Texas, killed for "organizing Negroes" (ibid.).

- Thomas J. Mackey of South Carolina, "one of the few white men to attend the state labor convention in Columbia in 1869" (ibid., p. 34).

- William Wallace Chisolm and John P. Gilmer, killed in Mississippi in 1877 in order that "confidence [be] restored between the races" (James D. Lynch, *Kemper County Vindicated: A Peep at Radical Rule in Mississippi* [New York, 1879], p. 319).

- Alexander Boyd, murdered in Eutaw, Alabama, "for too earnest inquiries into outrages committed against freedmen" (Black, pp. 47–8, citing the Greensboro, North Carolina *Republican*, 28 April 1870).

- John Walter Stephens of North Carolina, poor farmer, uncompromising activist in the struggle against white supremacy, whose lynching and the manner of it are described in Chapter 30 of Albion W. Tourgée's novel *A Fool's Errand* (1879; New York, 1961).

The ruling class strangled Reconstruction by sheer terror, but they could not forget the time when the impossible happened and a part of the European-American population arrayed itself against white supremacy. The consensus is that the proportion of this defection from the white-race function was insignificant. If it was so insignificant why the reign of terror against it? Was the terror not simply a new edition of the gag rules, the tar and feathers, and the interdiction of abolitionist mail that had been produced by the fears of abolitionism in the South in the pre-war decades?[88] And, in the end, had not those forebodings proved valid? Given the decision to continue the system of racial oppression, given the self-limiting advantages of rule by mere terrorism, given the dilemma-dictated reliance on African-American labor, given the constitutional leverage, actual or potential, now in the hands of the African-Americans – the matter of the intermediate stratum remained in urgent need of attention.

The immigrant labor supply fantasy

At some point on the road to the Hayes–Tilden deal, the plantation bourgeoisie was seized with the fantasy of recruiting Chinese laborers in numbers sufficient even to threaten the Negroes with marginalization.[89] The main problem with regard to the Chinese was that the Southern planters could not/ would not pay as much as those workers were earning building railroads in the West.[90] A few were procured for Louisiana plantations, but they ran away to work as fishermen or truck farmers around New Orleans. A number of Southern states established agencies to recruit laborers from Europe, especially Ireland and Germany. "There is one answer – *and one only* – WHITE IMMIGRATION," declared an Alabama editor.[91] Many Irish and German immigrants had come to New Orleans before the war. Perhaps, it was thought, the same sources would go a long way toward supplying the needed intermediate stratum.[92] The trouble in this case was that Germans and Irish would not be coming to work as field hands, but would have to be offered homesteads, and those homesteads would have to be cut out of the holdings of the plantation owners themselves. When that realization struck home, the whole idea lost its appeal. Indeed, the bourgeoisie did want "a wall betwixt" themselves and the laboring-class African-Americans; and, like the planters of Ulster, they were perfectly willing to provide some land for settlers when it could be taken from the native population. But to cut up their own land for giveaway freeholds would be to lose sight altogether of their lives' basic purpose.[93] Balancing social needs against economic interests, it seemed, would require exploration of other possibilities for shoring up the buffer middle stratum in the face of problems presented by Emancipation. The Irish and the Germans meantime paddleboated up the Mississippi in search of homestead prospects brighter than any they could expect in the South,[94] perhaps passing stranded Exodusters as they went. In the Exodus decade, 1870–79, in Kansas the foreign-born became the fastest-growing segment of the population (as compared with the native-born, African-American and European-American segments), while in Louisiana the foreign-born proportion of the population continued to decline.[95]

Homesteaders pay the price of Free Soil

White labor had, by accepting the white-skin privilege principle of Free Soil and the Homestead Act of 1862, rendered itself powerless to shape land policy; then, by turning its back on black labor's dream for land and loans for the freedmen, it had endorsed capitalist land monopoly in the South. The result was to foredoom opposition to land monopoly in the West. The industrial bourgeoisie, having consolidated its power by the Hayes–Tilden deal that perpetuated the system of racial oppression, proceeded unchecked to dispose of the "public lands" for railroad building enterprises and for other forms of direct and indirect exploitation of the land and its resources by large capitalist enterprises. By 1890, four times as much land had been given to the railroad capitalists as the total acreage of homestead entries made since 1862.[96]

Yet upon those tillers of the soil who did succeed in perfecting their homestead claims, the pressure of capitalist exploiters took a devastating toll. The homesteaders were always in debt; by 1890, in the five Plains states (Kansas, Nebraska, North Dakota, South Dakota and Minnesota) there was a ratio of more than one mortgage per family.[97] Then came an epidemic of foreclosures. Worst hit was Kansas, where between 1889 and 1893 eleven thousand farms were foreclosed; in some counties "as much as ninety per cent of the farm lands passed into the ownership of the loan companies," writes historian John D. Hicks. But the other Plains states were also heavily hit.[98]

By 1890, of the 8.4 million people engaged in agriculture in the United States, more than 35 percent were hired laborers, and another 18 percent were laboring-class tenants.[99] Land historian Fred A. Shannon comments thus:

> Equally certain as that railroad companies, private speculators, and loan companies profited most from the government's land policy, is the fact that the labor surplus became a constantly increasing factor in the national life after 1864.... The years of agricultural distress in the 1870s and 1880s were accompanied by an ever-increasing roll of unemployed in the cities. Even the pioneers on the homesteads, baffled by fortune and beaten by nature, edged their way back, more often than not, to the ancestral farms and from there to the factory and, too frequently, to the bread line.[100]

By shaping the homestead policy as a white-skin privilege, the ruling class had secured the acquiescence of laboring-class whites in the overthrow of black Reconstruction. Now it was time for the bourgeoisie to reveal the other side of its policy on the land question: the power of capital to expropriate a great proportion of the white farmers and cast them – racial privileges and all – into the ranks of the proletariat. But precisely because the white-skin privileges were sedulously preserved, history would present the farce of Populism as the sequel to the tragedy of Reconstruction.

As a general principle of social control the interests of the intermediate stratum conflict at points with those of the ruling class. This poses the possibility that the middle stratum, or a decisive part of it, might defect to the side of the oppressed masses. To insure against this possibility, certain inviolable spheres of development are apportioned to people of the middle stratum, which afford them an appropriate degree of independence and security. Typical are the Ulster Custom, the Homestead Law, and hereditary apprenticeship opportunities.

What had distinguished the ante-bellum South in this regard was the total absence of such guarantees from the ruling plantation-owning class to the non-owners of bond-labor, who made up three-fourths of the European-American population.[101] Scholars are agreed. The plantation social order "walled them up and locked them in ... blocked them off from escape or any considerable economic and social advance ... left them virtually out of account ... [and the ruling class] concerned itself but little if at all about making use of them as economic auxiliaries."[102] The better-off of them, the "yeoman," so-called, had little if any vital economic connection with the larger plantation society. He "might have devoted a few acres to one of the staples for a 'cash crop', but he directed most of his land and time to food crops for the subsistence of his own family."[103] In Louisiana in 1850, three out of five whites owned no land, and "white labor ... was excluded from the plantation economy." Before the advancing tide of plantations, "Yeomen had no choice but to move westward, or to retreat to ... the woods ... swamps or bayous."[104] They were "left out of the scheme of things ... on the fringe of civilization and in most respects were just tolerated ... [with] no place provided for them by those in social control."[105]

Unlike the Protestant tenant in Ulster, or the homesteader in the West, or the skilled craftsman in industry, the intermediate status of the poor whites hung by a single thread: the enslavement of the Negro and the concomitant fact of their own non-slave status. That did, of course, carry the privileges of keeping weapons, marrying, moving about freely in the public domain, becoming literate if they could, voting at elections, and the male white privilege of assuming familiarity with Negro females; but that all meant nothing in the way of property status or economic security. As one eastern Virginia plantation owner, "Civis", wrote of most of the poor whites in his area of the country, they had "little but their complexion to console them for being born into a higher caste."[106] Yet that one tie bound them to the plantation owners like hoops of steel, and made them "always ready to respond to any call of race prejudice, [so that they] voted with the planter, though the economic interests of the two parties of white men were as separate as the poles."[107]

Because of this about one million Southern poor whites marched off to a war from which more than one out of four would not return.[108] Those who did return found that the very foundation of their social status had been blasted away: the Negro was free, too. Adding to that were the effects of the war's desolation. For the planters there was a silver lining. The price of cotton in 1866 was more than two and a half times its level in the high-price half-decade before the war. Though it declined after 1866, it did not reach the pre-war level until 1875.[109] High prices made it attractive to raise cotton on the less fertile land in poor-white country. Poor whites became for the first time totally committed to cotton farming, and in fairly short order they were enmeshed in the credit system, reduced to tenants, on shares, less self-sufficient and as poor if not poorer than before it all began.[110] Most significant of all, they were on the same economic plane with freedmen tenants who were also striving to succeed as cotton farmers.

The prospect of the poor whites being put on a footing of equality with the African-American tenant and sharecropper, as would be pointed out by W. J. Cash, carried implications that "filled [the plantation bourgeoisie] with terror." For who could doubt that "intimate competition with the Negro would lead to social equality," and to the breakdown of "the convention of white superiority."[111]

> Who did not see again, that, despairing of their racial status ... these whites would eventually be swept fully into the bitterest class consciousness: that this slow impulse which the master class was at least aware of from the beginning [since Bacon's Rebellion?], would develop a power no barrier and no argument could hold back? Who could not see, in a word, that here was chaos?[112]

The Cotton Mill Campaign – the "way out"[113]

I have noted how the Industrial Revolution came to Ireland in the mold of Protestant Ascendancy. Industrialization was limited to Ulster while potentially profitable opportunities were ignored in the Catholic south and west on political grounds. The point was given emphasis by the deliberate decision of the British government to let the Famine run its course, with the resulting loss of one-fourth of the labor power of Ireland through death and emigration. Similarly, when the Industrial Revolution came to the United States South, it was cast in the mold of white supremacy in the most explicit way:

> The Poor Whites under slavery had been excluded, while slaves were cherished. Now the disinherited were read into the will. They had been unnecessary, now they were all-important. The bond of sympathy between whites of both classes was cemented against the common enemy, the Negro.[114]

In its "determination to find a way out for the South,"[115] meaning the continuation of racial oppression of the Negro in the United States, the bourgeoisie now wove the third strand into the post-Emancipation system of privileges of white workers – preference in industrial employment – by means of the Cotton Mill Campaign. It was not merely an investment strategy to take advantage of the poverty-level wages prevailing in the South, and to reduce the cost of cotton at the mill, although it was that, too. Capital investment in cotton manufacture in the South, which had grown at a rate of about $3 million per decade from 1840 to 1880, to a level of $17 million, rose to a total of $124.4 million between 1880 and 1900.[116] It was to be the foundation of a reconstructed system of social control.

From before the Civil War on up through the Reconstruction period, Southern mills generally employed African-American workers, often together with white workers.[117] In the 1850s Saluda mill, near Columbia, South Carolina, had a labor force of 128, including children, all African-Americans.[118] Supervisors who came from the North overcame their early prejudices upon finding that African-American bond-laborers worked "with equal efficiency and even superiority in many respects as compared with whites." The authoritative all-South journal *De Bow's Review*, based in New Orleans, at that time found the possibilities of "African labor" so promising for factory employment that an end should be put to schemes for its "emigration to other countries," an apparent reference to various proposals for "colonization" of Negroes outside the country.[119] A study done by De Bow in 1852–53 endorsed the use of African-American bond-laborers in textile manufacture throughout the South, basing the recommendation on favorable past experience.[120] After the war the "familiar practice" of employing African-Americans in cotton mills was continued.[121] Even as late as 1880, of the 100 workers at the Saluda mill, 25 were Negroes.[122]

The explosion of capital investment in the last two decades of the century was accompanied by a sixfold increase in the number of cotton mill operatives in the South, from 16,741 in 1880 to 97,559 in 1900. This was a period when cotton prices were falling; in the mid-1890s the price stood at about a nickel a pound, far less than half what it had been in 1880. A typical small tenant farm family might earn, say, $525 in a year's work. By going into the cotton mill, where again the entire family would be employed, the family income would be increased to $900.[123] It was a perfectly normal response when debt-ridden tenants "industrious and lazy alike flocked to the mill communities."[124]

What was not normal from the standpoint of lowering operating costs was to refuse to hire Negroes as cotton mill operatives, even though the mill owners believed that African-American laborers were perfectly capable of doing the work,[125] and possibly at lower cost (given the augmented labor pool, and assuming non-union conditions). It was altogether rational, however, in terms of the maintenance of bourgeois social control, one more instance of balancing the economic and the social aspects of rulership. The mill owners as a class had "recognized the fact that the mill life is the only avenue open ... to our poor whites, and we have with earnestness and practically without exception kept that avenue open to the white man alone."[126] The aim, said D. A. Tompkins, prominent cotton mill entrepreneur, had to be "to reestablish as quickly as possible respectability for white labor."[127] Prospective Cotton Mill investors were urged to rise above "purely mercenary considerations," and think of the thousands of jobs they would be providing for unemployed "white" women. Mitchell "explains": "whites, particularly women, could not compete with negroes in certain occupations, and in 'servile' ones would not."[128] At the conclusion of its investigation of the cotton mill industry, the United States Industrial Commission noted uncritically "[t]he finding ... that the white mill workers ought to be saved from negro competition; that this field ought to be reserved for white labor."[129] I leave aside here the frequent self-serving white-supremacist allusion to "social equality," except to note that the discrimination in employment was related to the white male privilege aspect of the system of social control peculiar to the United States, which it seems was regarded as certain to be undermined by white women and black men working together, especially in the same room! Undoubtedly, W. J. Cash was faithfully interpreting the mind of the South's mill owners in saying, ". . . we shall create a sanctuary for the falling common whites and place thousands of them in employment which by common agreement shall be closed to the Negro."[130] In earnest whereof, the mill owners had awarded the poor white an annual income differential *vis-à-vis* the African-American equal to the difference between the share-tenant's $525 and the mill worker's $900.

For some time now, official society has fled from the concept of affirmative action as a measure of fairness and equality for African-Americans and other not-"whites." Some opportunists have preeningly repudiated affirmative action. A chorus of white pundits have sung a steady dirge about "preferential treatment." One of them denounces affirmative action as "an ethnic spoils system."[131] One can only imagine how indignant they all would have been if they had been alive to witness the workings of the Cotton Mill Campaign!

White-skin Privilege as a Depressor of Wage Levels

The effects of the development of this discrimination in employment were ramified not only across the South, but throughout the United States. Cotton goods manufacture was the one factory industry in the South; it was necessarily a family affair, not like mining or logging, or other extractive industries. More than 90 percent of all African-Americans lived in the South; escape to the west and north, as we have seen in the story of the Exodus of 1879, was effectively cut off for all but the most hardy and lucky of them. Outside the South, industrial employers understood that the white-skin privilege employment policy, when combined with a corresponding racist immigration policy, was on the whole perfectly compatible with profitable operations, and that it served their long-range class interests as a preventive against class-consciousness in the North and in the West, no less than in the South. It had another very tangible effect outside the South: the gradual decline of the importance of the New England textile mills, due largely to the low wages paid in the South. Taking the combined number of active spindles in the two regions as an index, New England's share declined from 94 percent in 1880 to 75 percent in 1990; the decline continued until New England was destroyed as a textile region, along with its relatively higher wage scale.[132]

Textile mill wages in the South were not only low relative to those of New England, but absolutely low with reference to their own daily needs. Mitchell quotes mill owners as saying that the North–South cotton mill wage differential was about 25 percent.[133] But Vann Woodward cites a variety of more disinterested authorities who found that the wages of Southern mill hands were much lower than those given by Mitchell as a basis for comparison with New England wages. Instead of three to four dollars a week, the workers in North Carolina received from ten cents a day, for children, to fifty cents a day for men. In Alabama in 1885, male spinners got $2.53 a week and women $2.76. The work week was seventy hours.[134] The condition was self-perpetuating. Ordinarily the wages of operatives living in cotton mill towns were so low "that all available members of a family had to work in the mill, and the companies refuse[d] to let houses except to families which [could] furnish two, three or sometimes even four workers to a family."[135]

This historic persistence of low wages was not due, however, to the conditions of rural poverty of those tenant farmers and sharecroppers alone, or to the lack of opportunities for other industrial employment. It was bound to perpetuity because of the paralyzing effect of white-supremacism, *a barrier that could not be overcome without a facing of the issue*. That seems to be the clear conclusion to which the brothers Mitchell were led by their extensive studies in the field. They said: "Managements have encouraged the maxim that the cotton manufacture is a white man's industry; the implied danger of Negro invasion is supposed to render the operatives glad to hold what they have, rather than reach out for more."[136]

Of Parallels and Intertwining

It is a century now since the Populist Revolt and the Cotton Mill Campaign, a century that has merely underscored the judgment rendered by DuBois in 1935 that Reconstruction had "presented the greatest opportunity" we were likely to see for "many decades"[137] for breaking the mold the slaveholders made. Except for the consciousness-raising civil rights movement in the United States and in Ulster, dating from the Montgomery bus boycott, little of significance has been added to or subtracted from the message of the parallels drawn in these six chapters, to contribute to an understanding of the essential principles of racial oppression and their organic relationship to the problems of ruling-class social control.

These histories present not only parallels, however, but an intertwining which is no less valuable for its illumination of the social process of recruitment of Euro-Americans into the "white race" social control formation, and the resistance to that process, in the period between 1820 and 1860.

7

The Sea-change

I have been looking into an Irish mirror for insights into the nature of racial oppression and its implication for ruling-class social control in the United States. I conclude this volume with a look at a unique historical phenomenon associated with the massive Irish immigration into the arena of the ante-bellum struggle between racial slavery and freedom in the United States. The image passes through the looking-glass to become American reality; but as if governed by the mirror metaphor, it reappears as the opposite of its original self. Subjects of a history of racial oppression as Irish Catholics are sea-changed into "white Americans," into opponents both of the abolition of racial slavery and of equal rights of African-Americans in general.

Between 1820 and 1860 Ireland and America became interlinked by two historic developments: first, the maturation of the struggle that culminated in the overthrow of racial slavery; and, second, massive emigration from Ireland to the United States.

The Struggle over Racial Slavery

The issue of racial slavery versus freedom was undermining "compromises" three decades before William Seward named it "the irrepressible conflict."[1] The United States Constitution itself was the first "compromise": the Southern slaveholding states were given enhanced representation in Congress, based on the number of their bond-laborers, and a fugitive slave law, in exchange for the Northwest Ordinance barring slavery from the territory north and west of the Ohio River and the decision to end by 1808 the importation of African-American bond-laborers. Next the Missouri Compromise of 1820, seventeen years after the Louisiana Purchase and five years after the end of the War of 1812, admitted Missouri as a slave state but stipulated that thereafter the southern boundary of that state was to be the limiting latitude (36 degrees 30 minutes) of slave territory. The third was the Compromise of 1850 passed in the wake of the Mexican War. It revoked the 36 degrees 30 minutes limit on the extension of slaveholding and instead introduced "squatter sovereignty" whereby in new states African-Americans were to be enslaved or free according to the majority vote of European-Americans in the territory. Its second most significant provision was a drastic strengthening of the Fugitive Slave Law.

In the beginning, however, the Emancipationist mood had been in the ascendant; slavery was such a shameful thing that the Founders resorted to elaborate circumlocution to avoid the use of the word "slave" in the Constitution.[2] There was a sense that both lifetime and limited-term bond-servitude would die a natural economic death with the development of the reserve army of unemployed labor normal to the capitalist social system.[3] In earnest of that belief, they enacted a ban on the "importation" of African bond-laborers after 1807. Events, however, took a turn as tragic as it was unexpected.

The cotton gin

Never has a truism borne the test of scholarship more successfully than that of the epochal impact of the invention of the cotton gin by Eli Whitney in 1793. That simple device for separating seed from lint increased labor productivity tenfold when driven by foot treadle, or fiftyfold when driven by animal power,[4] and thereby suddenly presented the plantation bourgeoisie with a field of profitable capital investment of an unprecedented scale. Within ten years, by 1803, raw cotton production in the United States increased twelvefold, and by 1820 it was triple what it had been in 1803.[5] The price of bond-laborers rose sixfold relative to the price of cotton between 1805 and 1860.[6] Profits were sufficient to increase the demand for plantation bond-labor twentyfold between 1810 and 1860.[7] In 1860, the pro-slavery writer Thomas Prentice Kettell observed that the "civilized world [was] pressing on the small force of blacks" so sorely that "every straggler is turned into the fields, to add ten more bales to the annual crop." The same program of impressment was directed at bond-laborers engaged in "the non-productive employments of the cities" of the South, and their places were taken by wage workers brought from Ireland and Germany.[8] Since the rate of profit per bond-laborer varied but without a long-term trend,[9] while the price of bond-laborers rose relative to the price of cotton and no post-gin technical revolutions occurred in the plantation economy, it is clear that the maintenance of the rate of profit resulted from the intensification of the labor of the bond-laborers.[10] This intensification was achieved by physical compulsion, work-gang discipline, close supervision, and the fact that slavery was a form of racial oppression imposed on free, as well as bound, African-Americans.[11] This increased exploitation of African-American laborers, carried out on a vastly expanding scale, brought a new intensity and scope to the struggle between freedom and slavery, and made it indeed "the irrepressible conflict."

Events in the Caribbean added further heat and pressure to the unfolding issue in the United States. In 1804, after a thirteen-year struggle, the revolutionary abolition of slavery was finally and forever an established fact in Haiti. Thirty years later the bond-laborers of the British West Indies – with the support of the British abolitionists and the Irish Emancipation movement led by Daniel O'Connell – won Emancipation.[12] "Abolition agitation," said the Governor of South Carolina in 1845, made it necessary "to draw the reins tighter and tighter day by day," for fear that bond-laborers would "cut our throats."[13]

The pro-slavery phalanx

A pro-slavery political phalanx emerged on the national scene, comprising three chief elements. First of all, of course, there was the plantation bourgeoisie itself, which was as one in its adamant opposition to abolition, but which was divided on tactical assumptions.[14] There were those, typically from the Deep South, like John C. Calhoun of South Carolina who, with the traditional support of the majority of the racially privileged non-slaveholders, scorned time-buying apologetics and instead justified slavery as "a positive good."[15] There were others, typically from the border South, most notably represented by Henry Clay of Kentucky, whose asserted abhorrence of slavery was exceeded by their absolute rejection of the possibility of coexistence with African-Americans *except* under a condition of racial slavery. For them, the end of slavery was inconceivable without the "colonization" of all African-Americans outside the United States[16]: a concept more monstrous in scope than that of the Cromwellian "transplantation" of Catholics to "Hell or Connaught" in 1652.

The second rank was supplied by elements of the bourgeoisie of the North who shared with the slaveholders a general class prejudice against abolitionism on the ground of "property rights." But their position was most particularly based on their business relationships with the plantation bourgeoisie. A major center of such connections was New York,[17] where banks profited greatly as suppliers of the bills of credit that were indispensable for financing the production and export of the annual cotton crop. In the five years immediately before the Civil War, the value of cotton exports amounted to nearly $750 million, constituting more than half the value of all United States exports;[18] of this total, it was said that 10 to 15 percent became part of disposable income in the state of New York.[19] It was the boast of *De Bow's Review*, the South's main business organ, that New York was so dependent on slavery that without it the great metropolis would become a mere historical artifact.[20] The sale of manufactures and processed commodities provided another major basis for political sympathies with the slaveholders. At a time when textiles accounted for one-third of the value of all United States imports, New York merchants, enjoying a practical monopoly of the field, were able to exploit that advantage as the suppliers of textiles to the slaveholding states.[21] A wide variety of other goods, from boots to butter, from hardware to hard liquor, helped to raise to more than $130 million by 1859 the value of commodities supplied to the slave states by "the same men who financed their crops and carried them to England."[22] It was claimed that annual Northern profits from all transactions with the South on the eve of the Civil War reached the level of $231,500,000.[23]

There was an even more intimate and direct connection between New York business interests and the slaveholders. Various shipowners, shipbuilders, merchants and other entrepreneurs – operating with the general approval of the pro-slavery elements in official society – conducted a large-scale trade supplying African bond-laborers to Cuba and to the slaveholders of the southern United States. The volume of this increasing commerce is indicated by the fact that in just three months at the end of 1860, US naval cruisers operating on the high seas took more than three thousand Africans from these New York-based ships. Although this trade had been illegal since 1808, the profits were deemed worth the risk of capture, confiscation and prosecution. Late in September 1860, seven hundred Africans were taken from one of these slave ships by a US cruiser off the coast of Africa. The owner was arrested and returned to New York for prosecution, but he was allowed to escape with the patent though unpunished connivance of the Federal Marshal.[24]

Eighteen days after South Carolina seceded from the Union rather than stay in it under the elected Republican administration of Abraham Lincoln, Mayor Fernando Wood, in his annual message to the New York City Common Council, expressed his endorsement of the secessionist course. Noting that the New Yorkers for whom he claimed to speak had a "common sympathy" with "our aggrieved brethren of the Slave States," Wood proposed that New York City too "disrupt the bands which bind her to a venal and corrupt master" by seceding from the United States and becoming "a Free City" open for business with all comers.[25] This was no mere political demagoguery. Many New York merchants and Southern leaders shared a common commitment to free trade and white supremacy, Iver Bernstein writes in his recent thoroughly researched study of the New York City Draft Riots.[26] At a meeting of these New York merchant capitalists in December 1860, called to consider their course of action with regard to secession, one of the leaders asserted that their unity with the South was first and foremost a matter of "race," and that "the city of New York will stand by their brethren, the white race."[27]

In order to maintain their dominant position in the national government[28] in the face of the threat of the faster-growing wage-labor industrial system in the North and West, and the consequent dilution of the Southern presence in Congress, the slaveholders increasingly depended on their links to the laboring-class European-Americans. This was to be the third rank of the pro-slavery phalanx.

Early on in the sharpening controversy, during the discussion of the Missouri Compromise of 1820, John Randolph of Virginia hurled defiance at the Northern proponents of restricting the spread of slavery, boasting, "We do not govern them [the free states] by our black slaves, but by their own white slaves."[29] Randolph's challenge differed from the appeal to capitalist class solidarity which the plantation bourgeoisie regularly addressed to the Northern bourgeoisie. Rather, it represented the strategic extension of an old Southern custom of social control, dating from the end of the seventeenth century,[30] to forestall the emergence of a proletarian front in favor of abolition. The critical element of this political strategy was the defense of the "white" racial privileges of laboring-class European-Americans against the "threat" of equalitarianism implicit in abolition. Its basic "theoretical" principle was an intolerance of the presence of African-Americans as free persons.

This grossly manipulative strategy was adapted and articulated for the consumption of Northern white laborers in ways derived from both the "positive good" and the "colonization" variations on the anti-abolition theme. The "positive good" school argued that wage workers in the Northern United States were worse off (or, at least, no better off) than the Southern bond-laborers, thus establishing a rationale for European-American workers to ignore (or indeed to be hostile toward) the plight of the African-American workers held in chattel bondage and those who were fleeing from it. Governor and Senator J. H. Hammond of South Carolina and pro-slavery ideologue George Fitzhugh of Virginia were among those who sought to compare the lot of the slave favorably to that of the free wage worker of the North.[31]

Addressing his Northern colleagues in the United States Senate in March 1858, James H. Hammond contrasted the pitiable insecurity and starvation wages of the Northern white worker with the position of the African-American "slaves [who] are hired for life and well compensated." He crowned his argument by reproachfully pointing out, "Your slaves are white, of your own race – you are brothers of one blood."[32]

George Fitzhugh produced such "sociological" insights as this:

> The employers of free labor ... try to get the most out of them for the least hire. ...
> No slaveholder was ever so brutal as to boast of the low wages he paid his slaves, to pride himself on feeding and clothing them badly – neglecting the young, the aged, the sick and the infirm; such a man would be hooted from society as a monster. ... But disguise the process a little, and it is a popular virtue to oppress the free white people.[33]

Fitzhugh linked an incitation against "free negroes" with an argument designed to appeal to the white workingman's other claim to social status. When he cited the fact that, "We subject wives to the dominion of their husbands,"[34] Fitzhugh apparently thought it self-evident that both "free Negro" and "free wife" were subversive concepts.

These ideas were translated in the name of Northern "workingmen."[35] By the 1830s, the organized and unorganized protests of the Northern artisans and wage workers against the ferocity of the capitalist juggernaut that was consuming them alive[36] were almost always couched in terms of the conventional anti-abolitionist rationale, according to which the lot of the Negro plantation bond-laborer was on the whole better than theirs, or according to which racial slavery was at most a secondary matter which should not be allowed to interfere with the interests of "[white] workingmen."[37] One of the most prominent and typical of this tendency was George Henry Evans, in 1844 editor of *Working Man's Advocate*. "I was formerly ... a very warm advocate of the abolition of slavery," he wrote. "This was before I saw that there was *white* slavery."[38] His newspaper said that only free distribution of public lands could abolish all slavery: wage slavery and chattel slavery. Without that, it said, the African-American slave would be "the loser" if freed to become a wage worker like the European-American workers in the North.[39] This pretense of concern for all laborers, slave and waged, was apt to be belied by the coupling of references to the "pride and delicacy of the Caucasian," with the most hateful white-supremacist references to African-Americans.[40] Brother Basil Leo Lee, in his study of the social and political atmosphere prevailing in New York during the Civil War, paraphrased the "proletarian" form of this "well-off-slave-worse-off-wage-worker" propaganda thus: "Why worry about the wrongs of the negro when you have evils in your own cities;" the New England capitalist abolitionist, he alleged, merely "sought to draw attention to the negro so that he might oppress his wage slaves without notice."[41]

Although the very enormity of the proposed "colonization" of freed African-American bond-laborers outside the United States meant that it could never be more than a "white race" fantasy, the insistent agitation on the subject was calculated to serve as ideological reinforcement against the spread of abolitionism among laboring-class European-Americans. The "colonization" school proceeded from the premiss that the free white workers were *better off* than the African-American bond-laborers, and that all their hopes depended upon their being protected from competition with African-Americans, whether slave or free. Henry Clay of Kentucky, Whig statesman and party leader, who was perhaps the foremost advocate of "colonization," pretended that it would, among other things, "elevate the social conditions of the white laborer."[42] Then as now, however, the motivational emphasis was less on future vistas than on alleged present perils. He used all his prestige as Whig leader in the effort to present freedom for the African-American as a deadly threat to the "white" worker. "To make the black man free," he said in the summer of 1842, "it would virtually enslave the white man."[43] A year later, as he was preparing to make his great bid for the Presidency, in 1844, Clay gave instructions for the writing of a pamphlet to be used in his campaign.

[T]he great aim ... should be to arouse the ["white"] laboring classes in the free States against abolition. Depict the consequences to them of immediate abolition; they [emancipated African-Americans] being free would enter into competition with the free laborer; with the American, the Irish, the German; reduce his wages; be confounded with him, and affect his moral and social standing. And as the ultras go for abolition and amalgamation, show that their object is to unite, in marriage, the laboring white man, and the laboring black man, and to reduce the white laboring man to the despised and degraded condition of the black man.[44]

It is to be noted that by his reference to "marriage" Clay was invoking subliminally the "racial" and gender privileges of the "white" male proletarian.

Again, there was the "proletarian" echo. The typical arguments were summarized in resolutions adopted in the name of "workingmen" in January 1861, in that pregnant pause between the election of Lincoln in November and the firing on Fort Sumter in April. They linked a defense of the slaveholders with condemnation of the Republican government for intending "to reduce white men to a forbidden level with negroes."[45]

The Developing Front against Slavery

The anti-slavery front too comprised a number of elements. African-American bond-laborers fled north, to the Free States or to Canada, at the rate of a thousand a year, with the organized support of three thousand or more personnel of the Underground Railroad, the system established by abolitionists to aid escaping slaves.[46] Some resolved to fight where they were, as did Denmark Vesey of Charleston, South Carolina, in 1822, and as did Nat Turner in Southampton County, Virginia, nine years later. Some, 135 in number, shipped from Norfolk, Virginia, on 30 October 1841 bound for New Orleans on board the coastal slave-trade ship the *Creole*, rose in revolt on 7 November, took over the ship, and arrived as free people two days later in the British West Indies.[47] Other African-Americans – Shields Green, Osborne Perry Anderson, Dangerfield Newby, John A. Copeland, Lewis Sherrard Leary, and John Anderson – together with ten or so European-American comrades, under the leadership of John Brown made the daring raid on the federal arsenal at Harper's Ferry in 1859.[48] Others – born free, emancipated, self-bought or free by defiant flight, but still forced to contend with racial oppression even in "free" states – began what would eventually become the abolitionist movement as early as the closing years of the eighteenth century. When the *Liberator* was first founded by William Lloyd Garrison in 1831, its main subscriber base was made up of Northern African-Americans.[49] This is not the place even to attempt to call the roll of these African-American abolitionists; the widely available and forever valuable resource *Documentary History of the Negro*

People of the United States, edited by Herbert Aptheker, presents their story. Two of them, Charles L. Remond and Frederick Douglass, figure particularly in our discussion below of Ireland and Irish-Americans. Nor is this a place to try to list the European-American abolitionists whose equalitarian convictions and instincts, rooted in religious principles and/or in the democratic side of political tradition, led them into battle against racial slavery. Many of them also are found in Aptheker's *Documentary History*. Perhaps the richest sources are abolitionist journals, including the *Liberator*, the *National Anti-slavery Standard*, and the *North Star* (later called *Frederick Douglass' Paper*). What can and must be said about the abolitionists generally is that they were widely persecuted, even lynched, but they never stopped their agitation. In our present context there are two aspects of the abolitionist movement that should be especially noted.

First, the abolitionist movement articulated a far better understanding of the "class question" than the "white" labor apologists did of the "race question." Frederick Douglass saw through the false "proletarian" pretensions of "white" labor movements that excluded African-American workers and yet took offense when Negro workers could not respond to their notions of "labor solidarity."[50] At the same time, more than any "white" workers' organization the abolitionist movement, in a resolution adopted in 1849 by the Massachusetts Anti-slavery Society, articulated the essential principle of true solidarity in the United States, two decades before Karl Marx said, "Labour cannot emancipate itself in the white skin where in the black it is branded."[51]

> Whereas, the rights of the laborer at the North are identified with those of the Southern slave, and cannot be obtained as long as chattel slavery rears its hydra head in our land; and whereas, the same arguments which apply to the situation of the crushed slave, are also in force in reference to the condition of the Northern laborer – although in a less degree, therefore
>
> Resolved, That it is equally incumbent upon the working-man of the North to espouse the cause of the emancipation of the slave and upon Abolitionists to advocate the claims of the free laborer.[52]

Second, the American abolitionist movement – African-Americans and European-Americans together – faithfully supported the struggle of the Irish people, led by Daniel O'Connell, for repeal of the Union with England.

The Free Soil component

The abolitionists never succeeded in winning over a majority of the people of the North to their principles; they could never have brought about the end of racial slavery themselves. The end of slavery came because the abolitionists were moving with the tide of history, and thus became allies with others who were anti-abolitionist but who were opposed to the expansion of slavery.

In 1848, the Free Soil Party came into being with the limited aim of preventing the expansion of slavery, while leaving it undisturbed where it already existed. Its politically strategic significance was that it replaced the illusion of "colonization" of the African-American with a more practical-sounding illusion of "colonization" of the laboring-class European-American homesteaders in "whites-only" Western territories.[53]

This idea of solving the "slavery question" without abolishing slavery paradoxically made possible the formation in 1856 of the Republican Party, which six years later would lead the nation into the abolition of slavery. Despite its original disavowals of abolitionist intentions, the new party was rooted in the reality of the "irrepressible conflict" between two modes of capitalist production, one employing wage labor and the other employing bond labor.

The Slaveholders' Strategic Assessment

The slaveholders were only too aware that the reign of King Cotton was being eclipsed by the rapidly growing industrial system of the North. They perceived the prospective victory of the Republican Party as a death warrant for their system, and they were prepared to resist it by armed rebellion. But they were confident that the North would be impaled on a dilemma. If the Northern bourgeoisie declined to adopt the abolitionist course, the plantation bourgeoisie would ultimately win, if only by attrition, by exploiting politically, diplomatically and economically the essential moral parity of North and South, and by reliance on the African-American bond-labor force for maintaining production of the principal crops for export, and domestic food supplies. If, on the other hand, the Northern bourgeoisie did opt for abolition, the plantation bourgeoisie maintained the confidence of John Randolph that the Northern white worker would refuse to support such a course, and would instead defend the cause of the slaveholders.[54]

The Irish-American Immigrants

Three particular characteristics of the Irish immigration into the United States during the period 1820 to 1860 have a special significance for our treatment of the subject: (1) its massive volume, combined with the pattern of concentrated settlement which it produced; (2) the shared historic background of these immigrants in struggle against racial oppression in Ireland; and (3) its status as being a Catholic minority in a strongly Protestant society characterized by widespread anti-Catholic bigotry.

Extraordinary economic hardships in Ireland associated with the ending of the Napoleonic Wars, the destruction of cottage-weaving by a tardy Industrial Revolution (in Ulster), and above all the Great Famine of 1845–50, led to the emigration of more than 3 million people, accounting in considerable part for the decline of Ireland's population by over 1 million in the forty-year period to 1860.[55]

Among the Irish who made their exodus across the Atlantic, Catholics predominated to an extent greater than in Ireland itself; the disproportion was even more pronounced among those who came to the United States, since most of those who settled in Canada were Protestants.[56] By 1860, the number of Irish-born residents of the United States was 1.2 million, equal to one-fifth of the total population of Ireland itself.[57] In 1860, the population of New York City numbered nearly 814,000; nearly half, 47 percent, were foreign-born, and of these more than half were Irish.[58] For reasons I shall consider later, although these Irish immigrants were almost all from rural parts of Ireland, they, more than other immigrant groups, congregated where they landed, and settled into urban life rather than moving to the West or to agrarian regions nearer by.[59]

No immigrants ever came to the United States better prepared by tradition and experience to empathize with the African-Americans than were these Irish who were emerging directly from the historic struggle against racial oppression in their own country. If there was any people who had demonstrated a sense of the cruel injustices of such a system, it was the Catholic Irish, such as those who came to the United States in this period.

One of their number, an Irish laborer named John Hughes, expressed this kinship in a poem he wrote under the name "Leander" in 1825. He had brought memories of mistreatment and humiliations imposed on his father and himself at the hands of good ol' Protestant boys in Ulster, where, as his father saw it, "a Catholic farmer ranked below a Protestant beggar" in the social scale. He recalled that when his sister died, the priest was forbidden to enter the

Table 1 (A) The percentages, by country of nativity, of immigrants disembarked at New York between 5 May 1847 and 31 December 1860; (B) The percentages, by country of nativity, of the foreign-born population of New York City in 1860; and (C) The indicated dispersal index (A/B)[60]

	A	B	C
Ireland	41.4	53.1	0.78
Germany	36.7	31.3	1.17
England and Scotland	14.5	9.5	1.53
France	2.2	2.1	1.05
Switzerland	1.6	0.5	3.20
Scandinavia	1.0	0.4	2.50
Others	2.6	3.1	0.84

graveyard to conduct the graveside ceremony.[61] Hughes had been in the United States some seven or eight years when he wrote his poem, titled simply "The Slave."[62]

The Irish-American poet observes the African-American bond-laborer in the field working beneath the broiling sun, while the author and others, more "fair" of color, are allowed a respite in the shade. The observer dwells on the life of unremitting, unrewarded toil of the slave, under the brutal whip-wielding overseer. In an apostrophe to Columbia, as poets then were wont to call the United States, Leander pleads:

Wipe from thy code, Columbia, wipe the stain;
Be free as air, but yet be kind as free,
And chase foul bondage from thy Southern plain:
If such the right of man, by heaven's decree,
Oh, then let Afric's sons feel what it is – to be.

There is sad irony, however, in the comment made by Hughes's biographer that soon after the writing of "The Slave," "poetry was driven out of [Hughes's] mind by more important matters" connected with his entrance upon his clerical career.[63] Thereafter, Hughes became an "organization man" in a double sense: for the Church and for the "white race."

In Ireland the spirit of Leander lived in the abolition and repeal movements.[64] It lived in the kind reception given to African-Americans who toured Ireland campaigning for abolition. It lived, above all, in O'Connell, called by William Lloyd Garrison "that fearless eloquent champion of liberty" and by slaveholders "the greatest abolitionist in the world";[65] the person whose leadership of the struggle to end racial oppression and for Irish independence earned him the name "The Liberator" in his own country.

We have met O'Connell as the peerless leader of the fight against racial oppression in his own country, but still a conventional bourgeois revolutionary, so mistrustful of the masses that in the end he drew back from the logic of the movement he had created. Yet, though he cancelled at Clontarf the threat he had made at Mallow,[66] the fight that overthrew the system of Protestant Ascendancy in non-Ulster Ireland was led by O'Connell with courage, audacity and skill anchored in his inveterate hatred for racial oppression. Africans had never been held in bondage in Ireland and, O'Connell declared, "Ireland and Irishmen should therefore be forward in seeking to effect the emancipation of mankind."[67] He was proud that "the Irish nation almost unanimously" supported the abolition of slavery, and cited the fact that though the Irish delegation within the British Parliament was "divided on other points ... there is not a man of them ... of any sect, party or denomination, whose voice has been raised but to cry down negro slavery."[68] Saying "there is something Irish at my heart, which makes me sympathize with all those who are suffering under oppression," he promised to put his prestige at the service of "the abolition of slavery all over the world."[69]

And he did so without regard to the consequences. Drawing an image from the psalm, he said, "may my right hand forget its cunning, and my tongue cleave to the roof of my mouth, if, to save Ireland, – even Ireland, I forget the Negro one single hour!"[70] This was no mere rhetorical flourish of a fledgling member of the British Parliament, but a direct and explicit rebuff of the West Indies planters' offer of their parliamentary support of the program of the Irish Party in 1830 if O'Connell would abandon the abolitionist cause. Far from abandoning the abolitionist cause, he regarded the victory over slavery in the West Indies in 1833 as a lever to be used for overturning slavery in the United States.[71]

He accordingly continued the struggle, directing the most powerful and trenchant attacks at the American slaveholders and the entire system of white supremacism. He arraigned them with his matchless oratorical powers on the full range of abolitionist indictments: the plot to annex Texas and thus reduce it again to slavery, which had been abolished in the territory by Mexico in 1830; the treacherous treatment of Osceola, the Seminole chief, in the same pro-slavery expansionist cause; the refusal to abolish slavery even in the Federal District of Columbia; the terrorizing of abolitionists; the criminaliza- tion of Negro literacy; and, ever and again, the very notion of the con- stitutionality of "property in man," with all its train of human degradation, suffering and destruction of family life. He would not visit such a country. He would not welcome slaveholders in his country. He would not shake the hand of an American until he was assured it was not the hand of a slaveholder.

O'Connell was bent on ending not only slavery, but racial oppression in general. He continually contrasted the theory of the Declaration of Independ- ence with the denial of the presumption of liberty to free African-Americans, with the denial of their equal rights in voting, in public transportation, and other accommodations; and with the denial of their civil rights in general. He recognized as well as Burke before him had done in the letter to Langrishe (see p. 71) the monstrous absurdity of "plebeian aristocracy," characteristic of a social order based on racial oppression. The worst of all aristocracies, he said, "is that which prevails in America – an aristocracy of the human skin."[72] When the American notion of "colonization" came to his attention, he ripped it to shreds with scorn and derision. He likened it to proposals made to rid England of surplus peasantry by shipping them to Canada. The only difference in principle, he said, was that the Colonization Society was motivated by no other reason than "color" prejudice.

The barbs stuck and stung, and the United States ruling plantation bourgeoisie reacted. They roundly condemned O'Connell for "interference in American affairs," and in the South some voices were raised against Irish immigration, fearful of contamination with abolitionist ideas. The most specific counter-blow, however, was the refusal to give financial support to the cause of Repeal unless O'Connell desisted from his abolitionist ways. As he had done in the West Indies case, O'Connell scornfully spurned all such threats.

It is doubtful whether the withholding of slaveholders' support by itself could have brought down the repeal movement in the United States; every month, low-earning Irish-Americans were sending tens of thousands of dollars back to Ireland to help the people left behind.[73] Half a tithe of that amount would have made a sizable "Repeal Rent" from America. It was up to the repeal movement to win its portion. The threat, however, was buttressed with aspersions – supported by the Catholic press – against O'Connell's Protestant allies and, by association, the women's rights movement.[74] In the political arena, narrowly conceived, the Democratic Party sought to identify O'Connell's position with British (and by inference anti-Irish) policy, especially after the abolition of slavery in the British West Indies in 1833.

O'Connell did not seek to avoid such questions, but dealt with them directly, promptly and frankly. He acknowledged the doctrinal differences between himself, as a Catholic, and Dissenters. But he was not put off by the fact that it had been the Wesleyan Methodists who had taken the initiative in the abolitionist cause in Britain and Ireland. "It is to their honor," said the Catholic Liberator, "and not to their reproach that they have been persecuted. It is my wish to imitate them."[75]

He met head on the issue of women's rights as it arose within the abolition movement itself, even though doing so required self-criticism of his male ego. After the World Anti-slavery Convention held in London in 1840 voted to exclude women delegates, the American abolitionist and women's rights leader Lucretia Mott, one of those excluded, wrote to O'Connell criticizing his stand on the matter. He promptly re-examined his position, admitted his error and, not sparing his male ego, said he "easily perceived" that his vote to exclude the women delegates was based on fear of "the ridicule it [his support of their inclusion] might excite." This, he said, "was an unworthy, and indeed a cowardly motive." He accordingly reversed his opinion and, however belatedly, adopted Mott's point of view.[76]

As for whether British government policy was informed by an abolitionist disposition after 1833, to any extent that that may have been so it was the by-product of the long abolitionist struggle in which O'Connell played a part, which he could not have desired to repudiate.

The abolitionists' strategy to win the Irish-Americans

The American abolitionists were well aware of the dimensions and the significance of the almost universal anti-abolitionist stand of the leadership and the rank and file of the Irish-American population. Catholic Irish-Americans were almost totally tied into the Democratic Party, the openly avowed party of slavery.[77] Furthermore, by the early 1840s there was "fairly unanimous agreement" among the Catholic clergy and press in the United States that "the principles and methods of Garrisonian abolitionism were not only a threat to the safety of the country but also in conflict with Catholic ethics and ideals."[78] It was at this juncture, as the repeal campaign was mobilizing in Ireland, as the World Anti-slavery Convention was pressing forward, heartened by the victory over slavery in the British West Indies, that the abolitionist movement conceived a strategy for winning Irish-Americans away from the pro-slavery front. The attack was to be directed at the most vulnerable spot at which a decisive blow could be struck against the power of the slaveholders, namely the anomalous seam between Irish-America and the slaveholders. A choice was to be posed between O'Connell and Hughes; between Pope Gregory XVI's denunciation of slavery and the apologetics for it put forward by Bishop England of Charleston; and, within the "Irish-American heart," between the reverence for O'Connell, Catholic Liberator, embattled leader of the historic struggle for repeal of the Union, and the blandishments of white supremacy.

The implement chosen was conceived and shaped in Ireland by two American abolitionists, the African-American Charles Lenox Remond and the European-American John Anderson Collins, together with members of the Hibernian Anti-Slavery Society.[79] It was a simple device – an "Address from the People of Ireland to Their Countrymen and Countrywomen in America." For some four months, the Irish abolitionists and repealers organized and supported a campaign to collect signatures to the Address. In addition to O'Connell, signers included two other figures revered among Irish-American Catholics: the Capuchin father Theobald Mathew, of Tipperary and Cork, the leader of the campaign against alcohol addiction, and the historian of the rebellion of 1798, Richard Robert Madden.[80]

Remond was the tireless featured speaker at meetings throughout most of Ireland. Starting in Dublin, he enthralled and enthused audiences in Cork, Waterford, Wexford, Limerick, Belfast and elsewhere. Night after night, this descendant of American Revolutionary War forebears poured out testimony and logic and historical example against the chattel-bondage in which African-Americans were held in the South, and no less against the humiliation of the petty and gross racial discrimination to which African-Americans were systematically subjected in the "free" states of the North. Understandably given to bitterness, he was nevertheless energized by the warmth of his reception by the Irish people, and by the sympathetic coverage of his appearance in the Irish press. During Remond's tour, sixty thousand people subscribed their names to the Address, and in the following year another ten thousand did so. As Remond embarked for America at the end of his tour in mid-December, he said, "Never were my hopes higher, my expectations stronger, or my zeal more ardent, than at present. Since my travels in Ireland ..."[81]

Those high hopes, expectations and zeal were shared by the Boston abolitionists. Garrison said: "The Irish Address, I trust, is to be the means of breaking up a stupendous conspiracy, which I believe is going on between the leading Irish demagogues, the leading pseudo-Democrats and the Southern slaveholders."[82] Within days of Remond's return to America with the precious scroll, it was formally presented at a meeting of five thousand people, "a third of them Irishmen,"[83] at historic Faneuil Hall in Boston. The enthusiastic audience was addressed by Garrison, Wendell Phillips and George Bradburn, the "half-Irish" leader of the Massachusetts Anti-slavery Society. Thus began a campaign that would last for four years,[84] a strategy well conceived but one that failed in its purpose.

Indeed its only effect was an unintended one, the production of a terminal crisis in the American Repeal Association, which attempted to combine repeal with cordiality to the slaveholders. The American repealers were instructed by the National Loyal Repeal Association in Ireland that no anti-abolition conditions were to be attached to financial or political support for repeal. The American repealers held two national conventions, one in Philadelphia in February 1842 and the other in New York in September of the following year. Overriding the objections of a tiny number of courageous supporters of the anti-slavery Address, the conventions rejected O'Connell's attacks on American slaveholders. To emphasize the point, the second gathering chose as its presiding officer Robert Tyler, son of the slaveholding and slavery-upholding President John Tyler.[85] Thus, at the very moment the Repeal movement was confronting the British government with the most serious crisis it had ever faced in Ireland, the Irish-American repeal organizations were assailing O'Connell for his opposition to racial oppression. One copiously annotated study summarizes the outcome as follows: "O'Connell's repeated denunciations of American Negro slavery alienated segments of Irish American opinion ... [therefore] almost all Irish-American Repeal Associations, as well as Bishop John Hughes of New York ... repudiated O'Connell's statements, and some Repeal societies actually dissolved."[86] The delegates to the National Repeal Convention in Philadelphia in 1842 unanimously rejected "the connection of the two subjects," namely repeal and abolition. The chief debate was whether simply not to be diverted by O'Connell's abolitionism, while continuing to revere him as "the Liberator"; or explicitly to repudiate O'Connell on that issue regardless of "whatever the Irish may think." Irish-Americans were said to be "too grateful ... to the land of their adoption" to follow the Irish abolitionist lead.[87] O'Connell found a metaphor in the course taken by the head of the Philadelphia repeal organization who abandoned repeal work upon becoming married to a slaveowner.[88]

O'Connell and the Cincinnati Repeal Association

The controversy intensified between the American repealers and O'Connell even as the issue of repeal was reaching its climax in Ireland. Through it all – through a tiff with Garrison, through the catastrophe of Clontarf, through the rising challenge of the Young Irelanders, who questioned the priority given to abolition – through it all O'Connell continued to strike out against racial oppression and its corrupting influence on Irish-Americans. The matter was brought to a head by a letter from the Cincinnati Repeal Association, dated 28 August 1843. The Cincinnati repealers were blunt, speaking the language of the slaveholders without apology: the Negro was of a lower natural order than "whites", they said, slavery was his proper social condition, and, they asserted, "the two races cannot exist on equal terms under our government and institutions." The cause of repeal could not survive in America unless it repudiated O'Connell and the Address.

O'Connell delivered an impromptu oral refutation of the Cincinnati letter when it was read at a meeting of the Repeal Association in Dublin; a few weeks later, commissioned by the association, he sent a written reply.[89] The synopsis attempted here hardly suggests the perspicacity and passion of the statement; yet it may give an inkling perhaps of the oratorical power that could engage a throng of hundreds of thousands in rapt attention, although, with one exception, it omits the humorous sallies often displayed on those occasions. Even in synopsis it suggests the need for a more critical examination of the facile justifications put forth for the rejection of the Irish abolitionist Address, since those justifications are all there in the points made by the Cincinnati pro-slavery repealers, which O'Connell so effectively refutes. Moreover, taken in its context, it remains to this day an inspirational indictment of racial oppression.

"*How*, then, can you have become so depraved?" O'Connell asks the Cincinnati repealers. Their entire letter, he charged, was "an advocacy of human bondage." Was it true that their feelings had been "made so obtuse by the air of America"? It was astounding that they, who were non-slaveholders living in a free state and thus having no "pecuniary interest" in slavery, would take the side of the slaveholders against the African-Americans; the mass of Irish-Americans, "who have not even that futile excuse, and yet justify slavery, are indefensible."

I have chosen to present the exchange in the form of a series of the Cincinnati Repealers' "Allegations" and O'Connell "Rebuttals."

Allegation 1: The abolitionists have caused the treatment of the Negro to become more harsh. *Rebuttal 1*: Not true. But if it were true, it would add to the indictment of the slaveholder, who would punish an innocent person for the offense of a third party. *Allegation 2*: The great majority, in a country where the majority rules, favors slavery. *Rebuttal 2*: If public opinion rules then, as

"Irishmen ought to do," they should work to influence the public mind in favor of the oppressed!" instead of lauding "the master as generous and humane." *Allegation 3*: The aristocrats in England would more readily accept laborers as "sheet fellows," than would "whites" of any social class in the United States consent to accept Negroes "on terms of equality." "[H]owever much humanity may lament it, we make no rash declaration when we say that the two races cannot exist on equal terms under our government and our institutions." The Negro is naturally inferior to the "white." *Rebuttal 3*: How, where it is a crime to teach even a free Negro to read, can one presume a "natural inferiority" of those so deprived? Finally, on this point, there are Negro Catholic priests in Brazil, and in Rome, and one of their number delivered a sermon before Louis Philippe, King of France. "To judge properly of the negro you must see him as educated, and treated with the respect due to a fellow-creature, uninsulted, by the filthy aristocracy of skin." *Allegation 4*: "Black and white cannot live on equal terms under the United States Constitution." *Rebuttal 4*: That argument has been disproved in Jamaica by the post-Emancipation peaceful relations between blacks and whites. Perhaps, by the way, that fact reveals a superiority of Negroes in moral qualities considering the magnanimity they have shown toward their former masters, who are compensated while the Negroes, the injured party, are not. *Allegation 5*: The abolitionists are the cause of the slaves' restlessness, and even abet the crime of horse-stealing by escaping slaves. *Rebuttal 5*: As if the Negro would not otherwise know of the miseries of slavery. Even though his, O'Connell's, knowledge of casuistry was too deficient to decide whether that would be an excusable act or not, "we are of this ... quite certain, that not one of you ... if he were under similar circumstances, that is, having no other means of escaping perpetual slavery, would not make free with your neighbour's horse to effectuate your just and reasonable purpose." *Allegation 6*: The happiness of 15 million white Americans depends upon the slave economy. *Rebuttal 6*: The Benthamite principle of promoting the greatest good for the greatest number is valid, and counting the African-American population the balance would come down on the anti-slavery side. *Allegation 7*: There is no reproach due to the concept of "property in men." *Rebuttal 7*: It is as if "you were speaking of beasts of the field ... that makes us disclaim you as countrymen." *Allegation 8*: Many clergymen, especially Catholic clergymen, are ranged on the side of the slaveholders. *Rebuttal 8*: That is hard to believe; but in any case, "every Catholic knows how distinctly slave-holding, and especially slave-trading, is condemned by the Catholic church," as was emphasized by the recent pronouncement of Pope Gregory XVI. That condemnation of the slave trade certainly applies to the inter-state sale of slaves and most of all to "the diabolical raising of slaves for sale."

O'Connell urged the Cincinnati repealers, and by implication Irish-Americans in general, not to come out of America but to "come out of the councils of the iniquitous, and out of the congregation of the wicked;" assist the "free persons of colour," promote educational opportunities for them, avoid selfishness based on race with regard to the free African-Americans, and support their efforts to secure equal rights and to resist the Fugitive Slave Law. Work for the abolition of slavery. Repudiate by action the reputation of "being the worst enemies of the men of colour," in order that it "shall be atoned for, and blotted out and effaced forever."

8

How the Sea-change was Wrought

In 1842, Irish-American abolitionist James Canning Fuller sadly observed:

> ... however true to liberty an Irishman's heart is, when it beats on his own native soil, ... on his emigration to America, circumstances and influences by which he becomes surrounded, in too many cases warp his judgment, and bias his heart.[1]

Why? That is the question. How was wrought this sea-change in so many immigrant Irish-Americans? What were those fateful "circumstances and influences"?

Before proceeding, it must be emphasized that there *was* a change. Make due allowance for O'Connell's affiliations with the English Whigs. Make due allowance for the incident of O'Connell's "disavowal" of Garrison's brand of abolitionism, prompted by reports of anti-Catholic religious slights. Make due allowance for the Young Irelanders' criticism of O'Connell for, as they saw it, not giving the proper priority to the struggle for repeal over the cause of abolition. Make due allowance, finally, for the subsequent American "white backlash" that produced its effect to some degree in Ireland at the time of the Civil War in the United States.[2] Indisputable facts remain.

O'Connell's never-failing advocacy of abolition, while he lived, probably reached as many people in Ireland and Britain as did abolitionists in the United States. The Loyal National Repeal Association, the official repeal organization in Ireland, actively associated itself with the work of the Hibernian Anti-Slavery Society, the chief organized form of the abolitionist movement in Ireland. The Repeal Association published a collection of numerous of its denunciations of "the hideous system" of American slavery.[3] In the United States, on the other hand, as we have noted, the Repeal Associations overwhelmingly repudiated the call to stand with the abolitionists.

The majority of the signers of the Irish Address urging Irish-Americans to stand by the abolitionists were Catholics.[4] One collector claimed to have obtained the signatures of one Catholic bishop and seventy-two Catholic priests.[5] The "first inquiries" of a Catholic priest in Ireland to an American woman evangelist "were concerning American slavery. Its principles and practices he abhorred, and he could not comprehend its existence in a republican country."[6] But in the United States authoritative Irish-Americans, in the clergy, in the press and in the legal profession, maintained an unrelenting attack against abolitionists, coupling it with a "patriotic" defense of the "institution" of slavery on constitutional grounds.

Perhaps the most graphic illustration of the contrast is to be noted in the treatment of African-American abolitionists such as Charles Lenox Remond in 1841, and Frederick Douglass four years later. I have noted Remond's buoyant reaction to his four-month campaign as the guest of the Irish abolitionists. Douglass, at the end of his four-month lecture tour of Ireland, wrote to Garrison that he had spent "some of the happiest moments of [his] life since landing in this country." He went on to mention "the warm and generous cooperation ... the glorious enthusiasm with which thousands have flocked to hear [his message] ... the kind hospitality constantly proffered me by persons of the highest rank in society ... and the entire absence of every thing that looked like prejudice against me, on account of the color of my skin."[7] At a repeal meeting at Conciliation Hall in Dublin, Daniel O'Connell introduced Douglass as "the Black O'Connell of the United States."[8] But in their own homeland these men were not only subjected to the white-supremacist indignities that were the common lot of free African-Americans, but as African-American lecturers they were time and again subjected to special harassment, sometimes life-threatening.

These contrasts need to be stressed because the prevailing historiographical consensus takes note of O'Connell's abolitionism and the Irish "Address ... to Fellow Countrymen and Countrywomen in America" only to minimize their significance. Historians have apparently felt justified in this neglect by the mere fact that the anti-slavery appeals from Ireland were repudiated by Irish-Americans. Their explanation of the sea-change, therefore, tends to be little more than an uncritical acceptance of the self-justifying rationale advanced by the original repudiators themselves.

The Two-front Attack on Abolitionism among Irish-Americans

The Irish abolitionist Address was met by a two-pronged campaign, directed, as it were, against the "Catholic-Irish" front and the "white worker" front respectively. The main burden of the attack on the "Irish" front was carried by what may be called the Irish-American establishment, the Catholic hierarchy, led by John Hughes, bishop and archbishop, together with the official and the unofficial Irish Catholic press.[9] Reinforcement was supplied by certain Young Irelanders exiled following the defeat of the brief rising of 1848. Their role was circumscribed, however, as a result of the censure to which they were soon subjected by the Irish-American establishment for their "red republicanism."

John Mitchel and Thomas Francis Meagher were the most notable figures in this Irish nationalist contingent.[10] On the "white worker" front the counter-attack was carried mainly by the Jacksonian Democratic Party nationally, and its local New York form, Tammany Hall. The Democratic Party was the preferred party of the plantation bourgeoisie who, as we have noted, had benefited from almost unbroken ascendancy in the United States federal government from the beginning.

Attacking Abolitionism on the "Catholic-Irish" Front

Archbishop Hughes was a single-minded American organizer of Roman Catholicism, which in the interest of combining central authority with all-nation inclusiveness followed a strict policy of avoiding conflicts with authority, wherever the Church found acceptance of its own authority, under a commodious Caesar-and-God tent.[11] This was the root of a pandemic political conservatism, a tradition to which the American Catholic Church was determined to adhere. "The spirit of the Catholic Church is eminently conservative," said one typical pastoral letter, justifying the refusal to "take sides" on the slavery question on the grounds of preserving "the unity of spirit" of the Church.[12] John Kelly, the only Catholic member of the United States Congress, speaking in the House of Representatives in 1857 pledged that "the Catholics of the United States," responding to "a higher power which has commanded them to 'give unto Caesar the things that are Caesar's,'" would avoid the councils of the "Abolitionists" and "fanatics."[13] The New York Catholic newspaper *Freeman's Journal* thought that by rights *Uncle Tom's Cabin* ought to be put on the Vatican's index of forbidden books since its abolitionism was just an American version of "Red Republicanism."[14]

The proclivity to worship authority was no less fundamental to Protestants, but for them, with generally more homogeneous constituencies, centralist organizational authority was not the critical problem that it was for Catholicism. The Protestant tradition was one of a succession of hivings-off of dissenters from a previous church authority. Such schisms were much harder to accommodate in Catholicism, tolerated by constitutional guarantees but nevertheless beset by the erosive proselytizing efforts of the Protestant majority,[15] and by "anti-popery" fulminations on a local scale. Hughes met the situation by strict repression of even potential schismatic tendencies. In 1856, for instance, Hughes, by then Archbishop of New York and "the most prominent American Catholic prelate,"[16] advised Catholic periodicals "that they shall not presume to draw odious comparisons, and publish them, between the [Catholic] clergy of one section of the country and those of another."[17]

But the big problem was the abolition issue in a country whose government was traditionally dominated by slaveholders. Hughes could see that abolitionism, often with ministers themselves as its protagonists, was putting a divisive pressure on Protestant congregations of various denominations.[18] The New Orleans *Catholic Mirror* was proud that the Catholic Church in America had avoided the pitfalls of "Protestant moral theology . . . [that] varies with degrees of latitude."[19]

But American Catholic Church authorities found it politic to deny or ignore the degrees of *longitude* that increasingly separated them from the pronouncements of Church authorities in continental Europe, beginning with Pope Gregory XVI's Apostolic Letter of 1839 and followed by statements of national Church leaders. In the name of Christ, the Pope "vehemently admonish[ed] and adjure[ed]" Christians not

> to molest Indians, negroes, or other men of this sort; or to spoil them of their goods, or to reduce them to slavery; or to extend help or favor to others who perpetrate such things against them; or to exercise that inhuman trade by which negroes, as if they were not men, but mere animals, howsoever reduced to slavery, are . . . bought, sold, and doomed sometimes to the most severe and exhausting labors.[20]

Bishop England of Charleston, South Carolina, wrote a series of long letters to John Forsyth of Georgia, Secretary of State under both Jackson and Van Buren, which soon were edited for "our fellow citizens of Irish origin" in refutation of the abolitionism of Daniel O'Connell. England, like Hughes Irish-born, argued that the Pope was merely condemning the international slave trade, and meant nothing hostile to "domestic slavery,"[21] as if "chattels" would be other than objects of sale and purchase, when he knew well that capitalist commodity production based on slave labor could not possibly exist without "slave trading" such as regularly occurred virtually on his own doorstep. In sharp contrast, Madeleine Rice documents the fact that "Catholic opinion abroad was coming more and more to outright condemnation of slavery."[22]

If the Union itself were to be split into two nations over the deep-running moral issue of racial slavery, the American Catholic Church would be presented with a painful dilemma. Either the essential unity of the Church would be destroyed over a moral issue or, in either the South or the North, it would stand in minority opposition to the civil authority.[23]

And so it came to pass, at some point in his post-Leander career, that Hughes found it advisable to be an organization man in a second sense, in relating to the predominately Protestant American, slaveholder-dominated society in general, that is, the "white race." Leader and authority that he was, he became a most influential foe of abolition and defender of white-race privileges.

A dramatic encounter between Hughes and O'Connell occurred in 1840. The bishop secured an introduction to O'Connell in London, "with a determination," as Hughes later recorded, "to have a struggle" with O'Connell on the issue of his abolitionism.[24] The account, slightly abridged here, is as biographer Hassard found it set down by Hughes himself.

"[W]hile you have many friends in America," [said Hughes] "you have some who are much displeased with certain of your public remarks."

And he asked, "Which?"

"Well," I replied, ". . . [T]hey think you are too severe upon . . . slavery."

[O'Connell] paused, and said: "It would be strange, indeed, if I should not be the friend of the slave throughout the world – I, who was born a slave myself."

"He silenced me," Hughes wrote, "although he did not convince me."[25] Regrettably, this repression of his views did not last.

As archbishop, Hughes presented his view of the position of the Catholic Church in the United States (more especially the New York diocese) and his own role in it in a letter he submitted to the Vatican in 1858.

> . . . *my* lot was cast in the great metropolis. Catholics were surrounded by inducements to diverge from the unity of the Church. . . . [Therefore I] found it expedient to stand up among them, as their . . . chief; to warn them . . . to repel the spirit of faction. . . . [and] to convince their judgment . . . in regard to public questions. . . . [But due to my influence] New York acquired a certain kind of general predominancy in the minds of Catholics. What was done at New York, or said by me, was taken to be true for every place else as well as this. And thus, through the medium of the newspapers, rather than from any direct instruction or guidance on the part of the local ecclesiastical authority, a certain tone and feeling became prevalent among the Catholics.[26]

Hughes regarded the Irish immigrant as the "mainstay" of the Church in the United States.[27] He associated this belief with the fact that, "It is only when he has the consolation of his religion within his reach that he feels comparatively happy in his new position."[28] It was his assessment of the special importance of "the metropolis," and of the Irish as the basic membership of the diocese, that, it is generally believed, led him to disapprove sternly of proposals for the establishment of Catholic colonies[29] for the relief of the congested living conditions of the misplaced Irish peasants in New York.[30]

Though Hughes opposed the dispersal of New York Catholics by westward migration, he at the same time enjoined his Irish-American flock to "merge socially and politically with the American people." That he did mean white people was clear from the inveterate opposition he expressed toward abolitionists, and his "determination to struggle" with O'Connell on the question of slavery. As was the fashion among American Catholic prelates, Hughes would generally make a formal obeisance in the direction of Gregory XVI's anti-slavery edict by saying he was not an advocate of slavery. But the substance of his actions and of his frequent denunciations of abolitionism were not calculated to "convince the judgment" of Irish Catholics to oppose the bondage of the African-American; quite the contrary.

After visits to the Spanish sugar slave colony of Cuba and the American

South in 1853, and several other Southern visits during which he was a sometime plantation guest, Hughes defended the international slave trade in classical slaveholder terms.[31] In May 1854, Hughes delivered a sermon at St Patrick's Cathedral in which he spoke of his 1853 trip. Taking as his text John 10:11–16, he discussed slavery in terms of the slaveholder's endowment by God to be a shepherd over his flock of slaves. "Is not the father of the family invested with the power of god that he is a sovereign, commanding and expecting to be obeyed, as he should?" he analogized. All God demanded was that the shepherd exert a good Christian influence on the slaves. Hughes was convinced that the lot of the Africans was improved by being kidnapped and enslaved in America. He was reinforced in this opinion by the fact that when he had asked plantation slaves whether they would prefer to stay as they were in America or to go back to Africa, they had unanimously told him that they much preferred being slaves in America. He apparently did not ask them whether they would prefer freedom to bondage.[32] From the beginning of the Civil War, Hughes condemned the very idea that the abolition of slavery might be a war aim, saying Irish-Americans would not fight for such a cause, adding that if Lincoln had such an intention, he ought to resign the presidency.[33] Hughes denounced the Emancipation Proclamation before the ink was dry.[34] And he blamed the New York Draft Riots of the summer of 1863 on the belief that the government intended to make Negroes equal to white men.[35]

The Irish-American establishment was determined to prevent the spread of the influence of abolitionism through the Irish abolitionist Address. They first sought to asperse the authenticity of O'Connell's signature, and to impute fraud to the African-American bringer of the news and his fellow American abolitionists. They surely knew from Bishop Hughes's encounter with O'Connell in 1840 that this pretense could not be maintained. In any case, they quickly shifted to more substantive questions.

They demanded that Irish-Americans repudiate the Irish abolitionist Address on two general grounds, namely, loyalty to the United States and loyalty to the anti-Protestant interest. The Irish-Americans were to disregard the appeal to be brethren to the racially oppressed African-Americans because it was an unwarranted interference in American affairs, involvement in which would bring heavy censure upon Irish-Americans for being "un-American." At best this was advice to silently "pass by on the other side"[36] from where the Negro lay in chains. But among those who were not silent on the issue, there was almost unanimity in identifying American "patriotism" with support of the slavery-sanctifying United States Constitution.

The abolitionist cause was to be sternly resisted as a hive of anti-Catholicism, since many of the abolitionists, African-American and European-American, also held strong Protestant convictions. As noted above, O'Connell had no difficulty in dealing with the issue, and Pope Gregory XVI felt no need to bring the subject up. It was true, of course, that the relative strengths of the contending branches of Christianity in the United States were the opposite of what they had been in Ireland, where the Protestant evangelists were few and where the Protestant Ascendancy, the Church of Ireland and the yeomanry were not really interested in Protestantizing the Catholic masses. In the United States the Catholics were not only in a permanent minority, they were beset by the Know-Nothing movement and generally subjected to the prejudices of the general Protestant majority. Views hostile to the Catholic Church were evident among abolitionists.[37] O'Connell, in the course of his reply to the Cincinnati repealers, noted that "there are amongst the abolitionists, many wicked and calumniating enemies of Catholicity and the Irish, especially in that most intolerant class, the Wesleyan Methodists."[38] But it is fair to note that the abolitionists were no less severe with pro-slavery attitudes in Protestant churches. The New England Anti-slavery Society in 1841 made no Protestant exception in declaring that "the church and clergy of the United States, as a whole, constitute a gross brotherhood of thieves, inasmuch as they countenance the highest kind of theft, i.e., man-stealing."[39] Abolitionists were not interested in winning Catholics to Protestantism; they were busy trying to "convert" the whole population to the anti-slavery cause. On the other hand, most of the slaveholders and the political leaders were Protestant, even as the abolitionist leaders were. Evangelism may not have in all cases been the slaveholders' style, but when the Irish Address was first broached in the United States, some slaveholders even reacted by advocating an end to immigration from Ireland.[40] How then did the Irish-American mistrust of Protestantism come to be translated by the Irish-American establishment into fervent support of Protestant slaveholders? The apparent inconsistency is seen to be explained by the principle of "merger" with the "white" people. By this light, the Protestantism of the abolitionists was the threat to be stressed, rather than the Protestantism of the defenders of slavery.

Within the United States Catholic Church there was no desire to promote a revolutionary overthrow of British rule in Ireland, but when the time came it would support Vatican policy favoring encouragement of the United States as a counterweight to perfidious Albion.[41] To that extent they shared with some Young Ireland exiles the strategic principle that "the enemy of my enemy is my friend." Even though the Church anathematized the Young Irelanders as "red republicans," Young Irelanders in the United States reinforced the establishment's position; they condemned O'Connell's abolitionism for antagonizing the United States, from whom they expected to get direct or indirect support in throwing the British out of Ireland.[42] This was an open avowal of alliance with the slaveholders.

Some of the Young Irelander exiles in the United States entered into that spirit with a vengeance. John Mitchel, who considered O'Connell, "next to the British Government, the worst enemy that Ireland ever had, or rather the most fatal friend,"[43] was the most extreme example. He published a stridently anti-Negro weekly newspaper, the *Citizen*, in which he delivered himself of these sentiments:

> We deny that it is a crime, or a wrong, or even a peccadillo, to hold slaves, to buy slaves, to keep slaves to their work by flogging or other needful coercion.... we, for our part, wish we had a good plantation, well-stocked with healthy negroes.[44]

Another well-known post-1848 Irish exile, Francis Meagher, was a typical anti-Negro Democrat up to the time of the Civil War. He published the *Irish News* wherein he charged the abolitionists with "hostility to our republican form of government by their assaults on the domestic institutions of the South."[45]

The notable lack of success of this approach to Irish liberation by way of Anglo-American antagonism would seem to refute it as a strategy for overthrowing British rule in Ireland.[46] The anti-British angle served most significantly as an excuse for the pro-slavery stand among Irish-Americans, rather than as a cause of it. Most of the political exiles found "more practical and profitable ways to use their nationalism," says Kerby Miller. "Many former Young Irelanders drifted into Democratic politics, using their talents and reputations to cement emigrant loyalties to the party of Jackson."[47]

The Attack on the "White Worker" Front

The desire of the Protestant slaveholders to turn Catholic Irish-Americans against the abolitionism of the Catholic Liberator, O'Connell, has been noted. But that negative stimulus of withholding support for repeal was too little and too remote to account for the emergence of the predominant pro-slavery Irish-American politics of the ante-bellum and Civil War periods.

The America to which these Irish immigrants came was already constructed on the principle of racial oppression, including the white-skin privileges of laboring-class European-Americans. If Irish-Americans rejected the heritage represented by O'Connell and the Address, and if they were frequently identified with the most hostile actions against Negroes in the Northern cities, it was basically because they – like immigrants from Germany, France, England, Scotland and Scandinavia – accepted their place in the white-race system of social control and claimed the racial privileges entailed by it. Before the Civil War, the main basic white-skin privileges were: (1) the presumption of liberty; (2) the right of immigration and naturalization; and (3) the right to vote.[48] The first two of these were in place before the Jacksonian phenomenon, the third was crafted by it.

The presumption of liberty distinguished the poorest of European-Americans from the free African-American. Under the white-race system of social control, even the most destitute of European-Americans were expected to exercise this racial prerogative by supporting the enforcement of the Fugitive Slave Law.

The United States Constitution implicity made immigration a white-skin privilege, when in Article I, Section 9, Europeans were classed as migrants whilst Africans were classed as imports. Naturalization statutes enacted, amended and re-enacted before the Civil War repeated the phraseology of the original "Act to establish an uniform Rule of Naturalization" signed into law on 26 March 1790, providing that "any alien, being a free white person . . . may be admitted to become a citizen" of the United States.[49] Seen in historical context, this "whites"-only immigration policy was a corollary of another constitutional provision which was the basis of the Fugitive Slave Laws that effectively restricted the presumption of liberty to European-Americans, by providing that any "person held to service in one State . . . escaping into another . . . shall be delivered up" to the owner (Article 4, Section 2, paragraph 2).

This privilege of immigration carried with it a status entirely new to the newcomers; the moment they set foot on United States soil, however lowly their social status might otherwise be they were endowed with all the immunities, rights and privileges of "American whites." By the same token they were implicitly enrolled in the system of racial oppression of all African-Americans, which the ruling slaveowning plantation bourgeoisie first imposed during the country's colonial pre-history in order to maintain effective social control.

From "Irish" to "white American"

The Jacksonians made politics "practical" by means of the "spoils system," the egregious exploitation of political jobbery and systematic patronage. Jackson, the founder of the system, construed his obligation to the country in strictly partisan terms: "I can have no other view," he said, "but to administer the government in such a way as will strengthen the democratic party."[50] This practice was essential in launching the big-city machine politics in the United States.

Political scientists have long since identified Jacksonianism with the spoils system. But no one acquainted with the history of the Irish Protestant Parliament in the eighteenth century, or the open vote-buying and pocket boroughs that characterized English politics before the assertion of the Chartist influence in the nineteenth century, could be especially horrified by the corruption of Jackson's program for establishing the same sort of principle on a national scale in the United States. Indeed, Arthur M. Schlesinger Jr, author of the most popular history of the era, defends the practice as essential to Jackson's program, which Schlesinger views favorably as bringing about a "democratic" social transformation of United States politics.[51]

Regrettably, critics and defenders alike generally seem to ignore the most historically significant fact about the spoils system, namely that it was first of all a "white-race" spoils system. At the outset, it was given this character by the "manhood suffrage" laws (ending the property qualification for voting), adopted mostly between 1820 and 1830, which recognized only "whites" as "men." Either African-Americans were explicitly excluded from voting rights under this "sweeping democratic reform," or they were subject to special property qualification designed to have the same practical effect, even in states where they had historically exercised that right.[52] This policy was of key importance for recruiting a labor base in the North for slaveholder dominance of the United States government in general, and for assuring active or passive support in the enforcement of the Fugitive Slave Law as a constitutional principle.

In regard to "white" privileges in general, the Irish-American position did not differ from that of other European-Americans. The special significance of the Irish-American case was that: (1) they were the largest immigrant group in the ante-bellum period; (2) they explicitly rejected their own national heritage to become part of the system of "white" racial oppression of African-Americans; and (3) by virtue of their concentration in Northern cities – above all, New York, the locale of the most important Northern links with the plantation bourgeoisie – they became a key factor in national politics.

In the early 1820s, a discredited aristocratic pro-slavery leadership of Tammany Hall was replaced by a prototypical Jacksonian leadership: mass-oriented, "democratic," but again, aligned with the plantation bourgeoisie. Thenceforward, "Throughout the slavery agitation up to the firing on Fort Sumter," wrote historian Gustavus Myers, "the South had no firmer supporter than Tammany."[53]

This new departure at Tammany Hall coincided with the beginning of a sharp rise in Catholic Irish immigration and the granting of "white" manhood suffrage. The number of Irish immigrants nearly doubled on an average every half-decade from 1821 to 1850,[54] and they settled in New York in inordinate proportions. They came from an Ireland where Catholics had a long history of being aliens in their own land or, after 1829, only second-class citizens. But Catholics entered the United States eligible, under the general provisions of the naturalization laws, to receive the full and unlimited rights of citizenship, on an equal legal footing with Protestants. They came from an Ireland where, as a part of Catholic Emancipation, the voting rights of forty-shilling freeholders were taken away in 1829, after a period of thirty-six years, and a much more restricted franchise was imposed.[55] In the United States they were entering they would, on becoming citizens, be able to vote, without property qualifications.

"White" suffrage and African-American disfranchisement

Though barred from the militia many New York Negroes served as volunteers in the War of 1812 against Britain. They were among the African-American one-fourth of the American forces in Perry's command at the Battle of Lake Erie, 10 April 1813, under the famous pennant-borne resolve "Don't give up the ship!" For forty years African-Americans had been voting on the same basis as other men who paid taxes or owned fifty dollars' worth of real estate or paid an annual rent of five dollars. As voters, they gave their allegiance to the Federalist Party because of its stand in favor of ending slavery and for equal rights for free African-Americans. In more than one election (in 1810 in Brooklyn, and in 1813 in New York, for instance) the outcome was decided by the margin provided by African-American voters.[56] The 1821 New York State Constitutional Convention effectively disfranchised African-Americans by requiring them (and only them) to be freeholders worth $250.[57]

Resistance to this disfranchisement of African-Americans continued to play a central part in New York politics for a quarter of a century.[58] Attempts to restore those rights were made in constitutional conventions in 1826 and 1846, only to be defeated each time primarily by the exertions of Tammany Democrats. It would take a great civil war to repeal that discriminatory law, which was formally done in 1870, though still, however, against Tammany opposition.[59] Fox, the historian of the subject, notes two facts especially relevant to my thesis. The "white" laborers, he writes, "prized the luxury of feeling themselves better than the Negro." Second, the New York City wards in which "the anti-Negro vote was strongest, were the sixth and fourteenth, which had the largest number of immigrant citizens,"[60] and most of the new voters were Irish-Americans. This was certainly so in the Sixth Ward[61] which, in 1848, "gave the largest anti-Negro vote ... [and] was the very citadel of Tammany."[62]

The historical affinity of the generality of Irish-Americans and Tammany Hall[63] was thus from the beginning conditioned on denial of the rights of African-Americans, and on a concomitant attachment to the national program of the slaveholders. The Tammany machine did its part in a number of ways. It facilitated naturalization of Irish immigrants, with careless regard for the letter of the law, in order to hasten the inauguration of the Irish immigrants into slaveholder electoral service.[64] Graft-rich government contracts afforded benefits to Irish-American ward heelers, who had important local appointive powers, including appointment of the police in each ward.[65] The merest Irish voter was encouraged in his loyalty by little favors, especially at election time, such as early or temporary release from prison,[66] or by payments in money or in kind at the ward heeler's saloon.[67] (This chance to market his franchise was just what many an immigrant had lost as insurance against eviction in the wake of Catholic Emancipation.) The whitening effect in due course became manifest. Though the poor Irish-Catholics were not immediately delivered from their low-caste status in Protestant Anglo-America, these perquisites and privileges were intended and defended – not as Irish-American rights, but as "white men's" rights. Along the way, the sense of white-race identity was regularly reinforced by pro-slavery lectures sponsored by Tammany. Among the guests at celebrations of the slavery-extending Mexican War were such eminent Southerners as President James Polk and Sam Houston of Texas, along with Generals Henry Martin Foote and Leslie Combs, enthusiastic veterans of that invasion.[68]

Irish-American Voters and the Annexation of Texas

The counter-attack against the abolitionist appeals from Ireland, especially through the "white" spoils system, proved to be a key factor in one history-shaping political victory of the slaveholders, the presidential election of 1844, in which the leading question was whether or not the United States should annex Texas.[69]

American abolitionist opposition to annexation had the support of Daniel O'Connell who, despite opposition from Young Irelanders,[70] denounced the slaveholders' designs on Mexican territory as the scheme of a "gang of land pirates" which, among other ills, would increase the political base of the slaveholders in national affairs. He recommended that the Mexican government "form a colony of free persons of colour ... [which] would be a refuge for free men of colour of the United States who are naturally enough disgusted with the paltry injustice of being called 'free' while they are deprived of all the practical rights of freedom," to oppose the incursions of the "white monsters."[71]

The Democratic Party candidate, James K. Polk, was aggressively committed to annexation. The Democrats' hand was strengthened among Irish-Americans not only by their "white" spoils system, but specifically by success in linking anti-abolitionism with the anti-British cause, by playing up British support for the establishment of an independent Texas on abolitionist principles. The Whig Party candidate, Henry Clay, had forfeited the Northern anti-slavery vote by being (as historian Freehling calls him) "a Whig for all regions"[72] in his two-faced behavior regarding annexation. But, as noted above,[73] he was determined to compete with the Democrats for the vote of the "white workers," including explicitly the Irish and the Germans, by promising to protect their white-skin privileges *vis-à-vis* African-Americans.

The New York vote was expected to be crucial, and it proved to be so. Polk won with an electoral college vote of 170 to Clay's 105, the thirty-six New York votes supplying the margin of victory. Polk won in New York by a margin of only 5,016 out of a total popular vote of 470,000, of which

15,012 were cast for the abolitionist Liberty Party candidate, James G. Birney. In view of the calculated risk taken with regard to the anti-slavery voters, it is fair to say that New York's Irish-Americans, who (far more than German-Americans) voted solidly for the Democrats, decided the outcome of the national election. That conclusion is supported by the lament of Clay's vice-presidential running mate, Theodore Frehlinghuysen of New York, five days after the election.

> [T]he foreign vote was tremendous. More than three thousand, it is confidently said, have been naturalized in this city, alone, since the first of October. It is an alarming fact that this foreign vote has decided the great question of American policy.[74]

The Irish-American voters of New York had not only opted for the "filthy aristocracy of skin," but had become a key factor in national politics, all in fulfillment of the strategic plan of the slaveholders as formulated by John Randolph a quarter of a century before (see page 163).

Acting as "Whites"

Charles Spencer of Mississippi, spying out the North some five weeks after Lincoln's election in November 1860, reported that the slaveholders could "safely rely on" the Irish of New York because "they hate the [African-American] as they do the devil."[75] The die was cast for war, which began with secession of Southern states from the Union, followed by the rebel attack on the Federal Fort Sumter in April 1861. In effective coordination with the slaveholder Confederacy, pro-slavery, anti-Negro elements in the North intensified agitation on the "Catholic-Irish" and the "white worker" fronts. A major role in that effort was taken by the publications directed mainly at a Catholic Irish-American readership in New York, such as the *New York Freeman's Journal* (later *Freeman's Journal and Catholic Register*), *Irish-American*, *Irish News*, and *Citizen* (later *Caucasian*).[76]

The campaign produced a combination of white-supremacist rallies, anti-abolitionist exhortations, pronouncements aimed at undermining the anti-Confederate cause, physical assaults on African-Americans, a "dress rehearsal" riot in south Brooklyn in August 1862 and the culminating Draft Riot/"white" pogrom of July 1863.[77] The following selected chronology may serve to indicate the unrelenting intensity of the campaign.

7 January 1861 – The Democrat Mayor Fernando Wood, expressing the "common sympathy" felt for the slaveholders by the people he represents, proposes the secession of New York City from the United States.[78]

15 January 1861 – A mass meeting, "well attended", at Brooks Hall, is largely officered by "Irish personnel" and "engineered" by the infamous Democratic leader Isaiah Rynders, who is implicated as US Marshal in the escape of a convicted New York slave-trader; and by R. G. Horton, co-conspirator in the frustrated Confederate coup in New York of November 1864. The meeting denounces "the black Republican Party" for attempting to overthrow the Constitution in order "to reduce white men to a forbidden level with Negroes." Its manifesto opens with the call, "Workingmen Arouse!"[79]

7 May 1861 – Twenty-five days after the attack on Fort Sumter, and twenty-two days after Lincoln's call for 75,000 volunteers to fight the insurrection, Archbishop Hughes, writing to a Southern bishop, takes a stand of "non-interference" in the war; he neither encourages "Catholics to take part in it," nor advises them "not to do so."[80]

18 May 1861 – Archbishop John Hughes declares that any effort by the government to abolish slavery would be a violation of the United States Constitution, and that if such be the intention, President Lincoln should forthwith resign from office.[81]

16 June 1861 – The Democratic Party newspaper, the *Leader*, upon hearing that an African-American has been hired at the New York United States Custom Office in the place of a "white" man, threatens that if the report proves true, "it would take more than honied words to quiet ... the entire race of white men [who] would rise in vindictive rebellion against it."[82]

October 1861 – Archbishop Hughes writes to Secretary of War Simon Cameron that if "the purpose of the war is the abolition of slavery in the South," then "among a certain class [read, Irish Catholics], it would make the business of recruiting slack indeed."[83]

12 October 1861 – The *Metropolitan Record*, Archbishop Hughes's "official organ," in an editorial personally written by Hughes declares that Catholics will fight for the Union, but not for ending slavery, that slavery exists by "Divine permission of God's providence;" Hughes even defends the international slave trade, failing to see any "crime ... or moral transgression of the law of God" in such a transaction; rather, indeed, it is in the end a good way "for humane masters to ... take care of these unfortunate people." Although it is perhaps sad that the slavery should be transmitted to the children, that is no worse than the Divine command to eat bread in the sweat of the brow borne by "men who are living now who had no part in the commission of original sin."[84]

27 November 1861 – The Democratic Mayor of New York Fernando Wood denounces the federal government as having provoked the war.[85]

18 January 1862 – The *Metropolitan Record* declares that, for the "mechanics and labourers of our country," abolition of slavery, "would be the worst evil that could befall them," because "the influx of negro labour on the Northern market would reduce them to a condition worse than that of the pauperized operatives of Europe."[86]

4 July 1862 – The Grand Sachem, or highest officer, of Tammany Hall, Nelson J. Waterbury, declares that the fighting spirit of the Union soldiers requires that the President "set his foot firmly on abolitionism and crush it to pieces."[87]

26 July 1862 – The *Caucasian* warns "white" workers that free Negroes are taking "their" jobs, and publishes a letter on the subject, demanding: "White Men! mechanics and workingmen of New York! how long is this state of things to exist? If you are asleep, awake! If awake, arouse! When aroused from your slumbers, act!"[88]

4 August 1862 – Acting as "whites," a mob of from two to three thousand from an Irish-American Brooklyn neighborhood force two local tobacco factories to end the employment of African-Americans. The owners of Lorillard's, where for years 250 "colored and white ... worked harmoniously side by side," surrender to the demand, discharge the Negro workers, and agree never to hire African-Americans again. Watson's, the other factory, employing 50 persons, all Negroes, is attacked by the mob, who try to burn the building down. The workers retreat to the second floor and successfully defy the attackers until police arrive. But shortly thereafter the factory is shut down.[89]

9 October 1862 – The prominent Irish-American lawyer Richard O'Gorman, speaking before the Democratic Union Association, declares that constitutionally the federal government has no more authority to "alter the relation" of slaveholder and slave than it has to alter that between parent and child or husband and wife.[90]

12 October 1862 – The *Caucasian*, under the heading, "Archbishop Hughes's Thunderbolt Against the Abolitionists," publishes from the *Metropolitan Record* of the week before Hughes's long editorial condemning the Emancipation Proclamation (announced by Lincoln about three weeks before). Hughes equates Emancipation with highway robbery, arguing that to say that slavery is the cause of the war is like saying, "that a man's carrying money on his person is the cause of his being robbed on the highway."[91]

December 1862 – Presumably without violating the confidence of the confessional, Archbishop Hughes advises Secretary of State William H. Seward that "there are men ... who say rather that *their* fighting is to be done in the streets of this city."[92]

18 July 1863 – After four days of continuous rioting and lynching of African-

Americans, by mobs composed mainly of Irish-Americans, Archbishop Hughes, at the request of the Governor, speaks to an audience numbering three or four thousand whom he has invited to congregate by his residence. Identifying with them as a Catholic and an Irishman, he urges that the rioting cease. He is in a frail condition due to an illness from which he will die within a year, and does not make any reply to anti-Negro cries from the audience.[93]

18 or 19 July 1863 – Archbishop Hughes writes to Secretary of State Seward that the real cause of the riots was not the draft, but the prospect that powerful influences were at work, disposed "to make black labor equal to white labor," and that "black labor shall have local patronage over the toil of the white man."[94]

The "Labor Competition" Rationale Re-examined

The archbishop's comment was not adding anything new to the Secretary of State's knowledge. It had been the most common justification relied upon by the perpetrators of the white-supremacism in that period. A number of historians, even as they have made valuable contributions to the study of anti-Negro attitudes and behavior on the part of Irish-American workers in the ante-bellum and Civil War periods, have made the assumptions characteristic of the "labor competition" rationale, accompanied almost invariably by palliative allusions to "Negro strikebreakers."[95] The remainder of this chapter is chiefly intended to offer a more critical examination than is usually given to the "labor competition" thesis.

Competition among individuals for employment is a necessary condition of the wage-labor system. Moreover, groupings, unintentionally formed by family extension, language, or locality, are commonly projected into labor-pool groupings. Even within the ranks of Catholic Irish-Americans, job competition took the form of "many a bloody brawl" between men from Cork and men from Connaught, or, again, from Ulster.[96]

In the 1800s competition occurred between groups, formed with some degree of deliberation, as "native-born" and immigrants, when Irish immigrants "sought such occupations as offered; [and] they underbid labor."[97] The nativist movement sought restrictions on immigration and naturalization because, it was said, the influx of immigrants was driving wages down.[98] Nativism, drawing on the heritage of British and Ulster Protestant Ascendancy, was mainly directed against the Catholic Irish. The movement peaked about 1845,[99] having had only a limited effect on job competition; it never reduced the inflow of immigrants.

The "labor competition" commonly alluded to in reference to the anti-Negro attitude of Irish-American "white" laborers also involved a deliberate choice, but one profoundly more significant than that which produced conflicts between native-born and immigrant, even in their most violent Protestant-versus-Catholic form.

The latter was a quarrel between factions of the "white race," which did not threaten the fundamental Constitution of the country. The former was a fight for the system of white supremacy, on which the government was founded. The Catholic *St Louis Leader* defined the difference in essentially the same way. The ascendancy of Know-Nothingism, the paper said, would bring only "temporary and local" difficulties; but a victory of the "anti-slavery Republicans" would be a forerunner of the "general and final catastrophe."[100]

New York City's foreign-born population grew steadily; in 1855, the foreign-born actually made up more than half of the city's inhabitants. The number of foreign-born rose by over 57,000 in the next five years, to nearly 384,000, of whom over 53 percent were from Ireland.[101] Fifteen thousand people a year were settling in the city,[102] more than the *total* African-American resident population. Such a rate of immigration would, of course, tend to increase "labor competition." But why should it have been "racial"?

Leaving aside workers born in the United States, Table 2 shows that the number of foreign-born "white" competitors with the Irish for employment was greater in every category than the number of African-American competitors. The overall figures for the occupations covered by the table show a 5 to 1 ratio of foreign-born "whites" to African-Americans competing with the Irish immigrants for jobs. In the most critical socio-political category, laborers, there were four times as many non-Irish foreign-born "whites," European-

Table 2 The numbers of Irish and other workers in the occupations in which Irish workers were most numerous in New York City in 1855[103]

	Foreign-born European-Americans			African-Americans
	Total	Irish	Non-Irish	
Domestic servants*	29,470	23,386	6,084	1,025
Laborers	19,783	17,426	2,357	536
Dressmakers and seamstresses	6,606	4,559	2,047	111
Waiters	2,006	1,491	515	499
Coachmen	972	805	167	102
Total	*58,837*	*47,667*	*11,170*	*2,273*

*The notice "No Irish need apply" has been more effective in discrediting anti-Irish bigotry than it was in reducing the entry of Irish workers into domestic service employment.

Americans, in the labor market as there were African-Americans. If information showing the number of native-born workers in these categories were included, the ratios of non-Irish "whites" to African-Americans would be yet higher.

The "fear of Negro job competition," so much favored as an explanation of the concentration of Irish-American workers' hostility on the African-American minority of their non-Irish competitors thus had no basis in actual fact.[104] These Irish-American workers may have been led to believe that their interest depended above all upon the exclusion of the African-American workers. But that "fear" was no more justified than the exaggerated allegations of Jesse Helms's 1990 campaign concerning the horrific consequences to be feared by "white" workers from affirmative action employment programs; nor did the existence of such fears qualify a "white" pogrom against Negro men, women and children in July 1863 as a "working-class movement."

It does not help the "labor competition" case to speak of "Negro strikebreakers" when no special mention is made of "German strikebreakers," such as those who took the jobs of Irish workers striking for higher pay and shorter hours at the Atlantic Dock in Brooklyn in 1846,[105] or other European-American strikebreakers on the Erie Railroad docks in January 1863, or the Hudson River Railroad docks two months later.[106] Both African-American and European-American strikebreakers were employed at various times, but the murderous wrath of the strikers was reserved for those of "dark skin," who were pursued by the mob crying, "Drive off the damn niggers," and "Kill the niggers."[107]

Possible alternatives to that entire historically evolved scenario were suggested in two separate events, one of which became the rule, and one of which remained an exception. Naturalized European-American workers complained of being shut out by native Americans as if the former were no more than "foreigners." "If you don't include us to get better wages," said one of their number in a letter to a labor paper of the 1850s, "you needn't expect our help." In response the labor movement "aided the immigrants and in turn sought their cooperation."[108] African-Americans in the waiters' trade in New York in 1853 demanded and won an advance in wages which put them four dollars a month ahead of the wage paid to white waiters. A meeting was held at which the white workers considered measures to secure parity. A "Negro delegate" to the meeting encouraged the white workers in their campaign.[109]

If the opportunistic use of the label "strikebreaker" is to be so selectively applied in order to excuse the adherence by Irish-American or other European-American workers to what O'Connell called "the filthy aristocracy of skin," then there should be a name for the process that drove thousands of African-Americans from jobs and from the city of New York altogether in the age of Jackson and the *ante-bellum* period.

Labor competitions given an abnormal "racial" form

Prior to 1840, a wide range of industrial employments (from longshoring to coachman), service occupations (from stableman to table-waiting), as well as domestic service in New York were "almost wholly in the hands of" African-Americans. Their wages were good relative to those of other workers. The Irish, driven into exile by famine, competed for those jobs by taking lower wages, and by the early 1850s they had made extensive inroads into those fields of employment.[110] To *assume* that it was in the nature of the case that Irish would seek to drive Negroes out, off the job, and do so on the basis of an Irish claim to a "white" identity, is to assume the Jordan–Degler assumption, that "white over black" is a memory of the blood. But that is precisely the notion that the Irish Address denied, denounced and refuted. The Leanders of Ireland remembered what racial oppression meant: the Penal Laws which reduced them to aliens in their own country, the assaults on their families, the denial of education and apprenticeships, the daily humiliations at the hands of Protestants, however lowly in the social scale. If they appealed to their countrymen and countrywomen in America to be brethren to the Negro, and to enter the struggle for abolition, it was not out of ignorance of "race" as a social motive. To the extent that Irish-Americans rejected that appeal and opted instead to stand by the slaveholders on the grounds of fear of job competition from African-Americans, the cause was not actual "job competition." Rather, the problem of job competition was cast in the mold of white supremacy as an integral part of the social control system instituted by the American slaveholders in the days of William of Orange and Queen Anne and the opening of the Penal Laws era in Ireland.

Although there was widespread discrimination in public services against African-Americans, private employers in the ante-bellum North tended, by contrast, to act as straightforward buyers of labor-power, indifferent to "racial" considerations. It was only after the Civil War that the Northern employers adopted as their own the general principle of racial discrimination in industrial employment.[111] Nevertheless, there were powerful countervailing influences: constitutional guarantees, the "white" manhood suffrage laws, and the pervasive power of the Democratic spoils system, which served to encourage the extensions of the principle of "racial" preference in employment to the North. Special mention is due to the Custom House as a bell-wether in the effort to establish the principle of "racial" preference in hiring in the North.

Control of hiring at the United States Custom House was in the hands of the national government, and consequently most of the time in the hands of the Democrats. It was "the largest single federal office in the country and was the greatest source of patronage." The Collector "had at his disposal hundreds of relatively well-paying jobs which he could distribute to the advantage of the political party or faction he represented," and "[i]t was at the Custom House that the spoils system reached its highest form of development."[112] The Custom House therefore offered an opportunity not only to build up the pro-slavery political machine; by strictly keeping employment at this government facility as a white-skin privilege, it effectively was a Northern bastion of the principle that the Negro had no job rights that a "white" person was bound to respect.

When, in the first few months of Lincoln's administration, an African-American man, Robert Vosburgh, was hired at the New York United States Custom House, the editor of the Tammany paper, the *Leader*, erupted with vituperation. His editorial, titled "A [Negro] Appointed in the Custom House," began thus: "A startling rumor has reached us, which we can scarcely credit ... a *negro* has been appointed" to a job in the Custom House.[113] Since, according to long-established Democratic principles, Custom House jobs were for "whites" only, the editorial could only see Vosburgh's employment as a displacement of the "white" William O'Brien. By the fall of 1862, a number of other Negro workers had found jobs at the Custom House. A month after the issuance of the Emancipation Proclamation and ten days before the gubernatorial and congressional elections, Tammany's *Leader* thought it seasonable to charge that the continued employment of Negroes in the Custom House was a plot against the Democratic Party.[114] As we have noted, this incident was used by the Democrat press to call for "White" men to rise in "vindictive rebellion."

From true competition to "white" racial preference

In the context of the "white" spoils system, what began as a form of normally occurring wage labor competition soon developed on the Irish-American side into an assertion of the right of "white" preference. It will be noted that the Cincinnati Repeal Association spoke as "white" men in attacking O'Connell in 1843 for his denunciations of slavery; he, on the other hand, repeatedly called upon them as Irishmen to make the cause of the Negro their own. John Mitchel's *Citizen* declared in 1856, "He would be a bad Irishman who voted for the ascendancy of principles which proscribed himself, and which jeopardized the present system of a nation of white men."[115] In January 1860, the New York paper the *Irish American*, taking note of a Massachusetts cotton mill disaster which took the lives of scores of young Irish women, voiced their grievance in terms of an abuse of "white" workers.[116] A mass meeting made up mainly of Irish-American workers in New York in January 1861 declared labor to be the natural ally of the slaveholders, in opposition to any and all efforts "to reduce white men to a forbidden level with negroes."[117]

In the riots in Brooklyn and in New York to which I have referred, the mobs made up primarily of Irish-Americans did not express their demands and aims in terms of Irishness, but in the name of "white workingmen."

By 1863, "[a]lmost all longshoremen in New York City were Irish;" they were organized in the Longshoremen's Association, and resolved that dock work would be limited to "such white laborers as they see fit to permit upon the premises."[118] African-Americans were driven from the trade in which they had predominated twenty years before, not in the normal course of economic competition, but by Irish-Americans operating under the immunities of "whiteness." The African-American population had declined perhaps 16 percent between 1840 and 1860, "owing to the aroused hostility to Negroes," as one historian put it.[119] Then, between 1860 and 1865, it fell by another one-fourth, to less than ten thousand. It is sadly ironic that the Catholic proportion of the population of Belfast was reduced as a result of similar pogrom-like attacks by Protestant workers, as noted in Chapter 5.

Labor competition – the reality

It was said at the time, and has been stressed by historians, that the "white" workers were motivated mainly by a fear of the prospect of freed African-Americans coming to the North looking for work in such large numbers that the oversupply of labor would result in lower wages.[120] This explanation ignores the fact that more than two million European immigrants came into the United States in the decade before the Civil War, and two and three-quarters million in the ten years after the war,[121] of whom several hundred thousand remained in New York City. Yet no European immigrants were lynched, no "white" orphanages were burned, for fear of "competition" in the labor market. Second, to come North to escape slavery made sense, but to come North to escape freedom would not. To the extent that the Irish-American and the other "whites" were worried on this account, therefore, they should have supported the struggle of the African-American people and the abolitionists for an end to bond-servitude. This precise point was made at the time by the *New York Tribune*. The Irish-born Brigadier-General Richard Busteed directed the same argument at his fellow Irish-Americans in a speech in City Hall Park in August 1862.[122] General David Hunter, Union commander at Port Royal, South Carolina, offered free passes North for freedmen, but so few took up the offer that Hunter concluded that the idea of mass migration of freedmen was a "carefully fostered illusion." A special official investigation of the matter found that there was no basis for believing that freed Negroes were eager to leave the South.[123]

In short, strike off the chains of the African-American bond-laborers, apply the principle of "land to the tiller" with a land redistribution program in the South, and the main incentive to go North would dissolve. The story of the Negro Exodus of 1879 would in time bear out this judgment.[124] Only a protracted white-supremacist terroristic campaign intended to reimpose virtual bondage could convince African-Americans of the South to undertake a concerted effort to escape; and, then, the destination was not the Northern cities, but the farm lands of Kansas.

There was indeed a real competition between African-American bond-labor and Irish-American (and other "white") workers, that if understood would have provided a basis for a joint struggle against slavery. As DuBois put it, "[T]he black man enslaved was an even more formidable and fatal competitor than the black man free."[125] It was in the interest of the slave-labor system to maintain the white-skin privilege differential in favor of the European-American workers. At the same time, however, it was equally in the interest of the employers of wage-labor, as well as of bond-labor, that the differential be kept to no more than the minimum necessary for the purpose of keeping the European-American workers in the "white race" corral. To increase the differential beyond that degree would entail an unnecessary deduction from capitalist profits, which would be distributed by the workings of the average rate over the employers of bond-labor as well as employers of wage-labor. Furthermore, it would tend to increase the traffic on the Underground Railroad. The chains that bound the African-American thus also held down the living standards of the Irish-American slum-dweller and canal-digger as well. This underlying reality also gave a basis to the connection that the Catholic press, with hostile intent, alleged to exist between Free Soil and abolitionism. The "competition" for Western lands was between the bond-labor system and the wage-labor system. It was no coincidence that it was in 1862 that both the Homestead Act and the Emancipation Proclamation were promulgated in the interest of a war to abolish slavery.

The Pre-existing Logic

In 1864, the year that Archbishop Hughes died, Thomas Francis Meagher, with the fervor of the wartime convert to Lincoln's cause, pronounced a bitter judgment on his fellow Irish-Americans and, so it would seem, on his own former self:

> To their own discredit and degradation, they have suffered themselves to be bamboozled into being obstinate herds in the political field, contracting inveterate instincts, following with gross stupidity and the stoniest blindness certain worn out old path-ways described for them by their drivers, but never doing anything worthy of the intellectual and chivalrous reputation of their race.[126]

It was not the rank and file of Irish immigrants, however, who framed the issues in pro-slavery terms; Leander himself had proved that with his youthful poem. The white-supremacist and pro-slavery attitudes and behavior among Irish-Americans of "the metropolis," as universally recorded by historians of the ante-bellum and Civil War periods, were driven first by the Democratic Party's Tammany Hall, and then by the naturally conservative, "merger"-minded, Hughes-led American Catholic establishment – in the interest of the plantation bourgeoisie. It was chiefly they who brought about the rejection of the appeal by O'Connell and seventy thousand of their countrymen, in the Address, to "stand with the Abolitionists," and "treat the coloured people as your equals, as brethren." That is why a historian must move beyond the uncritical repetition of the catalog of self-justifications – "job competition" etcetera – as if that were an adequate explanation of the question.

But there is more involved here than merely setting the record straight. If the rationale was valid for the ante-bellum Irish-Americans and, *mutatis mutandis*, for European-Americans in general in that day, it is no less valid in its familiar modern-day forms: "preservation of property values" in "ethnic" neighborhoods, "quota" phobia the denunciation of affirmative action, etcetera.

Irish-Americans were not the originators of white supremacy; they adapted to and were adopted into an already "white" American social order. A modern Irish historian puts it in terms of later-arriving Catholic Irish imitating the example of earlier-arriving Ulster Protestants. The Catholic Irish who chose to follow the "pre-existing presbyterian logic" in seeking "popular rights," were met by the slaveholders' Jacksonian Democratic Party that "had to promote outsiders and small men."[127] Those "popular rights" of Irish-Americans were given the form of white-skin privileges, the token of their membership in the American "white race."

Then who were the originators, from whom the Jacksonians came; who were the first "bamboozlers"; who were the "drivers"; why did they have to "promote the small men"; why did they "promote" them to the "white race"?

I turn to that subject in Volume Two.

Appendix A

(see Introduction, note 46)

In the 1816 edition of the memoirs of his tour of duty, with the British military expedition to the West Indies in 1795–96, physician George Pinckard advocated the gradual emancipation of slaves and the social promotion of freedmen. Thus by an intermingling of "all shades," he believed, "the colored inhabitants would be made fellow-citizens with the whites and they would aspire to be Englishmen!" (George Pinckard, *Notes on the West Indies*, 2nd edn, 3 vols [London, 1816]; reprinted by Negro Universities Press, Westport, 1970, pp. 2:531–2.)

In 1787 the French Marquis de Chastellux, who had traveled extensively in the United States, proposed a way of blending Anglo- and African-American populations through a plan combining racist exile with sexual oppression. According to this idea, African-American women were to be taken to wife by Anglo-American men, while "a great number" of African-American males were to be "exported" (Marquis de Chastellux, *Travels in North America in the Years 1780, 1781, and 1782*, 2 vols, second edition [London, 1787; New York, 1968], pp. 199–200). Other French writers also suggested intermarriage as a general solution to the United States "race question" (cited in Winthrop D. Jordan, *White over Black* [Chapel Hill, 1968] p. 554 n. 17).

A modern monograph on relations between the French and the Canadian Indians in the sixteenth and seventeenth centuries reports that in 1666 Colbert, Louis XIV's chief minister, "recommended that the French and the Indians should be made one people by means of intermarriage." The author declares that, "Physical differences then were not ... a barrier of major importance to the miscegenation of the two races.... In Acadia the French had been encouraged to intermarry freely with the Micomac by the home government in order that the new land might be peopled without draining France of its inhabitants.... Miscegenation was general in settlement and hinterland ..." (Alfred Goldsworthy Bailey, *The Conflict of European and Algonkian Cultures, 1504–1700; a Study in Canadian Civilization* [Sackville, New

Brunswick, 1937], pp. 107, 110, 112, 113).

An English Royal Instruction was issued in 1719 providing for the grant of fifty acres of land, with a ten-year tax exemption, to any "white" Protestant British subject – woman or man – in Nova Scotia who would marry an Indian native of that province. This order was amended in 1749 to say "British" instead of "Protestant," probably out of consideration for Scots Dissenters; the tax exemption period was increased to twenty years; and a bonus of £10 sterling was added (Leonard Woods Labaree, collator and editor, *Royal Instructions to British Colonial Governors, 1670–1776*, 2 vols [New York and London, 1935], p. 2:470). Jordan takes note of these facts merely to stress what he sees as a difference in the English attitudes toward sexual union with African-Americans and with American Indians. Intermarriage with Indians might have been advocated, he says, but "never with Negroes" (p. 550 n. 61).

In 1815, William H. Crawford, then serving as Secretary of War in James Madison's cabinet, proposed a policy of merger by intermarriage of European-Americans and American Indians (Ulrich Bonnell Phillips, in Eugene D. Genovese, ed., *The Slave Economy of the Old South* [Baton Rouge, 1968], p. 24). Crawford had been a member of the United States Senate and, beginning in 1816, served as Secretary of Treasury for Madison and then eight years under Monroe. He was a nationally prominent figure as leader of the anti-Federalist party and candidate for President in 1816 and 1824.

In connection with their support of the Cherokees' resistance to expulsion from their southern lands, first the Methodist Church and then the Moravian, Baptist, Congregationalist and Presbyterian churches jointly expressed them-selves in favor of intermarriage "as a force for improvement" (Thurman Wilkins, *Cherokee Tragedy: The Story of the Ridge Family and the Decimation of a People* [New York, 1970], p. 219, citing the *Cherokee Phoenix*, a Cherokee-language newspaper, 18 February 1832, quoting the New York *Commercial Advertiser*).

Appendix B

(see Introduction, note 80)

In the mid-seventeenth century, Sir William Petty found the profitability of agricultural enterprise to be dependent upon the proportion of the number of laboring people to the amount of cultivable land, what might have been called the labor/land ratio. Because he believed bond labor, provided it could be secured, was cheaper than wage labor, Petty advocated slavery, and not only for thieves, vagabonds, etcetera, in England and Ireland ("A Treatise of Taxes and Contributions" [1652], in *The Economic Writings of Sir William Petty*, 2 vols, edited by C. H. Russell [1899; New York, 1967], 1:34 and 1:68).

By the early nineteenth century, at a time when slavery had been forced on the defensive, a reversal of the terms of the ratio provided a much-needed apology, which would in time come to be known as the land/labor ratio. Instead of the emphasis on "cheap labor," with its connotation of greed, the emphasis was placed on the other end, "cheap land." In this way the existence of slavery might be removed beyond questions of moral responsibility to the realm of topography, and made to appear not as a matter of choice, but of national necessity. At the same time it provided a parallel theme in "economic law" for the "paradox thesis" of United States democracy, according to which American liberties were necessarily predicated upon the slavery imposed on African-Americans. "Cheap land" was a good, whose potential could only be realized by resort to the evil of slavery.

The author of the land/labor ratio theory (although he did not give it that name) was Edward Gibbon Wakefield (1796–1862). Wakefield elaborated his idea in two books, *England and America, a Comparison of the Social and Political State of Both Nations* (New York, 1834; 1967), especially pp. 202, 206–8, and 212, and *A View of the Art of Colonization in Present Reference to the British Empire, in Letters Between a Statesman and a Colonist* (1849; New York, 1969), see especially pp. 322–9. "Superabundance of land," he argued, "has never led to great prosperity without some kind of slavery" (*England and America*, p. 212). He believed that "[slavery] happens wherever population is scanty in proportion to land" (*Art of Colonization*, p. 304). "The operation of superabundance of land in causing a scarcity of free labour and a desire for slaves" was, for Wakefield, an economic law (ibid., p. 326).

Eminent American historians writing in the late nineteenth and early twentieth centuries also ascribed the establishment of slavery to economic laws. Philip Alexander Bruce stated categorically, "The Institution of slavery sprang up [in Virginia] under the operation of an irresistible economic law" (Bruce, *Economic History of Virginia in the Seventeenth Century*, 2 vols [New York, 1895; 1935], 2:57). Ulrich Bonnell Phillips was in accord with Wakefield: "Land [in the plantation colonies] was plentiful and free," he said, "and men would not work as voluntary wage earners.... Finally the negroes were discovered to be cheap and useful laborers" ("Economics of the Plantation", *South Atlantic Quarterly*, Vol. 2, pp. 231–6 [July 1903]; reprinted in Eugene D. Genovese, *The Slave Economy of the Old South* [Baton Rouge, 1968], p. 118). Thomas J. Wertenbaker used a metaphor devised from natural laws: "the Black Tide," which, he asserted, brought such low labor costs that the free laboring person could not sustain the competitive struggle (*The Planters of Colonial Virginia* [Princeton, 1922], pp. 123–7 and 139–44).

Winthrop D. Jordan asserts that "there were social and economic necessities which called for some sort of bound, controlled labor" (*White over Black* [Chapel Hill, 1968], p. 61). And Edmund S. Morgan argues that the land/labor ratio hypothesis "would seem to be borne out by the developments under way in seventeenth-century Virginia" (*American Slavery/American Freedom* [New York, 1975], pp. 218 n. 11, 296).

Evsey D. Domar, in his 1970 article "The Causes of Slavery or Serfdom: A Hypothesis" (*Journal of Economic History*, Vol. 30, No. 1 [March 1970], pp. 18–32), found that land/labor ratio theorem ideally consistent with the history of bond-labor in Russia, Poland–Lithuania, western Europe and the United States. But when he came to consider the situation in plague-depopulated England in the latter half of the fourteenth century, he confessed with good-humored self-criticism, "my hypothesis is of little value," and he had no good alternate hypothesis to fit that situation (p. 28). The answer is, of course, that the old system of social control had broken down. The English villeins and wage workers of that period took hold of the "land/labor ratio" by the other end and used it to destroy serfdom in England, by walking away from their old obligations and by rebelling under Wat Tyler and John Ball. Contrary to the presumed economic laws and irresistible necessities upon which the land/labor thesis is based, it turned out that English cultivation continued to thrive through the fourteenth century, on the basis of leasehold and copyhold tenantry. (See Volume Two.)

Domar credits his own hypothesis particularly to the very substantial work on the land/labor theory of bond-servitude as presented in Herman J. Nieboer's *Slavery as an Industrial System* (1900; revised edition, The Hague, 1910). It is interesting to note that Nieboer (at least in the 1910 edition), did take into account the nullifying effect of laboring-class rebelliousness on the operation of the land/labor ratio (pp. 410–18).

Appendix C

(see Chapter 1, note 58 and Chapter 2, note 51)

The Portuguese in 1490 were the first to learn this fact of life. They were "disappointed in their hope of penetrating the interior by the way of the great [Congo] river for the states of the Congo resolutely barred their way" (Basil Davidson, *The African Slave Trade* [Boston, 1961], p. 150). Their efforts to penetrate adjacent Angola for purposes of establishing a plantation economy were likewise fruitless, because "their direct control of the country ... seldom extended more than a few miles from the coast" (ibid., p. 152). The Portuguese did establish a sugar plantation colony two hundred miles off the coast of West Africa on the island of São Tomé in 1506. But the bond-laborers were imported from the African continent (supplemented by two thousand Jewish children taken from their parents in Portugal). Despite the natural advantage typically devolving upon a sea-power ruling class in an insular colony, a massive slave revolt occurred in 1586 on São Tomé, which drove out many of the Portuguese owners and marked the beginning of the decline of the plantation economy there (Luis Ivens Ferraz, "The Creole of São Tomé," *African Studies*, 37 [1978]:3–68, cited in Orlando Patterson, *Slavery and Social Death* [New York, 1990], p. 465 nn. 51, 52, and 53).

In 1675 the British launched a crown colony, to be called Senegambia, on the west coast of Africa between the Gambia and Senegal rivers. The project was abandoned in 1783. (J. D. Fage, *A History of West Africa: An Introductory Survey* [Cambridge, 1969], pp. 77–8; Basil Davidson, *Africa in History* [New York, 1974], p. 202 and 202n.)

Since they were not powerful enough to occupy African territory, the Europeans established forts and "factories" (trading posts and detention pens for laborers purchased or otherwise procured). Although Africans entered into trading arrangements with the Europeans, the Africans would attack these alien enclaves with little or no hesitation, whenever they felt policy required it. On numerous occasions – at Kommenda in 1687, Sekondi in 1694, and Anomabu in 1701, for example – European forts fell to such attacks (W. E. F. Ward,

A History of the Gold Coast [London, 1935], p. 87; John and Awsham Churchill, comp., *Churchill's Voyages and Travels* . . ., 6 vols [London, 1732], p. 5:446; Davies, *The Royal African Company* [London, 1957], pp. 263 and 267).

The Dutch (specifically the Dutch East India Company) colony established at the Cape of Good Hope in 1652 represents a partial, technical exception, but one that proves the rule. The Dutch were not intending to establish a plantation colony there, but only a victualing station for ships in the Far East trade. Until the discovery of gold and diamonds in the second half of the nineteenth century, South Africa (the British takeover was begun in 1795 and completed in 1806) was primarily engaged in cattle-raising, an activity not typical of plantation economies, and one poorly suited for slavery, especially on continental territory. Holland in the seventeenth century did not have an exportable labor supply. (See Volume Two, Chapter 1, of this study.) In the first fifty-five years of the colony's existence only some 2,500 European immigrants arrived, and only half of that number were Dutch. Yet they were not able to enslave the Khoisan people native to the territory. The Dutch found that, "It would be impossible to obtain slaves here, for they will not for anything in the world dispose of their children or any of their relatives, having an outstanding love and regard for one another" (*The Early Cape Hottentots described in the writings of Olfert Dapper [1668], William Ten Rhyne [1686], and Johannes Gulielmus de Grevenbroek [1695]*, original text, with translation into English by I. Schapera and B. Farrington [Cape Town, 1933], p. 197, and n. 27). Although there were African slaves in the colony as early as 1658, they, as well as those later recruited, were brought in from the outside, from Angola, Madagascar and Mozambique. And of these early arrivals at least, a goodly portion were destined for transshipment to the Dutch colonies in the East Indies (*Journal of Jan Van Riebeeck*, edited by H. B. Thom, 3 vols [Cape Town and Amsterdam, 1952–58], pp. 2:267–8). European immigration was suspended in 1707, a ban that lasted till the British takeover nearly a century later. And, although a deliberate decision was made in 1717 to use African bond-laborers instead of Europeans, the colony grew very slowly so that in 1795 there were only 17,000 slaves and 16,000 free Europeans in the colony. By contrast, the population of the English colonies on the mainland of North America had grown to 50,000 within less than thirty-five years of the founding of Jamestown; the Anglo-American colony of South Carolina grew from a population of fewer than 400 in 1672 to a quarter of a million in 1790, of whom 107,000 were African-American bond-laborers (Theodore K. Rabb, *Enterprise and Empire: Merchant and Gentry Investment in the Expansion of England, 1575–1630* [Cambridge, Massachusetts, 1967], p. 99; Lewis C. Gray, assisted by Esther Katherine Thompson, *History of Agriculture in the Southern United States to 1860*, 2 vols [Washington, DC, 1932], p. 2:1025).

The Dutch were able to defeat the Khoisan peoples, thousands of whom succumbed to European diseases. Some simply retreated before the Dutch advance, but others were incorporated, though not assimilated, into the colony, generally on a peon-like basis, as low-wage herdsmen and laborers, and as militiamen. Thus the nature and the rate of growth of the colony were such that the decisive battles – with the Xosa and the Zulu peoples – for territory were not fought until late in the nineteenth century, well after the legal abolition of slavery in all British colonies.

Appendix D

(see Chapter 2, notes 42 and 73)

Technical military advantage having swung to the English side through improved organization and increased employment of cannon and firearms, the "plantation" campaigns became the occasion for English war by starvation, exile, extermination and terror against the resisting Irish. Certain events of the Munster campaign, familiar to students of Irish history, clearly indicate that no sense of "white Christian" affinity operated to moderate the cruelty of English racial oppression of the Irish.

The plantation of Munster was prepared by the repression of two (Desmond) rebellions. The first began in 1569, the year that Queen Elizabeth was excommunicated by the Catholic Church; it was ended in 1574. The second began in 1578 and lasted until 1583. In these wars Anglo-Irish and native Irish joined to oppose the English. During the first of these rebellions Humphrey Gilbert, the English commander, made it his aim not merely to subdue his Irish enemies, but to employ such terror in the process as would ever after deter the very thought of resistance to English rule; to spare neither sex nor age among his Irish foes, so that thenceforward the very name of "Englishman" should be more feared than the actual presence of a hundred Englishmen had been before. (Here I am following Professor Nicholas P. Canny's account [*The Elizabethan Conquest of Ireland* (New York, 1978), pp. 121–2]. Canny cites Great Britain Public Record Office, State Papers Office, n.s., *State Papers, Ireland, Elizabeth to George III*, 1:79, 1558–1580, p. 63/29/70.)

To this end, Gilbert instituted the following practice: at the close of each day's work, the severed heads of the Irish slain were arranged in two inward-facing rows to form a lane leading to the tent where Gilbert sat to receive the abject surrender of his enemies. In passing, the Irish were thus forced to see "the heads of their dead fathers, brothers, children, kinsfolke and friends lie on the ground before their faces." (From the eyewitness account of Thomas Churchyard, an English correspondent, in *Churchyard's Choise, a General Rehearsal of Warres* [London, 1578], cited by Canny, pp. 121–2; the quotation as given here modernizes the spelling.) In recognition of his services, Gilbert was shortly thereafter knighted by Queen Elizabeth and made Governor of Munster.

Following the second Desmond War, the man who served as secretary to the Lord Deputy propounded a historical theory of colonial war in Ireland: "Great force must be the instrument," he wrote, "but famine must be the meane [the principal element] for till Ireland can be famished it can not be subdued" (*A Breife Note of Ireland* [1598–99], in *The Works of Edmund Spenser, a Variorum Edition* [Baltimore, 1949], 10 vols Vol. 9 [special editor Rudolf Gottfried], p. 244).

Indeed, fire and sword were employed with such ferocity that, as the chronicles tell, "From Dingle [on the Kerry coast] to the Rock of Cashel [in Tipperary, a hundred miles distant], not the lowing of a cow was that year to be heard" (from the Gaelic Irish account in *The Annals of the Four Masters*, cited in William Edward Hartpole Lecky, *A History of Ireland in the Eighteenth Century*, 5 vols [London, 1893], 1:7). In just one year of such warfare, 1582, in that one Irish province of Munster more than 30,000 men, women, and children starved to death (*Pacata Hibernia* [1820 edition], p. 645, cited in Lecky, 1:7; Robert Dunlop, "The Plantation of Munster, 1584–89," *English Historical Review*, 3:269).

Appendix E

(see Chapter 2, note 58)

Domestically the basis had been laid by the expropriation of the copyhold peasantry (see Volume Two) By the early seventeenth century, English agriculture had been transformed from primarily an activity of independent peasantry to that of wage labor and capital. Even the loss of the trans-Channel markets for raw English wool, a result of the Spanish occupation of the Netherlands, was turned to advantage. With the help of Protestant refugee craftsmen from Flanders, England became an exporter of wool cloth, finished as well as unfinished, rather than raw wool. English cloth production was a capitalist operation from the outset, with cottage weavers working up yarn and thread supplied by capitalist "clothiers" (John Ulrich Nef, *The Conquest of the Material World* [Chicago, 1964], pp. 96–9). "The history of the change from medieval to modern England," writes Trevelyan, "might well be written in the form of a social history of the cloth trade" (G. M. Trevelyan, *A Shortened History of England* [Harmondsworth, 1942], p. 206).

The essential element in this social transformation was the accumulation of capital: primitive accumulation by expropriation, followed by normal reproductive accumulation. Implicit in the process were the principles of free trade in commodities and the free flow of capital according to the prospective rate of profit. Under the stimulus of these principles, England by the end of the sixteenth century was well advanced in what Nef has called the "Early Industrial Revolution" (Nef: see particularly the two essays: "The Progress of Technology and Growth of Large-scale Industry in Great Britain, 1540–1640," pp. 121–43, and "A Comparison of Industrial Growth in France and England from 1540 to 1640," pp. 144–212; Nef defines "Early Industrial Revolution" at pp. 220–21). Of England Nef observes:

During the last sixty years of the sixteenth century the first paper and gunpowder mills, the first cannon foundries, the first alum and copperas factories, the first sugar refineries, and the first considerable saltpetre works were all introduced into the country from abroad. The discovery of calamine, the ore of zinc, in Somerset and elsewhere, together with the first really effective attempts to mine copper ore, made possible the establishment of brassmaking and battery works for hammering brass and copper ingots into plates. (ibid., pp. 123–4)

(At this point Professor Nef supplies the names of two bibliographies, and lists a dozen particular indispensable works for the study of this early industrialization. To these must be added Nef's own *Rise of the British Coal Industry*.)

In addition to the advances in cloth-finishing, there were significant improvements in deep-mining of coal, iron-making, and shipbuilding, and in the production of glass, brass, salt, gunpowder, alum, saltpetre, dyes, and printed materials. New industries using water-powered machinery in factories began to turn out paper, saltpetre, and refined sugar. (Nef, *Conquest of the Material World*; see the particular items listed under "England" in the index.) England had been "something of a backwater" before 1540; but thereafter it forged rapidly to the fore (ibid., pp. 142–3).

Sir Francis Bacon, vaunting the united productive potential of England and Scotland as the promise of enrichment of the kingdom, made reference to an ancient saying: "Iron commands gold" (letter to Sir George Villiers – later Duke of Buckingham – 5 July 1616, in Spedding, ed., *The Letters and Life of Francis Bacon*, 7:175).

The link between the mundane and the legendary in all this, between the tradesmen and the crew of the *Golden Hind*, between the clothiers and the victors in the Channel, was supplied by the emergence in England of the joint-stock company for mobilizing capital for overseas commercial ventures and for colonization in Ireland and America. Commerce led the way, if for no other reason than that it promised quicker and more certain profits (Theodore K. Rabb, *Enterprise and Empire* [Cambridge, Mass., 1967], p. 38).

Appendix F

(see Chapter 2, note 77)

Moryson's *Itinerary* details more than a score of particular instances of the ruthless application of this starvation strategy.

In August of 1600, Mountjoy confiscated cattle, horses and sheep in Leix. With the example of their officers before them, initially hesitant soldiers proceeded to "cut downe with their swords all the Rebels corne to the value of ten thousand pounds and upward [about 80,000 bushels], the onely meanes by which they were to live." Sir Oliver Lambert took 1,000 cows, 500 horses, and "great store of sheep." Sir Arthur Savage "spoiled the Countrey and took great prey" (Fynes Moryson, *An Itinerary, Containing His Ten Yeeres Travell through the Twelve Dominions of Germany, Bohmerland, Sweitzerland, Netherland, Denmarke and Ireland*, 4 vols [London, 1617; Glasgow, 1907], 2:329–30). The English marveled that the land was so well cultivated and orderly fenced by such "barbarous inhabitants."

For a month, beginning at Christmas 1600, Mountjoy spoiled and ransacked what came to be County Wicklow, "swept away the most part of their cattle and goods, burnt all their Corne, and almost all their Houses, leaving little or nothing to relieve them" (ibid., 2:250). In February, Mountjoy crossed and recrossed the counties of Meath and Westmeath; before he moved on, "the greatest part lay waste." He devoted attention not only to planted fields, but sent his men into the woods "to fetch out the rebels corne, and to burn the houses, and such things for their reliefe." On 17 March, St Patrick's Day, Moryson says, "we burnt the houses and spoiled the goods of the inhabitants" in the northern part of County Meath (ibid., 2:355–6, 2:358).

In orders issued to the commander of the northern wing of a north–south pincers invasion of Tyrone, the Ulster stronghold, Mountjoy said "he should burn all the dwellings, and destroy the corne on the ground, which might be done by incamping upon it, and cutting it downe with swords, and other waies, [Mountjoy] holding it best they should spoile all the corne, except that which he could gather." Mountjoy made it a particular point that they should not be dissuaded from this course by the importunings of those of the Irish who submitted to the English (ibid., 2:399).

In a letter written on 19 July 1601, Mountjoy informed the English government that "he had destroied the rebels Corne about Armagh (whereof he found great abundance), and would destroy the rest, this course causing famine, being the only way to reduce or root out the Rebels." On the next day his forces "cut a field of Corne lying on the skirt of the Woods" near the site of the rebuilding of a fort on the Blackwater river. The next day after that, they "cut all the Corne by the Bogge and Wood side near our Fort, except that which our men had power to reape." Then, on 23 July, they marched "two little miles" out and "camped and cut downe the Corne on every side." Four days later three regiments from the same base cut down the corn, not only in open fields but in the woods as well, "burning many houses in the skirts of the woods," as they went. Six days later, Sir Henry Davers, "with three hundred foote, and fortie horse, was sent into a Fastnesse to burne some twentie faire timber houses" (ibid., 2:412, 2:413–14, 2:415–16).

So effectively was their work done that the English army itself was in short supply when victuals were slow to arrive from England. Already in June 1601, Mountjoy foresaw the danger. "Our only way to ruine the rebels," he said to the lords in England, "must be to make all possible wast[e] of the meanes for life," and therefore it was vital that for the future the shipments of victuals arrive in due time. By December he was reporting that they could not even feed their horses, and he requested the prompt shipment of 2,000 quarters of oats, without which the horses would starve. Three weeks later Mountjoy renewed his appeal, noting that "the whole Countrie is so harried and wasted, that it cannot yielde any reliefe." In May 1602, Mountjoy combined his report of wasting the countryside in Wicklow and Meath with the reminder that the English army could find themselves neither "victuals or any other necessary provision, but what we bring with us." In September a promised supply of victuals was more than a month past due, although the northern garrisons for whom they were intended were dependent upon them, particularly for bread and salt (ibid., 2:394; 3:67, 3:85, 3:157–8, 3:210–11).

Fynes Moryson was well situated to observe this Operation Starvation (as it would be called today). Moryson was Mountjoy's chief secretary and he had a brother, Sir Richard, who was a colonel in the field with the English forces. A decade after the event, drawing upon the eyewitness accounts provided by his brother, and Sir Arthur Chichester, as well as a number of other English commanders and officers; and the testimony of "many honest [English] Gentlemen" who were colonists in Ireland, Moryson described at length the "unspeakable extremities" to which Irish victims of the English war by famine had been driven in order to survive. But, he wrote,

[N]o spectacle was more frequent in the Ditches of Townes, and especially in the wasted Countries, than to see multitudes of these poore people dead with their mouthes all coloured greene by eating nettles, docks, and all things they could rend up above ground. (Ibid., 3: 281–3)

Appendix G

(see Chapter 2, note 108)

Professor J. A. Barnes, of Australia National University, has provided an illuminating analysis of the social control policies of the Western colonizing powers ("Indigenous Politics and Colonial Administration with Special Reference to Australia," *Comparative Studies in Society and History*, 2:133–49 [January 1960]). Centering his study on British colonial administration in Africa, Australia and Australian New Guinea, Barnes discerns a pattern of essential principles employed for effecting social control of conquered tribal peoples. "The distribution of authority characteristic of statelessness," he writes, "is incompatible with the hierarchical administration and judicial system" required by the colonizing power (p. 145). Therefore, in stateless societies, the colonizers more or less arbitrarily bring into being an intermediate stratum, since "no system of administration seems to be able to operate entirely without this buffer of local employees" (p. 143). Alternately, he says, some of the indigenous people of stateless societies are incorporated (without being assimilated) directly into the colony as "peons." Still others flee, "so long as the deserts are large enough and contain some wildlife and water, or the jungles are deep enough [so that] the old way of life can be continued" (p. 138).

On the other hand, Professor Barnes says, "where indigenous peoples live in a well ordered state with powerful centralized authority, it is economical for the conqueror to govern through the native rule." Barnes quotes a letter written from Uganda by an English colonial administrator in 1887, explaining this policy of indirect rule. Barnes notes, however, that this principle for ruling countries with pre-existing state systems did not originate with the English, but "goes back to the Romans, or even earlier" (p. 140).

Barnes's passing references to the European colonizers in the Americas conform to his general thesis. Although he makes no mention of the English colonization of Ireland, his general principles seem no less applicable to that case.

In Brazil, where the Portuguese encountered a stateless society, the course of relations was quite different. Due to a combination of resistance, including rebellion, by the indigenous population and their decimation by European diseases, early attempts to enslave them for plantation labor failed, and the Portuguese began to turn to African labor supplies. The Indians for the most part found safe refuge by retreat to the jungles of the interior (Charles R. Boxer, *The Portuguese Seaborne Empire* [New York, 1969], p. 88; Charles Edward Chapman, *Colonial Hispanic America: A History* [New York, 1933], pp. 77–80; Barnes, pp. 77–80; Marvin Harris, *Patterns of Race in the Americas* [New York, 1964], pp. 12–13).

E. G. Bourne traces statistically the extinction of the stateless Carib population of Hispaniola, from 300,000 in 1492 (when, as Columbus recorded it, the Spanish explorers were courteously greeted by the people there), to 60,000 in 1508, to 14,000 in 1514, and finally to 500, virtual extinction, in 1548 (E. G. Bourne, *Spain in America: 1450–1580* [New York, 1904], pp. 211–14).

"In the newly annexed Island of St Vincent," writes the English military historian Fortescue, "there was a fierce race of men known as the Black Caribs, indigenous to the Archipelago, and of negro slaves who had escaped, or, as tradition goes, had been wrecked on the coast and had taken refuge in the forest. . . . They claimed two-thirds of the best and richest land in the island . . . and were a great obstacle to settlement" (W. J. Fortescue, *A History of the British Army* [London, 1899–1930], 3:41–2). The Black Caribs rose in revolt against the British in 1795, but were defeated in 1796. Considered intractable for British social control purposes, the majority of the Black Caribs were deported from their homeland.

In an instance that was not a part of the Western colonizing activity, the Incas of pre-Columbian times were able to extend their empire over a territory two thousand miles long by the conquest of other state-organized societies. But they failed when they attempted to take over the stateless peoples in the Amazon basin (Harris, pp. 9–10).

Appendix H

(see Chapter 3, note 8)

The subject of Scottish slavery is generally ignored by historians of the Anglo-American colonies, although it is a phenomenon contemporaneous with colonial bond-servitude and closely kin in form. Abbot E. Smith does not allude to it in his *Colonists in Bondage* (Chapel Hill, 1947; New York, 1971). Winthrop D. Jordan, in his *White over Black* (Chapel Hill, 1968), mentions the relatively favored situation of Scots bond-laborers in the continental colonies, but he ignores the contrasting situation of bondmen in Scotland, and its possible implications for his thesis regarding the origin of racial slavery.

The Scots Poor Law was amended in 1597 to make vagrants and their children – together comprising one-tenth of the population of Scotland – subject to court sentence to lifetime servitude to private employers. In 1605, any member of the employing class was legally authorized to take such vagrant persons before the authorities, have them officially declared vagrants, and "set his burning iron upon thame and retaene thame as slaves"; this slavery was for life. The following year, the Scottish Parliament by law forbade any coal miner or salt-pan worker to leave his or her job without written consent of the employer. The same law authorized the owners of coal mines and salt works themselves to seize unemployed men, whether vagrants or not, and, without further legal formality, to force them to work for the owner as slaves. In 1607, owners of metal ore mines were granted the same powers. In 1617, children of poor parents – whether they were orphans or not – were made subject to serve masters until they were thirty years of age. It was the practical effect of this law that made the slavery of the coal miners not only perpetual, but hereditary. The law provided perpetual servitude for the adult miner after he or she had served the master for one year. The children of miners were customarily, and practically inescapably, bound to service by their parents through the acceptance from the master of a payment of "earnest money," or "arle," as it was sometimes called, usually at the christening of the child. The period of service being thirty years, the young miners, male and female, could not escape the system, since their common-law option to leave during their twenty-first year was superseded by the original thirty-year term into which their parents had sold them.

In 1649 Scottish law gave any British subject of Charles II the right to capture a vagrant and sell him or use him in servitude of unlimited duration, the subject's only obligation being to provide the slave with food and clothing. "It is impossible," says the author of the *Edinburgh Review* account, "to read this law in any other sense than as establishing a slave trade in Scotch vagrants, and throwing it open to the male inhabitants of the empire" ("Slavery in Modern Scotland," p. 131). In 1661 the Scottish Parliament extended slavery to workers around the mines, not just the miners themselves. In 1685 the Edinburgh authorities decreed lifetime servitude in manufacturing work for vagrants and unemployed persons over the age of five years. Scotland's criminals were at the beginning of the eighteenth century subject to be sentenced to slavery for life. There were various forms of the status of slavery in Scotland. Temporary slavery might mean eleven, fifteen or twenty-five years, but "slavery for life [was] commonest of all" (ibid., p. 140).

In 1698, the influential Scottish statesman Andrew Fletcher of Saltoun (1655–1716) criticized the notion that Christians could not be enslaved, and proposed that two hundred thousand Scottish beggars be made slaves for life to men of means (A. Fletcher, *The Political Works of Andrew Fletcher, Esq., of Saltoun* [Glasgow, 1749], "Second Discourse Concerning the Affairs of Scotland," [1698], pp. 87–8, 100). Whether or not Fletcher's advocacy of slavery as a cure for vagrancy, etcetera, received the "obloquy and disdain" that he anticipated, it seems not to have been given its due as a counter-argument to the land/labor-ratio theory of slavery as propounded by Wakefield and his disciples (see Appendix B).

The Scottish Habeas Corpus Act of 1701 expressly excluded coal-bearers and salters from its protection. Their slavery was reconfirmed in law by the Scottish Parliament in 1747, forty years after the union with England. This was "the last legal sanction given in the United Kingdom to the slavery of native Britons" ("Slavery in Modern Scotland," p. 142).

The last of the Scottish colliery slaves was finally freed in 1799, under the gradual emancipation act passed by the British Parliament in 1775 (*Statutes at Large from the thirteenth year of the Reign of King George the Third, to the Sixteenth Year of the Reign of George the Third* [London, 1776], 12:296–8 [15 Geo. III c. 28]). Although the preamble of this act deplored the immorality of holding "Colliers and Coal-bearers and Salters ... in a state of Slavery," the fact is that, as the *Edinburgh Review* put it, "They were emancipated in the same great cause they were enslaved in – the cause of low wages" ("Slavery in Modern Scotland," p. 144). With the coming of the Industrial Revolution, opportunities in free-labor jobs were opening up. As a result, in the words of the act, "many new-discovered Coals remain unwrought, and many not sufficiently wrought, nor are there a sufficient number of Salters for the Salt-works, to the great loss of the Owners and Disadvantage to the Publick" (15 Geo c. 28).

The moral factor derived strength, however, from the relation between the opposition to the slavery of Scottish people and the slavery of laborers of African descent in the British colonies. In 1769 a Scotsman named Steuart returned to Scotland from Virginia. He brought with him the African-American James Somerset, whom he claimed as his property. In 1771, Somerset emancipated himself by removing himself from Steuart's control. However, after a lapse of about two months, Steuart was able to seize Somerset and put him captive on board a ship, intending to take him to Jamaica to be sold as a slave. Somerset sued in court for a writ of habeas corpus, maintaining that he could not legally be held a slave under English law. The Chief Justice of the King's bench, Lord Mansfield, heard the case and rendered his historic decision:

> The state of slavery is of such a nature, that it is incapable of being introduced on any reasons, moral or political, but only by positive law.... It is so odious, that nothing can be suffered to support it but positive law. (Barnett Hollander, *Slavery in America* [New York, 1964], p. 2; A. Leon Higginbotham, *In the Matter of Color, Race and the American Legal Process, the Colonial Period* [New York, 1978], pp. 333, 353)

Somerset was freed, and in consequence of the same decision, the 14,000 to 15,000 Anglo-Africans then held as slaves in England won the right to be free. English abolitionists had been instrumental in carrying this case through to victory. Immediately thereafter the English abolitionist leader Granville Sharp (1735–1815) "was approached on the subject of a public agitation for the abolition of collier slavery in Scotland, and he would have probably undertaken the task had not some of the coalmasters themselves engaged to bring about the emancipation of their labourers" ("Slavery in Modern Scotland," p. 144). It is interesting to note that while Scottish colliers and salters were still enslaved, the Glasgow Court of Sessions in 1775 granted freedom to Joseph Knight, who had been brought from the West Indies by his owner, John Weddeburn, Esq. For all that he might have been a slave in the West Indies, said the Court, he had become a free man by the mere fact of being in Scotland (Chambers, 3:453–4).

It thus seems that the campaign for the liberation of persons of African ancestry in America and England supplied much of the moral force for the ending of the ancient slavery of the Scots colliers and salt-pan workers.

Appendix I

(see Chapter 3, note 46)

The English money wage for common labor in 1776 was about 18*d.* per day, on an average, winter and summer. The corresponding wage in Ireland was 6½*d.*, but the cost of necessaries was about half what it was in England (Arthur Young, *Tour in Ireland* [London, 1780], book 2, p. 28; W. E. H. Lecky, *History of England in the Eighteenth Century*, 8 vols [New York, 1878–90], 2:323, n. 3). In nominal money terms, therefore, the employers could hire Irish workers for 64 percent less than they paid English workers. However, in seeking the lowest possible limit of costs, the employers would have had to take into account the real wage level, which was only 28 percent less in Ireland than in England.

In continental Anglo-America near the end of the eighteenth century, the labor of lifetime bond-laborers hired out by the year cost £8 to £12, which was 80 percent of the annual outlay for wage labor (£10 to £15) doing the same sort of work (Lewis C. Gray, *History of Agriculture in the Southern United States to 1860*, 2 vols [Washington 1932; 1956], 1:468–9). Thus the employer's cost was reduced by 20 percent by hiring bond-labor instead of wage-labor. This was still less than the England/Ireland real wage differential. The fact that in continental Anglo-America in the eighteenth century real wages ranged from 30 percent to 100 percent above those in England (Richard B. Morris, *Encyclopedia of American History* [New York, 1982], p. 760) further strengthens the implication that labor costs in Ireland were at a level such that bond-labor would not have reduced.

Information provided by Arthur Young, however, shows that the actual annual money cost of most Irish common agricultural labor was only about half that which would have been represented by a wage of 6½*d.* per day (Young, Vol. 2, p. 28; in the remainder of this appendix I have relied on the same work, mainly Vol. 2, pp. 19–23).

At the conclusion of four years (1776–80) of observing Irish agricultural economics and social life, Young made certain generalizations concerning

"The Labouring Poor," particularly the cottiers, who constituted the majority of the Irish laboring people. The cottier, with a wife and typically five children, lived mainly by renting a plot of ground, usually, but not always, provided with a single-room shack ("cabbin and garden"); and by wages earned by working for the landlord. Rental on the land was £5 10s. 2d. per Irish acre (equal to about 1.6 English acres). The average cottier paid £1 13s. 10d. ground rent, the indicated average holding thus being less than one-third of an Irish acre, less than half an English acre. For the graze of one cow, the cottier paid £1 11s. 3d., the total thus costing the cottier £3 5s. 1d.

Working for the landlord 250 days a year at $6\frac{1}{2}d.$, the cottier could earn £6 7s. 1d. per year. The staple diet of the cottier family was the potatoes they raised in the family's plot (the man being able to work at it less than one day a week [County Derry; Young, Vol. 1, p. 364]). These, together with the buttermilk left after the butter-fat products had been reserved for paying the landlord his rent, and a bit of oatmeal when the potatoes were gone, was their food.

Such a family needed sixty 280-pound barrels of potatoes per year. The average output of potatoes on one acre was 82 barrels per year (one barrel containing four English bushels). Obviously, one-third of an acre could provide less than half the potato requirement of the cottier family.

Wages were paid every six months, in some cases, and at the end of the year in others. The £3 2s. difference between what the landlord collected from the cottier in rent and the wages he paid to the cottier represents the annual labor cost per cottier. At 2s. 8d. per barrel, the difference between the price of sixty 280-pound barrels of potatoes and the 28-barrel yield of the cottier's $\frac{1}{3}$-acre "garden," amounting to £4 5s. 4d., was supplied perhaps by wages earned by other members of the family at fractional rates, by keeping another cow, a pig, some poultry, and by going hungry to the point of starvation in bad crop years. (With regard to the calculated function of beggary, see Lecky, 2:251, n. 1.)

Even worse off were the *spalpeens*, the landless laborers, living on casual cash-wage employment, at annual wages of £3 to £4 for men, and £1 2s. for "maids" (the *spalpeen* figures were those for the Castle Lloyd locality).

Appendix J

(see Chapter 4, note 107)

For reasons more than just that I am a foreigner, I am deterred from expressing a personal judgment about Daniel O'Connell's views regarding revolutionary violence in Ireland. When he sought to apply to Ireland the principle that "[N]o human revolution is worth the effusion of one single drop of human blood" (W. E. H. Lecky, *Leaders of Public Opinion in Ireland*, 2 vols [London, 1903], pp. 263–4), he was expressing the attitude of the Irish bourgeoisie, lay and clerical, in general. O'Connell was a uniquely powerful leader; perhaps no other individual could have brought matters to such a climax as that of Clontarf. But if there had been another leader of the bourgeois class, it is certain that their decision would have been the same. The behavior of the Irish bourgeoisie in this situation was typical of that of their class confronted with similar crises in the nineteenth century. We, as citizens of the twentieth century, cannot easily dismiss O'Connell's assertion that "Human blood is no cement for the temple of human liberty" (ibid.). So much has been done in the twentieth century in the name of proletarian liberation that has only gone to show that we are still unprepared for the role that Marx prescribed, that we cannot disregard O'Connell's dictum as if it were a self-evident fallacy.

Still, there are questions that an American student may ask. If he had lived so long, would O'Connell, the unwavering enemy of African-American slavery, have rejected the stand ultimately taken by Lincoln that a righteous God could hold that "every drop of blood drawn with the lash, shall be paid by another drawn with the sword" (Second Inaugural Address, 4 March 1865)? To follow Lincoln a bit further: O'Connell's aversion to embracing an armed Irish peasantry was no greater than was Lincoln's aversion in 1860 to freeing, arming, and enlisting African-American bond-laborers to fight the white rebels. He could have had a peace that would have saved hundreds of thousands of lives. If Lincoln had done so, would he have received the same approbation that many historians have bestowed upon O'Connell for his Clontarf decision, even though chattel bond-servitude would thereby have been prolonged indefinitely?

We can ask, as others have before us, was it in a pacifist spirit that O'Connell sent his own son Morgan to fight under Bolívar in South America? Was it, then, aversion to bloodshed, or rather the imminent involvement of the propertyless masses that he in the end could not embrace? (This despite his repeated oratorical invocations of Byron: "Hereditary bondsmen! know ye not,/ Who would be free, themselves must strike the blow" [*Childe Harold*, canto 2, stanza 76].) Was he tacitly distinguishing a war between Spanish colonists and the Spanish government, over issues in which the mass of the super-exploited Indios were not involved, from the situation in Ireland in which the laboring classes would have been involved as the main force in any revolution? When, speaking at a "monster meeting" at Mallow on 11 June 1843, O'Connell said, "The time is come when we must be doing … you may soon have the alternative to live as slaves or die as freemen," did he think only to create a propitious attitude in Westminster, and not to suggest that the thousands of his listening fellow countrymen suit actions to the words? (The text of O'Connell's Mallow speech as reported in the Young Ireland *Nation* [Dublin] 17 June 1843, cited in Kevin P. Nolan, *The Politics of Repeal* [London, 1965], p. 48).

Historians seem to believe that the alternative was a bloody civil war which the British would have won quickly and decisively by slaughtering tens of thousands of poorly armed and untrained Irish peasants and laborers. However awkward and however politically damaging to O'Connell, it is said, surrender was the only sensible course in the face of the British government's monstrous provocation (see, for example, R. F. Foster, *Modern Ireland* [New York, 1989], p. 313). Of course, the Young Irelanders rejected this rationale, and split with O'Connell over the issue, a stand not generally supported.

Yet, even if the criticism of Young Ireland is correct in this regard, there is another aspect of the matter that seems to deserve more consideration than it has had. Two years after Clontarf, the Great Famine began. Within five years the population of Ireland had been reduced by one-fourth; of that two million gone, *one million had died of starvation* or starvation-induced disease. This catastrophe must be attributed not only to the history of English landlordism in Ireland, but to the British government's response to the Famine by deliberate malign neglect more destructive of life than even Mountjoy's strategy of conquest by famine in the closing years of the Tyrone War. If the British government had got its war and won it in 1843, might it not thereby have so seriously damaged its moral position in the world that it could not, as it actually did, sacrifice *hundreds* of thousands of Irish men, women and children on the altar of *laissez-faire*, or as it is said today, "free market forces" operating without "government interference"? If so, would the self-sacrifice of *tens of* thousands fighting for equality have been in vain? Is such quantification of quick and dead unspeakable? Did not O'Connell himself set the example?

"A living friend," he estimated, "is worth a churchyard full of dead ones" (Robert Dunlop, *Daniel O'Connell* [New York, 1900], p. 353; O'Connell was riposting the Horatian slogan, "Sweet it is to die for one's country"). O'Connell died during the Famine, in 1847. Did he at the end ever speculate along such lines? May not we ourselves do so, without forgetting lessons our own century has taught us?

Appendix K

(see Chapter 7, note 62)

The Slave

by Leander (John Hughes)

Hard is the lot of him who's doomed to toil,
Without one slender hope to soothe his pain,
Whose sweat and labor are a master's spoil,
Whose sad reward a master's proud disdain.
Wipe from thy code, Columbia, wipe the stain;
Be free as air, but yet be kind as free,
And chase foul bondage from thy Southern plain:
If such the right of man, by heaven's decree,
Oh, then let Afric's sons feel what it is – to be.

In hot meridian day of late, I hied
To court the covert of a spreading oak;
I sat beneath – and thence in pity eyed
The negro moiling at his daily yoke.
And still he plied the dull, desponding stroke,
Beneath the scorching of the noon-tide sun,
Sullen and silent, or if words he spoke,
I could not hear; but ever and anon
I heard the lash – which even brutes are fain to shun.

The ruthless driver soon was forced to yield:
Though strong of sinew, still he could not bear

The tyrant labors of the parching field,
But sought the shade to breathe a cooler air;
Whilst, less inhuman, but alas! less fair,
The drudging slave began to pour his song
Upon the heedless wind, and breathe despair.
He sung the negroes' foul, unpitied wrong,
Sad and ironical – late he felt the thong.

"Hail Columbia, happy land!
Where freedom waves her golden wand,
    Where equal justice reigns
But ah! Columbia great and free
Has not a boon for mine and me,
    But slavery and chains.
Oh! once I had a soothing joy,
    The hope of other years,
That free Columbia would destroy
    The source of these my tears.
        But pining, declining,
    I still drag to the grave,
        Doomed to sigh till I die,
    Free Columbia's slave.

"Hail Columbia, happy land!
Whose sons, a free, a heaven-born band,
    Will free us soon with blows.
If freeman's freest blood were shed,
Could it be purer or more red
    Than this of mine that flows?
'Twas freeman's whip that brought this gore
    That trickles down my breast;
But soon my bleeding will be o'er,
    My grave will yield me rest.
        I will, then, until then
    Abide my hard and hopeless lot;
        But there's room in the tomb
    For freemen too to rot.

"Hail Columbia, happy land!
Where those who show a fairer hand
    Enjoy sweet liberty.
But from the moment of my birth,
I slave along Columbia's earth,

Nor freedom smiles on me.
Long have I pined through years of woe
   Adown life's bleeding track,
And still my tears, my blood must flow,
   Because my hand is black.
     Still boiling, still toiling,
   Beneath the burning heats of noon,
     I, poor slave, court the grave;
   O Columbia, grant the boon!

"Hail, Columbia, hap–"

He ceased the song, and heaved another sigh
In silent, cheerless mood – for ah! the while
The driver's hated steps were drawing nigh;
Nor song of woe, nor words dare then beguile
The goaded sorrows of a thing so vile.
Yet such the plaintive song that caught my ear,
That cold humanity may blush to smile,
When dove-eyed mercy softly leans to hear,
And Pity turns aside to shed another tear.

Appendix L

(see Chapter 7, note 80)

Address from the people of Ireland to their Countrymen and Countrywomen in America[1]

You are at a great distance from your native land! A wide expanse of water separates you from the beloved country of your birth – from us and from the kindred whom you love, and who love you, and pray for your happiness and prosperity in the land of your adoption.

We regard America with feelings of admiration; we do not look upon her as a strange land, nor upon her people as aliens from our affections. The power of steam has brought us nearer together; it will increase the intercourse between us, so that the character of the Irish people and of the American people must in future be acted upon by the feelings and disposition of each.

The object of this address is to call your attention to the subject of slavery in America – that foul blot upon the noble institutions and the fair fame of your adopted country. But for this one stain, America would, indeed, be a land worthy your adoption; but she will never be the glorious country that her free constitution designed her to be, so long as her soil is polluted by the footprint of a single slave.

Slavery is the most tremendous invasion of the natural, inalienable rights of man, and of some of the noblest gifts of God, "life, liberty, and the pursuit of happiness." What a spectacle does America present to the people of the earth! A land of professing christian republicans, uniting their energies for the oppression and degradation of three millions of innocent human beings, the children of one common Father, who suffer the most grievous wrongs and the utmost degradation for no crime of their ancestors or of their own!

---

1. The Address as published in the *Liberator*, 25 March 1842.

Slavery is a sin against God and man. All who are not for it, must be against it. None can be neutral! We entreat you to take the part of justice, religion and liberty.

It is in vain that American citizens attempt to conceal their own and their country's degradation under this withering curse. America is cursed by slavery! We call upon you to unite with the abolitionists, and never to cease your efforts, until perfect liberty be granted to every one of her inhabitants, the black man as well as the white man. We are all children of the same gracious God; all equally entitled to life, liberty, and the pursuit of happiness.

We are told that you possess great power, both moral and political, in America. We entreat you to exercise that power and that influence for the sake of humanity.

You will not witness the horrors of slavery in all the states of America. Thirteen of them are free, and thirteen are slave states. But in all, the pro-slavery feeling, though rapidly decreasing, is still strong. Do not unite with it: on the contrary, oppose it with all the peaceful means in your power. Join with the abolitionists everywhere. They are the only consistent advocates of liberty. Tell every man, that you do not understand liberty for the white man, and slavery for the black man: that you are for liberty for all, of every color, creed, and country.

The American citizen proudly points to the national declaration of independence, which declares that "All mankind are born free and equal, and are alike entitled to life, liberty, and the pursuit of happiness." Aid him to carry out this noble declaration, by obtaining freedom for the slave.

Irishmen and Irishwomen! treat the colored people as your equals, as brethren. By all your memories of Ireland, continue to love liberty – hate slavery – cling by the abolitionists – and in America, *you will do honor to the name of Ireland.*

Chronological Finding Aid
for Users of this Volume

Below are listed the main Irish historical periods as defined by the Irish Royal Academy, together with sub-periods as noted and characterized in this work.

Medieval Ireland (1169–1534)

1169–ca. 1216   Papal-sponsored English "overlordship"
ca. 1217–1315   English option for racial oppression
ca. 1315–1534   Scots invasion; defeat of racial oppression; eclipse of English power

Early Modern Ireland (1534–1691)

1534–1603   Breaking of tribal power; English opt for religio-racial oppression
1594–1603   Tyrone War
1603–1641   English encroachment by plantation, most notably in Ulster
1641–1652   Irish are involved in the War of the Three Kingdoms, climaxed by the Cromwellian conquest
1652–1656   Irish Catholics are subjected to mass exile, expropriation and "transplantation"
1660–1689   Stuart Restoration; Irish hopes are revived
1689–1691   Jacobite War; defeat of the Irish Catholic cause by Protestant Dutch-English King William III

Eighteenth-century Ireland (1691–1800)

1691–1700   Williamite expropriations of Catholic lands
1704–1829   Penal Law system of religio-racial oppression of the Catholic Irish
 ca. 1760   Mitigation of the Penal Law system is begun
1782–1798   Anglo-Irish Protestant independence movement; United Irishmen rebellion is defeated
1792–1800   British overtures to Irish Catholics to counter Anglo-Irish radicalism

Ireland Under the Union (I) (1801–1870)

     1801   Union of Great Britain and Ireland Act
ca. 1811–1829   Catholic Emancipation struggle
1829–1845   Catholic Emancipation permits Catholics in the British Parliament, but restricts suffrage. A period of adjustment: tithe war; defeat of Repeal; Catholic bourgeoisie is incorporated into the British colonial social control system, racial oppression is replaced by national oppression (except in Ulster)
1845–1850   The Great Famine; depopulation by starvation, disease, and mass emigration
     1870   First fruits of the War for the Land, Gladstone's first Land Reform Bill

Notes

Introduction

1. The term "Peculiar Institution" was a euphemism for the socio-economic system based on the lifetime, hereditary, chattel bond-servitude of African-Americans, which existed in the continental Anglo-American colonies and in the United States until the ratification of the Thirteenth Amendment to the Constitution in 1865, mainly in the Southern plantation region.

2. *Report of the National Advisory Commission on Civil Disorders* (New York, 1968), pp. 206–7. Pronouncements made by Presidents Kennedy and Johnson reflected the spirit of the time. According to Kennedy, "[Negroes] are not fully free ... [therefore] this nation ... is not fully free...." "[V]ictory for the American Negro," Johnson asserted, "is a victory for the ... nation" (Civil Rights Address by Kennedy and Johnson's speech on passage of the Civil Rights Act of 1965, respectively, *New York Times*, 12 June 1963 and 7 August 1965).

3. Peter H. Wood, "'I Did the Best I Could for My Day': The Study of Early Black History during the Second Reconstruction, 1960–76," *William and Mary Quarterly*, 3rd series, 35:185–225 (April 1978), p. 189.

4. Regarding "the origins of slavery ... contemporary attitudes have affected the positions historians have taken on the subject" (Raymond Starr, "Historians and the Origins of British North American Slavery," *Historian*, 36:1–19 [1973–4], p. 16).

5. Eric Williams, *Capitalism and Slavery* (Chapel Hill, 1944), p. 7.

The "equal-but-separate" doctrine was promulgated in an 1896 decision by the United States Supreme Court in the case of *Plessy v. Ferguson*, holding that "racial" segregation could not be interfered with provided only that the accommodations offered were of equal quality. Under a Louisiana state law, Homer Plessy, an American of African ancestry, had been forced from a "white" railroad coach under provisions of Louisiana state law, because he was not "white." Plessy sought relief from the courts for deprivation of civil rights protected by the post-Civil War Fourteenth Amendment of the United States Constitution. The *Plessy* decision remained the ruling precedent until it was overturned in 1954 by the Supreme Court in the case brought by Oliver Brown against the Board of Education in Topeka, Kansas, against school segregation. The *Brown v. Board of Education* decision held that racial segregation is in itself a denial of equal rights. The historic United States civil rights crusade originated a year later, on 1 December 1955 when Mrs Parks, an African-American worker, refused to give up her seat to a white fellow bus passenger, and was arrested for that violation of a Montgomery city law. The incident led to the historic year-long Montgomery bus boycott by African-Americans, which ended with another Supreme Court order based on the principle of the *Brown* decision.

6. Recognition among historians of the signal significance of Williams's contribution is represented in Barbara Lewis Solow and Stanley L. Engerman, eds, *British Capitalism and Caribbean Slavery: The Legacy of Eric Williams* (New York, 1987). The editors' preface cites as the first of four Williams themes that "slavery was an economic phenomenon; and thus racism was a consequence, not the cause, of slavery."

Two helpful bibliographies of this controversy are: Joseph Boskin, *Into Slavery, Racial Decisions in the Virginia Colony* (Philadelphia, 1976), pp. 101–12; and James M. McPherson, Laurence B. Holland, James M. Banner, Jr, Nancy J. Weiss and Michael D. Bell, eds, *Blacks in*

America: Bibliographical Essays (Garden City, New York, 1971), especially pp. 26–8 and 39–44. See also: Alden T. Vaughan, "The Origins Debate: Slavery and Racism in Seventeenth-Century Virginia," *Virginia Magazine of History and Biography,* 97:311–54 (July 1989), for a more recent, avowedly partisan, analysis of the state of the discussion; and Raymond Starr's earlier review of the discussion, cited in n. 4.

7. Oscar and Mary F. Handlin, "Origins of the Southern Labor System," *William and Mary Quarterly,* 3rd series, No. 7 (1950), pp. 214 and 220–21.

8. See, for example: James Curtis Ballagh, *A History of Slavery in Virginia* (Baltimore, 1902), especially pp. 28–32; Ulrich Bonnell Phillips, *American Negro Slavery* (New York, 1933), pp. 74–7, and "Racial Problems, Adjustments and Disturbances," in *The South in the Building of the Nation,* 13 vols (Richmond, 1909–13), VI:194–241, reprinted in Eugene D. Genovese, ed., *The Slave Economy of the Old South: Selected Essays in Economic and Social History by Ulrich Bonnell Phillips* (Baton Rouge, 1968), pp. 23–64, also pp. 26–7; and John H. Russell, *The Free Negro in Virginia, 1619–1865* (Baltimore, 1913), Chapter 2, "The Origin of the Free Negro Class."

9. Russell, pp. 16–17.

10. Winthrop D. Jordan, "Modern Tensions and the Origins of American Slavery," *Journal of Southern History,* 28:18–30 (February 1962), p. 20.

11. The most recent general review of the state of the discussion is Vaughan. He refers to and makes comments on some forty works published since 1976, the year following the date of Boskin's bibliography, also cited in n. 6. Vaughan's review, however, is in the form of an essay wherein the author "takes a stand" on the general Jordan–Degler psycho-cultural side of the issue, namely that pre-colonial anti-black prejudice in England predetermined the enslavement of African-Americans in Anglo-America. He summarizes what he sees as three points upon which consensus has been reached: (1) the numbers of African-Americans in Virginia and Maryland in the seventeenth century; (2) the ambiguity of the legal status of these African-Americans; and (3) the tightening of restrictions on African-Americans late in the seventeenth century; and four points of remaining fundamental disagreement: (1) the status of most African-Americans before the 1660s; (2) the amount of anti-Negro discrimination before the 1660s; (3) the reasons the African-Americans were enslaved; and (4) the point at which ethnocentrism became racism directed at the African-Americans. The reader will be able to infer quite clearly from the present work points at which I disagree with, agree with, or have reservations about Vaughan's presentation. In the main the differences derive from my particular approach to the entire question of the origin of racial slavery, indicated in the third paragraph of this Introduction.

Just one note: Vaughan mentions my *Class Struggle and the Origin of Racial Slavery* (1975) and says that my argument, along with those of Edmund S. Morgan (1972 and later) and Timothy Breen (1972 and later), quickly "succumbed" to "a withering fire" by economic, labor-supply, and skilled/unskilled labor-differentiation theses put forward by Russell Menard (1977) and David W. Galenson (1981). Speaking for myself, while my interpretation of the political and social significance of economic facts presented by Menard and Galenson may vary from theirs in some, even important, respects, the reader will judge whether it has "succumbed."

12. Carl N. Degler, "Slavery and the Genesis of American Race Prejudice," *Comparative Studies in Society and History,* Vol. II, No. 1 (October, 1959), pp. 49–66; and No. 4 (July 1960), pp. 488–95. *Neither Black Nor White: Slavery and Race Relations in Brazil and the United States* (New York, 1971).

13. Winthrop D. Jordan, *White over Black: American Attitudes Toward the Negro, 1550–1812* (Chapel Hill, 1968).

14. Degler, *Neither Black Nor White,* pp. 287 and 290. Degler's conviction on this point finds expression in the title of his latest book, *In Search of Human Nature: The Decline and Revival of Darwinianism in American Social Thought* (New York, 1991), a thesis in defense of socio-biology, that is, the search for biological explanations of social behavior. To the extent that that is intended to "explain racism," it would seem to merit the mistrust expressed by Doctor Ross (Dorothy Ross, *American Historical Review,* April 1992, pp. 608–9).

15. Jordan, *White over Black,* pp. 582 and 584.

16. As will be further noted in Volume Two, the fact that the term "free Negro" does not appear in court record references to African-American non-bond-laborers in the early decades (with one exception in which a deponent so describes himself) would tend to show that

African-Americans at that time shared the presumption of liberty with European-Americans. With the one exception, the first use found was in a record of hog marks dated 29 April 1699 ("Cattle and Hog Marks, 1665–1707," pages which somehow got inserted at the back of *Northampton County Records, 1651–54*, Virginia State Archives, Richmond).

17. Jordan, *White over Black*, p. 75. Here Jordan seems to disregard his own express caution against "reading the past backwards," (p. ix), and thus falls into a common error of historians on both sides of this argument. That is the error of casually fixing the label "white," on people who never identified themselves as such. Furthermore, he would seem to have less excuse than some others, since he himself tells us that the term "white" was not current in Virginia before 1680 (p. 97). In this seemingly insignificant detail is revealed the key to the whole puzzle of the origin of racial slavery.

18. Degler, "Slavery," p. 49; *Out of Our Past, The Forces that Shaped Modern America* (New York, 1959), pp. 27–30 and 36–8; and *Neither Black Nor White*, which in its entirety is a development of this point.

19. Degler, *Out of Our Past*, pp. 30 and 38; and "Slavery," p. 52. Some time later Degler sought to emphasize the perhaps subtle point of his case. He did not intend to say that prejudice caused slavery, but simply that it caused slavery to be *racial* (Degler, letter to *New York Review of Books*, 22 January 1976).

20. Degler, *Out of Our Past*, pp. 30–31.

21. Oscar James Campbell and Edward G. Quinn, *The Reader's Encyclopedia of Shakespeare* (New York, 1966), particularly "Othello – sources." John Gassner, *Masters of the Drama*, 3rd edition (New York, 1951), p. 232.

22. John Lambert, *Travels through Canada, and the US*, 2:138, cited in Jordan, *White over Black*, p. 405.

23. Irene A. Wright, *Documents Concerning English Voyages to the Caribbean, 1527–1568*, Works Issued by the Hakluyt Society, 2nd series, LXII (London, 1928), pp. 7, 14, 18–19.

24. Irene A. Wright, ed., *Documents Concerning English Voyages to the Spanish Main, 1569–1580*, Works Issued by the Hakluyt Society, 2nd series, LXXI (London, 1932), pp. xxxvii–xxxix, 72, 258–9 and 279.

25. Ibid., pp. 21, 24, 170, 324 and 310.

26. E. G. R. Taylor, ed., *The Original Writing and Correspondence of the Two Richard Hakluyts*, Works Issued by the Hakluyt Society, 2nd series, LXXVI and LXXVII (London, 1935), pp. 17, 142–3, and 318. English policy, said Hakluyt, should be to "use the naturall people there [on the Spanish Main in America] with all humanitie, curtesie, and freedome . . . [so that] with the Symerons a few hundrethes of this nation [England under Elizabeth] may bring greate things to passe" (p. 318).

27. Edmund S. Morgan, *American Slavery, American Freedom: The Ordeal of Colonial Virginia* (New York, 1975), pp. 10–17.

28. Richard Jobson, *The Golden Trade or a Discovery of the River Gambra, and The Golden Trade of the Aethiopians* (London, 1623; Teignmouth, 1904).

29. Basil Davidson, *The African Slave Trade: Precolonial History, 1450–1850* (Boston, 1961), p. 5.

30. Sir John Davies, "Microcosmos," (spelling modernized) in a two-volume collection of Davies's writings made by Alexander Balloch Grosart in 1878. This John Davies (1565?–1618) is not to be confused with the better-known John Davies (1569–1626), who served James I as English solicitor-general and attorney-general in Ireland, and is referred to later in this work, who was also a poet collected by Grosart.

31. Since Degler brought Shakespeare into it, he might have tipped his hat to Shylock (whose name was the English transliteration of the Hebrew word for "cormorant," a symbol in Christendom of the "pervert" usurer) and to a century-by-century anti-Jewish lineage from the folktale of poor murdered Christian Hugh of Lincoln to Chaucer's Prioress, and to Marlowe's *Jew of Malta*. He might have mentioned how the Irishman Macmorris in *Henry V* (Act 3, Scene 2) is had to repeat the characterization of his own nation as "villain and a bastard, a knave and a rascal." And Degler might have put this remark in the context of the English attitude toward the Irish as expressed, say, from the fourteenth-century Statute of Kilkenny to the eighteenth-century Penal Laws, which I shall have further occasion to note in Chapter 3. Any discussion of this point would have benefited by reference to James O. Bartley's analysis of stereotypical presentations of the Irish, Welsh and Scots in English

plays (James O. Bartley, *Teague, Shenkin and Sawney, Being an Historical Study of the Earliest Irish, Welsh and Scottish Characters in English Plays* [Cork, 1954]).

32. Marvin Harris, *Patterns of Race in the Americas* (New York, 1964), pp. 69–70. P. E. H. Hair, "Protestants as Pirates, Slaves and Missionaries: Sierra Leone 1568 and 1582," *Journal of Ecclesiastical History*, 21:203–24. Canny was equally specific in his criticism of Jordan in this regard. See his "The Permissive Frontier: The Problem of Social Control in English Settlements in Ireland and Virginia, 1550–1650," in K. R. Andrews, N. P. Canny and P. E. H. Hair, *The Westward Enterprise: English Activities in Ireland, the Atlantic and America, 1480–1650* (Detroit, 1979), p. 35.

33. This well-known thesis is identified with the names of social anthropologists Frank Tannenbaum, author of *Slave and Citizen* (New York, 1947), and Gilberto Freyre, author of *The Masters and the Slaves* (New York, 1956).

34. See Great Britain Public Record Office, *Calendar of State Papers, Colonial*, Vol. I, pp. 123, 152–3, 168, 201–3, 247–9 and 277–8. Unfortunately, historians on both sides of the issue commonly fail to grasp the significance of this central aspect of the history of Providence Island. Jordan mentions it in a footnote, but for the purpose of emphasizing the enslavability of heathens, rather than the non-enslavability of Christians (*White over Black*, p. 92, n. 112).

35. Degler, *Out of Our Past*, p. 31.

36. Philip Alexander Bruce, *Economic History of Virginia in the Seventeenth Century: An Inquiry into the material condition of the people, based on original and contemporaneous records*, 2 vols (New York, 1895), 2:74–7. It was not until after the Treaty of Breda in 1667, ending the Second Anglo-Dutch War, that the English had direct access to the African labor-supply coast. It was only in mid-1680s that the direct Africa-to-Virginia bond-labor trade began in ships exclusively used for that purpose (Bruce, 2:84).

37. Jordan, "Modern Tensions," p. 21.

38. Jordan expressed his dissatisfaction with all previous attempts to deal with the origin of racial slavery. He specifically mentioned the "virtually opposite" views of the Handlins and Degler on the relation of "slavery and prejudice" (*White over Black*, p. 599), and claimed to hold "a still different view." But he differed differently from those respectively polar positions. His difference with the Handlins was substantial; his difference with Degler was technical, designed to make more effective historiography's service to the proposition that white racism could never be eliminated by purposive social action.

39. Jordan, *White over Black*, p. 80. It is interesting that throughout his book, Jordan puts "prejudice" in quotation marks (other instances are found at pp. 276, 281, 565, 568 and 569). Perhaps he felt that this was merely being consistent with his thesis that "white over black" is not a matter of judgment, or prejudgment, but of instinct.

40. Jordan titled Chapter 2 of *White over Black* "Unthinking Decision: Enslavement of Negroes in America to 1700." Although he did not use the term "unthinking decision" in the 1962 article "Modern Tensions," the explication there is nearly verbatim that in the book.

41. Jordan, *White over Black*, p. ix.

42. In the epilogue to his book, Jordan concludes: ". . . the most profound continuities ran through the centuries of change. Particularly there were the tightly harnessed energies of a reckless, trafficking, migrating people emerging from death and darkness into plenty and enlightenment. These were a people of the Word, adventuring into a New World; they sought to retain their identity – their identity as a peculiar people" (*White over Black*, p. 574).

43. African immigrants were barred from the United States. By contrast, in the decade following the abolition of slavery in British Guiana, some eleven thousand African workers came there as wage-workers (Walter Rodney, *A History of the Guyanese Working People, 1881–1905* [Baltimore, 1981], pp. 33, 97 and 241).

44. "The western states," said George Washington in 1784 "(I speak now from my own observation) stand as it were on a pivot. A touch of a feather would turn them either way" (letter to Governor Harrison of Virginia, 10 October 1784, cited in Benjamin Horace Hibbard, *A History of Public Land Policies* [New York, 1924: republished by University of Wisconsin Press, 1965], p. 34).

45. Jordan, *White over Black*, Chapter XV, "Toward a White Man's Country," especially pp. 542 and 569.

46. See Appendix A.

47. Eric Williams wrote that persons of joint European-African ancestry in the Caribbean, "In training and in outlook . . . retain little or no trace of their African origin, except the color of their skin. . . . When they go 'home' every four years to enjoy a well earned holiday . . . they imply by 'home' not Africa, but England, France, even Spain" (Eric E. Williams, *The Negro in the Caribbean* [New York, 1942], p. 60).

In Jamaica in the immediate post-emancipation period, "The people of color were very conscious of their European heritage and extremely proud of it," according to Philip D. Curtin (*Two Jamaicas: The Role of Ideas in Tropical Society, 1830–65* [Cambridge, Massachusetts, 1955], p. 45). Curtin cites three nineteenth-century sources, including "A Protest of the [Jamaica] House of Assembly," dated June 1838.

See also: Douglas Hall, "Jamaica," pp. 199–200; and Jerome S. Handler and Arnold A. Sio, "Barbados," pp. 236–8, and 256–7, in David W. Cole and Jack P. Greene, eds, *Neither Slave Nor Free* (Baltimore, 1972). See also: Elsa V. Goveia, *Slave Society in the British Leeward Islands at the End of the Eighteenth Century* (New Haven, 1965), pp. 223 and 232; and Jerome S. Handler, *The Unappropriated People, Freedmen in the Slave Society of Barbados* (Baltimore, 1974), pp. 75–6, 91–2, 94–5, 109, 216–17.

48. Jordan, *White over Black*, pp. 141 and 175.

49. Ibid., Chapter 15, passim.

50. Ibid., pp. viii–ix. As is made more explicit at the other end of his book (p. 582), Jordan intended an epitaph to aspirations for the achievement of equal rights of, by and for African-Americans in the United States.

51. Jordan does say that his book "is not about Negroes" (ibid., p. viii). But he does not say explicitly that it is not a book *for* Negroes. It would seem that elementary sensitivity, if no other consideration, should have led him to distance himself more consistently than he does from some of the racist "attitudes" he dug up in the course of his research ("The Negro's admittedly unattractive characteristics", which were supposedly an embarrassment to opponents of slavery [p. 305]; "No wonder Linnaeus backed away" from the conclusion that the Negro was a different species [p. 236]; "[C]ertain superficial physical characteristics in the West African Negro helped sustain (and perhaps helped initiate) the popular connection with the ape" [p. 237]; "During the seventeenth century there had been little progress on the scientific problem of the Negro's blackness" [p. 242]). Perhaps Jordan's failure to do so validates his own observation that "an historian's relationship with the raw materials of history is a profoundly reciprocal one" (ibid., p. vii). In choosing his subtitle, "The American Attitude Toward the Negro," Jordan, consciously or not, was in tune with the sentiment expressed by Thomas Dixon Jr, whose book *The Clansman* was made into the movie *Birth of a Nation*. "[W]ho thinks of a Negro when he says American?" said Dixon (*Saturday Evening Post*, 19 August 1905, pp. 1–2, cited in Stanley Feldstein, ed., *The Poisoned Tongue: A Documentary History of American Racism and Prejudice* [New York, 1972], p. 200).

52. Reviewers were typically kind, though some of them expressed serious reservations. Richard D. Browne saw "intuitive generalizations . . . not sustained by the evidence" (*New England Quarterly*, 41:447–9 [September 1968]). The evidence occasionally fails to carry the burden, wrote David H. Fowler (*Journal of American History*, 56:344–5 [September 1969]). Challenging a number of Jordan's themes, including his assumption of an immemorial "revulsion-for-blackness," J. H. Plumb counterposed the proposition that "Racism does not cause slavery. It is an excuse for it" (*New York Review of Books*, 12:3 [13 March 1969]).

53. In his "Essay on Sources," Jordan avowed his deliberate avoidance of comparisons between English and other European colonies in the Americas. Displaying unusual acerbity, Jordan dismissed as worthless the body of scholarly work accumulated in the period after World War Two that attempted to shed light on racism and slavery in North America by comparison with non-English colonies. "Virtually all such studies," Jordan said, were done by people who were "ignorant" of their subjects. In such hands, he said, "the comparative approach proved to be extremely dangerous" (*White over Black*, pp. 604–5). It seems all the more regrettable therefore that Jordan was not able to set a better example of the comparative approach in its application to English colonies in the Caribbean, as an illuminator of the nature of racial slavery in the continental colonies and the United States.

54. Jordan, *White over Black*, Chapter 4, "Fruits of Passion," *passim*; especially sub-chapters 1 and 6. The quoted phrase is at p. 137.

55. Ibid.

56. Philip D. Curtin, *Two Jamaicas*, p. 45.

57. The human sexual drive, Jordan says by way of explication, overrides not only the "sense of difference between two groups of human beings [but also that] . . . between themselves and animals" (*White over Black*, p. 138). One wonders at Jordan's seeming gradation of English lapses from the libidinal norm: "interracial" sex, then interspecies sex.

58. Ibid., p. 141.

59. Donald L. Horowitz, "Color Differentiation in the American System of Slavery," *Journal of Interdisciplinary History*, vol. 3, no. 3 (Winter 1973), pp. 509–41; p. 528, citing: James Stewart, *View of the Past and Present State of the Island of Jamaica* (Edinburgh, 1823), p. 333; and Edward Long, *The History of Jamaica or, General Survey of the Ancient and Modern State of That Island*, 3 vols (London, 1774), Vol. II, Book 2, p. 328.

60. A convenient brief account of the prevalence of "interracial" sex in the Southern slave states is presented in Kenneth Stampp's *The Peculiar Institution: Slavery in the Ante-bellum South* (New York, 1956), pp. 350–61. Jordan's desire-versus-aversion-in-a-sea-of-blacks scenario seems a relic of the nineteenth-century thesis that "going native" bore the seed of the fall of the British Empire.

61. Jordan, *White over Black*, p. 167.

62. Ibid., pp. 175 and 177.

63. Allen D. Candler, comp., *The Colonial Records of Georgia*, 26 vols (Atlanta, 1904–16), Vol. 18, Statutes of the Royal Legislature, p. 659.

64. James Ramsay, *An Essay on the Treatment and Conversion of African Slaves in the British Sugar Colonies* (London, 1784), pp. 288–9.

65. Alan Burns, *History of the West Indies* (London, 1954), pp. 446–7.

66. Sidney Greenfield, *English Rustics in Black Skins: A Study of Modern Family Forms in a Pre-Industrial Society* (New Haven, 1966), pp. 42 and 46.

67. Jordan, *White over Black*, p. 169 (emphasis added).

68. Long, *History of Jamaica*, Vol. 2, Book 2, pp. 270, 327, 332–7.

69. Jordan, *White over Black*, p. 177.

70. Ibid.

71. "In many areas one of the major concerns of responsible men was the effective control of masses of slaves" (Ibid., p. 102).

72. Horowitz, "Color Differentiation," pp. 529–30.

73. Jordan notes in passing: "The only rebellions by white servants in the continental colonies came before the firm entrenchment of slavery" (*White over Black*).

74. Oscar and Mary F. Handlin, "Origins of the Southern Labor System," p. 208.

75. From Degler's final letter in the exchange with the Handlins, published in *Comparative Studies in History and Society*, Vol. 2 (1959–60), No. 4 (July 1960), p. 495.

76. Williams, *Capitalism and Slavery*, pp. 201–2. The crisis, according to Williams, began in 1823 when the home government sought to impose limitations on the harshness and brutality of treatment of bond-laborers in the British West Indies. The sugar bourgeoisie resisted, even threatening secession from the Empire. The tide was turned by the numerous insurrectionary actions of the bond-laborers themselves (inspired by the Santo Domingo example of 1804), climaxing in revolts in Antigua and in the biggest sugar colony, Jamaica, in 1831. Their intervention transformed the question from that of abating the owners' cruelties to ending the ownership itself. Faced with the alternatives of "emancipation from above, or emancipation from below" (Williams, p. 208), the British Parliament resolved the crisis in 1833 by decreeing the end of slavery in the West Indies.

77. Ibid., pp. 19–20.

78. The cost of transporting a cargo of African bond-laborers from São Tomé to Barbados in 1693–94 was ten pounds ten shillings per laborer ("A Journal of a Voyage in the Hannibal of London, Ann. 1693, 1694 from England to Africa and so Forward to Barbadoes, by Thomas Phillips, Commander of the said Ship," in John and Awsham Churchill, comp., *A Collection of Voyages and Travels* [Churchill's Voyages], 6 vols [London, 1704–32], 6:171–239, p. 236). "Never during the colonial period did it cost more than five or six pounds sterling to transport a servant to the plantations" (Abbott Emerson Smith, *Colonists in Bondage: White Servitude and Convict Labor in America, 1607–1776* [Chapel Hill, 1947; New York, 1971], p. 35). See also Bruce, 1:629–30.

79. "Will the manager with the two or three bookkeepers he has to assist him attempt ... to enforce the obedience of 200 or 300 negroes?" (Viscount Hamrick speech, 14 May 1833, in United Kingdom, *Hansard Parliamentary Debates*, 3d series (1830–91), vol. 18, cols 1231–59; 1255.)

80. See Appendix B.

81. Interestingly, Morgan did not present his work as a contribution to the controversy over the origin of racial slavery. His aim, rather, was to explore the symbiosis of racial slavery and the Jeffersonian freedom doctrines. Nevertheless, most reviewers tended to consider *American Slavery/American Freedom* (New York, 1975) in the context of the controversy, believing that Morgan's account of the emergence of racial slavery was the strongest part of his book. See for instance: J. H. Plumb (*New York Review of Books*, 27 November 1975); Peter H. Wood (*New York Times Book Review*, 21 December 1975); Rhys Isaac (*Reviews in American History*, Vol. 4, No. 1 (March 1976); and Theodore William Allen (*Monthly Review*, March, 1978). Carl N. Degler, in a letter commenting on Plumb's review, limited his criticism to what he called Morgan's "flawed" argument regarding the rise of racism (*New York Review of Books*, 22 January 1976).

82. Morgan, p. 309. For a telling criticism of Morgan in this negation of the African-American bond-laborer, see Peter Wood's review, cited in n. 81.

83. Morgan, pp. 296–7.

84. "The Myth of the Friendly Master" is a chapter title in Harris's *Patterns of Race*.

85. Morgan, p. 328.

86. Ibid.

87. Ibid., p. 331.

88. Ibid., p. 344.

89. Ibid., pp. 331–3 and 344.

90. Ibid., pp. 330–31.

91. Ibid., p. 380.

92. Ibid., p. 386.

93. Letter of Thomas Ludwell and Robert Smith to Charles II, 18 June 1676, Henry Coventry Papers at the Bath Estate at Longleat, Vol. 77, f. 128 (American Council of Learned Societies British Manuscripts Project, microfilm reel no. 63, Library of Congress).

94. Jackson T. Main, "The Distribution of Property in Post-Revolutionary Virginia," *Mississippi Valley Historical Review*, 1954–55, 41:241–58, p. 248, n. 21; Jackson T. Main, *The Social Structure of Revolutionary America* (Princeton, 1965), especially pp. 42, 47, 54–57, and 61; D. Alan Williams, "The Small Farmer in Eighteenth-century Politics," *Agricultural History*, 43:91–101 (January 1969); Gloria L. Main, "Inequality in Early America: The Evidence from Probate Records of Massachusetts and Maryland," *Journal of Interdisciplinary History*, 7:559–81 (Spring 1977). Although Morgan cites some of these sources he apparently does not see them in the light intended here.

95. "Strange is the situation of our community in Eastern Virginia, where more than one-half the population is born to absolute slavery, and fully half the other with little but their complexion to console them for being born in a higher caste" ("Civis," writing in the *Richmond Enquirer*, 4 May 1832).

96. In addition to the early-nineteenth-century English traveller Sir Augustus John Foster, cited by Morgan (p. 380), other notable antecedent expressions of fondness for this "paradox" are found in the commentaries of Edmund Burke, Thomas R. Dew, Lyon G. Tyler and Henry A. Wise (see Theodore William Allen, "Slavery, Racism and Democracy," review of Morgan's *American Slavery/American Freedom*, in *Monthly Review*, March 1978).

97. Jordan, *White over Black*, p. 134.

98. We have the familiar testimony of Chastellux, who traveled in America in the early 1780s, concerning "the state of poverty, in which a great number of white people live in Virginia ... [where] I saw poor persons [in America] for the first time ... [and where] miserable huts are often to be met with, inhabited by whites, whose wan looks and ragged garments bespeak poverty" (François Jean, Marquis de Chastellux, *Travels in North America in the Years 1780, 1781, and 1782*, trans. and ed. Howard C. Rice Jr [Chapel Hill, 1963], 2:190). The historian John B. MacMaster's research led him to conclude that between 1810 and 1820, "Although the population of the seaboard had grown but slowly, the pauper, dependent, and petty criminal class had multiplied with what seemed alarming rapidity ... [and, in 1817] one-seventh of the population [of New York] were actually living on charity" (John B. McMaster, *History of the People of the*

United States from the Revolution to the Civil War, selected and edited by Louis B. Filler [New York: Farrar, Straus and Company, 1964], pp. 211 and 214).

99. Timothy H. Breen, "A Changing Labor Force and Race Relations in Virginia 1660–1710," *Journal of Social History*, Fall 1973, pp. 3–25.

100. Ibid., pp. 10–12 and 17.

101. Timothy H. Breen and Stephen Innes, *"Myne Owne Ground", Race and Freedom on Virginia's Eastern Shore, 1640–1676* (New York, 1980).

102. Breen, "Changing Labor Force," pp. 13–14.

103. Allan Kulikoff, *Tobacco and Slaves: The Development of Southern Cultures in the Chesapeake, 1680–1800* (Chapel Hill and London, 1986), pp. 4–5, 79.

104. Jacob M. Price, "The Economic Growth of the Chesapeake and the European Market, 1697–1775," *Journal of Economic History*, 24(1964):496–516, p. 498.

105. Breen, "Changing Labor Force," p. 16.

106. Breen, "Changing Labor Force," pp. 15–16.

107. Lerone Bennett Jr., *The Shaping of Black America* (Chicago, 1975), pp. 76–8.

108. See Stanley Garn, *Human Races*, rev. 2nd printing (Springfield, Illinois, 1962), and Theodosius Dobzhansky, *Mankind Evolving: The Evolution of the Human Species* (New Haven and London, 1962).

109. W. E. B. DuBois, *Black Reconstruction* (New York, 1935), p. 577.

1 The Anatomy of Racial Oppression

1. "A great deal, of course, depends on what one means by race. I take the racial factor to mean the assumption of innate differences based on real or imagined physical or other characteristics" (O. Patterson, *Slavery and Social Death* [New York, 1990], p. 176). What other, "non-physical," characteristics are meant, Patterson does not say at this point (pp. 176–8) in his discussion. Elsewhere his presentation may justify the inference that he had in mind considerations of presumed mental, temperamental, or moral attributes.

2. David Brion Davis, *The Problem of Slavery in Western Culture* (Ithaca, 1966), pp. 23–4. Davis makes this comment in the context of a critical examination of the views of George Bancroft as expressed in his *History of the United States, from the Discovery of the American Continent*, 10 vols, 14th edn (Boston, 1850–74). Davis cites from 1:159–61, 2:451. Bancroft (1800–91), a fervent Jacksonian and US expansionist, served as Secretary of the Navy, 1845–46, and was Ambassador to Britain from 1846 to 1849.

3. Charles Edward Chapman, *Colonial Hispanic America: A History* (New York, 1933), p. 118.

4. Marvin Harris, *Patterns of Race in the Americas* (New York, 1964), p. 59.

5. US Department of Commerce, Bureau of the Census, *Historical Statistics of the United States, 1789–1945* (Washington, DC, 1975), Series B 40–47 and n. 1. Walter Rodney, *A History of the Guyanese Working People, 1881–1905* (Baltimore, 1981), p. 143.

6. Franklin W. Knight, "Cuba", in David W. Cohen and Jack P. Greene, *Neither Slave Nor Free* (Baltimore, 1972), p. 280, n. 8.

7. Cited in June Purcell Guild, *Black Laws of Virginia* (1936; Negro Universities Press reprint, 1969), from the Virginia Statutes for the given years.

8. "What Makes You Black?", *Ebony*, 38:115–16 (January 1983).

9. *Boston Globe*, 17 September 1983. In an apparent misprint, the *Globe* says the Conservatives took their stand on "1/164," which I have taken the liberty of inferring to have intended "1/64." I do so not out of any pro-Conservative bias, but simply because of the fact that 164 is not a power of two. See also the *New York Times*, 6 July 1983.

10. In Louisiana in 1970 a lawyer went down to the Legislature to lobby for a definition of "Negro" sufficiently limited to leave a client of his on the "white" side of the line. "I got into a hassle with some of them," he later said; "... they started off at one one-hundred-and-twenty-eighth, and just to have some bargaining power I started off with ... an eighth. We finally struck the bargain at one thirty-second, and it sailed through" (*New York Times*, 30 September 1982).

11. The essential difference between racial and national oppression is the following. In the system of racial oppression, social control depends upon the denial of the legitimacy of social distinctions within the oppressed group. In the system of national oppression, social control depends upon the acceptance and fostering of social distinctions within the oppressed group.

12. See my discussion of Winthrop D. Jordan's view in the Introduction.

13. Henry Hallam, *Constitutional History of England from Henry VII to George II* (London, 1827), 3:401.

14. William Edward Hartpole Lecky, *A History of England in the Eighteenth Century*, 8 vols (New York and London, 1878–90), 2(1882):103.

15. W. K. Sullivan, *Two Centuries of Irish History, 1691–1870*, Part I, *From the Treaty of Limerick to the Establishment of Legislative Independence, 1691–1782*, edited by James Bryce (London, 1888), pp. 39–40.

16. Letter from Marx (London, 9 April 1870) to S. Meyer and A. Vogt, revolutionary German exiles in the United States (*Karl Marx and Friedrich Engels on Britain* [Moscow, 1962], pp. 551–2); emphasis in original.

17. Lewis P. Curtis, *Anglo-Saxons and Celts* (Bridgeport, Connecticut, 1968), p. 81, citing W. R. W. Stephens, *The Life and Letters of Edward A. Freeman*, 2 vols (London, 1895), 2:242.

18. Notable contributions to this field of study include: David Beers Quinn, "Sir Thomas Smith and the Beginning of English Colonial Theory," *Proceedings of the American Philosophical Society*, 89:543–60 (1945); David Beers Quinn, "Ireland and Sixteenth-century European Expansionism," in T. Desmond Williams, ed., *Historical Studies*, 1:20–32 (Papers Read before the Second Irish Conference of Historians, London, 1958); David Beers Quinn, *The Elizabethans and the Irish* (Ithaca, 1966); Howard Mumford Jones, "The Origins of the Colonial Idea in England," *Proceedings of the American Philosophical Society* (1949); Howard Mumford Jones, *O Strange New World: American Culture, the Formative Years* (New York, 1964); Nicholas P. Canny, "The Ideology of English Colonization: from Ireland to America," *William and Mary Quarterly*, 3rd series, 30:575–98; Nicholas P. Canny, *The Elizabethan Conquest of Ireland: A Pattern Established, 1565–76* (New York, 1978); and James Muldoon, "The Indian as Irishman," *Essex Institute Historical Collections*, 3:267–89 (October 1975).

19. Quinn, *Elizabethans and the Irish*, p. vii. See particularly pp. 20–27 for an example of Quinn's presentation of this point.

20. Wesley Frank Craven, *White, Red, and Black: The Seventeenth-century Virginian* (Charlottesville, 1971; New York, W. W. Norton reprint, 1977), pp. 39–40.

21. Muldoon, p. 270.

22. George M. Frederickson, *White Supremacy: A Comparative Study in American and South African History* (London University Press, 1981), p. 15.

23. Canny, "Ideology of English Colonization," p. 596 (repeated almost verbatim in his *Elizabethan Conquest of Ireland*, pp. 160, 576).

24. Canny, "Ideology of English Colonization," p. 596.

25. Michael Hechter, *Internal Colonialism: The Celtic Fringe in British National Development, 1536–1966* (Berkeley, 1975), pp. xvi–xvii. Cf. Raymond Crotty, *Ireland in Crisis: A Study in Capitalist Colonial Undevelopment* (Dover, New Hampshire, 1986), p. 38.

Sociologist Richard Williams makes a signal contribution along this line by bringing a study of history to a trenchant critique of misleading American sociological categories, which he believes impede the struggle for equality. He starts with the proposition that "race and ethnicity are social designations rather than natural categories" (Richard Williams, *Hierarchical Structures and Social Value: The Creation of Black and Irish Identities in the United States* [New York, 1990], p. ix).

26. Quinn, *Elizabethans and the Irish*, p. 26.

27. In 1978, Alden Vaughan questioned the validity of the Irish parallels, but he found no satisfactory alternative rationale for the contempt shown by Elizabethan Englishmen toward the American Indians. But whatever it may have been, he is convinced that it was not a matter of color prejudice, "for Englishmen believed the Virginia Indians to be approximately as white as themselves" (Alden T. Vaughan, "'Expulsion of the Savages': English Policy and the Virginia Massacre of 1622," *William and Mary Quarterly*, 3rd series, 35:57–84 [January 1978], p. 59, n. 3). Might it not have been that the earliest Anglo-Americans "believed the Virginia Indians to be as white as themselves" for the simple reason that they had not yet identified themselves as

"whites"? Later, Vaughan returned to the subject, and noted a shift in the English color perception of Indians beginning in the late seventeenth century, corresponding to the beginning of the usage "white" to distinguish Europeans and European-Americans from Indians; but he excludes African-Americans in making this observation, implying that where European-Americans and African-Americans were involved the former were immemorially designated "whites" (Alden T. Vaughan, "From White Man to Redskin: Changing Anglo-American Perceptions of the American Indian," *American Historical Journal*, 87:917–53 [October 1982]. For his exclusions of African-Americans from his generalization, see p. 931.) Instances in which the seventeenth-century Virginia court records seem to contradict him in this regard will be considered in Volume Two of this study. It is encouraging to note that by 1989 Vaughan had come to believe in the germaneness of "possible parallels and contrasts between English–African and English–Irish relations" (Alden T. Vaughan, "The Origins Debate," *Virginia Magazine of History and Biography* 97:311–54 [July 1989], p. 353, n. 129).

28. Canny, "Ideology of English Colonization," pp. 575–6, 588–92.

29. Canny, *Elizabethan Conquest of Ireland*, pp. 133–4, citing Essex to Privy Council, Additional Manuscripts 48015, fols 305–14.

30. Canny, *Elizabethan Conquest of Ireland*, p. 134, citing a letter of Leicester to (Sir William?) Fitzwilliam, 24 August 1572. Canny also cites another Elizabethan as likening Sidney's mission in Ireland to that of the Spanish in America, as one of "brideling the barbarous and wicked."

31. Cornwallis to the Spanish Council, 16 October 1609. Great Britain Public Record Office, *Calendar of State Papers relating to Ireland of the Reign of James I*, vol. 3 (1608–10) (London and Edinburgh, 1874), edited by C. W. Russell and John P. Prendergast, 3:83. When it had suited their Reformationist purposes a quarter of a century earlier, however, the English ruling class published the writings of Bartolomeo de las Casas exposing and condemning the usages of the Christian conquistadors in the Americas (Bartholomew de Las Casas, *The Spanish Colonie, Or Briefe Chronicle of the Acts and gestes of the Spaniards in the West Indies, called the newe World for the space of xl yeeres* [London, 1583; Readers Microprint Corporation, 1966; see the Foreword for the history of the appearance of this English edition of writings of Las Casas]. See, for instance, sigs A, A2, B2, B3.)

32. In a letter to Hercules Langrishe, 3 January 1792, *The Works of the Right Honorable Edmund Burke*, 6th edition (Boston, 1880), 12 vols, 6:305.

33. Lecky, *History of England*, 2:280.

34. Philip Dormer Stanhope, Fourth Earl of Chesterfield (1694–1773), who had served as Lord Lieutenant of Ireland (1745–46), writing to the Bishop of Waterford on 1 October 1764 (cited in Philip Henry Lord Mahon, *History of England from the Peace of Utrecht to the Peace of Versailles*, 7 vols [London, 1858], 5:123).

35. From a speech given at a meeting of the Catholic Board, Shakespeare Gallery, Exchequer Street, Dublin, 8 January 1814 (*Select Speeches of Daniel O'Connell, M. P., edited with historical sections by his son John O'Connell, Esq.*, 2 vols [Dublin, 1865], 1:408).

36. *Hansard's Parliamentary Debates*, 3rd series, 71:391 (8 August 1843). Brougham, an English abolitionist but an opponent of Irish independence, knew that the slaveholding Tyler family was playing politics with the repeal issue in the United States (see Chapter 8).

37. Richard Price, ed., *Maroon Societies: Rebel Slave Communities in the Americas* (Garden City, New York, 1973), p. 20; C. L. R. James, *The Black Jacobins: Toussaint L'Ouverture and the San Domingo Revolution* (revised edition, New York, 1963), pp. 17, 19.

38. Alfred H. Stone, "The Mulatto Factor in the Race Problem," *Atlantic Monthly*, 91:658–62 (1903), p. 660. Stone pegged his thesis on a distinction between "mulattoes" and "negroes." However, his awareness of social distinctions among Africans who were to be declassed in plantation America is worth noting. Terry Alford's *Prince Among Slaves: The True Story of an African Prince Sold into Slavery* (New York, 1977) is the history of Ibrahim, who is identified (p. 61) as "Rahahma" in a context which makes it apparent that he is the same person to whom Alfred H. Stone referred as "Rahamah." Stone also mentions "Otman dan Fodio, the poet chief of the Fulahs" as among distinguished Africans brought as slaves to plantation America.

39. E. S. Abdy, *Journal of a Residence and Tour in the United States of North America, from April 1833 to October 1834*, 3 vols (London, 1835), 3:346–8.

40. H. M. Henry, *Police Control of the Slave in South Carolina* (Emory, 1914), p. 11, citing

Nott and McCord (Law): *Witsell v. Parker*; and 2 Strobhart (Law), 43: ex parte Boylston.

41. Adam Smith, *Theory of Moral Sentiments*, 6th edition, 2 vols (London, 1790), 2:37.

42. US Supreme Court decision in *Dred Scott v. Sanford*, March 1857.

43. *Address of the Colored Convention to the People of Alabama*, published in the *Daily State Sentinel*, 21 May 1867 (James S. Allen, *Reconstruction: The Battle for Democracy [1865–1876]* [New York, 1937], pp. 237–8).

44. Major Ridge, who was not the richest man in the Cherokee nation, and who was not on the delegation, had an estate at this time of $22,000, not counting his thirty African-American bond-laborers and his interest in a trading post business (Thurman Wilkins, *Cherokee Tragedy: The Story of the Ridge Family and the Decimation of a People* [New York, 1970], pp. 183–4). An official census in 1835 found that of the population of the Cherokee nation (in contiguous areas of Georgia, North Carolina, Alabama and Tennessee) numbering 17,000, 1,600 were African-American bond-laborers (Samuel Carter III, *Cherokee Sunset, A Nation Betrayed: A Narrative of Travail and Triumph, Persecution and Exile* [Garden City, 1976], p. 22). The phrase "Cherokee planter-merchant" is Carter's (p. 23).

45. Opinion of Chief Justice John Marshall in *Cherokee Nation v. State of Georgia*, 30 US (1831), in Wilcomb E. Washburn, *The American Indian and the United States: A Documentary History*, 4 vols (New York, 1973), p. 2558. On Jackson's attitude, see ibid., pp. 2352–3, 2461–2, 2554, 2603; and Carter, pp. 216–17.

46. The Methodists having first taken the lead, the Moravians, Baptists, Congregationalists and Presbyterians, in concert, denounced the "white" incursions against Cherokee tribal lands and individual rights, attacks that became especially aggressive after the discovery of gold on Cherokee land in 1828. These Christian missionary workers "attached value to intermarriage as a force for improvement" (Wilkins, pp. 35, n. 58, 202–3, 219).

In 1815, William H. Crawford of Georgia, Secretary of War in Madison's cabinet, proposed a policy of merger by intermarriage of European-Americans and American Indians (see Introduction, n. 54). See Wilkins, p. 145, citing *Christian Herald*, Vol. 10, p. 468 (20 December 1823).

47. Wilkins, p. 145, citing *Christian Herald*, Vol. 10, p. 468 (20 December 1823).

48. "The [Scots] invasion [of Ireland] by Edward Bruce in 1315 has been recognized as the turning point of English influence in medieval Ireland" (G. H. Orpen, *Ireland Under the Normans*, 4 vols [Oxford, 1911–20], 4:160).

49. In a Gaelic-language article, a modern Franciscan historian, Canice Mooney (Cainneach O Maonaigh) finds in this Anglo-Norman policy a "racist" precedent of what occurred "yesterday in Birmingham, Alabama, or earlier in Sharpeville, South Africa" ("Racialism and nationalism in the Irish church, 1169–1534," *Galvia*, 10:4–17 [1954]). I am indebted to Brother Quinn of Iona College for translating this article for me. F. X. Martin characterizes Mooney's article as an "Irish nationalist interpretation" ("John, Lord of Ireland, 1185–1216," in *A New History*, 2:147, n. 3). The abbreviation *A New History* is used throughout this work to refer to *A New History of Ireland*, *under the auspices of the Royal Irish Academy*, planned and established by the late T. W. Moody, 10 vols (Oxford, 1976–), of which all but vols 1, 6, and 7 were published as of 1992. The volumes, composed by a select group of Irish scholars, are variously edited thus far by Art Cosgrove, T. W. Moody, F. X. Martin, F. J. Byrne, W. E. Vaughan. The citations will note the name of the contributor and the contribution, with locations cited by volume number and page number.

50. Jocelyn Otway-Ruthven, "The Request of the Irish for English Law, 1277–80," *Irish Historical Studies*, 6:261–70 (1948–49), pp. 264–5; Jocelyn Otway-Ruthven, "The Native Irish and English Law in Medieval Ireland," *Irish Historical Studies*, 7:1–16 (1950–51), pp. 14–15.

51. Sir John Davies, *A Discovery of the True Causes why Ireland was never Entirely Subdued* ... (London, 1612; 1969) p. 116. Orpen noted that Davies's comment was even more applicable to the earlier rejection of the Irish petition for enfranchisement (*Orpen*, 4:23, n. 3).

52. Edmund Curtis and R. B. McDowell, eds, "Remonstrance of the Irish Princes to Pope John XXII, 1317," in *Irish Historical Documents* (London, 1943), p. 41.

53. Otway-Ruthven, "Native Irish and English Law," p. 6. The complaint of the Irish "free" classes of the thirteenth century was despairingly echoed five centuries and three conquests later, during the early years of the Penal Laws era, by a Gaelic poet raging against a trinity of oppressions: the poverty from which escape was forbidden; the systemic frustration of all hope of social recognition; and, above all, "the contempt that follows it, for which there is no cure" (cited and translated in T. W. Moody and J. C. Beckett, *Ulster Since 1800, second series, a social*

survey [London, 1957], p. 171).

Daniel O'Connell, looking back in about 1815, reminisced: "It was easy to tell a Catholic in the streets by his subdued demeanour and crouching walk. So deeply had the iron of oppression entered into their souls" (a paraphrase given by Robert Dunlop, *Daniel O'Connell* [New York, 1908], p. 45).

54. Speaking of kinship societies in general, Orlando Patterson says, "Land was corporately owned" (Patterson, *Slavery and Social Death*, p. 241). A fairly recent comprehensive bibliography makes it manifest that the central problem of "land reform" in colonial, neo-colonial and post-colonial Africa is the conversion from tribal land ownership to individual (corporate or personal) title (*Land Tenure and Agrarian Reform in Africa and the Near East: an Annotated Bibliography*, compiled by the staff of the Land Tenure Center Library, Madison, Wisconsin, under the direction of Teresa Anderson, Librarian [Boston, 1976]). For the view of an early Pan-Africanist and pioneer of "African socialism," see J. E. Casely-Hayford (African name, Ekra Agiman), *The Truth about the West African Land Question* (London, 1971), with an Introduction by E. U. Essien-Udom, Department of Political Science, University of Ibadan. Casely-Hayford (Ekra Agiman) was " a member of the Anona clan, Ghana." "He was not opposed to modernization as such, but he wanted it to take place within the framework of 'African humanism'" (Professor Essien-Udom's Introduction). See also the Senate testimony of Major J. W. Powell of the American Bureau of Ethnology, Smithsonian Institution, at hearings on the Allotment Act of 1881 (Washburn, pp. 1751–2). The Irish case is discussed at length below.

55. The term and concept "social death," credit for which is given to Michel Izard, was used in a seminar on slavery in pre-colonial Africa held in Paris in 1971 under the auspices of the Institut international africain. Orlando Patterson found it appropriate to his general critique of slavery, to which he gave the title *Slavery and Social Death*. See Claude Meillassoux, ed., *L'Esclavage en Afrique précoloniale* (Paris, 1975), pp. 21–2.

56. The quoted phrases are in Meillassoux, p. 21.

57. ". . . colonists soon enough develop a sense of their own interests" (Liam de Paor, *Divided Ulster* [Harmondsworth, 1970], p. 24).

58. See Appendix C.

59. "By the sixteenth century, for example, much of the land of Europe was in the private possession of a landowning class. In West Africa, even today, most of the land is not so divided" (Basil Davidson with F. K. Bush and the advice of Ade Adayi, *A History of West Africa to the Nineteenth Century* [New York, 1966], p. 176).

See also Williams, *Hierarchical Structures and Social Value*, pp. 55–6.

60. Orlando Patterson, "Slavery and Slave Revolts: A Sociological Analysis of the First Maroon War, 1665–1740," in Richard Price, ed., *Maroon Societies*, p. 283. Patterson's article was originally published in *Social and Economic Studies*, 19:289–325 (1970).

In contrasting the situation of the African captives and the American Indians in the Anglo-American colonies, Phillips notes that the former were more vulnerable because "they were completely broken from their tribal stems" (Ulrich Bonnell Phillips, *Life and Labor in the Old South* [Boston: Little, Brown and Company, 1929], p. 160).

61. "The chief circumstance upon which the planters based their hope of security was the diversity of language and race among the negroes" (Vincent T. Harlow, *A History of Barbados, 1625–1685* [Oxford, 1926], p. 325). See Patterson, "Slavery and Slave Revolts," pp. 256, 261, 263, 282–3.

62. After the war against the Powder River Sioux in 1866, General John Pope testified on the basis of his own personal participation in this cynical program of spoliation of the Indian: ". . . the peace commissioners promise the Indians, in the first place, that the whites shall not go into the Indian country, knowing well that it is impossible to fulfill any promise of the sort; the parties who make these treaties know they must be broken; I have broken them, and I have known for twelve months that war would come out of it" (Washburn, *American Indian and the United States*, pp. 1508, 1522).

63. *Ibid.*, pp. 1134, 1158. In December 1827 the Georgia legislature nullified the treaty-based land rights of the Cherokees and declared them tenants-at-will subject to dispossession by the colonists (Wilkins, *Cherokee Tragedy*, p. 196). This reduction of natives to colonial tenants-at-will was a re-enactment of the treatment of the native Irish under the Plantation of Ulster (see Chapter 5). Ulster Protestant settlers were numerous in the original Cherokee territory, but whatever record

there may be of contemporary references to this parallel has escaped this author.

64. Washburn, p. 2484.

65. Ibid., quoting an editorial in the St Louis *Republican*.

66. Ibid., p. 1752.

67. Ibid., p. 68.

68. Ibid., p. 1230.

69. Ibid., p. 1429.

70. Haymarket Square in Chicago was the scene of a rally on 4 May 1886, held in support of the eight-hour-day campaign and specifically to protest the police brutality against an assembly of strikers on the previous day. A large contingent of armed police came to stop the meeting. A bomb went off, resulting in the death of eight of the police. Eight anarchist leaders were convicted, who became known to labor history as the "Haymarket martyrs." Of the eight, four were hanged, and one died in jail, a suicide it was said. In 1893, the remaining three were freed from prison by Illinois Governor Peter Altgeld, who declared that they had been tried unfairly.

In the United States the term "robber barons" is applied to capitalist entrepreneurs who, in the latter part of the nineteenth century, accumulated (and occasionally lost) vast fortunes by unabashed fraud, bribery and force, including the brutal repression of working-class resistance. There were railroad barons, timber barons and cattle barons, who were licensed by a corrupt Congress and state legislatures to privatize (as today's Conservatives would say) public lands taken by force and fraud from Indian tribes, and to loot the public treasury. They enacted a reversion to the primitive accumulation period of the English enclosures of the sixteenth century and the plunder of Aztec and Inca treasures by the conquistadors. The reader is referred to the old but still champion history of this United States phenomenon, Gustavus Myers, *History of the Great American Fortunes* (New York, 1907, republished 1937). See also Matthew Josephson, *The Robber Barons: The Great American Capitalists, 1861–1901* (New York, 1934).

71. Washburn, 1:422. Morgan's views can be found in ibid., pp. 1:424–5.

72. Graven in my consciousness is the caution offered by Professor Eoin MacNeill regarding "the sort of fallacy common enough when the history of a nation or description of its customs is undertaken by foreigners" (Eoin MacNeill, *Celtic Ireland* [Dublin, 1921], p. 116). I am a student of Irish history, but not a scholar in it as are those whose works I cite are. I have tried to stay clear of controversies in this field. In some instances, where it appears that I am involved willy-nilly, I have sought to present the contrary views fairly, and to defend my own. My focus here is always on the nature and extent of the structural differences between the Anglo-Norman social order and the Gaelic–Celtic social order as they confronted each other in Ireland – and their significance for an understanding of racial oppression.

73. D. A. Binchy, "Ancient Irish Law," *Irish Jurist*, new series, 1:85–92 (1966), p. 89. Estimates of the number of *tuaths* for later periods may reflect a demise of weaker tribes, as cattle raids concentrated wealth in the hands of the strong tribes (Kenneth Nicholls, "Gaelic Society and Economy in the High Middle Ages," in *A New History*, 2:414–15.

74. Professor Eoin MacNeill, who made some of the most important investigations of the records of ancient Ireland, argued that the term "tribe" should not be applied to early Irish society because he thought it invidiously suggested a comparison with the societies found among the "Australian or Central African aborigines" in the modern day (Eoin MacNeill, *Phases of Irish History* [Dublin, 1919], pp. 288–9; Eoin MacNeill, *Early Irish Laws and Institutions* [Dublin, 1935], pp. 24–5). MacNeill categorized the ancient Irish as "European white men" (*Celtic Ireland*, Preface). P. W. Joyce regularly used the term "tribe," although he made reference only to "Aryan" parallels (*A Social History of Ancient Ireland* [1913], 1:167). Kenneth Nicholls, however, points a footnote at an African parallel ("Gaelic Society and Economy in the High Middle Ages," p. 425). Students of early Irish history will recognize the validity of the parallels with Africa apparent in *Land Tenure and Agrarian Reform in Africa and the Near East*, the bibliography cited in n. 54.

Other Irish historians, before and after MacNeill, who have found the terms "tribe" and "tribal" appropriate include: D. A. Binchy, cited above, n. 73; W. K. Sullivan ("permission of the tribe council"), cited by his contemporary George Sigerson at p. 8 of *History of the Land Tenures and Land Classes of Ireland with an account of the Various Secret Agrarian Confederacies* (London, 1871), a work recommended highly by MacNeill; Sigerson himself, ("another tribe" [ibid., p. 9]); Alexander George Richey, ed., *Ancient Laws of Ireland* (Dublin and London, 1879), Vol. VI, Glossary (*fine* = "tribe"; "it is probably impossible to use any word in translation that will not be liable to a misconception; the translator renders it mostly by tribe, but also by family"); ibid., Vol. IV, *Brehon Law Tracts*, p. cxvii ("a system of tribe law"); Standish O'Grady, in "The Last Kings of Ireland," *English Historical Review*, 4:286–303 (1899), uses "tribe," "tribal," "clan"; Irish Texts Society, *A Smaller Irish–English Dictionary for the Use of Schools* (1932) (*fine* = "tribe; family"); and *A New History*, 8:11 (*tuath* = "people, tribe, tribal kingdom ...").

75. Gearoid Mac Niocaill, *Ireland Before the Vikings* (Dublin, 1972), p. 67; Nicholls, pp. 397–8.

76. In Gaelic Ireland in the sixteenth century, the chiefs exercised their privileges in the matter of the customary land redistribution in ways that "tended to concentrate land ownership" in their own hands. Furthermore, the conveyance of land rights, by inheritance or otherwise, was subject to such heavy assessments by the chiefs that the land in question often passed into the hands of the chief. Most common of all was the takeover of lands that the landholder had mortgaged to a chief (lord) for stock. If the charges were not met, the client (tenant) lost his holding. Whilst the tenant had a theoretical right to pay up and reclaim his land, "the conditions for redemption were ... often virtually impossible of fulfillment" (D. B. Quinn and K. W. Nicholls, "Ireland in 1534," in *A New History*, 2:34–5). See also: Joyce, 1:186–7; and George Sigerson, pp. 6–7.

77. Joyce, 1:156–60, 1:194–5.

78. Mac Niocaill, pp. 68–9.

79. Joyce, 1:163–4.

80. Ibid., 1:193, 1:195. Mac Niocaill, pp. 63, 65.

81. For all its Gaelic appearance, the term *betagh* does not seem to have appeared until it was used by the Anglo-Norman settlers to describe the native Irish of the laboring classes, who like the English villein (serf) were *adscriptus glebae*, that is, not free tenants for a term of years or at-will, but bound hereditarily to the land of their lord.

82. This section on the *derbfine* is based on (1) Mac Niocaill, pp. 49–53; (2) MacNeill, *Celtic Ireland*, p. 151; (3) MacNeill, *Phases of Irish History*, pp. 296–7; and (4) Sigerson, pp. 8–11.

83. "This constitution of the clans was one of the evils of ancient Ireland. It weakened the power of the kings or supreme chieftains" (James Henthorne Todd, ed., *The War of the Gaedhil with the Gaill; or the Invasion of Ireland by the Danes and other Norsemen* [originally a twelfth-century work], in *Chronicles and Memorials of Great Britain and Ireland during the Middle Ages* [London, 1867], vol. 48, p. cxviii).

84. See Joyce, 1:187–8, 2:282–4, for a discussion of the practical arrangements for sharing the use of common lands.

85. Standish O'Grady, "The Last Kings of Ireland," pp. 287, 291. This view is supported by Brian Cuiv in *The Course of Irish History* (Cork, 1967), pp. 120–22; and by F. J. Byrne, "The Trembling Sod," in *A New History*, 2:4–5.

86. In 1155, or within a few years thereafter, Pope Adrian, the only Englishman ever elected pope, in an act that came to be known as the Donation of Adrian granted Ireland to Henry II and commanded the Irish to submit to the English king. Rome was particularly interested in rooting out unacceptable practices by the Celtic clergy, such as rejection of celibacy, and the hereditary succession to office. In parallel with the temporal authorities, this pope intended to secure "the abandonment of features of Gaelic society going back to pre-Christian times" (F. X. Martin, "Diarmait Mac Murchada and the Coming of the Anglo-Normans," in *A New History*, p. 56).

87. Kathleen Hughes, Introduction to Jocelyn Otway-Ruthven, *A History of Medieval Ireland* (New York, 1986), p. 14.

88. Otway-Ruthven, *History of Medieval Ireland*, p. 102. It is interesting to note that during the Norse occupations of parts of Ireland, from the end of the eighth century to the middle of the eleventh, though many were the battles between the "Gaedhil" and the "Gaill," the Irish and the foreigners, land tenure principles were not at issue. Possibly that was in part due to the fact that the Scandinavians were primarily raiders and traders rather than cultivators. But it would seem equally due to the fact that "The Norse system [of land tenure] resembled the Irish in a marked manner" (Sigerson, p. 12).

The French views of land tenure certainly differed from those of the Algonkian people inhabiting Canada in the two centuries after the French made their first appearance on that coast in 1504. But since the French were soon primarily concerned first with fishing and then with the fur trade, their relations with the Algonkians were little troubled by land tenure issues (Gary B. Nash, *Red, White, and Black: The Peoples of Early America* [Englewood Cliffs, NJ, 1974], pp. 107–8). See also Alfred G. Bailey, *The Conflict of European and Algonkian Cultures, 1504–1800* (St John, New Brunswick, 1937); and William Eccles, *The Canadian Frontier, 1534–1670* (New York, 1969).

89. R. E. Glasscock, "Land and People, c. 1300," in *A New History*, 2:226.

90. Mac Niocaill cites an instance of annual rent on twenty-four milk cows; it included: one cow, three calves, a pig, a sheep, cream and butter, a flitch of salt pork, lard, suet, and three handfuls of candles (*Ireland Before the Vikings*, p. 64). P. W. Joyce noted a later record which showed the tenant paying an annual rent of one animal for every seven (*Social History of Ancient Ireland*, 1:188–9).

91. MacNeill, *Celtic Ireland*, p. 169.

92. "In Anglo-Norman society ... all land was held of someone, of the king in chief, or of someone on a ladder leading to the king." (The major exception – Church land – was to disappear under Henry VIII.) The settlers "had no interest in the theoretical basis of Irish land-tenure, and were fully aware of having overthrown the Irish order." The quotations are from Mac Niocaill, *Irish Jurist*, new series, 1:293 (1966).

93. MacNeill, *Celtic Ireland*, p. 170.

94. See Hughes, pp. 4–14.

95. Speaking of warring by cattle raids, O'Grady writes, "ownership of land divested of cattle or other exchangeable property meant subjugation; permanent military occupation of such territory was not necessary" (O'Grady, p. 300.) So it remained three centuries later, and these wars involved "rent and tribute ... [but] little interference in the internal affairs of the tributary" (O'Domhnaill, "Warfare in Sixteenth-century Ireland," *Irish Historical Studies*, 5 [1946–47]: 29–54, p. 29). See also Mac Niocaill, pp. 53, 54. MacNeill, *Celtic Ireland*, p. 122.

96. Mac Niocaill, p. 54.

97. Early Brehon Law provided that orphan brotherless "daughters should obtain all the land with obligation to perform service of attack and defence, or the half of it, without obligation to perform service of attack and defence; and there is a power over them to compel them to restore the land after their time" (Alexander George Richey, ed., *Ancient Laws of Ireland*, vol. IV, *Brehon Law Tracts* [Dublin, 1879], p. 41): Under this law, the woman would seem to have had no heirs, so that, upon her death, her land "fell back into the common fund of land out of which it had been taken" (Richey's Introduction, p. cxix). Mac Niocaill, referring to a later period (the latter half of the seventh century), suggests that this return to the common fund was made by way of the woman's son or sons, if she had any, or otherwise the "nearest male member" of the kinship group (*Ireland Before the Vikings*, p. 52).

98. Ibid., p. 58.

99. D. A. Binchy, *Crith Gablach* (Dublin, 1941), pp. 80–81. Noting that when women married they "passed to their husband's *fine* for the duration of the marriage," Mac Niocaill adds parenthetically, "some marriages were merely temporary arrangements" (*Ireland Before the Vikings*, p. 51).

100. Ibid., pp. 55, 58.

101. For this characterization of English family custom, I have relied on Lawrence Stone, *The Crisis of the Aristocracy, 1558–1641* (London, 1967), pp. 594–605. See also John P. Prendergast, *The Cromwellian Settlement of Ireland* (New York, 1868), pp. 17–18.

102. Mac Niocaill, pp. 58–9. Etymological note: "gossipred" is derived from "god-sib," god-child.

103. The practice of the stronger party demanding and holding hostages of the weaker one was regular in these times, Ireland being no exception. See O'Grady, "The Last Kings of Ireland," pp. 292, 294, 297, 301. Ordinary captives were a source of wealth, according to O'Grady, "for war captives were then [in the 12th century] sold into slavery" (p. 302).

104. G. J. Hand, *English Law in Ireland, 1290–1324* (Cambridge, 1967), p. 202.

105. Sir John Davies, *A Discovery of the True Causes why Ireland was never entirely Subdued, nor brought under Obedience of the Crowne of England, Untill the Beginning of his Majesties happie Raigne* (London, 1612).

Despite his anti-Irish bias, Davies brought to his task experience as a lawmaker and colonial administrator, a good literary style, a legal concern for precision, and a reverence for history. This work of some three hundred pages ranks in these respects with Francis Bacon's *History of the Reign of King Henry VII.*

106. *Discovery of the True Causes . . .*, p. 167.

107. Ibid., pp. 167–8.

108. Ibid., p. 169.

109. Ibid., pp. 170–73.

110. Ibid., p. 182.

111. Ibid., pp. 174, 179.

112. F. X. Martin, "Diarmait Macmurchada," pp. 57–9.

113. F. X. Martin, "Overlord Becomes Feudal Lord, 1172–85," in *A New History*; 2:111; F. X. Martin, "John, Lord of Ireland, 1185–1216", in *A New History*, 2:128.

114. Martin, "Diurmait Macmurchada," pp. 64, 65; Martin, "Overlord," p. 117.

115. Otway-Ruthven, *History of Medieval Ireland*, p. 102. As is often noted, the chronicle of Giraldus Cambrensis (Gerald of Wales – who accompanied King John to Ireland in 1185) both recorded and concurred with the supercilious and disdainful Anglo-Norman references to the Irish and their way of life. But that cannot explain the English resort to racial oppression in Ireland; sooner or later, the same chauvinistic attitude was directed by the English at the Welsh and the Scots, in whose countries a fundamentally different system of English domination was instituted.

116. Davies, p. 116.

117. See Martin, "John, Lord of Ireland," pp. 147, 150–53.

118. Immanuel Wallerstein, *The Modern World-System: Capitalist Agriculture and the Origins of the European World-Economy in the Sixteenth Century* (New York, 1974), pp. 68–9.

119. Martin, "John, Lord of Ireland," pp. 150–51.

120. Ibid., p. 153.

121. In insisting on the relevance of the parallel between incidents so widely separated in time, I appeal to the example of the Irish historian James C. Beckett. Speaking of the resentment felt by the Anglo-Irish toward English "newcomers," Beckett argues: "This parallel between the fourteenth century and the eighteenth is not merely adventitious. It indicates a real continuity of tradition. . . . The constitutional programme of the Anglo-Irish patriots in the reign of George III was consciously derived from precedents set by the 'English in Ireland' three or four hundred years earlier" (J. C. Beckett, *The Anglo-Irish Tradition* [Ithaca, 1976], p. 25).

122. See Introduction, n. 16.

123. Hand, p. 194.

124. Ibid., p. 188.

125. Phillips, *Life and Labor in the Old South*, p. 162.

126. John P. Prendergast, *The Cromwellian Settlement of Ireland*, second, enlarged edition (Dublin, 1875), p. 21, n. 2.

127. 4 Hening 132–3 (1723).

128. Hand, pp. 201–2.

129. "Remonstrance of the Irish Princes to Pope John XXII," 1317, p. 43.

130. *Neale v. Farmer* in *Reports of Cases in Law and Equity Argued and Determined in the Supreme Court of the State of Georgia from August 1850–May 1851*, Thomas R. Cobb, reporter, Vol. IX (Athens, Georgia, 1851), pp. 555–84. The court, far from considering this fact a loophole in the law, held it an indispensable principle because, "If [the Common Law] protects the life of the slave, why not his liberty? and if it protects his liberty, then it breaks down at once the *status* of the slave" (p. 579). The same principle had been written into law in colonial Virginia in 1723 (4 Hening 133).

131. Prendergast, p. 2, n. 1, citing Sir John Davies, *Discovery of the True Causes . . .*

132. Washburn, *The American Indian and the United States*, pp. 2669–70, 2676. The Dred Scott decision rendered by the United States Supreme Court in 1857 held that Negroes were not citizens of the United States, and in the words of Chief Justice Roger B. Taney, had "no rights which a white man is bound to respect" (Richard D. Heffner, *A Documentary History of the United States, An Expanded Edition* [New York, 1956], p. 131).

133. 4 Hening 326–7 (1732).

134. J. C. Beckett, *A Short History of Ireland* (New York, 1968), p. 22; Orpen, *Ireland Under the Normans*, 4:259–60; Otway-Ruthven, " Native Irish and English Law," p. 3; Otway-Ruthven, "Anglo-Irish Shire Government in the Thirteenth Century," *Irish Historical Studies*, 5:1–7 (1946).

135. Otway-Ruthven, "Native Irish and English Law," p. 6.

136. Douglas Hall, "Jamaica," in Cohen and Greene, eds, *Neither Slave Nor Free*, p. 201;

Charles Edward Chapman, *Colonial Hispanic America*, pp. 118–19.

137. Hand, p. 207. Compare Otway-Ruthven, "Native Irish and English Law," pp. 6–7.

138. The eclipse of English power in Ireland in the fourteenth and fifteenth centuries, touched only in passing in this chapter, is dealt with in Chapter 2.

139. *Hansard Parliamentary Debates*, 2d series, vol. 72 (1844), 1172. The subject was "The State of Ireland."

140. Sean O'Domhnaill, "Warfare in Sixteenth-century Ireland," p. 46.

141. Ibid., p. 30.

142. Sigerson, *History of Land Tenures*, pp. 24–5.

143. Aidan Clarke, "The Irish Economy, 1600–60," in *A New History*, 3:169–70. The word "plantation," as found in this work, has two meanings, derived from two kinds of "planting": the planting of colonies of settlers, and the planting of agricultural crops. The British Board of Trade was for a time called, in the first sense, the "Lords of Trade and Plantations." In the Anglo-American context the term acquired its second meaning. There, at first, the term "plantation colonies" had the same colonial connotation as it did with regard to the plantation of Ulster. In time, the terms "plantation" and "plantation system" came to refer to a system of agricultural operations producing staple crops on large tracts of privately owned land.

144. J. C. Beckett, *The Anglo-Irish Tradition*, p. 131.

145. The "Act for the Settling of Ireland," commonly called the Act of Settlement, was passed on 12 August 1652 (*Statutes and Ordinances of the Interregnum, 1642–1660*, collected and edited by C. H. Firth and R. S. Raitt, 2 vols [London, 1911], 2:598–603).

The full title of the Act of Satisfaction is informative: "An Act for the speedy and effectual Satisfaction of the Adventurers [London merchants and other capitalists backers of the English war effort] for Lands in Ireland, and of the [English] Soldiers there, and of other Publique Debts, and for the Encouragement of Protestants to plant and inhabit Ireland" (ibid., 2:722).

146. Vincent Gookin, *The Great Case of Transplantation in Ireland Discussed; or Certain Considerations, wherein the many great inconveniences in the transplanting the Natives of Ireland generally out of the three provinces of Leinster, Ulster, and Munster, into the Province of Connaught, are shewn* (London, 1655), p. 26.

147. Richard Lawrence, *The Interest of England in the Irish Transplantation, Stated . . . Being chiefly intended as An Answer to a scandalous seditious Pamphlet, intituled, The great case of Transplantation, discussed* (Dublin, 1655), p. 12.

148. Ibid., p. 25.

149. According to William Petty, the native Irish population of about 850,000 was reduced to around 700,000 in the course of the war. Gardiner estimates that some 180,000 were males twenty-five years of age or older. According to Petty, 35,000–40,000 Irish soldiers, that is, approximately one-sixth of the adult male population, were sold abroad to serve in the armies of Spain, France, Flanders, etcetera (William Petty, *The Political Anatomy of Ireland* [1672] in Charles Henry Hull, ed., *The Economic Writings of Sir William Petty*, 2 vols [1899; New York, 1963], p. 150; Samuel Rawson Gardiner, "The Transplantation to Connaught," *English Historical Review*, 14:700–734 [October 1899], p. 703; Gookin, *The Great Case of Transplantation*, p. 22). Spain was probably the chief first destination of these transported men under conduct of their officers. Many were abandoned there among a hostile population. Of those enrolled in actual Spanish units, thousands deserted to France because of neglect and ill-treatment suffered under the Spanish. Some were shipped to be sold as plantation bond-laborers in Barbados, St Christopher and elsewhere, possibly Virginia in Anglo-America (Richard Bagwell, *Ireland under the Stuarts and during the Interregnum* 3 vols, [London, 1909], pp. 2:303–4, 2:310; A. E. Smith, *Colonists in Bondage: White Servitude and Convict Labor in America, 1607–1776* [Chapel Hill, 1947; New York, 1971], pp. 163–5; *The Petty Papers: Some Unpublished Writings of Sir William Petty*, edited from the Bowood Papers by the Marquis of Lansdowne, 2 vols in 1 [London, 1927; New York, 1967], p. 2:229; Philip Alexander Bruce, *Economic History of Virginia in the Seventeenth Century, An Inquiry into the Material Conditions of the People based upon Original and Contemporaneous Records*, 2 vols [New York, 1895; reprinted 1935], pp. 1:608–9).

Rather than be the primary financier of the process, the Parliamentary government worked through intermediaries, former Irish officers, English officers willing to invest in it as a business proposition, or enterprising Spanish officers, but with the King of Spain as the main ultimate payer (Robert Dunlop, ed., *Ireland under the Commonwealth, Being a Selection of Documents Relating to the Government of Ireland from 1651 to 1659* [Manchester, 1913], 2 vols; 1:177, 1:238, 2:310, 2:430; Bagwell, 2:303; Day's Proceedings, Council of State, 10 December 1652 and 9 April 1653, Great Britain Public Record Office, *Calendar of State Papers, Domestic, 1652–53*). So eager was the English government to dispose of these Irish fighters that when the Spanish Crown, or some other customer or merchant, failed to make prompt payment, the government would underwrite the process to keep it moving (Dunlop, 2:310, 2:370). During the war launched by Cromwell against Spain for the West Indies in 1655, no Irish could be sent to Spain, but, by that time the process had been completed to the general satisfaction of the English government. In August 1657, Oliver Cromwell himself, writing to the Lord Deputy and Council in Ireland, appears to be concerned only with seeing to it that proper financial settlements be made with those shippers and contractors who were unpaid as a result of the war "between us and the Spaniard" (ibid., 2:669–70). The following year, after Oliver's death, his son and successor Richard Cromwell, in the course of discussing the same subject of unresolved debts, speaks of the advantage that had been gained by "transporting into Spain very great numbers of Irish soldiers, pestering our good people of Ireland and endangering the peace of that nation" (Richard Cromwell to the Lord Deputy and Council [in Ireland], 9 November 1658, ibid., 2:689–90).

150. Gookin, pp. 22, 26.

151. Prendergast, *Cromwellian Settlement of Ireland*, p. 98. "The object was to de-grade the evicted upper-tenant or landlord to a lower condition . . . of cultivators" (Sigerson, *History of Land Tenures*, p. 80).

152. Aidan Clarke, *The Old English in Ireland, 1625–1642* (London, 1966), pp. 26, 236; Aidan Clarke, "Irish Economy, 1600–60," p. 169; Karl S. Bottigheimer, *English Money and Irish Land: The "Adventurers" in the Cromwellian Settlement of Ireland* (Oxford, 1971), p. 5, n. 1.

153. For the provisions of the Act of Settlement, see Firth and Raitt; and Gardiner, "Transplantation to Connaught."

154. W. F. T. Butler, *Confiscation in Irish History* (London, 1918), pp. 132, 156. Butler (p. 156) says that in 1641 Catholic landowners numbered at least eight thousand, or even twelve thousand. Clarke, on the other hand, says that the total of all "proprietors" could not have been more than six thousand, of whom about four thousand were Old English or Irish, presumably Catholics (Clarke, "Irish Economy, 1600–60," p. 170). A possible clue to the discrepancy may be supplied by Butler (p. 198, n. 59). Speaking of two thousand Catholics who were assigned Connaught land, he said that, "possibly many of these had only been tenants or leaseholders in 1641." Perhaps Clarke's "freeholders" do not include tenants. While in England and in Ireland most English were "freeholders" having hereditary leases, Catholic tenants generally did not have hereditary leases; they were tenants, but not freeholders. Perhaps the Butler and the Clarke figures can be reconciled on this basis. I have chosen to use Butler's in this instance, but a picture of mass expropriation is indicated in either case, and is corroborated by all historians of the period. J. G. Simms's criticisms of Butler's estimates, whatever their validity, do not impair the argument being made here as to the significance of the massive expropriation of Catholic lands (J. G. Simms, "Land Owned by Catholics in Ireland in 1688," *Irish Historical Studies*, 7:180–90 [1950–51]).

155. As a further concession to their religio-racial status, Protestants were later allowed to pay money fines instead of forfeiting lands. But they combined to spurn even that condition, and in the end the English government simply left them alone (Dunlop, 1:cxlix–cl.)

156. Dunlop, 1:cxlvi. The history of the continuous transplantation of the American Indians by the United States government, which began with the Indian Removal Act of 1832, was in many respects a virtual re-enactment of the transplantation to Connaught.

157. Butler, pp. 157–8. "The number of transplantees who finally held land west of the Shannon . . . [was] above 580" (ibid., pp. 198–9).

158. The data for Catholic-held land presented in this paragraph are drawn from Butler, especially p. 162; and Simms, especially pp. 180, 182, 189–90. Of the total land, about seven out of every ten acres (71 per cent) were profitable (Simms, p. 180, citing William Petty). About five out of every eight acres of profitable land belonged to Catholics in 1641 (Butler, p. 162; Simms, pp. 180, 189).

159. Simms, pp. 182, 189.

160. The Irish historian and revolutionary martyr of 1916 James Connolly declared that Ireland lost this struggle because the Irish leaders refused "to raise the standard of the Irish nation instead of an English faction" (James Connolly, *Labour in Irish History* [New York, 1919], pp. 20–21).

161. Simms, pp. 189–90. After losing 615,000 (Irish) acres in the Williamite confiscations, the Catholics owned 1,086,000 acres. Simms says the Penal Law toll amounted to as much as the Williamite confiscations, indicating that by the middle of the eighteenth century only 471,000 of some 7.5 million acres of profitable land was still Catholic-owned. Butler, *Confiscation in Irish History*, says that the Williamite confiscations had already reduced the Catholic share to no more than one out of every twenty acres (p. 237). It is commonly accepted that Catholics owned only 5 per cent of the land at the close of the eighteenth century. Catholics made up four-fifths of the population of Ireland at the beginning of the eighteenth century (see p. 77).

162. Speech in the Irish Parliament in 1789. By this reminder, Fitzgibbon was warning his independence-minded fellow members of the Irish Parliament to reflect on the possible consequences of withdrawing from British authority (Quoted in E. M. Johnston, *Ireland in the Eighteenth Century* [Dublin, 1974], p. 161).

163. Prendergast, *Cromwellian Settlement*, pp. 180–81.

164. John Locke (1632–1704), son of a Cromwellian soldier, member of the Board of Trade and Plantations, and philosophic patron saint of the American and French Revolutions, endorsed the rationale of this anti-Catholic persecution. In the first of four famous *Letters on Toleration*, he excluded Roman Catholics from the right of toleration on the ground that they "deliver themselves up to the protection of a foreign prince . . . and [are] soldiers against the government."

165. Butler, p. 237.

2 Social Control and the Intermediate Strata: Ireland

1. For Anglo-American examples, see: 3 Hening 459; and A. Leon Higginbotham Jr, *In the Matter of Color: Race and the American Legal Process, the Colonial Period*, pp. 194–96 (South Carolina, 1740), and p. 254 (Georgia, 1755). For the insecurity and lack of legal defense of the Catholic tenant-at-will in Ireland, see Chapter 3.

2. See 2 Hening 267. Literally, *coverture* means "concealment"; the male-supremacist legal lexicography uses this term to class married women with minors as lacking independent legal standing.

3. W. K. Sullivan, *Two Centuries of Irish History, 1691–1870* (London, 1888), part I, pp. 20–21.

4. See John Collier's moving account *Indians of the Americas* (New York, 1948), pp. 104–5, 135–7. For documentary materials see the annual reports of the United States Commissioners of Indian Affairs for 1891 and 1901. Wilcomb E. Washburn, *The American Indian and the United States: A Documentary History*, 4 vols (New York, 1973), especially 1:560–69, 1:712–14.

5. As did the anti-Catholic Penal Laws in Ireland under which Catholic merchants and other middle-class elements suffered "[e]xclusion from local politics and from formal civic life" (David J. Dickson, "Catholics and Trade in Eighteenth-century Ireland: An Old Debate Renewed," in T. P. Power and Kevin Whelan, eds, *Endurance and Emergence: Catholics in Ireland in the Eighteenth Century* [Dublin, 1990], p. 91). Archbishop William King wrote to the Archbishop of Canterbury in April 1719 expressing anxiety about the possible risks to the security of his Protestants in this exclusion. "How will the protestants secure themselves," he said, "when all the commonalty are all papists?" (Thomas Bartlett, "The Origins of the Catholic Question in Ireland, 1690–1800," in Power and Whelan, p. 3).

6. Lewis C. Gray, assisted by Esther Thompson, *History of Agriculture in the Southern United States to 1860*, 2 vols (Washington DC, 1932; Peter Smith reprint, 1958), 1:478–80; Robert William Fogel and Stanley L. Engerman, *Time on the Cross: The Economics of American Negro Slavery* (Boston: Little, Brown, 1974), pp. 192–4; Robert William Fogel, *Without Consent or Contract: The Rise and Fall of American Slavery* (New York: W. W. Norton, 1989), pp. 72–80.

7. Fogel, pp. 78–9. In regard to the "overseer problem" as seen from the plantation owner's point of view, see Ulrich Bonnell Phillips, "The Origin and Growth of the Southern Black Belts," *American Historical Review*, 11:798–816 (July 1906); 11:808, n. 13.

8. Gray, 2:794, citing agricultural journals of the 1840s.

9. Bartholomew de Las Casas, *The Spanish Colonie, Or Briefe Chronicle of the Acts and*

gestes of the Spaniards in the West Indies, called the newe World for the space of xl yeeres (London, 1583; Readers Microprint Corporation, 1966 – see the Foreword for the history of the appearance of this English edition of writings of Las Casas), sigs A, A2, B2, B3; E. G. Bourne, *Spain in America: 1450–1580* (New York, 1904), pp. 211–14; C. L. R. James, *Black Jacobins: Toussaint L'Ouverture and the San Domingo Revolution,* 2nd revised edition (New York, 1973), pp. 9–24, 36–42.

10. J. C. Beckett, *A Short History of Ireland,* 6th edition (London, 1973), p. 24.

11. In one of a number of studies which he did on English plantation projects in Ireland, Robert Dunlop found that the failure to induce English tenant farmers and laborers to migrate to Ireland was "the weakest point of the whole scheme" ("The Plantation of Munster, 1584–89," *English Historical Review,* 3:250–69, p. 269).

12. Sir John Davies, *A Discovery of the True Causes why Ireland was never entirely Subdued, nor brought under Obedience of the Crowne of England, Untill the Beginning of his Majesties happie Raigne* (London, 1612), pp. 118–20. Compare G. H. Orpen, *Ireland Under the Normans,* 4 vols (Oxford, 1911–20), 2:332–4.

13. Davies, pp. 119–20.

14. The invasion of Ireland by Edward Bruce in the year 1315 marks a major turn in the story of English influence in medieval Ireland (James Lydon, "The Impact of the Bruce Invasion, 1315–27," in *A New History,* pp. 296–302; Orpen, 4:160).

15. Edmund Curtis, *A History of Medieval Ireland from 1086 to 1513* (London, 1938; reprinted 1968), p. 277. See also Richard Bagwell, *Ireland Under the Tudors, with a Succinct Account of the Earlier History,* 3 vols (London, 1885–90), 1:65, 1:80; and J. C. Beckett, *The Making of Modern Ireland 1603–1923* (New York, 1966), p. 15.

16. Orpen, 4:161.

17. The term "Anglo-Irish" is, strictly speaking, anachronistic here, as it was not in use until the nineteenth century (see Beckett, *Short History* p. 15, n. 1). But already in the course of the medieval era the Norman character was superseded by the English, as the definition of the distinct interest of the English colonists emerged.

18. Curtis, p. 277.

19. Ibid., pp. 203, 219, 372.

20. Richard Bagwell, 1:70–71; Beckett, *Short History,* p. 15; Curtis, pp. 219, 255, 299; Davies, p. 211; Seamus MacManus, *The Story of the Irish Race: A Popular History of Ireland* (New York, 1944), pp. 337–9.

21. Curtis, p. 255.

22. *Statutes and Ordinances and acts of the parliament of Ireland, King John to Henry V,* edited by H. F. Berry (Dublin, 1907), pp. 431–69, excerpted in Edmund Curtis and R. B. McDowell, eds, *Irish Historical Documents* (London, 1943), p. 52.

23. Curtis and McDowell, eds, pp. 52–6. The proscribed Irish mode of riding was the bareback style.

24. Ibid.

25. Bagwell, 1:123. In conceding the situation, King Henry VII said that since Ireland could not rule Kildare, then Kildare must rule Ireland (Curtis, p. 338).

26. George Hill, *An historical account of the Plantation in Ulster at the commencement of the seventeenth century, 1608–1620* (Belfast, 1877; reprinted Shannon: Irish University Press, 1970), pp. 21–2, n. 21. Hill cites the preface to the *Calendar of Patent Rolls,* Elizabeth [I], p. xvii.

"... Mr Allen, Master of the Rolls, reported to the King [Henry VIII], that his laws were not obeyed twenty miles from the capital" (John Fitzgibbon, Earl of Clare, Lord Chancellor of Ireland, addressing the Irish House of Lords, 10 February 1800, in support of the Union of Great Britain and Ireland; pamphlet in the collection at New York Public Library Research Libraries, p. 5).

27. Bagwell, 1:84; D. B. Quinn, "'Irish' Ireland and 'English' Ireland," in *A New History,* 2: 633; D. B. Quinn, "The Hegemony of the Earls of Kildare," in *A New History,* 2:647; J. A. Watt, "The Anglo-Irish Colony under Strain, 1327–1399," in *A New History,* 2:369–70; D. B. Quinn, "The Re-emergence of English Policy as a Major Factor in Irish Affairs," in *A New History,* p. 675.

28. Kenneth W. Nicholls, "Gaelic Society and Economy in the High Middle Ages," in *A New History,* 2:408–9; Art Cosgrove, "The Emergence of the Pale, 1399–1447," in *A New History,* 2:552–3; Curtis, *A History of Medieval Ireland* (1923 edition), pp. 202, 417.

29. Bagwell, 1:134–5, citing *State Papers, Henry VIII*, 12, 14, 18. (The letter of instruction on this subject sent by Henry VIII to Lord Deputy Sir Anthony St Leger was dated 23 September 1541.) G. A. Hayes-McCoy, "The Ecclesiastical Revolution, 1534–47," in *A New History*, 5:48.

30. It is to be noted that the terms of tenure attendant upon these regrants to the Irish and the Catholic Old English were more burdensome than those allowed to Protestant New English colonists (Karl S. Bottigheimer, *English Money and Irish Land: The "Adventurers" in the Cromwellian Settlement of Ireland* [Oxford, 1971], p. 11, n. 1).

31. Gerard Anthony Hayes-McCoy, "Conciliation, coercion, and the protestant reformation, 1547–71," in *A New History*, 3:79. For a highly interesting and well-documented account of the workings of the surrender-and-regrant policy told vicariously from the point of view of the participating chieftain class, see N. C. Macnamara, *The Story of an Irish Sept, their Character & Struggle to Maintain their Lands in Clare, by a Member of the Sept* (London, 1896), pp. 148–71.

32. Robert Dunlop, "The Plantation of Leix and Offaly," *English Historical Review*, 6:61, citing Commissioner Anthony St Leger to Thomas Cromwell (1537), in Great Britain Public Record Office, State Paper Office, *State Papers, Henry VIII*, 2:526.

33. Macnamara, p. 148, citing *Calendar of State Papers, Henry VIII*, 1520.

34. Eoin MacNeill, *Phases of Irish History* (Dublin, 1919), 298–9.

35. George Hill, *An historical account of the Plantation in Ulster at the commencement of the seventeenth century, 1608–1620* (Dublin 1877; 1970), p. 30.

36. Though the Irish were firmly supportive of Mary Tudor for her promotion of Catholicism, they regarded her administration of affairs, particularly her failure to restore confiscated lands to Catholic owners, as injurious to Ireland (Francis Peter Plowden, *An Historical Review of the State of Ireland from the Invasion of that Country under Henry II to its Union with Great Britain on the first of January 1801*, 5 vols [Philadelphia, 1805], 1:63).

37. Karl S. Bottigheimer, "Kingdom and Colony: Ireland," in K. R. Andrews, N. P. Canny, and P. E. H. Hair, eds, *The Westward Enterprise: Essays in Tribute to David Beers Quinn* (Detroit, 1979), p. 51. Karl S. Bottigheimer, *English Money and Irish Land*, p. 11.

38. D. B. Quinn, *The Elizabethans and the Irish* (Ithaca, 1966), p. 108.

39. G. A. Hayes-McCoy, "The Completion of the Tudor Conquest and the Advance of the Counter-reformation, 1571–1603," in *A New History*, 3:96–7.

40. Quinn, *The Elizabethans and the Irish*, p. 108, citing Historical Manuscripts Commission, De l'isle and Dudley MSS., II, 12–15.

41. Bottigheimer, *English Money and Irish Land*, p. 26.

42. See Appendix D.

43. Hayes-McCoy, "Completion of the Tudor Conquest," pp. 102–3.

44. Hill, pp. 42 n. 45, 48–50, 62.

45. G. A. Hayes-McCoy, *Irish Battles* (London: Longman Green, 1969), chapter entitled "The Yellow Ford," especially pp. 118–28; P. W. Joyce, *A Concise History of Ireland from the Earliest Times to 1837*, 6th edition (Dublin, 1897), pp. 162–8.

"The English from their first arrivall in that Kingdome, never had received so great an overthrow" (Fynes Moryson, *An Itinerary, Containing His Ten Yeeres Travell through the Twelve Dominions of Germany, Bohmerland, Sweitzerland, Netherland, Denmarke and Ireland*, 4 vols (London, 1617; Glasgow, 1907), 2:217. Moryson (1566–1629) served as chief secretary to the English Lord Deputy Mountjoy in Ireland from November 1600 until he returned with his employer to England in 1603. His *Itinerary* devotes 650 pages to "The Rebellion in Ireland."

46. Moryson, pp. 218–20, 273–4.

47. As did his despairing Red Cross Knight in *The Faerie Queene*, Book I, Canto ix, Stanza 35, line 111.

48. Queen Elizabeth's recommendation of Spenser to be Sheriff was overtaken by events, and the poet never actually served in that post. His "Breife note" to the queen was composed in Cork, where he had taken refuge with other English colonists (Pauline Henley, *Spenser in Ireland* [Cork, 1928; reissued New York, 1969], pp. 144, 153–6, 165).

49. "A Breife Note of Ireland," in Greenlaw et al., eds, *The Works of Edmund Spenser*, 10 vols (Baltimore, 1949), 9:236, 9:244.

50. F. X. Martin, "Medieval Ireland," in *A New History*, 2:lx; R. E. Glasscock, "Land and People, c. 1300," *A New History*, 2:225.

51. See Appendix C.

52. Basil Davidson with F. K. Bush and the advice of Ade Adayi, *A History of West Africa to the Nineteenth Century* (New York, 1966), p. 213.

53. Kenneth G. Davies, *The Royal African Company* (London, 1957), p. 284.

54. *John Fitzgibbon Lord Clare speech to the Irish House of Lords in support of the Act of Union of Great Britain and Ireland, 10 February 1800*, p. 4 (pamphlet in the New York Public Library Research Libraries).

55. Theodore K. Rabb, *Enterprise and Empire, Merchant and Gentry Investment in the Expansion of England, 1575–1630* (Cambridge, Massachusetts, 1967), p. 40.

56. A. L. Rowse, *The Elizabethans and America* (New York, 1959), p. 24.

57. Moryson, 2:170. Did Karl Marx know of this old prophecy? "If England is the bulwark of landlordism and European capitalism," he wrote in 1869, "the only point where one can hit official England really hard is *Ireland*" (Resolution of the International Workingmen's Association, 1 January 1870, *The General Council of the First International, 1868–70 – Minutes* [Moscow, n. d.], pp. 399–405; 403).

58. See Appendix E.

59. Moryson, 2:229, 2:277.

60. Ibid.

61. Mountjoy (1536–1606) was made Earl of Devonshire in 1603 in recognition of his services in Ireland. He was an instance of the one in fifty of the gentry and nobility in England between 1575 and 1630 who invested in joint stock companies for overseas ventures (Rabb, pp. 26–7, 248).

62. Moryson, Vol. 2, pp. 222–4, 276, 360, 369–72; Vol. 3, 36, and (for summary figures) 341–2.

63. John Ulrich Nef, *The Conquest of the Material World* (Chicago, 1964), p. 127. See also p. 181.

64. Moryson, 2:407–8, 3:53–4, 3:61, 3:72–5. See also 2:456, 3:110, 3:256.

65. Moryson, 3:143. Since the soldiers had to pay for their food and clothing, or have the costs docked from their pay, the actual costs to the exchequer were much less.

66. Nef, pp. 126–7, 195–7.

67. Moryson, 2:410.

68. "Muster of the Army at Dundalk" (ibid., 2:334–6). Compare the illustration of the siege of Kinsale (17 October 1601 to 9 January 1602) in which the pikemen appear in a far greater proportion than they do in the muster at Dundalk (ibid., 3:96–7, foldout).

69. Nef, p. 114, n. 109. Spanish tools and arms that came into the hands of the English during the siege of Kinsale were so much superior to those of the English that Moryson complained, "… the sight of them would have put her Majesties Ministers of the Ordinance to shame, who for private gaine sent sale ware to us, unfit to be used" (*Itinerary*, 3:55).

70. Moryson, 2:241–2 (Essex to Queen Elizabeth I, 25 June 1599), 3:152 (Mountjoy to Privy Council, 5 May 1602). Mountjoy suggested Scots be sent as reinforcements because they "would in all likelihood better endure the winters hardnesse … than such new men as come usually from England" (ibid., 2:210, Mountjoy to Privy Council, 12 September 1602).

71. Ibid., 2:172–3, 2:174, 2:228. For a summary of expenditures, see ibid., 3:341–2. For joint stock investment figures, see Rabb, Table 5, p. 66 and the concluding paragraph of n. 96.

72. "Breife Note of Ireland," p. 244.

73. See Appendix D.

74. Moryson, 2:241, 2:311. "Rebels," was the official English designation for the Irish fighters against English colonization.

75. In the five-point indictment that had started the Earl of Essex toward the executioner's block, it was charged that he had dishonored the English Queen by conferring "in equal sort" with O'Neill, "a bush Kerne, and base [bastard] sonne of a Blacksmith" (Moryson, 2:313–14). For Moryson's version of the relevant O'Neill genealogy, see ibid., 2:176–8.

76. Ibid., 3:208–9 (Mountjoy to the Lords in England, 10 September 1602).

77. Ibid., 2:270–71. See Appendix F.

78. Ibid., 2:423, 2:424. "To add to Ulster's attractiveness, war had decimated the population. The whole of Ireland had suffered during Elizabeth's wars … the reduction in population encouraged the idea of plantation" (M. Perceval-Maxwell, *The Scottish Migration to Ulster in the Reign of James I* [London and New York, 1973], p. 17).

79. Moryson, 3:200, 3:207.

80. "The English succeeded, principally by playing off one of a family or sept against another, and holding out bright prospects to their Irish adherents" (Hill, *Plantation in Ulster*, p. 56).

The list of their Irish adherents, in which the great Ulster family names were represented, included: Mulmorie O'Reilly, who died fighting for the English at Yellow Ford; Connor Roe Maguire, O'Neill's son-in-law, who sought the chieftaincy of the Maguires of Fermanagh; Sir Arthur O'Neill, his brother Tirlogh and Henry Og O'Neill (of a rival branch of the O'Neills). Sir Donnell Ballagh O'Cahan, (another son-in-law of the Irish leader Hugh O'Neill, Earl of Tyrone) and Neil Garve O'Donnell (aggrieved at having been passed over in his tribe's choice of chief) rendered indispensable service to the launching of the English second front on Ulster's northern coast. Sir Cahir O'Doherty, angry at not being elected to succeed his father as chieftain, helped the English conquer Donegal in return for a promise that he would be given that territory at the end of the war (ibid., pp. 60–63, 96 n. 3, 318 n. 221; Moryson, 2:308–9, 332–3, 352, 357, 379; 3:179–80, 206, 302).

81. Moryson, 2:309, 2:421, 2:425.

82. Ibid., 3:259 (Mountjoy to the Lords in England, 9 January 1603).

83. Ibid., 2:410.

84. Indeed, when the war was over, English officials looked upon Irish veterans with undiminished hostility and suspicion. When the plantation of Ulster was begun in 1609, plans were made and executed to round up many of these men and sell them to Sweden. See Chapter 5.

85. Davies, *Discovery of the True Causes*, pp. 6–7.

86. Moryson, 3:292–3 (Mountjoy to Cecil, 25 March 1603); 3:300 (O'Neill's oath of submission, 31 March 1603); 3:302 (the Mountjoy grant to the Earl of Tyrone, same day). Hugh's grandfather Conn, the first Earl of Tyrone, had likewise foresworn the title and name of "the O'Neill," under a surrender-and-regrant pact with Henry VIII in 1541 (Hayes-McCoy, "Completion of the Tudor Conquest," p. 50).

Similar terms were allowed to Rory O'Donnell, who had succeeded to the chieftaincy after the death of his brother Red Hugh in Spain in 1602 (Moryson, 3:232, 3:328).

87. Ibid., 3:341–2.

88. Ibid., 3:337.

89. On Sir John Davies's views see p. 65, and Great Britain Public Records Office, *Calendar of State Papers relating to Ireland of the reign of James I*, Vol. 3, *1608–10*, edited by C. W. Russell and John P. Prendergast (London and Edinburgh, 1874), 3:17. See also pp. 115–16. On the attitudes of English landlords, see p. 76 and Chapter 3, n. 39. On the Privy Council, see Hill, *Plantation in Ulster*, p. 408.

90. As noted above (p. 53 and n. 11) the studies of two other eminent scholars, Beckett and Dunlop, arrive at the same conclusion as Hill (ibid., p. 407, n. 56).

91. William Knowlson, *The Earl of Strafford's Letters and Dispatches, with an Essay towards his Life, by Sir George Radcliff, from the Originals in the Possession of his Great Grandson, the Right Honourable Thomas, Earl of Malton, Knight of the Bath*, 2 vols (London, 1739), 1:264.

92. Hugh F. Kearney, *Strafford in Ireland, 1633–41: A Short Study in Absolutism* (Manchester, 1959), pp. 100–101. In 1639 Wentworth conveyed his mistrust of native Irish soldiers as "children of habituated rebels" (Wentworth to Secretary of State Windebank, cited in Richard Bagwell, *Ireland Under the Stuarts and During the Interregnum* (London, 1909), 1:287).

93. Another one-third was held by the Catholic Anglo-Irish (Aidan Clarke, *The Old English in Ireland, 1625–1642* [London, 1966], pp. 26 and 236; Bottigheimer, *English Money and Irish Land*, p. 5, n. 1).

94. Robert Dunlop, ed., *Ireland under the Commonwealth, Being a Selection of Documents relating to the Government of Ireland from 1651 to 1659*, 2 vols (Manchester, 1913), 1:cxxxiv, cliv–clv; Bagwell, *Ireland Under the Stuarts*, 2:347.

95. Beckett, *Making of Modern Ireland*, p. 1109.

96. *A Collection of State Papers of John Thurloe, containing authentic materials of the English affairs from the year 1638 to the Restoration of King Charles II*, 7 vols (London, 1742); 5:558, t70–71, correspondence of Henry Cromwell and Colonel Moore, November 1656 (cited in Bagwell, *Ireland Under the Stuarts*, 2:351).

97. "Ireland was the great capital out of which all debts were paid, all services rewarded, and all bounties performed" (Edward Hyde, 1st Earl of Clarendon, *The Life of Edward, Earl of*

Clarendon ... [and the] Continuation of the History [1672; London, 1759], p. 116 [cited in Bagwell, *Ireland Under the Stuarts*, 2:338]).

98. Dunlop, *Ireland under the Commonwealth*, 1:clvi, 1:clx.

99. Bottigheimer, *English Money and Irish Land*, pp. 135, 140.

100. "A Treatise of Taxes," in C. H. Hull, ed., *The Economic Writings of Sir William Petty*, 2 vols (1899; reprinted 1963), 1:1–97; p. 6. By chargeable armies, Petty appears to have meant armies whose costs could be paid out of revenues generated in the occupied country.

101. Bagwell, *Ireland Under the Stuarts*, 3:179; *A New History*, 8:249–50.

102. Sir William Petty, "A Treatise of Taxes," in Hull, ed., *The Economic Writings of Sir William Petty*, 2:545–621; p. 559.

103. Petty, "Treatise of Taxes," p. 561.

104. Ibid., pp. 551, 555.

105. Ibid., pp. 555, 557, 558, 560–61, 563–5.

106. Ibid., p. 559.

107. "Petty's transplantation scheme (within limits) would not have appeared to his contemporaries quite so fantastic as it does to us. ... Cromwell's Settlement, though never carried out in its entirety, was founded on a general transplantation of the Irish to Connaught and a 'plantation' of English soldiers in their stead" (*The Petty Papers: Some Unpublished Writings of Sir William Petty*, edited from the Bowood Papers by the Marquis of Lansdowne [London, 1927], Editor's Note, 1:47).

108. See Appendix G.

109. For an authoritative treatment of the Mexican case, see Charles Gibson, "The Aztec Aristocracy in Colonial Mexico," *Comparative Studies in Society and History*, 1:169–96 (January 1960). See also John K. Chance, *Race and Class in Colonial Oaxaca* (Stanford: Stanford University Press, 1978).

110. *The Commentaries of the Great Afonso Dalboquerque, Second Viceroy of India*, translated and edited by Walter deGray Birch, 4 vols (London: Hakluyt Society, 1875–84), 4:204, 4:206; Marguerite Eyer Wilbur, *The East India Company and the British Empire in the Far East* (New York, 1945), p. 56. E. E. Rich and C. H. Wilson, editors of *The Economy of Expanding Europe in the Sixteenth and Seventeenth Centuries* (Cambridge, 1967), vol. 4 of *The Cambridge Economic History of Europe*, note, pp. 309, 328–9, but with undisguised bias, the same unique Portuguese attitude. See Basil Davidson, *The African Slave Trade: Precolonial History, 1450–1850* (Boston, 1961), pp. 22–3. Davidson makes clear in his Chapter 4, however, that this policy did not prevent the Portuguese from being just as unprincipled as other European colonizers in their dealings in Africa.

111. Most of the Africans taken as laborers to the Americas came from West Africa. Two-thirds of those taken by British traders came from West Africa (Davidson, *African Slave Trade*, p. 104; J. D. Fage, *A History of West Africa*, 3rd edition [Cambridge, 1969], p. 79).

112. Sigerson, *History of the Land Tenures and Land Classes of Ireland with an account of the Various Secret Agrarian Confederacies* (London, 1871), p. 35.

3 Protestant Ascendancy and White Supremacy

1. *The Statutes at Large, Passed in the Parliaments held in Ireland from the Third year of Edward the Second, AD, 1310 to the Twenty Sixth year of George the Third, AD 1786 inclusive with Marginal Notes, and a Compleat Index to the Whole*, continued through the fortieth year of George Third, 1800, 20 vols. Published in 20 volumes (Dublin 1765–1800), hereinafter noted as *Irish Statutes*. The list of the religio-racist Penal Laws includes principally the following enactments, reenactments, and amended acts: 7 Will III c. 4, c. 5, c. 17; 9 Will III c. 1, c. 3; 10 Will III c. 13; 2 Anne c. 3, c. 6, c. 7; 6 Anne c. 13; 8 Anne c. 3; 2 Geo I c. 10; 4 Geo I c. 9; 6 Geo I c. 6; 12 Geo I c. 3; 1 Geo II c. 2, c. 12, c. 20; 7 Geo 2 c. 4, c. 6; 15 Geo II c. 4; 17 Geo II c. 9; 19 Geo II c. 7, c. 13; 23 Geo II c. 7, c. 10; 25 Geo II c. 7; 29 Geo II c. 2; 31 Geo II c. 4; 33 Geo II c. 3; and 1 Geo III c. 4, c. 12.

W. K. Sullivan says that with the passage of 8 Anne c. 3 (1709), "the Penal Code was now practically complete" (*Two Centuries of Irish History, 1691–1870* [London, 1888], Part I, p. 39). Edmund Curtis (*A History of Ireland*, 6th edition [London, 1950], p. 277) says that it was completed in 1727 (1 Geo II). Beginning about 1760, certain modifying amendments were enacted, but the body of the Penal Laws was repealed by act of the British Parliament only in 1829.

2. Burke, letter to Hercules Langrishe, 3 January 1792, in *The Works of the Right Honorable Edmund Burke*, 6th edition (Boston, 1880), 4:241–306, 4:249–52, 4:305.

3. See Chapter 5.

4. Recent welcome exceptions include: Michael Hechter, *Internal Colonialism: The Celtic Fringe in British National Development, 1536–1966* (Berkeley, 1975); and Richard Ned Lebow, *White Britain and Black Ireland: the Influence of Stereotypes on Colonial Policy* (Philadelphia, 1976).

5. Curtis, *History of Ireland*, p. 251; James Anthony Froude, *The English in Ireland in the Eighteenth Century*, 3 vols (London, 1881), 1:130.

6. Gerard Anthony Hayes-McCoy, "The Completion of the Tudor Conquest, and the Advance of the Counter-reformation, 1571–1603," in *A New History*, 3:96–7.

7. Petty, *A Treatise of Taxes and Contributions* (1662), in Charles Henry Hull, ed., *The Economic Writings of Sir William Petty*, 2 vols (1899; New York, 1963), 1:68–9.

8. "Slavery in Modern Scotland," *Edinburgh Review*, 189:119–48 (January 1899). John Ulrich Nef called that essay, "the most important treatment of the subject" (*The Rise of the British Coal Industry*, 2 vols [London, 1932], 2:157). In the following comments I have relied principally upon that *Edinburgh Review* article, and secondarily upon the following works: Robert Chambers, *Domestic Annals of Scotland*, 3 vols (London and Edinburgh, 1861); Henry Grey Graham, *Social Life of Scotland in the Eighteenth Century* (1899; London, 1950); Henry Hamilton, *An Economic History of Scotland in the Eighteenth Century* (Oxford, 1963). See Appendix H to this volume.

9. Scotland, Privy Council, *Registry of the Privy Council of Scotland*, 14 vols, edited by John Hill Burton (vols 1 and 2) and David Masson (vols 3–14) (Edinburgh, 1877–98), 7:434 (July 1606).

10. Chambers himself personally knew Scotsmen who had been slaves in their youth. He also relates an anecdote told to him by a mining engineer concerning old Moss Nook who "had been a slave, and was exchanged for a pony" (Chambers, *Domestic Annals*, 3:250).

According to Hamilton, the wife and her children, along with the collier himself, "were listed in colliery inventories, like machinery, stocks, or gin horses. Wives, and often sons and daughters, acted as bearers and carried coal in baskets on their heads from the coal face to the surface. At Dunmore colliery there were 28 colliers, 23 bearing wives, 17 bearing sons, 29 bearing daughters" (Hamilton, p. 369). A nimble climber would carry $1\frac{1}{2}$ tons of coal per day up from the working face to the surface (ibid.).

11. "Slavery in Modern Scotland," p. 132.

12. A. E. Smith, *Colonists in Bondage: White Servitude and Convict Labor in America, 1607–1776* (Chapel Hill, 1947; New York, 1971), p. 146.

13. Armagh, Derry, Fermanagh, Tyrone, Cavan and Donegal. See Chapter 5.

14. The plantation of Ulster will be further discussed in Chapter 5.

15. Sir Robert Jacob [King James' Solicitor] to Lord Salisbury, Dublin, October 1609, *Calendar of State Papers relating to Ireland of the Reign of James I*, vol. 3, 1608–10 (London and Edinburgh, 1874), edited by C. W. Russell and John P. Prendergast, 3:299. (For subsequent notes this series will be abbreviated to: *Cal. S. P., Ireland, James I, [date] [vol. no.]*).

16. Sir John Davies, then Attorney-General of Ireland, suggested the English settlement at Jamestown in Virginia as a possible exile for these Irish "swordsmen" (*Cal. S. P., Ireland, James I, 1608–10, vol. 3*, p. 416, answer to queries from the Privy Council [?], 14 March 1610). See Chapter 5.

17. Petty, *The Political Anatomy of Ireland*, in Hull, 1:151. *The Petty Papers: Some Unpublished Writings of Sir William Petty*, edited from the Bowood papers by the Marquis of Lansdowne (London 1927; 1967), 2:229. Vincent Gookin, *The Great Case of Transplantation in Ireland Discussed; or Certain Considerations, wherein the many great inconveniencies in the transplanting the Natives of Ireland generally out of the three provinces of Leinster, Ulster, and Munster, into the Province of Connaught, are shewn* (London, 1655), p. 22. Richard Bagwell, *Ireland under the Stuarts and during the Interregnum* (London, 1909), 3 vols, 2:304–5. Samuel

Rawson Gardiner, "The Transplantation to Connaught," *English Historical Review*, 14:700–734 (October 1899), p. 703. Commenting on a problem raised by Gardiner (ibid. pp. 708–9), Robert Dunlop suggests that an additional 80,000 Irish persons liable to be hanged, under terms of the Act of Settlement, were instead sent into exile (*Ireland under the Commonwealth, Being a Selection of Documents Relating to the Government of Ireland from 1651 to 1659*, 2 vols (Manchester, 1913), 1:cxxxiii, n. 1).

18. A. E. Smith, *Colonists in Bondage*, p. 165. Aubrey Gwynne presents extensive documentation of the social control problems in the English colonies that arose from the presence of transported Irish. Three of his Barbados documents, dated 1655–57, suggest that the Irish mentioned might be exiled soldiers (Aubrey Gwynne, SJ, *Analecta Hibernia*, Irish Manuscripts Commission [Dublin: Stationery Office], No. 4 [October 1932], pp. 234–8).

19. Letter written from Spain, 4 March 1653, cited in Bagwell, 2:301, n. 1.

20. Hull., 1:151.22.

21. Dunlop, 2:310, 2:370; John Patrick Prendergast, *Ireland from the Restoration to the Revolution* (Dublin, 1887), pp. 11–13.

22. Great Britain Public Record Office, *Calendar of State Papers, Domestic, 1652–53*, pp. 21, 270 (Day's Proceedings, Council of State, 10 December 1652 and 9 April 1653). Dunlop, 1:177, 1:240. Bagwell, 2:303.

23. *Journals of the House of Commons*, vol. 7 (15 August 1651–16 March 1959), p. 123.

24. Smith, p. 166. With regard to the propriety of applying the term "slave trade" to this dealing in Irish laborers, see: John P. Prendergast, *The Cromwellian Settlement of Ireland*, 2nd edition (Dublin, 1875); and Patrick Francis Moran, *Historical Sketch of the Persecutions Suffered by the Catholics of Ireland Under the Rule of Cromwell and the Puritans* (Dublin, 1884). Moran's Chapter 7, "Irish Exported as Slaves," cites a number of references to the Irish victims of this English policy as "slaves." Moran, writing in Australia, made the point of saying "white Slaves" (p. 332). But it is to be noted that Smith distances himself from the idea by putting the phrase "Irish slave trade" in quotation marks and insisting that "there was never any such thing as perpetual slavery for any white man in any English colony" (*Colonists in Bondage*, pp. 163, 171). My copy of *A Smaller Irish English Dictionary* (compiled and edited by Patrick S. Dineen) translates *sclabha* as "slave"; and *sclabhuide* as "slave; labourer; peasant." These are of course cognates, Latin-derived. What then would the Irish have called their life of plantation servitude but *sclabhaideacht*, "slavery"? It seems, furthermore, that they would not have felt it necessary to distinguish their servitude from any other plantation servitude. It is only a "white" habit of mind that reserves "slave" for the African-American and boggles at the term "Irish slave trade."

25. Smith, p. 167.

26. Dunlop, 2:655–6.

27. Prendergast, p. 238.

28. "... mercenaries without a fatherland in the armies of kings in whose quarrels they had no interest ..." (Sullivan, 1:16). As to the numbers of such exiles, see Robert Dunlop, *Ireland from the Earliest Times* (Oxford, 1922), p. 129; and William Edward Hartpole Lecky, *History of England in the Eighteenth Century*, 8 vols (New York, 1878–90), 2(1882):286.

29. In the United States in the period after the Civil War, employers of agricultural labor in the South were able to institute what was a tenancy-at-will system, called "contract labor," later transmuted to a system of sharecropping peonage, under which the African-American laborers saw no more of cash wages than they and their forebears had seen before under chattel bondage (Charles Wesley, *Negro Labor in the United States* [New York, 1927], pp. 126–7, 130–35).

30. Prendergast, pp. 307–8.

31. J. C. Beckett, *The Making of Modern Ireland: 1603–1923* (New York, 1966), pp. 132, 135.

32. Petty, *Political Anatomy*; 1:102.

33. Sigerson, *History of the Land Tenures and Land Classes of Ireland with an account of the Various Secret Agrarian Confederacies* (London, 1871), p. 132.

34. *Mist's Weekly Journal*, 30 September 1721. Cited in Herbert Davis, ed., *Major British Writers*, enlarged edition, 2 vols (New York: Harcourt Brace, 1954), 1:642, n. 13. The view was confirmed by R. C. Dallas who had observed West Indies life first-hand. Speaking of the plantation bond-laborers' housing, he declared, "In structure and comfort, these cottages certainly surpass the cabins of the Irish peasants" (R. C. Dallas, *History of the Maroons*, 2 vols [London, 1803], 1:cviii).

35. Lecky, 2:317; Philip Henry Lord Mahon, *History of England from the Peace of Utrecht to the Peace of Versailles*, 7 vols (London, 1858), 5:123.

36. Lecky, 2:265.

37. Ibid., 2:198. A study made in County Tyrone in 1802 found that in general the cottier was allowed half an acre for oats, one-eighth to one-fourth of an acre for potatoes, one-eighth of an acre for flax, graze for a cow, turf for fuel, and "sometimes" a small garden. The rent amounted to £5 to 5 guineas, which the cottier paid by work in the landlord's fields, the time of payment being scheduled to fall in the busiest seasons of the year (John M'Evoy, *A Statistical Survey of the County of Tyrone, with Observations on the Means of Improvement, Drawn upon the Years 1801, and 1802, for the Consideration, and Under the Direction of The Dublin Society* [Dublin, 1802], pp. 99–100). This was the condition of the typical Catholic tenant-at-will, not of the Protestant Scots-Irish leaseholder (see Edward Wakefield [père], *An Account of Ireland, Statistical and Political*, 2 vols [London, 1812], 2:589–90, 2:730, 2:744).

38. Ibid., 2:241–2.

39. Sigerson, p. 35, citing *A Briefe Description of Ireland; made in this yeare 1589, by Robert Paine, unto xxv of his Partners [in England], for whom he is undertaker there [in Ireland]*, in Irish Archaeological Society, *Tracts Relating to Ireland*.

40. Sullivan, *Two Centuries of Irish History*, 1:47.

41. Jonathan Swift, *A Modest Proposal for preventing the children of poor people in Ireland, from being a burden to their parents; and for making them beneficial to the public* (Dublin, 1729).

42. Lecky, 2:239.

43. Sullivan, 1:47.

44. Lecky, 2:274.

45. Francis Lewis Plowden, *History of Ireland from the invasion of Ireland during the reign of Henry II to the Union of England and Ireland/An Historical Review of the State of Ireland from the Invasion of that Country under Henry II to its Union with Great Britain on the first of January 1801*, 5 vols (Philadelphia, 1805), 3:146.

46. See Appendix I.

47. *A New History*, Ancillary Volume II, *Irish Historical Statistics: Population, 1821–71* (Dublin, 1978), edited by W. E. Vaughan and A. J. Fitzpatrick, cites the gamut of estimates of the population of Ireland in the eighteenth century.

48. W. E. H. Lecky, *History of Ireland in the Eighteenth Century*, 5 vols (London, 1893), 2:198–200; 2:221 n. 1, 2:255. J. C. Beckett, *The Anglo-Irish Tradition* (Ithaca, 1976), p. 64. Hugh Boulter, *Letters Written by His Excellency Hugh Boulter, D. D., Lord Primate of All Ireland, &c., Containing An Account of the Most Interesting Transactions which passed in Ireland from 1724 to 1738*, 2 vols, edited by "G.F." (George Faulkner?), (1770; Oxford: Clarendon Press, 1969–70), 2:10. Arthur Young, *A Tour in Ireland* (1780), vol. 2, book 2, p. 33.

49. T. P. Power and Kevin Whelan, eds, *Endurance and Emergence: Catholics in the Eighteenth Century* (Dublin: Irish Academic Press, 1990), p. 102; Lecky, *History of Ireland*, 2:315–16.

50. The most rapid rate of population increase occurred during the last quarter of the century, while a statistically offsetting conversion bulge occurred in the third quarter of the century (T. P. Power, "Converts," in Power and Whelan) after a quarter-century marked by severe famine conditions (J. L. McCracken, "The Social Structure and Social Life, 1714–1760," in *A New History*, 4:34). A doubling of the population in the century, which is the assumption made for this calculation, represents a compound annual rate of increase of 0.7 percent.

51. For comparative figures in regard to the Americas, see David W. Cohn and Jack B. Greene, eds, *Neither Slave Nor Free: The Freedman of African Descent in the Slave Societies of the New World* (Baltimore, 1972), Appendix. Even in the Lower South (principally South Carolina, Georgia, Alabama, Mississippi, Louisiana and Texas, the chief areas for the production of cotton by bond-labor) where free African-Americans were in an especially precarious position, the emancipation ratio was eight times what it was in Ireland (ibid.). Patterson provides a similar set of tables, citing the Cohn and Greene appendix among other sources (Orlando Patterson, *Slavery and Social Death* [New York, 1990] Appendix C, and Tables for Notes to Appendix C).

52. "Apostasy was the first step in the path of ambition" (Lecky, *History of England*, 2:315–16). "Of the upper classes a fairly large number adopted Protestantism, and so became identified with the ruling caste, while preserving a certain amount of sympathy with their Catholic kindred" (W. F. T. Butler, *Confiscation in Irish History* [London, 1918], p. 246). See also: J. G.

Simms, "The Establishment of Protestant Ascendancy, 1691–1714," in *A New History*, 4:19; and Power and Whelan, p. 124.

Because they were by law forbidden to purchase land, or to take long leases, Catholic entrepreneurs were most often merchants and graziers, and prospered there more than in other lines of endeavor (Lecky, *History of England*, 2:245. See also Sullivan, 1:43–4.)

53. Butler, p. 246.

54. Beckett, *Anglo-Irish Tradition*, p. 65.

55. The exploitation of Irish labor was so relatively intense that landlords in Ireland were able to "make as much or more of their estates than any in the three kingdoms [England, Scotland and Ireland] while the [Irish] lands, for equal goodness, produced the least" (Lecky, *History of England*, 2:264, citing Bush, *Hibernia Curiosa*, p. 33).

56. Lecky, *History of England*, 2:311–12, citing the Irish *Commons Journal*, 20 June 1709. A quarter-century later, says Lecky, the sentiment was repeated (Irish *Commons Journal*, 17 December 1735).

57. 10 Will c. 13 (*Irish Statutes*).

58. 1 Geo II c. 20 (1728) (*Irish Statutes*).

59. Lecky, *History of England*, 2:311.

60. Sullivan, 1:36.

61. Maureen Wall, *The Penal Laws, 1691–1760* (Dundalk, 1961), p. 9.

62. Boulter favored the abandonment of the highly questionable "Wood's halfpence" monetary reform proposal precisely because the widespread opposition to the measure had been the occasion for "intimacies between Papists and Jacobites [Scots-Irish Presbyterians] and Whigs [the Anglo-Irish opposition party]" (Boulter to the Duke of Newcastle, 19 January, 1724/5, in Ambrose Phillips, ed., *Letters Written by His Excellency Hugh Boulter, D.D., Lord Primate of All Ireland &c. to Several Ministers of State in England, and some others containing an account of the most interesting transactions which passed in Ireland from 1724 to 1731 (to 1738)*, 2 vols in one [Dublin, 1770], 1:7). Sullivan cites this letter as an illustration of "one of the chief maxims of British rule in Ireland, and one which [Boulter] carefully followed – keep the different sections and parties of the nation asunder" (Sullivan, 1:45).

63. Lord John Beresford to William Eden Lord Auckland, 9 August 1798 (W. Beresford, ed., *Correspondence of the Right Honourable John Beresford*, 2 vols [London, 1854], 2:169–70). Beresford (1738–1805), an Anglo-Irish member of the English Privy Council, enjoyed such influence in the Irish Parliament that he was called "king of Ireland." He displayed his power in securing the dismissal of William Fitzwilliam as Lord Lieutenant of Ireland in 1795, on the grounds that Fitzwilliam was soft on Catholics (Dunlop, *Ireland from the Earliest Times*, p. 151).

64. This apparent absurdity – private encouragement of a tendency publicly anathematized – has its present-day manifestation. The Catholic establishment in Ireland prefers the continuation of Protestant Ascendancy in Northern Ireland rather than accept the disestablishment of religion in the rebirth of a united Ireland.

65. Thomas Smith, *De Republica Anglorum, a Discourse on the Commonwealth of England* (1583; New York, 1906), p. 139 (bk 3, ch. 9).

For a greater appreciation of the importance attached to this issue in the social and economic development of plantation Anglo-America, see: Patterson, pp. 70–76; David Brion Davis, *The Problem of Slavery in Western Culture* (Ithaca, 1966), pp. 13–24, 85–90, 165–73, 222 and 294; and Winthrop D. Jordan, *White Over Black* (Chapel Hill, 1969), pp. 190–215.

66. *Calendar of State Papers, Colonial*, 1:202.

67. Richard Ligon, *A True and Exact History of the Island of Barbadoes* (London, 1673), p. 85; Vincent T. Harlow, *A History of Barbados, 1625–1685* (Oxford, 1926; New York, 1969), p. 84; E. E. Rich and C. H. Wilson, eds, *The Cambridge Economic History of Europe*, vol. IV, *The Economy of Expanding Europe in the Sixteenth and Seventeenth Centuries* (Cambridge, 1967), pp. 334, 338, 344 and 347.

68. Harlow, pp. 338–9.

69. Ligon, p. 50.

70. Virginia County Records, *Northumberland County Record Book, 1652–58*, p. 85 (21 July 1656); *Northumberland County Order Book*, pp. 80 (20 January 1655/6) and 97 (?) (21 July 1656). For a discussion and documentation of this case see "The Elizabeth Key Case," in Volume Two of this work.

71. 2 Hening 26, 170, 260.

72. Peter H. Wood, *Black Majority: Negroes in Colonial South Carolina from 1670 through the Stono Rebellion* (New York: Norton Library, 1975), p. 137.

73. 28 Henry VIII, c. 15, sec., 15. *The Statutes at Large, passed in the Parliaments held in Ireland from the Third Year of Edward the Second, AD 1310, to the First Year of George the Third, AD 1786 inclusive with Marginal Notes, and a Compleat Index to the Whole*, 20 vols (Dublin, 1765–1800). Richard Mant, *History of the Church of Ireland from the Reformation to the union of the Churches of England and Ireland, January 1, 1801*, 2 vols (London, 1840), 1:292–3.

74. Edmund Spenser, *A View of the State of Ireland* [1596], in Edwin Greenlaw, Charles Grosvenor Osgood, and Frederick Morgan Paddelford, eds, *The Works of Edmund Spenser, a Variorum Edition*, 10 vols (Baltimore: Johns Hopkins University Press, 1966), 9:119.

75. *Calendar of State Papers, Colonial*, 10:611 (8 October 1680).

76. The first use in a Virginia statute of the term "white" to designate European-Americans as a social category occurred in 1691 (see 3 Hening 87). The Irish Penal Laws were inaugurated with two acts passed by the Irish Parliament in 1695 (7 Will III c. 4 and c. 5).

77. Lyon G. Tyler, reviewing Philip Alexander Bruce, *Social Life of Virginia in the Seventeenth Century*, in *William and Mary Quarterly*, series 1, 16(1907–8):145–7. Other book reviews, earlier and later, made the same point almost verbatim (*William and Mary Quarterly*, series 1, 6[1897–98:202–3]; 25[1916–17]:145–6).

78. Plowden, *History of Ireland*, 1:199.

79. Wall, *Penal Laws*, p. 9.

80. Sigerson, *History of Land Tenures*, p. 117.

81. Denys Scully, *A Statement of the Penal Laws, which Aggrieve the Catholics of Ireland: With Commentaries* (Dublin, 1812), p. 334. Sullivan (*Two Centuries of Irish History*, pp. 59–60) cites a mid-eighteenth-century case in which the judge decided against a Catholic by precisely the legal formula quoted.

82. Despite the racist restrictions of the Penal Laws and the general spirit of the Protestant Ascendancy, Catholics, by evasion or taking advantage of loopholes in the system, did find some success in trade and leasehold farming and livestock. As the detente between the Catholic bourgeoisie and the British government matured in the closing decades of the eighteenth century, a Catholic middle class was able to make some economic headway. See: Maureen Wall, "The Rise of a Catholic Middle Class in Eighteenth-century Ireland," *Irish Historical Studies*, vol. 11, no. 42 (September 1958); Louis M. Cullen, "Catholic Social Classes Under the Penal Laws," in Powers and Whelan, pp. 58–63. A number of historians have sought to redress the neglect of "the presence of a significant number of propertied catholics who not only survived but prospered and increased in number even before 1782" (Cullen, p. 62). The "Catholic relief act of 1782" allowed Catholics to acquire land.

83. "The penal code, as it was actually carried out, was inspired much less by fanaticism than by rapacity" (Lecky, *History of Ireland*, 1:312).

84. All the Penal Laws relating to Ireland cited in this section are, of course, to be found in *Irish Statutes*.

85. Sigerson, p. 118.

86. 2 Hening 280–81. In time there were African-American owners of bondmen and bondwomen throughout the South, except in Delaware and Arkansas, where that practice was legally barred to African-Americans on "race" principles (Kenneth M. Stampp, *The Peculiar Institution* [New York, 1956], pp. 194–5, citing Carter G. Woodson, *Free Negro Owners of Slaves in the United States in 1830* [Washington, DC, 1924]; and Helen Tunncliff Catterall, ed., *Judicial Cases Concerning American Slavery and the Negro*, 5 vols [Washington: Carnegie Institution, 1926–37; Octagon Books reprint, 1968], 4:215 and 5:257). In 1832 Virginia also made it illegal for an African-American to acquire bond-laborers (except through inheritance), other than the purchaser's own wife or husband, parent or descendant (Luther Porter Jackson, *Free Negro Labor and Property Holding in Virginia, 1830–1860* [New York, 1942], p. 23).

87. Philip Alexander Bruce, *Economic History of Virginia in the Seventeenth Century* (New York, 1895), 2:51–2, 89–90. Not all African-American bond-laborers were bound for life; as limited-term bond-laborers they were priced comparably with European-American bond-laborers (ibid., 2:51–3).

88. 2 Hening 86–7; 3 W & M Act 16 (Virginia).

89. In 1670 the 750 acres left by Anthony Johnson in Accomack County were escheated on the grounds that he was "a Negroe and by consequence an alien" (*Virginia Miscellany, Foreign Business and Inquisitions, 1665–1676*, Library of Congress Manuscript Collection. Photocopy at Virginia State Library, Archives Division. Access number: 22388). I am indebted to Robert Clay of the Virginia State Library Archives for bringing this item to my attention, and to Fred Dornan who exhumed it from the Jefferson Manuscripts at the Library of Congress. Whether this became a precedent and, if so, for what period of time, this writer cannot say. It had ceased to be Virginia law sometime before 1830 (see Jackson). The Mississippi Black Code, a short-lived attempt to nullify the Thirteenth Amendment, in 1866 forbade Negroes to acquire farm land (John Hope Franklin, *Reconstruction After the Civil War* [Chicago, 1961], p. 50).

90. *Irish Statutes*: 7 Will III c. 5; 10 Will III c. 8, 13; 2 Anne c. 6; 8 Anne c. 3; 2 Geo I c. 10; 6 Geo I c. 10; 1 Geo II c. 9; 9 Geo II c. 3; 17 & 18 Geo II c. 2; 15 Geo III c. 21. One English statute, 3 W & M c. 2, belongs in this list. The citations of laws passed by English (or, after 1700, British) Parliaments refer to (1) *The Statutes at Large from Magna Charta ... to 1807*, 46 vols in 52 (London 1762–1807), the title to be abbreviated *English Statutes*; and (2) *The Statutes of the United Kingdom*, 46 volumes in 52 (London, 1807–69). Citations are by reign and chapter.

91. Scully, p. 333.

92. From the decision of Chief Justice Roger B. Taney for the Supreme Court in 1857, and cited here from Richard D. Heffner, ed., *A Documentary History of the United States* (New York, 1956), p. 131.

93. 3 Hening 298 (4 Anne c. 19, sec. 31 [Virginia]). Catholics were by law required to abandon allegiance to the Church of Rome, to accept the authority of the Anglican Protestant church, and regularly to attend its services. Offenders were "recusants." A "recusant convict" was any person officially declared guilty of the offense.

94. In August 1831 three score African-American bond-laborers in Southampton County, Virginia, rose in rebellion under the leadership of Nat Turner. Around sixty "whites" were killed by the rebels. Twice that number of African-Americans were killed in the repression of the rebellion, mostly randomly and summarily. Nat Turner and sixteen others, including three free Negroes, were executed after trial. However, the rebellion brought the issue of abolition to a level of attention that it had not held before in the United States, and thus may be said to mark the beginning of the pre-Civil War period (see: Herbert Aptheker, *Documentary History of the Negro People of the United States*, [New York, 1951], pp. 119–25; John Hope Franklin, *From Slavery to Freedom: A History of Negro Americans*, 6th edition [New York, 1988], pp. 133–5; William Freehling, *The Road to Disunion*, vol. I, *Secessionists at Bay* [New York, 1990], especially pp. 178–81; William Loren Katz: *Eyewitness: The Negro in American History: A Living Documentary of the Afro-American Contribution to US History* [New York, 1967], 120–22).

95. 3 Hening 102 (4 W & M Act 3 [Virginia]); Stampp, pp. 224–8; Jackson, p. 22.

96. Sullivan, 1:37.

97. 1 Geo II c. 6, sec. 7 (Ireland).

98. 3 Hening 172, 238 (11 Will III, Act 2, and 4 Anne c. 2, sec. 3 [Virginia]).

99. 4 Hening 133–34 (9 Geo I c. 4, sec. 3 [Virginia]).

100. 8 Anne c. 3, sec. 16. The name of the offense was "praemunire," that is, following an authority other than that of the queen. Catholic priests were assumed to be guilty of praemunire simply by virtue of their affiliation with Rome. Hedgerow schools were indeed taught by Catholic priests illegally. This law simply treated Catholic Irish teachers as if they were all in fact priests.

101. David J. Dixon ("Catholics and Trade in Eighteenth-century Ireland: An Old Debate Revisited," in Powers and Whelan, *Endurance and Emergence*, pp. 85–100) believes that the apprenticeship restrictions were little more than a nuisance to Catholic tradespeople, and that it was the ban on urban leasing by Catholics that was the most serious handicap to the urban Catholic bourgeois's aspirations (p. 91).

102. Lecky, *History of England*, 2:309, citing *The case of the Roman Catholics of Ireland*, drawn up by the Reverend Doctor Nary in 1724.

103. Lecky, *History of England*, 2:309–10.

104. Young, *Tour in Ireland*, bk 2, p. 34.

105. "No person, not even the master, was to teach a slave to read or write, employ him in setting type in a printing office, or given him books or pamphlets" (Stampp, p. 208).

106. Frederick Douglass, *Life and Times of Frederick Douglass, Written by Himself, His Early*

Life as a Slave, His escape from Bondage, and his complete History, revised edition (1892; New York: Collier Books, 1962), p. 79.

107. Jackson, pp. 19–21.

108. Lecky, *History of Ireland*, 1:308, n. 1; Richard B. Morris, *Government and Labor in Early America* (New York, 1946), p. 183, citing New York Common Council Records.

109. Morris, pp. 182–8.

110. Leon F. Litwak, *North of Slavery: The Negro in the Free States, 1790–1860* (Chicago, 1961), p. 17.

111. Douglass, pp. 179–85, 210–11. An irony to which I shall return is to be found in the identical nature of the treatment suffered by Douglass in these instances at the hands of "white" workers, including Irish immigrant workers in the United States, and the hostility often directed against Irish (and not just Catholic Irish) immigrant laborers in England and Scotland. (See J. H. Treble, "Irish Navvies in the North of England 1830–50," *Transport History*, 6:227–47 [1973], especially, p. 239, for an incident reminiscent of Douglass's experience in the Baltimore shipyard.)

112. Young, bk 2, p. 29.

113. Sigerson, p. 130. Sigerson draws this inference from a list of eight "Particular Clauses of Leases," in M'Evoy, *Statistical Survey of the County of Tyrone*, pp. 102–3. See also Robert Dunlop, *Daniel O'Connell* (New York, 1900), pp. 45–6. Compare Louis M. Cullen, "Economic Development, 1750–1800," in *A New History*, 4:171–2.

114. Boulter, letters to the Bishop of London, the Archbishop of Canterbury and the Duke of Newcastle, an English secretary of state, in May 1730 (in his *Letters*, 2:9–12).

115. So termed by Primate Boulter (*Letters*, 2:103).

116. Lecky, *History of England*, 2:219. I have relied much on Lecky's work, pp. 218–23.

117. Writing in 1888, Sullivan remembered how "Charter School kidnappers [served] as a bogey for wayward children" (*Two Centuries of Irish History*, 1:53).

118. Denys Scully, *A Statement of the Penal Laws, which aggrieve the Catholics of Ireland: with Commentaries*, 2nd enlarged edition (Dublin, 1802), p. 267.

119. Lecky, *History of England*, 2:219.

120. *Commons Journal* (1788), cited in Scully, pp. 268–9.

121. 2 Geo I, c. 17, sec. 11 (*Irish Statutes*).

122. Lecky, *History of England*, 2:276–7.

123. Ibid., pp. 221, 222. The English imperial historian J. A. Froude had not the slightest objection to the racial oppression aspect of the Charter School system. He seems to suggest that a stricter enforcement of the Penal Laws would have made it possible for the Charter Schools to succeed. But as it was, he said, they were "choked in Irish society, as wholesome vegetables are choked in a garden when the weeds are allowed scope to spring." The reader is left to apply the weed-and-vegetable metaphor to the following intelligence, added by Froude in a footnote: "The industrial training, so excellent in conception, degenerated by negligence into a system in which the children became the slaves of the masters and grew up in rags and starvation" (*The English in Ireland in the Eighteenth Century*, 4 vols [London, 1871–74]; 2:12 n. 1).

124. Lecky, *History of England*, 2:223. What the Protestant Ascendancy produced by way of the Charter Schools was emulated by American white supremacy in many respects through the United States Indian education program initiated about 1879. See John Collier, *Indians of the Americas* (New York, 1948), p. 134; and Wilcomb E. Washburn, *The American Indian and the United States: A Documentary History*, 4 vols (New York, 1973), under the index entries, "Education, Indian: outing system; purposes of; and schools." See especially, 1:430, 1:433–4.

125. Thomas Harris Jr and John McHenry, *Maryland Reports, being a Series of the Most Important Law Cases argued and determined in the Provincial Court and Court of Appeals of the then Province of Maryland from the Year 1700 down to the American Revolution* (New York, 1809), Vol. 1, p. 563; henceforth referred to as Harris and McHenry.

126. Stampp, *Peculiar Institution*, p. 343. The African-American family resisted with determination, courage and historical persistence. Stampp related the details of several such instances. But for a fuller treatment of the generations of African-American family tradition see Herbert Gutman, *The Black Family in Slavery and Freedom, 1750–1925* (New York: Vintage Books, 1977). For some interesting citations of Irish/Negro parallels drawn by nineteenth-century commentators, see particularly pp. 199–301 in that work. For Gutman's critique of the writings of other historians

(including Stampp, Elkins and Genovese) regarding the struggles of the African-American under bondage, see pp. 304–19.

127. 3 Hening 86–87 (3 W & M Act 16 [Virginia]).

128. Royal Instructions to the Governor of Nova Scotia in 1719 offered a grant of fifty acres, to be exempt from quit-rent for ten years, to "every white man . . . and every white woman" who married a native "Indian." This order was reissued in 1749, raising the inducement to intermarriage to a payment of £10 sterling and exemption from quit-rent for twenty years. Genetic imperatives upon which Winthrop Jordan relies to explain racial exclusionism, and blinding sexual passion by which he accounts for "interracial" mating, seem not to have entered into consideration in the framing of these instructions. The orders were officially said to be intended as "a further mark of [the Royal] good will towards the said Indian nations." This order remained in effect until 1773 (Leonard Woods Labaree, collator and editor, *Royal Instructions to British Colonial Governors, 1670–1776*, 2 vols [New York and London, 1935], p. 470). Jordan refers to these orders in a footnote, emphasizing that the scope of the orders was limited to Nova Scotia, and that they did not mention African-Americans (*White over Black*, p. 163 n. 61).

129. Washburn, 2:1429.

130. Ibid., 4:2723–4.

131. Judge Dulany, Maryland Provincial Court, 1767 (1 Harris and McHenry, p. 562.)

4 Social Control: From Racial to National Oppression

1. 1 W. & M. c. 2. John William Fortescue, *A History of the British Army*, 13 vols (London, 1899–1930), 3:11.

2. Fortescue, 3:10, 3:40. In 1779, Henry Burg, a member of the Protestant Anglo-Irish Parliament, said, "Ireland is not at peace; it is a smothered war" (P. W. Joyce, *A Concise History of Ireland from the Earliest Times to 1837*, 6th edition [Dublin, 1897], pp. 253–4).

3. In the 1780s, the cost of the military forces required to collect the hearth tax and the tax on "private distilleries" by special "still-hunting" detachments of the cavalry was as much as the amount of the taxes collected. "Throughout the eighteenth century the army played a crucial role in the internal peace of Ireland" (Kevin Boyle, "Police in Ireland before the Union," *Irish Jurist*, 7[1972]:115–37; pp. 125, 134).

When faced with the threat of a French invasion of Ireland in 1796, the British commander in Ireland sent an urgent request for reinforcements, because "his troops were so much dispersed on police-duty" (Fortescue, 4:518).

4. Maureen Wall, *The Penal Laws, 1691–1760, Church and State from the Treaty of Limerick to the Accession of George III* (Dundalk: Dundalgan Press, 1961), pp. 26–8. Lecky, *History of England in the Eighteenth Century*, 8 vols (New York, 1878–90), 2(1882):370. Of the 14,000 inhabitants of Galway in 1762, only 350 were Protestants (Maureen Wall, "Catholics in Economic Life," in L. C. Cullen, ed., *The Formation of the Irish Economy* (Cork, 1969), p. 47.

5. See Robin Blackburn, *The Overthrow of Colonial Slavery, 1776–1848* (London and New York: Verso, 1988), pp. 220–51. Blackburn's book is an excellent comprehensive treatment of the title subject.

6. R. B. McDowell, "The Age of the United Irishmen: Revolution and the Union, 1794–1800," in *A New History*, 4:357. Although in the absence of source citations it is not possible to reconcile differences in the numbers given for the size of the repressive force (Bottigheimer says 40,000 yeomanry, plus 25,000 Irish militia, and only 7,000 regular troops were employed), McDowell's conclusion is consonant with Bottigheimer's: "How viable was a state so palpably dependent upon the 'foreign' power of Britain to preserve it from the ravages of its own unruly population?" (Karl S. Bottigheimer, *Ireland and the Irish: A Short History* [New York, 1982], p. 157).

7. Burke to Langrishe, 3 January 1792, in *The Works of The Right Honorable Edmund Burke*, 6th edition (Boston, 1880), 4:265.

8. Thomas Bartlett, "The Origin and Progress of the Catholic Question in Ireland," in T. P. Powers and Kevin Whelan, eds, *Endurance and Emergence: Catholics in Ireland in the Eighteenth Century* (Dublin: Irish Academic Press, 1990), p. 8.

9. Ibid.

10. See Chapter 2. Two voices were still being raised in the British Parliament in May 1805 warning that Irish Catholic families secretly kept maps showing their ancestral lands in anticipation of regaining them upon Emancipation (cited by Connolly, in "Aftermath and Adjustment," in *A New History*, 5:29–30). Keeping to the safe side, indeed, the eventual Catholic Emancipation Act of 1829 required each Member of Parliament to swear an oath to "defend to the utmost of my Power the Settlement of Property within this Realm, as established by the Laws" (10 Geo. IV, c. 7, sec. 2).

11. 2 Anne c. 6., sec. 5.

12. Bartlett, p. 6.

13. Preamble to 17 & 18 Geo. III, c. 21 (1777–78), c. 49 (*Irish Statutes*), "An act for the relief of his Majesty's subjects of this kingdom professing the popish religion."

14. L. M. Cullen, "Catholic Social Classes under the Penal Laws," in Powers and Whelan, pp. 58–63. The law, 11 & 12 Geo. III (*Irish Statutes*), was called the "Bogland Act."

15. The first of these new laws, 17 & 18 Geo. III, c. 6, allowed to Catholics the right to be accepted for 999-year leases, a right hitherto reserved for Protestants. The second, 21 & 22 Geo. III, c. 24, permitted Catholics to acquire land, except in parliamentary boroughs. This last formal restriction was repealed only with Catholic Emancipation in 1829.

16. "The mass of the people lived on the borders of penury and starvation, [as] tenants at will ..." (Boyle, p. 127). Forty years after the Union, twelve years after Catholic Emancipation, still the census of Ireland showed that 76 percent of employed males were poor peasants (17.6 percent) or laborers (58.8 percent), with an average holding of less than two acres, comprising only one-eighth of the total acreage. Landlords, capitalist farmers and "comfortable farmers" had average holdings of 350 acres, 80 acres and 50 acres respectively, and their shares of the country's total acreage were 17.5 percent, 20 percent, and 25 percent (Cormac O'Grada, "Poverty, Population, and Agriculture, 1801–45," in *A New History*, 5:114).

17. L. M. Cullen, "Catholic Social Classes," p. 58; L. M. Cullen, "Economic Development, 1691–1750," in *A New History*, 4:128.

18. "The concessions to catholics in 1792 and 1793 were a product of fear rather than philanthropy" (Bartlett, p. 14).

19. Cited by R. B. McDowell, 4:307–8. Home Secretary Henry Dundas's exact words, as cited, were "sharers in the general predilection with which moderate men are accustomed to contemplate the existing government."

20. Patrick Rogers, *The Irish Volunteers and Catholic Emancipation, 1778–1793* (London, 1934), pp. 306–7, 312. Bartlett's assertion "The catholics were bought off" ("Origin and Progress," p. 14) might seem too harsh. But we have the corroborating testimony of Daniel O'Connell himself on the subject. Speaking of the critical years 1792 and 1793, O'Connell recalled "the spirit of republican phrensy" that was spreading throughout Ireland. He continued: "had not England wisely and prudently bought all the Catholic nobility and gentry, and the far greater part of the Catholic people out of the market of republicanism, that which was but a rebellion, would most assuredly have been a revolution. The Presbyterians and the Catholics would have united" (*The Select Speeches of Daniel O'Connell, MP, edited with historical sections Etc., by his son, John O'Connell, Esq.*, two vols [Dublin, 1865], 1:198 [15 June 1815]).

21. Hereward Senior, *Orangeism in Ireland and Britain, 1795–1836* (London: Routledge & Kegan Paul, 1966), p. 13.

22. Ibid.

23. Ibid., pp. 16–18, 29–30, 48.

24. Ibid., pp. 83, 88, 97–8, 102, 104.

25. "A restoration of the Irish parliament as it had been before 1801 was one thing; the creation of an independent parliament in the wake of catholic emancipation and a possible reform of the electoral system was quite another" (S. J. Connolly, "Aftermath and Adjustment," 5:22).

26. Bartlett, p. 17.

27. It was "a strange kind of arithmetical comfort" whereby the Irish Catholics "might be told that though they went to bed a majority, yet by the magic of a piece of parchment they awoke in a minority." So argued the Whig member Hobhouse in the House of Commons, adding that it would "provoke the indignation" of its presumed beneficiaries (*Cobbett's Parliamentary History of England ... 1066 to 1803*, 36 vols [London, 1806–20], 34:471 [14 February 1799]).

28. "... [G]iving stipends to the Roman Catholic priesthood, from the public funds ... was the measure contemplated by Mr Pitt in 1801." The speech of Home Secretary Robert Peel, on 5 March 1829, introducing the government's Measure for the Removal of Roman Catholic Disabilities (which came to be known as the Catholic Emancipation Act upon its enactment on 13 April 1829) took four hours to deliver; it required over fifty columns to print (*Hansard Parliamentary Debates*, 2d series, 20:727–80). In subsequent references, it will be called Peel's "Emancipation" speech.

29. The Irish Catholic prelacy "thankfully accepted" the proposal of the "Government of an independent provision for the Roman Catholic clergy of Ireland ... [in return for which the Irish Catholics agreed that] ... in the appointment of prelates of the Roman Catholic religion[, if] Government have any proper objection against such candidates" for bishop, then the Irish Catholics were to proceed "to the election of another candidate." The resolution was signed by all four of the archbishops and thirteen of the nineteen bishops. It was endorsed in quick succession by the other bishops and the generality of the priesthood (T. Dunbar Ingram, *A History of the Legislative Union of Great Britain and Ireland* [Dublin, 1887], pp. 146–58). The text of the resolution, with the names of the signers, is reprinted at pages 148–9. This proposition was consistently supported by the Vatican, even after most Irish Catholics had repudiated it.

It was Lord Grenville (1759–1834) who, referring back to the tacit pledges made to secure the support of the Irish Catholic hierarchy, said that the churchmen had been "justified in entertaining great and sanguine expectations that the measure would lead to the consequences anxiously desired" (*Cobbett's Parliamentary Debates 1803–12*, 22 vols [London, 1804–12], 4:659–60 [10 May 1805]).

30. "The people of Ireland are unable to understand why one system of government should be adopted in Canada, and another of a totally opposite character should, greatly to their disadvantage, be applied to Ireland" (William Smith O'Brien, Irish Protestant Liberal and nationalist Member of Parliament, speaking in a debate on "The State of Ireland," 4 July 1843 [*Hansard Parliamentary Debates*, 3d series, 70:669]).

Oliver Macdonagh (in his Introduction to Volume 5 of *A New History*: 5:lii–liii) makes a comment which seems relevant to the "relativity of race" theme in the present work. "Ireland in 1801–70 was dwindling into a colonial condition," he says. But noting the failure of Ireland to attain responsible government and the fact of its representation in the British Parliament, he concludes that Ireland "differed from the British colonies of white settlement." Translation: the Protestant ("white") sector of the colony was too small to function as the intermediate social control stratum, except in a gerrymandered Ulster; there, from 1922 to 1972, the Protestants ("whites") did have a separate parliament, and a "responsible government" in which their dominance was guaranteed, à la Canada and Australia.

31. Edward Wakefield, *père* (1774–1854) was of the opinion that one of the customs that legal reforms would not eradicate was the practice among "country gentlemen" of "making 'pets' of protestant yeomen, or in common language giving them the preference in every occurrence of life" (Edward Wakefield, *An Account of Ireland, Statistical and Political*, 2 vols [London, 1812], 2:589–90).

32. For example, W. E. H. Lecky, *Leaders of Public Opinion in Ireland*, 2 vols "new edition" (London, 1903), 2:70, 2:97. James Reynolds, *The Catholic Emancipation Crisis in Ireland, 1823–29* (Westport, Connecticut, 1954), p. 164.

33. Lecky, *Leaders of Public Opinion*, 2:101.

34. In its most common usage, "Catholic Emancipation" is understood to mean the passage of the Roman Catholic Relief Act (10 Geo IV, c. 7) in 1829, removing the religious test oaths which under the Penal Laws barred Catholics from Parliament and from trades and professions. The reader will notice that the qualification "so-called" given here to this historic term is here put in ironic quotation marks. The reason is that, while what was eventually accomplished under this heading was historically quite significant – the overthrow of racial oppression outside of Ulster – yet that still left Catholic Ireland under British domination as an oppressed nation, a point most tragically demonstrated in the conduct of the British government during the Great Irish Famine, which began in 1845. Moreover, it still left religio-racial oppression intact in Ulster. And it still left the masses of Irish Catholic peasants without the tenant-right of Protestant Ulster.

35. See especially Sections II, V, XIV, XXII, and XXIII of the Catholic Emancipation Act (10 Geo. IV, c. 7). "Emancipation was essentially the demand of a rising Catholic middle class,

of gentry owning or holding land, lawyers and journalists, merchants, shopkeepers, small and large tenant farmers, a broad and growing class which demanded a full share in local and central government and of which O'Connell himself ... was a perfectly representative member" (Angus Macintyre, *The Liberator: Daniel O'Connell and the Irish Party, 1830–1847* [New York, 1965], p. 12).

36. *Cobbett's Parliamentary Debates*, 4:659–60 (10 May 1805), and 4:101–2 (25 March 1805).

37. "[T]he moment we have resolved on the admission of the Roman Catholics to Parliament," said Peel in his "Emancipation" speech (5 March 1829), "[t]he eligibility of the Roman Catholic for civil office, becomes a 'security' for the Protestant establishments" (*Hansard Parliamentary Debates*, 2d series, 20:762).

38. "We must have the Irish rent spent in Ireland. We must have no foreign landlords. Let those who will not live in Ireland sell their Irish estates. The rents of Ireland *must* be spent in Ireland! Irish affairs must be managed by Irishmen; and, indeed, they *certainly* will be so soon as hope becomes extinct in the Orange leaders" (letter from Daniel O'Connell to P. V. FitzPatrick, 17 September 1833, emphasis in original; in Maurice R. O'Connell, ed., *The Correspondence of Daniel O'Connell*, 8 vols [Dublin: Irish University Press, 1973–80]).

39. To Prime Minister Robert Peel, repeal of the Union involved "not merely the repeal of an act of Parliament, but the dismemberment of this great empire," and he said he was prepared to launch a civil war to prevent it (*Hansard Parliamentary Debates*, 3d series, 4:24–5 (9 May 1843]).

40. See Daniel O'Connell's letter to John Campbell, then Irish Lord Chancellor, 9 September 1843, at the height of the Repeal campaign, in which O'Connell urged Campbell, a Whig, to promote a series of British reform measures for "conciliating the Irish nation and strengthening the British empire" (W. J. Fitzpatrick, ed., *The Correspondence of Daniel O'Connell, The Liberator*, 2 vols [London, 1888] 2:290–91). See also Campbell's letter of 16 September to his brother George Campbell, acquainting him with the contents of O'Connell's letter, and saying it showed that O'Connell would be "glad of a pretext for relaxing from Repeal agitation" (*Life of Lord Campbell, Lord High Chancellor of Great Britain, consisting of his autobiography, diary and letters*, by his daughter, Mrs Hardcastle, 2 vols [London, 1881], 1:179–80).

41. Robert Dunlop, *Daniel O'Connell* (New York, 1900), pp. 16–17. "[The Irish peasantry] favour Repeal in the hope of change" from "the poverty of the tenantry, and of the exactions of landlords and their agents" (letter of Home Secretary Sir James Graham to Prime Minister Robert Peel, 17 October 1843, in Charles Stuart Parker, ed., *Sir Robert Peel, from his Private Papers*, 3 vols [London, 1899], 3:64).

42. Gustave de Beaumont, the liberal-minded contemporary and fellow countryman of Alexis de Tocqueville, traveled extensively in America before visiting Ireland. In his Irish account he devoted an entire chapter to the poverty he encountered there. He wrote that he had thought that the condition of the driven-out American Indians and the enchained African-Americans must represent the ultimate in human deprivation, until he saw "the lot of poor Ireland" (Gustave de Beaumont, *L'Irelande sociale, politique et religieuse*, 2 vols [Paris, 1839], 1:204).

43. According to Daniel O'Connell, probably not one of the agrarian rebels was a qualified voter (O'Connell to Lord Duncannon, 14 January 1833, in O'Connell, ed., *Correspondence of Daniel O'Connell*, vol. 5, item 1949).

44. S. J. Connolly, "Mass Politics and Sectarian Conflict, 1823–30," in *A New History*, 5:92–3. Following the passage of the Catholic Emancipation Act, "the prevailing feeling of the ... masses in Ireland was undoubtedly that the victory they had achieved was only the forerunner of armed rebellion which was to break down English dominion in Ireland" (Lecky, *Leaders of Public Opinion*, 2:98).

45. James Connolly, *Labour in Irish History* (New York, 1919), p. 87; Brian O'Neill, *The War for the Land in Ireland* (London, 1933), pp. 37–8.

46. Reynolds, *Catholic Emancipation Crisis*, p. 155; *Hansard Parliamentary Debates*, 3d series, 13:1206 (2 July 1832); Robert Kee, *The Green Flag* (London, 1972), p. 205.

47. Angus Macintyre, *The Liberator*, pp. 180–81. "O'Connell ... fully justified the conspiracy to refuse ... payment [of the tithe]" (Lecky, *Leaders of Public Opinion*, 2:128). However, he and the other Catholic politicians and clergy were uncompromisingly opposed to the peasants' resorting to violence; they worried that the tithe war would get out of hand and become involved in anti-landlordism.

48. Historian S. J. Connolly's judgment regarding the O'Connell party and the development of the Catholic Emancipation campaign applies generally to the entire twenty-year period from the founding of the Catholic Association in 1823 to the miscarried Repeal Year of 1843: "[T]he catholic leaders took up the characteristic stance of bourgeois politicians throughout early nineteenth-century Europe, seeking to use popular discontent to further their own political aims, while at the same time holding back from the point at which that discontent would erupt into uncontrollable violence" (S. J. Connolly, "Mass Politics and Sectarian Conflict," 5:94).

49. Ibid., 5:84. A convenient source for brief biographical notes on many of the Irish figures of the seventeenth and eighteenth centuries is R. F. Foster, *Modern Ireland, 1600–1972* (New York, 1989), whose index italicizes the page numbers to show where the note is to be found, e.g., Sheil, p. *307*; Wyse, p. *297*. For more extensive notes on Sheil and Wyse and other Irish figures mentioned in this study see Alfred Webb, ed., *A Compendium of Irish Biography* (Dublin, 1878); Henry Boylan, ed., *Dictionary of Irish Biography* (New York: Barnes and Noble, 1978). See also Lecky, *Leaders of Public Opinion*, 2:57–8, and his sketch of Sheil, ibid., 2:58–9. Both Sheil and Wyse would eventually part with O'Connell on the issue of repeal of the Union. O'Connell, writing to Sheil at that time, referred to himself as having been "once your co-leader" (W. J. Fitzpatrick, ed., *Correspondence of Daniel O'Connell, The Liberator*, 2 vols [London, 1888], 2:323 [Richmond Bridewell prison, 19 June 1844]).

50. Fergus O'Ferrall, "'The only lever ...': The Catholic Priest in Irish Politics," *Studies* (Dublin), 70(1981), pp. 313, 317, and 322 n. 37.

51. Peel said: "We were watching the movement of tens of thousands of disciplined fanatics, abstaining from every excess and indulgence, and concentrating every passion and feeling on one single object" (Reynolds, p.158 n. 111).

52. Ibid., p. 149.

53. Ibid., pp. 149–50; 150 n. 75.

54. "... either restraints in Ireland unknown in the ordinary practice of the constitution, or concession in some form or other ..." (Duke of Wellington, as Prime Minister, to Robert Peel, Home Secretary, 12 December 1828, cited in Reynolds, p. 164).

55. Lecky, *Leaders of Public Opinion*, 2:99.

56. Even so, the government was apprehensive concerning the high percentage of Catholics among the troops (Reynolds, pp. 146, 149). See also Lecky, *Leaders of Public Opinion*, 2:83.

57. S. J. Connolly, "The Catholic Question, 1801–12," in *A New History*, 5:39.

58. J. G. Simms, "The Irish on the Continent," in *A New History*, 4:650. O'Ferrall, p. 314. Testifying in favor of the subsidy for Maynooth in 1825, Daniel O'Connell saw Maynooth as a way "to take away the temptation and necessity of foreign education, which I take to be dangerous in the event of the continuance of the existing order of things" (*The Evidence taken before the Select Committees of the Houses of Lords and Commons appointed in the Sessions of 1824 and 1825 to inquire into The State of Ireland* [London, 1825], p. 547).

59. S. J. Connolly, "Catholic Question," 5: 31–2, 5:36. Despite Ascendentist obstructionism, the commitment to the support of Maynooth remained an essential element of British policy (Oliver MacDonagh, "Politics, 1830–45," in *A New History*, 5:186; W. E. Vaughan, "Ireland, c. 1870," in *A New History*, 5:726). The hook in the Maynooth grants was always in "giving the State at once a control over the education and a hold upon the affection or the interests of the Roman Catholic priesthood" (Lord Edward Stanley to Sir Robert Peel, 21 October 1843 [Parker, 3:66]).

60. S. J. Connolly, "Catholic Question," 5:37.

61. Reynolds, pp. 161–2. S. J. Connolly, "Mass Politics and Sectarian Conflict," 5:95, 5:101. The "two-wings" bill was defeated in the House of Lords by a vote of 178–130 (*A New History*, 8:306–7).

62. The change was signaled by the defeat of two Protestant lords seeking parliamentary seats from Waterford and Louth, respectively, when forty-shilling freeholders defied custom by refusing to vote for their landlords' candidates (S. J. Connolly, "Mass Politics and Sectarian Conflict," 5:97–100; Lecky, *Leaders of Public Opinion*, 2:72–5).

63. Reynolds, p. 165; S. J. Connolly, "Mass Politics and Sectarian Conflict," 5:106.

64. Peel's "Emancipation" speech, *Hansard Parliamentary Debates*, 2d series, 20:769, 20:772.

65. Senior, *Orangeism*, p. 281.

66. Irish representation in the British Parliament was increased from 100 to 105 in 1832 (2 &

3 Will. IV, c. 88), and the Irish delegation elected that December included about forty repealers. Although Ireland contained 30 percent of the population of the United Kingdom, only 16 percent of the seats in the Reformed Parliament were allotted to Ireland.

67. "The limited Irish £10 franchise was an obstacle, for it gave the advantage to [O'Connell's] opponents" (Kevin B. Nowlan, *The Politics of Repeal: A Study in the Relations between Great Britain and Ireland, 1841–50* [London, 1965], p. 23).

68. S. J. Connolly, "Mass Politics and Sectarian Conflict," 5:106.

69. Reynolds, p. 168.

70. James O'Connor, *The History of Ireland, 1798–1924*, 2 vols (London, 1925), 1:229.

71. Report of the Select [Parliamentary] Commission on Tithes (1831–32), 21:294, 327, 381, cited in Macintyre, *The Liberator*, p. 176.

72. Oliver MacDonagh, "The Economy and Society, 1830–45," in *A New History*, 5:222–3. MacDonagh's comment is completely consonant with Wellington's characterization of the tithe war (see p. 98). See also Macintyre, pp. 175–6. For a contemporary account of the inception of the anti-tithe movement, see the speech of Mr Stanley in the House of Commons, 13 March 1832 (*Hansard Parliamentary Debates*, 3d series, 11:135–42).

73. Ibid. Lecky, *Leaders of Public Opinion*, 2:130.

74. Lecky, *Leaders of Public Opinion*, 2:131–2. For an account of the unspeakably inhuman conditions to which the transportees were subjected, and the related impact on the original population of the country, see Robert Hughes, *The Fatal Shore* (New York: Alfred A. Knopf, 1986).

75. MacDonagh, "Economy and Society, 1830–45," 5:223–4. An intermediate step toward turning the collection over to landlords was taken in 1832 with "tithe composition" legislation (2 William IV, c. 119). See Macintyre, p. 198.

76. MacDonagh, "Economy and Society, 1830–45," 5:225. Assign this role to the landlords, said O'Connell, "and the spirit which had continued the present agitation for seventy years, would be applied to rent" (*Hansard Parliamentary Debates*, 3d series, 21:596, 20 February 1834; cited in Macintyre, p. 190).

77. See Father John F. Broderick, SJ, *The Holy See and the Irish Movement for the Repeal of the Union with England, 1829–47* (*Analecta Gregoriana*, Cura Pontificiae Universitatis Gregoriana edita, Vol. IV, monograph Series Facultatis Historiae Ecclesiastiae, Rome, 1951). See also Donal A. Kerr, *Peel, Priests and Politics* (Oxford, 1982), Chapter 2, "The Irish Clergy and Politics," especially pp. 75–85.

78. Kerr, p. 85.

79. L. A. McCaffrey, *Daniel O'Connell and the Repeal Year* (Lexington, 1966) pp. 62–3.

80. Broderick, pp. 125–54.

81. Ibid.; Lecky, *Leaders of Public Opinion*, 2:239; Kee, pp. 204–5. Such estimates might be exaggerated where made by Repeal partisans, but whatever the actual numbers, they were sufficient to move the government to desperate countermeasures.

82. Lecky, *Leaders of Public Opinion*, 2:253.

83. Ibid., 2:239. For a concise, flavorful, and well-documented account of the Repeal campaign, see McCaffrey, *Daniel O'Connell and the Repeal Year*, especially Chapter 2.

84. Reynolds, *Catholic Emancipation Crisis*, p. 146 n. 53.

85. Senior, *Orangeism*, p. 279.

86. Ibid., pp. 200, 217, 279; S. J. Connolly, "Union Government, 1812–23," in *A New History*, 5:71.

87. Reynolds, p. 146. Two years before the death of William IV, an Orange plot was discovered aimed at awarding the succession to Ernst Augustus, Duke of Cumberland (1771–1851) King of Hanover (Germany), fifth son of George III. The Duke himself was a militant anti-Catholic spokesman in the House of Lords, and titular head of the Orange Order. In 1835 the Radical Joseph Hume, head of an investigating committee of the House of Commons, charged that there were two hundred thousand armed Orangemen in Ireland, who met in armies numbering in the tens of thousands (see Senior, pp. 266–71; and O'Connor, *History of Ireland*, 1:229).

88. Senior, p. 245.

89. MacDonagh, "Economy and Society, 1830–45," 5:224.

90. MacDonagh, "Ideas and Institutions, 1830–45", in *A New History*, 5:213–14; Vaughan, "Ireland c. 1870," 5:741.

91. In the wake of the tithe war, the constabulary and magistracy were deliberately reconstituted, "federalized" and "professionalized," to be free of the domination of Ascendancy types (MacDonagh, "Politics, 1830–45," and "Ideas and Institutions," in *A New History*, 5:180, and 5:214).

Within the highest levels of British authority, the last hurrah fittingly came from the Iron Duke, Wellington. In the summer of 1843, he asked for the formation of an armed yeomanry under crown-commissioned officers to confront the Repeal campaign. The British government rejected the proposal because it believed such a step would inevitably unleash a religious war (Kevin B. Nowlan, *Politics of Repeal*, p. 52).

92. Peel's "Emancipation" speech, *Hansard Parliamentary Debates*, 2d series, 20:746 (emphasis added).

93. Ibid., 3d series, 74:1026 (18 April 1845). Privately, Peel had even earlier conceded that in Ireland, "mere force ... will do nothing as a permanent remedy for the social evils" (Peel Papers. British Museum, Additional Manuscripts, 40449, ff. 105–6 [19 October 1843], cited in Kerr, *Peel, Priests and Politics*, p. 121).

94. When it came to the question of armed struggle, for O'Connell South America was one thing, Ireland another. He cheered on the independence campaign of Bolivar in South America, and sent off his son Morgan to fight in that war. There the conflict was not likely to get out of hand, but would remain a quarrel between Spain and the Spanish colonists; the masses of the superexploited "Indios" would not be dealt a hand in the game. But in Ireland the impoverished peasantry had dealt themselves in.

95. Kee, *The Green Flag*, p. 185.

96. The remainder of this paragraph is conveniently based on Reynolds, *Catholic Emancipation Crisis*, pp. 151–4.

97. "While rebellion was no part of their program, they had to keep popular passions at a fever pitch in order to intimidate and extort" (ibid., p. 153).

98. *A New History*, 8:309. This and similar orders subsequently issued were often overborne by the force of the movement and by the power of O'Connell's argument that the best hope for Catholicism lay in the liberation struggle (see Kerr, Chapter 2).

99. "O'Connell and his colleagues ... never broke with the notion of accepting emancipation as a boon from an upper-class legislature rather than as a right won by the people" (ibid., p. 169).

100. *Hansard Parliamentary Debates*, 3d series, 16:264 (5 March 1833). O'Connell documented his case with statistics showing a decline in "agrarian crime" in Ireland between 1823 and 1829, as proof of "the effect of establishing the Catholic Association."

101. MacDonagh, "Economy and Society, 1830–45," 5:224; *A New History*, 8:313.

102. Maurice R. O'Connell, ed., *Correspondence of Daniel O'Connell*, vol. 5, letter no. 1949 (14 January 1833).

103. Cited in James Connolly, *Labour in Irish History*, p. 85.

104. Lecky, *Leaders of Public Opinion*, 2:133, citing, *Life of Dr Doyle*, 2:452. "Blackfeet" was one of the names under which the secret peasant societies operated. My veiled allusion is, of course, to Psalms, 146:3: "Put not your trust in princes ..." For a sketch of Bishop Doyle's life, see *Compendium of Irish Biography*, compiled by Alfred Webb (Dublin, 1878), pp. 155–6.

In the House of Commons in 1838, O'Connell too declared his opposition to trade unionism, saying that there was "no tyranny equal to that which was exercised by the trade unionists in Dublin over their fellow labourers" (cited in James Connolly, *Labour in Irish History*, p. 101).

105. At a time when he was Solicitor-General in the British government, the Whig John Campbell told of an exchange he had had with O'Connell. O'Connell, he said, indicated his readiness to accept Campbell's insincerely proffered notion that O'Connell could get a separate Irish Parliament if "he were to agree that it should be subordinate to our [British] Parliament ... like the House of Assembly in Jamaica" (letter to Campbell's brother George, 23 March 1833, cited in Mrs Hardcastle, ed., *Life of John Lord Campbell*, p. 34).

106. James S. Donnelly, Jr., "A Famine in Irish Politics," in *A New History*, 5:357.

107. See Appendix J.

108. The generalizations made in this regard do not, of course, apply to the Protestant-majority area of Ulster, which will be treated in Chapter 5.

109. Oliver MacDonagh, "The Age of O'Connell, 1830–45," in *A New History*, 5:158–9. In recapitulating MacDonagh's thesis, I have combined his point four (the ending of "total

reliance on protestant ascendancy") with point one ("broadening the base of loyalism").

110. See Macintyre, *The Liberator*, pp. 142, 144, 145.

111. Ibid., pp. 152, 154. The "Irish Party" was not a formal party but an informal coalition of the Irish Parliamentary fraction, some repealers, some not (see ibid., pp. xiii–xvi).

112. Ibid., p. 104, citing Wellesley Papers, Additional MSS, 37307, pp. 217–20. Compare Vaughan, "Ireland c. 1870," 5:741–2.

113. "... the old Whig regime in Ireland was not to be resurrected" (Macintyre, p. 146).

114. Ibid., pp. 154, 163. "To do something for Ireland" seems to have been a common phrase at that time. For an abbreviated use of it by O'Connell, see *Hansard Parliamentary Debates*, 3d series, 50:201.

115. Macintyre, pp. 145, 165.

116. Ibid., p. 147; MacDonagh, "Politics, 1830–45," 5:178.

117. Macintyre, p. 161.

118. Macintyre, p. 158; MacDonagh, "Politics, 1830–45," 5:175, 5:180.

119. Oliver MacDonagh, ibid. 5:179.

120. Oliver MacDonagh, "Ideas and Institutions, 1830–45," in *A New History*, 5:212–14.

121. "Both in Parliament and outside of it, the necessity of reform for Ireland was now [February 1844] generally admitted" (Kerr, *Peel, Priests and Politics*, p. 116).

122. For a reference to examples of this ruling-class policy in regard to peasant uprisings in England in 1549 and 1607, see "A Consideration of the Cause in Question before the Lords touching Depopulation" (5 July 1607). If concessions were not to be avoided, the Lords concluded, they should be delayed for a couple of years, if possible, "lest encouragement move the people to seek redress by like outrages" (Eric Kerridge, *Agrarian Problems in the Sixteenth Century and After* [London: Allen and Unwin, 1969], pp. 200–203; Kerridge cites British Museum Cottonian Manuscripts, Titus F. iv, ff 322–3).

123. Kerr, p. 108.

124. MacDonagh, "Politics, 1830–45," 5:186–7.

125. Kerr, pp. 11–12.

126. In November 1843, a parliamentary commission (the Devon Commission) was appointed to look into the conditions of the peasantry and the possibility of agrarian reform. Its work, of course, was to be of no help to the Irish laboring classes in the holocaust of famine that loomed just ahead. Limited as the commission was in its purpose and outlook, its report, when made in 1845, gave legitimacy to the issue of landlordism in Ireland.
Speaking of the Irish priesthood of the nineteenth century, S. J. Connolly states: "the great majority of Maynooth priests, like those trained elsewhere in Ireland or abroad, were the sons of substantial tenant farmers or of the lower middle and middle classes of the towns and cities" (S. J. Connolly, *Religion and Society in Nineteenth-Century Ireland* [Dundalk, 1985], p. 40).

127. Parker, ed., *Sir Robert Peel, from his Private Papers*, 3:53–7: Peel to James Graham, 16 July 1843 (emphasis in original); Peel to De Grey, 24 July 1843; De Grey to Peel, 18 August 1843; Peel to De Grey, 22 August 1843. In due course, Peel's persuasion took effect and De Grey did make the recommended appointment (ibid., p. 60).

128. MacDonagh, "Age of O'Connell," 5:189.

129. Arthur Young, *A Tour in Ireland (1780)*, book 2, p. 34; Lecky, *History of England*, 2:261.

130. S. J. Connolly, *Religion and Society*, p. 30.

131. R. V. Comerford, "Ireland 1850–70: Post-Famine and Mid-Victorian," in *A New History*, 5:388–9. For the letter quoted above, see Emmet Larkin, *The Making of the Catholic Church in Ireland, 1850–1860* (Chapel Hill, 1980), pp. 445, 447. Larkin says that the letter gives a "thoughtful and accurate measure of what Cullen had achieved."

132. Vaughan, "Ireland c. 1870," 5:741.

133. Ibid., 5:740–2.

134. By the mid-Victorian period, Ireland witnessed "the enforcement throughout the land of order based on the rule of law and publicly administered in the courts" (Comerford, 5:390). The police-to-population ratios are given by Comerford, or derived from his presentation (ibid., 5:389).

135. O'Connell said his party's collaboration with the Whig government had made possible "... having troops [from Ireland] to spare for [rebelling] Canada, and for putting down the disturbances in England." Lord John Russell, Whig leader in the House of Commons and future

Prime Minister, praised O'Connell's steadfast support of the British government in these two crises. T. B. Macaulay expressed appreciation for the fact that "the Catholics of Ireland had remained true in all things to the general Government of the Empire," so that troops could be spared from Ireland to suppress the insurrections in England and in Canada (*Hansard Parliamentary Debates*, 3d series, 50:201–2 [O'Connell, 12 August 1839]; 72:707 [Russell, 13 February 1844]; and 72:1178–9 [Macaulay, 19 February 1844]).

Ireland would serve as an "excuse of the English Government for maintaining *a big standing army*, which in case of need they send against the English workers, as has happened after the army became turned into praetorians in Ireland" (Karl Marx, Resolution adopted by the General Council of the International Workingmen's Association, 1 January 1870, in *The General Council of the First International, Minutes*, 4 vols [Moscow, n.d.], vol. 2 [1868–70], p. 404; emphasis in original).

136. Quoted by Lord John Russell from a speech made by Fox, 14 May 1805 (*Hansard Parliamentary Debates*, 3d series, 70:109, 11 July 1843).

137. W. Burghardt Turner and Joyce Moore Turner, eds, *Richard B. Moore, Caribbean Militant in Harlem: Collected Writings 1920–1972* (Bloomington, Indiana, 1988), p. 29.

138. Wilfred D. Samuels, *Five Afro-Caribbean Voices in American Culture, 1917–1929* (Bloomington, Indiana, 1977), p. 3.

139. Robert A. Hill, *The Marcus Garvey and Universal Negro Improvement Association Papers* (Berkeley, California, 1983), 1:xxxvii–xxxviii. Garvey thought that the American Negroes were better for the "[r]acial caste oppression" to which they were subjected in the United States, according to editor Hill; on that account, Garvey said, the Americans were blessed with a "race consciousness" that the West Indians lacked (ibid.). Ira De A. Reid, looking at the matter somewhat differently, believed, "The Negro immigrant is beyond doubt more radical than the native" (Ira De A. Reid, *The Negro Immigrant: His Background, Characteristics and Social Adjustment, 1899–1937* [New York, 1939], p. 221).

140. Norwell Harrigan and Pearl I. Varlack, "The US Virgin Islands and the Black Experience," *Journal of Black Studies*, 7:387–410 (June 1977), 389–91.

141. Hubert H. Harrison, "The Virgin Islands," pp. 5–6, 12–13. Cited by Jeffrey Babcock Perry in his forthcoming (Louisiana State University Press) biography of Harrison.

142. Reid, pp. 216, 226.

143. Wilfred D. Samuels, *Five Afro-Caribbean Voices in American Culture, 1917–1929* (Boulder, 1977), p. 22.

5 Ulster

1. This question lies beyond the scope of the present work. The essence of the matter, however, was presented nearly sixty years ago by W. E. B. DuBois in his *Black Reconstruction*, most particularly in Chapter 2, "The White Worker."

2. Irish writers and social activists for more than thirty years now have been pointing out the pertinence of the United States/Ulster analogy to the struggle for equal rights. See, for example, the forceful statement of the general parallel of the Ulster and the United States situations today in Liam de Paor, *Divided Ulster* (Harmondsworth, England, 1970), p. 13. Recollect the Irish civil rights marchers of 1969 going into battle singing "We Shall Overcome."

3. Instructions by Arthur Chichester, Lord Deputy in Ireland, to Sir James Ley and Sir John Davys [Davies], 14 October 1608 (Great Britain Public Record Office, *Calendar of State Papers, relating to Ireland of the reign of James I*, vol. 3, *1608–10*, edited by C. W. Russell and John P. Prendergast [London and Edinburgh, 1874], 3:54–65; p. 64). (In subsequent notes this series will be abbreviated to *Cal. S. P., Ireland, James I, [date] [vol. no.]*.)

More than half of the investors in Irish plantations in this period were also stockholders in the Virginia Company (Theodore K. Rabb, *Enterprise and Empire: Merchant and Gentry Investment in the Expansion of England, 1575–1630* [Cambridge, Massachusetts, 1967], p. 108).

4. *Cal. S. P., James I*, 3:17.

5. Ibid., 3:xiv.

6. Fynes Moryson, *An Itinerary, Containing His Ten Yeeres Travell through the Twelve Dominions of Germany, Bohmerland, Sweitzerland, Netherland, Denmarke and Ireland,* 4 vols (London, 1617; Glasgow, 1907), 3:302, 328.

7. George Hill, *An historical account of the Plantation in Ulster at the commencement of the seventeenth century, 1608–1620* (Belfast, 1877; republished [with an introduction by John G. Barry] Shannon: Irish University Press, 1977), pp. 58–9.

8. Ibid., p. 61; Aidan Clarke with Dudley Edwards, "Pacification, Plantation, and the Catholic Question, 1603–23," in *A New History,* 3:196.

9. Hill, p. 61.

10. Ibid. Clarke with Edwards, 3:199 n. 5a.

11. Hill, p. 57.

12. Geographically Ulster included nine counties: Antrim, Down, Coleraine (Derry), Donegal, Tyrone, Fermanagh, Cavan, Armagh and Monaghan. Neither Antrim, Down nor Monaghan was included in the escheated lands of the "rebel" earls O'Neill and O'Donnell. By 1609, however, parts of Antrim and Down were already rather heavily settled by Scots, ancient settlers, as well as by the newcomers lodged on lands granted to James's fellow countrymen James Hamilton and Hugh Montgomery. Antrim and Down were to remain the main base of Protestant Ulster from that day to this.

13. In his *Confiscation in Irish History* (London, 1918), W. F. T. Butler speculates that the Irish chiefs would have been no less grasping than their Scottish counterparts, who had "reduced all their clansmen to the condition of tenants at will." He implies that English government sincerely wanted to draw the Irish chiefs into the English-style social structure as the Scottish chiefs had been drawn into it. At that point, however, Butler cuts short his "speculation as to what might have been." But the general tenor of Butler's study would seem to cast doubt on the depth of the sincerity of the British government toward such a reconciliation with the Irish chieftains.

14. Hill, pp. 60–64; 97; 109–10 nn. 79, 82; 112; 229; 300 n. 166; 347; 360; 411 n. 61. Moryson, 2:348–9. *Cal. S. P., Ireland, James I, 1608–1610,* 3:364. Aidan Clarke, "Plantation and the Catholic Question, 1603–23," in *A New History,* 3:199 n. 6(e).

15. When, in time, the chieftain class had been disposed of as a social force, the English found gavelkind serviceable for dispersing such Catholic landholding as remained. In 1704 it was made mandatory that such inheritance was "to be by the rule of gavelkind" (6 Anne c. 6, sec. 10).

16. Hill, pp. 37, 42, 49, 83, 318 n. 221. Moryson, 3:311–33. Clarke with Edwards, "Pacification, Plantation, and the Catholic Question, 1603–23," in *A New History,* 3:206–8.

The use of the term "Briton" in these early-seventeenth-century documents anticipates by a century the Act of Union of 1707, uniting England and Scotland in one state, Great Britain.

17. For deserting to the English side in 1598, Sir Tirlough McHenry O'Neill (half-brother of the leader of the Irish rebellion, Hugh O'Neill, Earl of Tyrone) and Sir Henry Oge O'Neill (Tyrone's son-in-law) were granted English land titles that were exceptional in two ways. The grants were exceptionally large, Sir Tirlough receiving 9,900 acres and Sir Henry Oge 4,900 acres. Second, while other native grantees were obliged to move to other lands in order to get their allotted acreage, Sir Tirlough and Sir Henry Oge were allowed to have the lands they had always occupied. Sir Henry died in battle against O'Doherty's revolt in 1608, and his lands were distributed to his wife and six sons (an opportune English show of regard for the rule of gavelkind, whereby the few exceptionally large family landholdings that still existed could be broken up) (Hill, pp. ii n. 1, 115, 318–19).

18. W. F. T. Butler gives their number as 280, but notes that "the numbers differ in the various lists" (*Confiscation in Irish History,* p. 50). Aidan Clarke says that no more than fifty natives in each of the six counties were allotted any land (Clarke with Edwards, 3:202). A perusal of the documents relating to grants and grantees for the year 1610, as reprinted by Hill, shows 231 "native grants" in the five counties (not including Coleraine/Derry) (*Plantation in Ulster,* pp. 309–48). The estimated total adult population of Ulster at this time was between 25,000 and 40,000 (M. Perceval-Maxwell, *The Scottish Migration to Ulster in the Reign of James I* [London, 1973], p. 17). Obviously, however large one estimates the size of the families to have been, the overwhelming majority of them were left landless.

19. Clarke, with Edwards, 3:202.

20. Patrick J. Corish, "The Rising of 1641 and the Catholic Confederacy, 1641–45," in *A New History,* 3:289. See also Hill, pp. 348–9, for a number of specific instances of the pressured

passing of land titles from Irish to British hands.

21. T. W. Moody, *The Ulster Question, 1603–1973* (Dublin and Cork, 1974), p. 5.

22. Hill, p. iii n. 2. *Cal. S. P., Ireland, James I,* 3:299 (Sir Robert Jacob to Lord Salisbury, 18 October 1609). Compare Hill, p. 205 n. 40.

23. *Cal. S. P., Ireland, James I,* 3:299 (Sir Robert Jacob, King James's Solicitor, to Lord Salisbury, October 1609); 3:287 (Lord Deputy Chichester to Lord Salisbury, 18 September 1609); 3:304–5 (Chichester to the Privy Council, 31 October 1609); 3:458–60 (Privy Council to Chichester, 8 June 1610; and 3:496 (Chichester to Privy Council, 23 September 1610). For a recurrence in 1619 of this proposed solution of the "woodkerne" problem, see Hill, p. iii n. 2 (citing MS *State Papers,* vol. 35, No. 60).

24. For African references see: Letter of John Lyle to Secretary of State Joseph Williamson, 16 September 1667, Great Britain *Cal. S. P., Dom., 1667, Charles II*; Narcissus Luttrell, diary entry 5 March 1701/2, cited in George M. Trevelyan, *England under Queen Anne,* 3 vols (London, 1934), 2:149; John and Awsham Churchill, compilers, *A Collection of Voyages and Travels . . . ,* 6 vols (London, 1704–32), 6:219.

25. *Cal. S. P., Ireland, James I,* 3:287, 3:458–60, 3:496; T. W. Moody, "Sir Thomas Phillips of Limavady, Servitor," *Irish Historical Studies,* 1:251–72 (1938–39), pp. 256–8.

26. Moody, "Sir Thomas Phillips," p. 257; Hill, p. 189; John J. Silke, "The Irish Abroad, 1534–1691," in *A New History,* 3:593. (Moody's transcription from the Cecil Manuscripts varies in some details from the version printed in *The Cecil Papers,* published by the Great Britain Public Record Office. But the discrepancies, mainly relating to the daily allowance for maintenance of the transportees, do not seem important.)

27. T. W. Moody, "Sir Thomas Phillips," 1:260–61.

28. Lord Deputy Sir Arthur Chichester, Instructions to Lord Chief Justice Sir James Ley and Sir John Davys [Davies], 14 October 1608 (*Cal. S. P., Ireland, James I,* 3:63).

In the contemporaneous fledgling colony of Virginia, such settlers were called "officers." Like the Ulster servitors, they were recruited from surplus veterans, who were "truly bred in that nursery of Warre, the Lowe countries" and, indeed, in some cases in Ireland itself (John Rolfe, *Relation of Virginia* [1616], reprinted in part in Alexander Brown, *The First Republic in America* [Boston, 1898], p. 227; Alexander Brown, *The Genesis of the United States,* 2 vols [Boston, 1890], 2:1065; and ibid., appended "Brief Biographies". See also Volume Two of this study.

29. *Cal. S. P., Ireland, James I,* 3:211–12.

30. Ibid., 3:68 (Lord Deputy to Privy Council, 14 October 1608); 3:41 ("A Brief of the Proceedings of the Commissioners for the Plantation of Ulster . . .," 19 March 1610).

31. Ibid., 3:63.

32. The quit-rent rates payable to the Crown per 1,000 acres were to be as follows: undertakers (barred from engaging native tenants or laborers), £5 6s. 8d.; servitors, if engaging only English or Scots tenants or laborers, the same as undertakers, but 50 percent more if engaging natives as tenants or laborers, i.e., £8 and native landholders, twice the undertaker rate, namely, £10 13s. 4d. (*Cal. S. P., Ireland, James I,* 3:490.)

33. Hill, *Plantation in Ulster,* pp. 310–48, 445–590.

34. "Without the succession of King James VI to the throne of England, it is unlikely that Scots would have been able to colonize any significant districts of Ireland" (W. H. Crawford, "Ulster as a Mirror of Two Societies," paper delivered at the Social Science Research Council of Great Britain Conference on Irish–Scottish Development, Strathclyde University, 16–18 September 1981, in T. M. Devine and David Dickson, eds, *Ireland and Scotland, 1600–1850, Parallels and Contrasts in Economic and Social Development* [Edinburgh, 1982(?)], p. 61). "The Ulster problem, it will be generally agreed, begins with the Plantation of Ulster in the early seventeenth century" (A. T. Q. Stewart, "The Mind of Protestant Ulster," in David Watt, ed., *The Constitution of Northern Ireland, Problems and Prospects* [London, 1981], p. 32).

35. For a discussion of the Scots "kindly tenant" status, and its disappearance as money rent superseded rent in kind, and of the emergence of "feu-farming" and the consequent prevalence of tenancy-at-will, see I. F. Grant, *The Social and Economic Development of Scotland before 1603* (Edinburgh, 1930; 1971). Section II, Chapter I, Parts VIII and IX; and Chapters IV and V. "Feuing was primarily undertaken as a method of increasing revenue. The cash nexus was predominant" (ibid., p. 279).

36. J. D. Mackie, *A History of Scotland* (Harmondsworth, England, 1964), Chapters 12 through

16; Curtis, *A History of Ireland*, 6th edn (London, 1950) pp. 288, 293, 310.

37. Curtis, pp. 397–8.

38. Moody, *Ulster Question*, p. 7. Perceval-Maxwell, *Scottish Migration*, p. 33.

39. Perceval-Maxwell, p. 33.

40. Ibid., p. 26.

41. *Edinburgh Review*, 159 (1899):126.

42. For the eighteenth-century contrast in Scotland, see Mackie, *A History of Scotland*, pp. 285 ff. For the English case, see: Eleanora Carus-Wilson, ed., *Essays in Economic History* (New York: St Martin's Press, 1966), 2:268–9; Leslie A. Clarkson, *The Pre-industrial Economy in England, 1500–1750* (New York, 1972), pp. 114–16; W. E. Lunt, *History of England*, 4th edition (New York, Evanston and London, 1957), pp. 485–8; and George M. Trevelyan, *English Social History: A Survey of Six Centuries, Chaucer to Queen Victoria* (London, 1942), pp. 141, 284–9.

43. *Encyclopedia Britannica*, "Scotland. – Population."

44. Andrew Fletcher, "Second Discourse concerning the affairs of Scotland" (1698) in *Andrew Fletcher of Saltoun, Selected Political Writings and Speeches*, edited by David Daiches (Edinburgh, 1979), p. 55.

45. Ibid., p. 58.

46. "The Scottish colonists ... should be regarded as displaced people superfluous to the economic and social needs of the colonizing society" (Crawford, p. 61). See Perceval-Maxwell, pp. 26–7.

47. A. T. Q. Stewart, p. 35; Moody, *Ulster Question*, p. 7; Perceval-Maxwell, pp. 25–6.

48. Perceval-Maxwell, p. 27.

49. A. T. Q. Stewart, Reader in Irish History at Queen's University, Belfast, and a defender of partition, says that the Revd Stewart's comment is "sometimes maliciously quoted" ("The Mind of Protestant Ulster," p. 35). Since Stewart is seeking to make the point that the English and Scots did not seize "the richest and most fertile of the Ulster lands from the Gaels," he includes in his citation a sentence which is often omitted, and which speaks of the Scots immigrants planting lands which were previously unoccupied, or at least uncultivated. That some did so may well be true, but all the documents concerning the plantation make it clear that the official purpose was precisely to displace the native population, not to coexist with them. The fact that this "ethnic cleansing," as it might be called today, was not fully accomplished is another matter.

50. Perceval-Maxwell, p. 277.

51. Ibid., p. 278.

52. Ibid.

53. Ibid., pp. 31–3. Impoverished Scots immigrants "received farms at low rents in order to colonize Ulster" (Curtis, p. 287).

54. "The seventeenth century was to elapse before there were sufficient British farmers in Ulster to generate significant competition for land" (Crawford, p. 61).

55. Great Britain, *Parliamentary Papers*, vols 19–22 (1845), "Reports from Her Majesty's Commissioners of Inquiry into the State of the Law and Practice in Relation to the Occupation of Land in Ireland" (the Devon Commission Report) (Dublin, 1845) 19:545/483. (There are two sets of page numbers, a confusion that I did not resolve.) Testimony of John Hancock, Esq., land agent to the Right Hon. Lord Lurgan, a magistrate of the Counties of Armagh, Down and Antrim, 23 March 1844.

56. Hill, *Plantation in Ulster*, pp. 447–8 n. 2. The measure failed of its basic purpose of displacing the native population because it was so widely disregarded. Instead, it served only to provide grounds a decade later for still other self-aggrandizing British landgrabbers to challenge the titles of earlier British occupiers (ibid.). The three-fourths Protestant quota served to emphasize the government's early awareness of the paradox that too much conversion would threaten Protestant rule, by diluting the privileges of the laboring-class Protestants.

57. "... the Irish were too hard to displace, the colonists too glad to find tenants on the spot.... But the plantation none the less meant a social revolution in Ulster, a clean sweep of all the traditional property-rights of the occupying Irish. The great mass of Ulster Irish remained on their former lands, but degraded to the status of tenants-at-will" (Moody, *Ulster Question*, p. 5). See also: Hill, p. 454 n. 13; Butler, *Confiscation in Irish History*, pp. 45–6; de Paor, *Divided Ulster*, p. 21.

58. Hill, p. 501 nn. 144 and 145. See also ibid., p. 447 n. 2; and Butler, p. 47.

59. "The tenant-right of Ulster, when considered economically, is only . . . the right of the tenant to the fair profit of the capital vested by him by purchase or expenditure . . . or to the inherited profit arising from such improvements made by some of his ancestors" (William Nelson Hancock, Esq., [brother of John Hancock, Esq., quoted in n. 55] barrister-at-law, *The Tenant Right of Ulster considered economically, being an essay read before the Dublin University Philosophical Society* [Dublin, 1845], pp. 33–4).

60. Hill, pp. 447–8 n. 2.

61. For a comprehensive discussion of the evolution of the Ulster tenant-right, presented in relation to its detailed historical context, see W. H. Crawford, "Landlord–Tenant Relations in Ulster, 1609–1820," in *Irish Economic and Social History*, 2:5–21 (1975).

62. Hill, p. 311.

63. Perceval-Maxwell, pp. 274, 284, 314–15. J. H. Andrews, "Land and People, c. 1685," in *A New History*, 3:459, 3:461.

Even within Ulster, sufficient as this Protestant implantation was in normal times for keeping watch over and repressing the hostile and excluded natives, it could not prevent the northern province from being the first to rise in rebellion in 1641. Then the British position was restored not by local militia but by a regular army of Scots under General Munro. "The situation [of the British settlers in Ulster for most of the seventeenth century] has often been compared to that of the early colonists in North America, whose little settlements lived under the threat of Indian attack . . . [like] white farmers in Kenya watching their Kikuyu workers and thinking of the midnight advent of the Mau-Mau" (de Paor, pp. 21, 23).

64. The siege of Protestant Derry by the forces of the Catholic James II was lifted in 1689. British Protestant units from Ulster distinguished themselves in the defeat of the Catholic forces at the Battle of the Boyne in 1690 (John Gerald Simms, "The War of the Two Kings, 1685–91," in *A New History*, 3:492–3, 3:497–8).

Ulster Protestant tradition, we are told, holds that the defenders of Derry found strength in "pride of race" as well as anti-Catholicism (Simms, 3:492).

65. John Patrick Prendergast, *Ireland from the Restoration to the Revolution* (London, 1873), p. 98. W. Macafee and V. Morgan, "Population in Ulster, 1660–1760," in Peter Roebuck ed., *Essays in Ulster History in honour of J. L. McCracken* (Belfast, 1981), pp. 47, 58.

66. Devon Commission Report, 19:14–15. The Devon Commission asked a John Andrews of County Down, land agent of the Marquess of Londonderry, if the "curtailment of the tenant-right [could] be carried without danger to the country." Andrews replied that the Protestant tenants of Down would resist such a curtailment as violently as the Catholics of Tipperary were wont to resist their landlords: "You would have a Tipperary in Down if it was attempted to be carried out" (ibid., 19:608/546, 27 March 1844).

67. Ibid.

68. "In Ulster . . . [there] was this bond between [the Presbyterian Scot] and his landlord that each was an intruder and knew he was looked upon as such. . . . [They] were Protestants, belonging to the conquering race" (James O'Connor, *History of Ireland*, 2 vols [London, 1924], 2:27–8).

69. Crawford, "Landlord–Tenant Relations," 2:13–16.

70. Crawford, "Ulster as a Mirror," pp. 62–4.

71. Ibid. See also Crawford's "Landlord–Tenant Relations," 2:16.

72. Such were the terms of Poyning's Law, enacted in 1494. It was of course no coincidence that, after 287 years, the 1782 law (21 & 22 Geo. III c. 47) was approved by the British government within nine months after the British surrender at Yorktown, ending the military phase of the American Revolution.

73. The cited laws are acts of the English Parliament.

74. James G. Leyburn, *The Scotch-Irish, A Social History* (Chapel Hill, 1962), pp. 157, 168–9.

75. A. T. Q. Stewart, *The Ulster Crisis* (London, 1967), p. 29.

76. From the United Irishmen's plan for parliamentary reform, 15 February 1794 (*Journals of the House of Commons of the Kingdom of Ireland* [Dublin, 1753–1800], vol. 17, p. 888; reprinted in Charles Carlton, *Bigotry and Blood: Documents on the Ulster Troubles* [Chicago, 1977], pp. 45–6).

77. Crawford, "Landlord–Tenant Relations." See especially Table I, p. 13.

78. De Paor, *Divided Ulster*, p. 43.

79. National Library of Ireland, Lake MSS 56, quoted in Hereward Senior, *Orangeism in*

Ireland, 1795–1836 (London, 1866), p. 67.

80. Great Britain, *Parliamentary Papers*, 1825, vol. VIII, *State of Ireland, with Four Reports of the Evidence taken in the Present Session*, pp. 688–9 (18 May 1825). See also: Kenneth Charlton, "The State of Ireland in the 1820s: James Cropper's Plan," *Irish Historical Studies*, 17:320–39 (March 1971); and R. F. Foster, *Modern Ireland, 1600–1972* (London, 1988), pp. 321–2.

81. L. C. Cullen, ed., *The Formation of the Irish Economy* (Cork, 1969).

82. Raymond Crotty, *Ireland in Crisis: A Study in Capitalist Colonial Development* (Dover, New Hampshire, 1986), p. 52; George O'Brien, *The Economic History of Ireland from the Union to the Famine* (London, 1921), p. 444.

83. T. M. Devine and David Dickson, "In Pursuit of Comparative Aspects of Irish and Scottish Development: A Review of the Symposium," in their *Ireland and Scotland*, p. 271.

84. Cullen, p. 105; T. A. Jackson, *Ireland Her Own* (New York, 1947), p. 188.

85. See Roy Foster's discussion of the question Why did Ireland, outside Ulster, fail to industrialize? (*Modern Ireland*), p. 321–2.

86. Crawford, "Landlord–Tenant Relations," 2:12–18.

87. De Paor, pp. 63–4.

88. Ibid., p. 66. See also: Stewart, *Ulster Crisis*, p. 30; O'Connor, *History of Ireland*, 2:28; Moody, *Ulster Question*, p. 17.

89. J. C. Beckett et al., *Belfast: The Making of the City* (Belfast, 1983), pp. 153–4, 159–60.

90. "... in Ulster alone was landlord help sufficiently widespread to reduce mortality in a poor county to a figure similar to that obtaining in the wealthier counties of eastern Ireland.... Only in Ulster were excess mortality rates below 7.5%" (S. H. Cousens, "The Regional Variations in Mortality During the Great Irish Famine," *Proceedings of the Royal Irish Academy*, Vol. 63, Section C [1963], p. 146). See also, Cousens, "Regional Death Rates in Ireland During the Great Famine from 1846 to 1851," *Population Studies*, Vol. 14, No. 1 (July 1960), pp. 55–7. With regard to the deliberateness of England's genocidal policy as rationalized by a government infatuated by laissez-faire economics and population theories, as first laid down by Adam Smith and Malthus, and elaborated and applied by such social theorists as Nassau Senior and Spencer, see: Thomas P. O'Neill, "The Organization and Administration of Relief, 1845–52," in R. Dudley Edwards and T. Desmond Williams, *The Great Famine* (New York, 1957), pp. 209–63; and Joel Mokyr, *Why Ireland Starved: A Quantitative and Analytical History of the Irish Economy, 1800–1850* (London, 1983), especially, pp. 290–92.

91. Beckett, pp. 44–7.

92. O'Connell to Revd Dr Paul Cullen, Rector of Irish College, Rome, 9 May 1842, in Maurice R. O'Connell, ed., *Correspondence of Daniel O'Connell*, 7:157.

93. A. C. Hepburn and B. Collins, "Industrial Society: The Structure of Belfast, 1901," in Peter Roebuck, ed., *Plantation to Partition*, p. 211; Leslie Clarkson, "The City and the Country," in Beckett, p. 153; D. J. Cowan, *History of Belfast* as quoted by Constantine Fitzgibbon, *Red Hand: The Ulster Colony* (London, 1971), p. 340.

94. "Abstract labour" is of course Marx's phrase, used to distinguish labor as value-creating as against labor as productive of particular items of use, "concrete labour." It also implies labor in general, regardless of the particular national, religious, or other characteristics of the laborers (see *Capital*, Vol. I, Chapter 1, Section 2, "The twofold character of the labour embodied in commodities"). The second quotation is from Abraham Lincoln's "Reply to the New York Workingmen's Democratic Republican Association," 21 March 1864 (Mario M. Cuomo and Harold Holzer, eds, *Lincoln on Democracy: His Own Words with Essays by America's Foremost Historians* [New York, 1990], p. 315).

95. These words are taken from the concluding sentence of James Connolly's *Labour in Irish History*, which was first published as a book in Dublin in 1910, having previously appeared in serial form in the Edinburgh *Socialist* and the New York *Harp* (*A New History*, 8:383). The cited passage appears on p. 137 of the 1919 New York printing.

96. Beckett, p. 136.

97. Ibid., pp. 174–7. A century later, concerned scholars in Northern Ireland note that the still-prevailing practice of hiring workers on the informal recommendation of friends and family of the employee "tend[s] to reproduce the existing patterns of job distributions both in terms of religion and geographical area." They urge adoption of the principle that "The company should not recruit new

employees on the recommendations of existing employees" (R. J. Cormack and R. D. Osborne, eds, *Religion, Education and Employment: Aspects of Equal Opportunity in Northern Ireland* [Belfast, 1983], pp. 160, 218). Although Catholics make up only one-third of the economically active population of Northern Ireland, they are the majority of the unemployed (ibid., p. 40).

98. Beckett et al., pp. 173–4. The authors were here referring to the 1901 census data. In 1974 one commentator, taking note of the prevalence of sectarian conflict in Belfast, offered the opinion that "Residential segregation may thus be viewed as a necessary, if unpleasant, way to preserve civic peace" (M. A. Busteed, *Northern Ireland*, in the series Problem Regions of Europe, General Editor D. I. Scargill [New York, 1974], p. 101). No thought was given apparently to whether the systematic segregation of Protestants in better housing might contribute to civic unrest.

99. A. C. Hepburn and B. Collins, "Industrial Society: The Structure of Belfast, 1901," in Roebuck, *Plantation to Partition*, p. 217. Was there not some anti-Catholic Moynihan type, as yet unknown to the present author, who felt obliged to address the social problems of Northern Ireland with a treatise on "The Breakdown of the Catholic Family Leading to Increased Dependency on the Dole," and "The Pathology of Matriarchy"? See Daniel Patrick Moynihan, *The Negro Family: The Case for National Action* (Washington: Office of Policy Planning and Research, United States Department of Labor, 1965), reprinted in Lee Rainwater and William L. Yancey, eds, *The Moynihan Report and the Politics of Controversy* (Cambridge, MIT Press, 1967).

100. Geoffrey Bell illustrates the point with selected official statistics, covering the period from 1871 to 1971, regarding wages and wage differentials, job classification, unemployment and housing conditions (*The Protestants of Ulster* [London: Pluto Press, 1976], pp. 18–30).

101. Ibid., pp. 18–19. Bell cites: *British Parliamentary Papers*: 1893, Vol. 83, Pt 2; 1897, Vol. 84; and 1899, Vol. 70.

102. South Africa is the extreme case, where the differential between "white" and African earnings is of such proportions as could not be supported even in the United States (see Robert H. Davies, *Capital, State and White Labour in South Africa, 1900–1960, An Historical Materialist Analysis of Class Formation and Class Relations* [New York: Humanities Press, 1979], p. 352). In the United States, historically, wages in the skilled trades (from which African-Americans have been excluded) have been lower in the South, where African-American workers have mostly lived and been most systematically kept down. Yet the wage differential between skilled workers and laborers has been greater there than in other regions of the country.

103. Beckett, pp. 147–9. See Henry Patterson, "Independent Orangeism and Class Conflict in Edwardian Belfast: A Reinterpretation," *Proceedings of the Royal Irish Academy*, Vol. 80c, pp. 1–27 (1980).

104. See Ian Budge and Cornelius O'Leary, *Belfast: Approach to Crisis, a Study of Belfast Politics, 1613–1970* (London, 1973), pp. 89–95; de Paor, *Divided Ulster*, pp. 49, 61; Hepburn and Collins, p. 211.

105. Great Britain, *Parliamentary Papers*, 1887, Vol. 18, "Report of the Belfast Riots Commission ...," p. 321. Historian A. T. Q. Stewart, however, states flatly that the cause of the riots was "the influx of a considerable Catholic and nationalist population into Belfast ... and the topography of their settlement ..." ("Mind of Protestant Ulster," p. 42).

106. See *British Parliamentary Papers*, 1887, Vol. 18, "Report of the Belfast Riots Commission...."

107. *British Parliamentary Papers*, 1887, Vol. 18, p. 267.

108. Hepburn and Collins, p. 211. The Catholic population of Belfast increased in absolute numbers by some 42,000 in this period. This, however, represented only a 1.7 percent annual increase, possibly no more than the natural increase, as contrasted with an approximate 5.1 percent annual increase during the first six decades of the century. (This calculation applies the percentage figures given by Hepburn and Collins to the population figures given by D. J. Cowan [*History of Belfast*] for 1861 and 1901, together with the figure for the year 1800, given at p. 131, above.) Historian Brenda Collins notes that rural Ulster Catholics in this period chose to emigrate rather than go to Belfast. "This attitude," she writes, "was scarcely surprising in view of the repeated demonstrations of anti-catholic feeling at intervals during the nineteenth century, which often resulted in rioting" ("The Edwardian City," in Beckett, p. 173).

109. Roy Jenkins, *Asquith, Portrait of a Man and an Era* (New York, 1964), pp. 315–23.

110. George Bernard Shaw, *John Bull's Other Island and Major Barbara* (New York, 1926), pp. xxi, xxv, xxx.

111. Keegan's last speech.

112. R. F. Rattray, *Bernard Shaw: A Chronicle* (London, 1951), pp. 158–9.

113. *Labour in Irish History*, concluding paragraph. "North East Ulster," *Forward* 2 August 1913; reprinted in P. Berresford Ellis, ed., *James Connolly; Selected Writings* (New York: Monthly Review Press, 1973), pp. 264, 265.

114. Liam de Paor, *Unfinished Business: Ireland Today and Tomorrow* (London: Hutchinson Radius, 1990), pp. 147, 150.

115. The histories of the other provinces, where social control required the sending of an army to do it, provide the negative confirmation.

6 Anglo-America: Ulster Writ Large

1. The French did not have to face this problem on the North American continent because they were primarily hunters and trappers in the fur trade, which did not involve any attempt to displace the Indian population, but rather led to the development of a cooperative relationship with the Indian tribes.

2. See Volume Two.

3. Jackson, report to Tennessee Governor Blount, 31 March 1814, *Correspondence of Andrew Jackson*, Carnegie Institution of Washington Publication 371, edited by John Spencer Bassett, 7 vols, 1926–1935; 1:492.

4. Jackson's parents were Ulster Scots who emigrated to America in 1765, it is said. Whether or to what extent this circumstance may hold some special significance, the version of "democracy" prevalent in the Protestant-majority Ulster Protestant Ascendancy seems to lose nothing in Jacksonian translation in America. "Jackson, race-obsessed authoritarian, believed upper-class control must end at the color line," writes a modern historian. "[He] aimed at institutionalizing classic herrenvolk democracy: both the complete equality of white men and the absolute superiority of whites over non-whites" (William W. Freehling, *Road to Disunion*, 2 vols; Vol. 1, *Secessionists at Bay, 1776–1854* [New York: Oxford University Press, 1990], p. 262).

5. Michael D. Green, *The Politics of Indian Removal: Creek Government and Society in Crisis* (Lincoln: Nebraska University Press, 1982), pp. 42–3; Angie Debo, *A History of the Indians of the United States* (Norman, Oklahoma, 1970), p. 112; Samuel Carter III, *Cherokee Sunset: A Narrative of Travail and Triumph, Persecution and Exile* (New York: Doubleday, 1976), pp. 2–3.

6. Thurman Wilkins, *Cherokee Tragedy: The Story of the Ridge Family and the Decimation of a People* (New York, 1970), p. 227. The report of the meeting was originally published in the New York *Commercial Advertiser* (date not given) and was reprinted in the Cherokee newspaper *Cherokee Phoenix*, 18 February 1832. See also Debo, p. 113.

7. See Carter, chapters 17, 18 and 19.

8. Wilkins, pp. 202–3.

9. Rather than risk the social instability of ruling without an intermediate stratum, the English ruling classes in the early sixteenth century deliberately chose to accept the economic cost of preserving a yeoman section of the laboring peasantry from expropriation to serve as a buffer social control group (see Volume Two). The option for racial oppression in Ireland and in continental Anglo-America, however, meant that the social control solution could not be achieved simply by the act of preserving a middle class.

10. Ulrich Bonnell Phillips, "The Slave Labor Problem in the Charleston [South Carolina] District," *Political Science Quarterly*, 22:416–39 (September 1907), 422.

11. See further details and discussion in Volume Two.

12. *Acts of Assembly Passed in the Island of Nevis, from 1664 to 1739, inclusive*, printed by Order of the Lords Commissioners of Trade and Plantations (1740), p. 37. *The Colonial Records of the State of Georgia*, edited by Alan D. Candler, 26 vols (Atlanta, 1904–16), 1:58.

13. See Volume Two.

14. For the Irish case, see pp. 81–2, 85–6. For further mention and discussion of cases in the Anglo-American colonies see Phillips, p. 423; Great Britain Public Record Office, *Calendar of*

State Papers, Colonial, 7:141 (14 December 1670); and *Colonial Records of the State of Georgia*, 1:58.

15. Letter of William Byrd, II, of Westover to Mr Ochs, "about 1735," *Virginia Magazine of History and Biography*, 9:22–6 (January 1902); 4 Hening 78 (1720).

16. Letter of William Byrd, II, of Westover to Lord Egmont, president of the trustees of Georgia, 12 July 1736, in *American Historical Review*, 1:88–90. Kenneth W. Porter, "Negroes on the Southern Frontier, 1670–1763," *Journal of Negro History*, 33:53–78 (1948); pp. 58–9, 60, 67, 76, 77–8. *Journal of the Earl of Egmont, Abstract of the Trustees Proceedings for Establishing the Colony of Georgia, 1732–1738*, edited by Robert G. McPherson (Atlanta, 1962), p. 83 (entry for 23 April 1735), approval of a law "prohibiting the use of negroes" in the Georgia colony.

17. *Congressional Globe*, 29th Congress, 2nd Session, Appendix, p. 317.

18. Benjamin Horace Hibbard, *A History of the Public Land Policies* (Madison: University of Wisconsin Press, 1965), pp. 300, 354.

19. Elizabeth Cady Stanton, Susan B. Anthony and Matilde Joselyn Gage, eds, *History of Woman Suffrage*, 2nd edition, 3 vols (Rochester, 1889), Vol. 1, pp. 69, 71, 74, 115–17.

20. Hibbard, p. 354.

21. Kansas was admitted to the Union as a free state on 29 January 1861, sixty-six days before the outbreak of the Civil War.

22. *Frederick Douglass' Paper*, 15 September 1854. See Philip S. Foner, *The Life and Writings of Frederick Douglass* (New York, 1950), 4 vols; 2:311–15.

23. Benjamin Quarles, *The Negro in the Civil War* (Boston, 1953), p. xii. The late Isabella Black generously allowed me to draw upon her scrupulously researched manuscript, as yet not accepted for publication, which she titled "Home-made Yankees, a South-side View of the War for the Union, 1860–1877." The data on the number of European-Americans from the slaveholding states who enlisted in the Union armies are summarized in that work at pp. 128–9.

24. South Carolina, Constitutional Convention, 1868: *Proceedings of the Constitutional Convention* ... (Charleston, 1868), pp. 105–7 (cited by Black, pp. 240–41). *Official Proceedings of the Convention for Framing a Constitution for the State of Louisiana* (New Orleans, 1867–68), pp. 110, 266–7, 306 (cited by Roger W. Shugg, *Origins of Class Struggle in Louisiana: A Social History of White Farmers and Laborers during Slavery and After, 1840–1875* [Baton Rouge: Louisiana State Press, 1966], p. 243 n. 40). Clara M. Thompson, *Reconstruction in Georgia, Economic, Social, Political, 1805–72* (New York, 1915), p. 204. B. F. Perry, who had served as Provisional Governor of South Carolina during the brief period of Presidential Reconstruction, expressed the fear that the poor whites of that state would "unite with the Negro in parceling out the lands of the State" (letter to the Columbia [SC] *Phoenix*, reprinted in the Charleston *Courier*, 4 May 1867; quoted in Paul Lewinson, *Race, Class and Party: A History of Negro Suffrage and White Politics in the South* [New York: Russell and Russell, 1924; reissued, 1969], p. 39).

25. Charles Sumner to John Bright, 13 March 1869, in Edward L. Pierce, ed., *Memoir and Letters of Charles Sumner*, 4 vols (Boston, 1893), 4:229.

26. Stevens made this proposal in a speech in his home town, Lancaster, Pennsylvania, on 7 September 1865. It was published in the New York *Herald* Supplement, 13 December 1865 (cited by Ralph Korngold, *Thaddeus Stevens, a Being Darkly Wise and Rudely Great* [New York, 1955], pp. 282–3).

27. George W. Julian, *Political Recollections, 1840–1872* (Chicago, 1884), p. 240.

28. Paul Wallace Gates, "Federal Land Policy in the South," *Journal of Southern History*, 6:303–30 (August, 1940), pp. 309–10.

29. Ibid.

30. Charles H. Wesley, *Negro Labor in the United States, 1850–1925, a Study in American Economic History* (New York, 1927), p. 138. Wesley cites Report of Hon. T. D. Eliot to the House of Representatives, 10 March 1868 (House Report, No. 121, 41st Congress, 1st Session, p. 486).

31. Gates, p. 310.

32. "In 1859 infants were valued at from $7 to $10 a pound" (Lewis C. Gray, *History of Agriculture in the United States to 1860* [Washington, 1932; Peter Smith reprint, 1958], 2 vols; 2:664).

33. *De Bow's Review*, 4:587–8 (December 1867) (cited in Shugg, p. 243). Lewinson, p. 39 n.

34. Robert William Fogel, *Without Consent or Contract: The Rise and Fall of American Slavery* (New York: W. W. Norton, 1989), pp. 307–10. John Francis Maguire, *The Irish in America*

(London, 1868; Arno Press reprint, 1969), Chapter XI. Jurgen Kuczynski, *A Short History of Labor Conditions under Industrial Capitalism*, 4 vols (in 6); Vol. 2, *The United States of America, 1789 to the Present Day* (New York, 1943), p. 57. John B. MacMaster, *History of the People of the United States from the Revolution to the Civil War*, selected and edited by Louis B. Filler (New York: Farrar, Strauss, 1964), pp. 211, 214. Matthew Carey, *The Public Charities of Philadelphia* (cited by Gustavas Myers, *History of the Great American Fortunes* [New York, 1907; 1937], p. 81). Matthew Carey, *Appeal to the Wealthy of the Land* (3rd edition), pp. 3–5, 33 (cited in Arthur Schlesinger Jr, *The Age of Jackson* [Boston, 1945], pp. 132–3). Matthew Carey, *Letters on the Condition of the Poor* (2nd edition), pp. 16–17 (cited by Schlesinger, pp. 132–3).

35. Liam de Paor, *Divided Ulster*, p. 49.

36. Clarence H. Danhof, "Farm-making Costs and the 'Safety-valve,' 1850–1860," *Journal of Political Economy*, Vol. 49 (1941), pp. 317–59, reprinted in Vernon C. Carstensen, ed., *The Public Lands, Studies on the History of the Public Domain* (Madison, 1968), pp. 253–96; see particularly pp. 269–70.

37. Willie Lee Rose, *Rehearsal for Reconstruction: The Port Royal Experiment* (New York: Vintage Books, 1967), p. 331.

38. Address of the Colored People's Convention of the State of South Carolina held in Charleston, 20–25 November 1865, to the people of South Carolina, *Congressional Globe*, 41st Congress, Session 2, *Senate Miscellaneous Documents*, No. 8.

39. John Hope Franklin, *Reconstruction: After the Civil War* (Chicago, 1961), p. 114.

40. Address of the Colored Convention to the People of Alabama, published in the *Daily State Sentinel*, 21 May 1867; in James S. Allen, *Reconstruction, Battle for Democracy* (New York, 1937), p. 240.

41. "To the honorable the Senate and House of Representatives of the United States of America," 6 December 1869 (Senate Miscellaneous Document No. 8, 41st Congress, 2nd Session). The convention was attended by more than two hundred elected representatives of African-American workers in twenty-three states (Wesley, *Negro Labor in the United States*, pp. 179–80).

42. John R. Commons and Associates, *Documentary History of American Industrial Society*, 10 vols (1910), 9:160–64. The convention was held in Baltimore in August 1866.

43. Ibid., pp. 190–91.

44. Address delivered at Sunbury, Pennsylvania, 16 September 1868 (in *The Life, Speeches, Labors and Essays of William H. Sylvis*, edited by James C. Sylvis [1872; 1968], pp. 231–49, 235–6).

45. Letter to the editor of the Philadelphia *Evening Advocate*, 17 January 1868 (ibid., p. 313).

46. "To Abraham Lincoln, President of the United States of America," *Documents of the First International*, 4 vols (Moscow, 1964); 1:53. The document was approved at the meeting of the Council of the Association on 29 November 1864; it was published in the *Beehive* newspaper, 7 January 1865.

47. *Congressional Globe*, 38th Congress, 2nd Session, p. 286 (16 January 1865). Kelley was perhaps the most explicit of all governmental figures in his advocacy of complete racial equality and in his scorn for white supremacism. He liked to advert (as he did in the speech cited here) to the imposition of white male privileges against Negro women, in denunciation of the white racist scare words concerning "miscegenation." In a later speech, he championed voting rights of African-American "laboring people and republican soldiers," among whom were "descendants of the kings of Dahomey and of American Congressmen, Senators, Presidents, and Cabinet ministers" (*Congressional Globe*, 39th Congress, 1st Session, p. 183 [10 January 1866]). It was only much later in his career that Congressman Kelley was tagged with the unexpungeable soubriquet "Pig Iron Kelley," as a result of his strong advocacy of tariff protection for American manufacturers. Those interested in learning about Kelley as a foe of white supremacism would do well to start with Ira V. Brown, "William D. Kelley and Radical Reconstruction," *Pennsylvania Magazine of History and Biography*, 85:316–29 (July 1961).

48. Stanley P. Hirschson, *Farewell to the Bloody Shirt: Northern Republicans and the Southern Negro, 1877–1893* (Bloomington, 1962), p. 21.

49. Of course, the bourgeoisie was not a monolith: the defeat of Reconstruction did not silence all bourgeois advocates of Negro rights; the subject of Negro rights became intermixed with factional and partisan concerns; the reversion to rule by the Democratic Party in the South, aided

by open terrorism against African-Americans, was mediated by proto-populist Southern "Independents" and their Northern counterpart, the Mugwumps.

But the will of the ruling class as a whole was made unmistakable by such signal events as the following: (1) the repeal of the Southern Homestead Act in 1876, it having been vitiated from the start by a lack of financial assistance to the freedmen; (2) the Hayes–Tilden deal of 1877 when, after negotiations at the highest level of the government, Hayes (who had received 250,000 fewer votes than Tilden [the Democrat]) was allowed to be president for one term in return for (a) agreeing to withdraw federal troops from the South (leaving the African-Americans there completely at the mercy of organized white terrorism), (b) extending substantial financial aid (such as was never granted to aid the freedmen to realize on the promise of "forty acres and a mule") to the overthrowers of Reconstruction to finance "internal improvements," (c) promising of public and private aid for the construction of a railroad from the South to the Pacific, and (d) appointing a Southern Democrat as Postmaster-General, dispenser of many patronage jobs and contracts; (3) a series of Supreme Court decisions rendered between 1873 and 1883, striking down constitutional and statute protections of civil rights (for a convenient notation on these decisions see Robert Cruden, *The Negro in Reconstruction* [Englewood Cliffs, 1969] pp. 140–41.)

50. Charles Nordhoff, *The Cotton States in the Spring and Summer of 1875* (New York, 1876), p. 19.

51. John Pool, *Address to the People of North Carolina* (Raleigh, 1867), p. 4, cited in Black, "Home-made Yankees," pp. 186–7. Black points out that it was not uncommon for Southern Republicans to vote for Negro suffrage for this reason, while at the same time refusing to support the right of Negroes to testify in court or to serve on juries.

52. In 1876 President Grant submitted to Congress a list of four thousand cases of murder, maiming and whipping committed by white terrorists since 1868. William Murrell, an African-American former member of the Louisiana state legislature, testified that 2,115 Negroes had been killed in the course of the white-supremacist repression of the Reconstruction regime in Louisiana between 1866 and 1875 (John G. Van Deusen, "The Exodus of 1879," *Journal of Negro History*, Vol. 21, No. 2 [April 1936], pp. 112–13).

53. For principal primary sources, see the following Congressional reports: 42nd Congress, 2nd Session (1871–72), *Testimony Taken by the Joint Committee to Enquire into the Condition of Affairs in the Late Insurrectionary States*, Vol. 2 (13 parts); 43rd Congress, 2nd Session (1874–75), *House Reports 101; 261 (Testimony) Condition of Affairs in the South (Louisiana)*; and, *Testimony 262 (Alabama)*; 44th Congress, 1st Session (1875–76), *Senate Report 527 (Mississippi)*; 44th Congress, 2nd Session (1876–77), *House Miscellaneous Document 31: Recent Election in South Carolina*; 44th Congress, 2nd Session, *Senate Miscellaneous Document 48 (South Carolina)*, 3 vols.

54. "Capitalists up to this time have been afraid to go to the South, owing to the disturbed condition of affairs politically and this very race question. A man does not want to carry his money down there and put it in a country that might be involved in riots or disturbances." (From the testimony of John Caldwell Calhoun, 13 September 1883. See Senate Committee on Education and Labor Committee *Report upon the Relations between Labor and Capital*, 5 vols, [Washington, 1885], 2:169.)

55. The principal primary source for information about the Negro Exodus of 1879 is the three-part Senate Report 693, 46th Congress, 2nd Session (1879–80), *Report and Testimony of the Select Committee of the US Senate to Investigate the Causes of the Removal of the Negroes from the Southern States to the Northern States*, henceforth referred to as *Exodus Hearings*. The chief secondary source is Nell Irvin Painter, *Exodusters: Black Migration to Kansas after Reconstruction* (New York, 1977). Especially valuable for putting the Exodus in a national political context is Hirshson, *Farewell to the Bloody Shirt*. See also Van Deusen.

56. See Douglass, "Address before the Convention of the American Social Science Association" (Saratoga Springs, New York, 12 September 1879). The address is reprinted in Foner, *Life and Writings of Frederick Douglass*, 4:324–42.

57. Painter, pp. 75, 109. Professor Painter, who presents the most exhaustive study of the Exodus, stresses that black migration from the Southern and border states to Kansas totaled much more than the number who migrated there in the "Kansas Fever Exodus of 1879." But the Exodus of 1879, concentrated in the period of a few months, was "the most remarkable migration in the

United States after the Civil War" (pp. 147, 184).

58. Ibid., p. 87. Van Deusen, pp. 119–20.

59. "I asked my wife did she know the ground she stands on. She said, 'No.' I said it is free ground; and she cried like a child for joy" (John Solomon Lewis, Leavenworth, Kansas, cited in Painter, p. 4).

60. The reference to John Brown is in Painter, p. 159. Painter seems to have made the most particular investigation of the numbers: see pp. 146–7, 158, 184, 184 n. 1, 185, 201. Compare Hirshson, p. 282; Van Deusen, p. 122.

61. Quoted in Hirshson, p. 70, from the *Journal of Commerce*.

62. For particulars regarding these supportive efforts, see Hirshson, pp. 64–5, 68; and Van Deusen, pp. 125–7.

63. Painter, p. 152.

64. Painter, pp. 200–201. Van Deusen, pp. 123–4.

65. Bristow to John Murray Forbes, New York, 1 October 1879 (Forbes Papers, Massachusetts Historical Society, quoted by Hirshson, p. 71). Bristow served for two years as Secretary of the Treasury in President Grant's first administration.

66. "I decided some time ago that if the GOM [Grand Old Man, Prime Minister William Gladstone] went for Home Rule, the Orange card would be the one to play" (letter of the Conservative leader Randolph Churchill to the Irish Lord Chief Justice Fitzgibbon, February 1885 [cited in Winston Spencer Churchill, *Lord Randolph Churchill*, 2 vols (New York, 1906), 2:59]). This resolve of Churchill *père* is, of course, only too familiar to students of Irish history.

67. Painter, p. 3; Hirshson, pp. 66–7.

68. Painter, pp. 155, 196, 197.

69. Hirshson, pp. 68–71.

70. Hirshson, pp. 68–9.

71. Painter, pp. 185–6, 197–200.

72. Van Deusen, p. 125. Among those who were diverted from Kansas was a group that ended up in Greencastle, Indiana. A white mob drove them from the town and burned the house they had lived in (testimony of the Sheriff of Putnam County, Indiana, M. T. Lewman, *Exodus Hearings*, 1:176–8).

73. Broadus Mitchell, *The Rise of the Cotton Mills in the South*, Johns Hopkins University Studies in Historical and Political Science, xxxix, No. 2 (Baltimore, 1921; Peter Smith reprint, 1966), p. 178.

74. US Department of Commerce, Bureau of the Census, *Statistics of the Population at the Tenth Census* (Washington, DC, 1883).

75. Hirshson, pp. 70–71.

76. Hirshson, p. 3.

77. For instances of terroristic imposition of white male privilege, see the testimonies of Henry Adams and Benjamin Singleton, in Part II, pp. 177–8, and Part III, pp. 382–3, respectively, of Senate Report 693, 46th Congress, 2nd session.

78. US Senate Education and Labor Committee, *Report upon the Relations Between Labor and Capital*, 2:157–88, henceforth referred to as the "Calhoun testimony."

79. Calhoun testimony, 2:157. In March 1869 in South Carolina, where black voters outnumbered white voters by 30,000, a State Land Commission was established to purchase land and sell it in parcels of from 25 to 100 acres to freedmen and poor whites. In Arkansas, African-Americans constituted only about 25 percent of the population; and in 1869 no Republican, not even the governor, felt safe from assassination by white-supremacists (Richard Nelson Current, *Those Terrible Carpetbaggers* [New York, 1988], pp. 140, 142, 222–3).

80. Calhoun testimony, pp. 178–9. "Once, I suppose there were 150 negroes, perhaps more, on the bank of the [Mississippi] river.... We notified all the boats coming up the river not to land at this point" (p. 179).

81. Calhoun testimony, p. 169.

82. Ibid., p. 160.

83. Commons, *Documentary History of American Industrial Society*, 9:158–9.

84. This observation occurs in one of a series of articles by Sorge published in the German Social Democratic organ *Neue Zeit* during the years 1890–96, under the general title of *Die Arbeiterbewegung in den Vereinigten Staaten*. The quotation here is from *Neue Zeit*, 2:243 (1891–92).

85. Ibid., 2:244.

86. See *Socialist Labor Party of America Records*, microfilm edition, State Historical Society of Wisconsin, 1970.

87. The great value of the late Isabella Black's work "Home-made Yankees" is its collection of the stories of these whites who risked their lives, fortunes and sacred honor to join hands with the African-Americans in the Reconstruction cause. Black's work is the product of years of exhaustive research, which took her to state archives throughout the South. It is enriched by reference to secondary works, mainly biographical, long practically forgotten. In just one chapter, Chapter Seven, "The Year of Jubilo," this reader encountered some degree of record of the actions and points of view of some forty-five such individuals, representing every one of the states that had been in rebellion.

88. Freehling, *Secessionists at Bay*, pp. 103, 308–36.

89. Charles H. Wesley, *Negro Labor in the United States*, pp. 196–7; Shugg, *Class Struggle in Louisiana*, pp. 254–60.
"... even if it forced them to retire like the Indians to unwanted land," said the *Opelousas Courier* of Louisiana, 21 August 1869 (cited in Shugg, p. 254). "The desire to weaken the negro by increasing the white population, was one of the considerations in seeking mill operatives [from] outside the South" (Mitchell, *Rise of the Cotton Mills*, p. 200).

90. Shugg, p. 255. The pay in California was said to be ninety cents to $1.50 per day; in the South they would get only twenty dollars a month (Wesley, p. 197). Calhoun, in the testimony cited above, said wages for field hands in his section were ten to twenty dollars a month, or seventy-five cents to one dollar by the day.

91. Mobile *Register*, 19 July 1873. Cited in Allen Johnston Going, *Bourbon Democracy in Alabama, 1874–1898* (Tuscaloosa, 1951), p. 122.

92. The South Carolina Immigration Office wanted "to get rid of the negro and bring in whites to take his place." The most famous effort was made in 1906, but, as Mitchell puts it, "the newcomers were not so well content as to form a satisfied nucleus which would automatically attract relatives in future years" (*Rise of the Cotton Mills*, pp. 206–7, nn. 91, 92).

93. Shugg, pp. 255–61.

94. Ibid., pp. 256–8.

95. Ibid., p. 258, citing census reports.

96. Fred A. Shannon, "The Homestead Act and the Labor Surplus," in Carstensen, *The Public Lands*, p. 298.

97. John D. Hicks, *The Populist Revolt: A History of the Farmers' Alliance and the People's Party* (University of Nebraska Press, 1961), pp. 23–4.

98. Ibid., pp. 82–5.

99. Shannon, p. 307.

100. Ibid., pp. 307–8.

101. Kenneth M. Stampp, *The Peculiar Institution: Slavery in the Ante-bellum South* (New York, 1956), p. 30.

102. W. J. Cash, *The Mind of the South* (New York, 1941), p. 23.

103. Stampp, p. 29.

104. Shugg, pp. 33, 85, 86, 92, 95.

105. Broadus Mitchell and George Sinclair Mitchell, *The Industrial Revolution in the South* (Baltimore, 1930), pp. 241, 242.

106. *Richmond Enquirer*, 4 May 1832.

107. Mitchell and Mitchell, p. 244 (paraphrasing Walter Hines Page, of North Carolina, editor and US diplomat). A small minority of the poor whites were known to favor abolition of slavery; they ranged in opinion from violent white-supremacism to thoroughgoing and militant equalitarianism. Hinton Rowan Helper's opposition to slavery was coextensive with his hatred of the Negro, and he expressed this point of view as author of a number of books, including *The Negroes in Negroland; the Negroes in America; and Negroes Generally. Also the Several Races of White Men, Considered as the Involuntary and Predestined Supplanters of the Black Race* (New York, 1868). The equalitarian abolitionists were outstandingly represented by John Fairfield of Virginia, a "conductor" on the Underground Railroad, the system established to aid escaping slaves, for more than twenty years, who died while taking part in a slave insurrection in 1861 in Tennessee (Fernando G. Cartland, *Southern Heroes: The Friends in War-time* [Cambridge, Massachusetts,

1895], p. 86, cited in Black, "Home-made Yankees," p. 11).

108. James M. McPherson, *Battle Cry of Freedom: The Civil War Era* (New York, 1988), pp. 306–7 n. 41, 854.

109. Ben F. Lemert, *The Cotton Textile Industry of the Southern Appalachian Piedmont* (Chapel Hill, 1933), p. 27.

110. Cash, pp. 149–52, 160–61; Mitchell, *Rise of the Cotton Mills*, pp. 174–6.

111. Cash, pp. 175, 176.

112. Ibid., pp. 176–7.

113. The still standard monograph on the Cotton Mill Campaign is Broadus Mitchell, *The Rise of the Cotton Mills in the South*, Johns Hopkins University Studies in Historical and Political Science, xxxix, No. 2 (Baltimore, 1921; Peter Smith reprint, 1966). See also: Broadus Mitchell and George Sinclair Mitchell, *The Industrial Revolution in the South* (Baltimore, 1930); August Kohn, *The Cotton Mills of the South*, letters written to the Charleston *News and Courier*, October December 1907; *United States Industrial Commission on the Relations and Conditions of Capital and Labor Employed in Manufactures and General Business, Reports*, (Washington, DC, 1901) Vol. xiv, "Review of the Evidence", p. lii. See also the treatments of the subject by: W. J. Cash, *The Mind of the South* (New York, 1941); C. Vann Woodward, *Origins of the New South, 1877–1913* (Baton Rouge, 1952); and William M. Brewer, "Poor Whites and Negroes in the South Since the Civil War," *Journal of Negro History*, 15:26–37 (January 1930).

114. Mitchell and Mitchell, p. 148.

115. Cash, p. 195.

116. Mitchell, p. 232, citing US Census of Manufactures, 1900. The rate of increase was rising before 1880; half the increase between 1840 and 1880 occurred in the final decade.

117. Mitchell, pp. 25, 210, 211, 212 n. 100, 213.

118. Ibid., p. 211.

119. Ibid., p. 211 n. 100.

120. Ibid.

121. Ibid., p. 213.

122. Ibid., p. 214.

123. Kohn, pp. 27–8.

124. Mitchell, p. 174.

125. Testimony of Lewis W. Parker at hearings held by the House of Representatives Judiciary Committee, 29 April 1902, pp. 11f. Cited in Mitchell, pp. 136–7.

126. Ibid. To say that the cotton mill investors were motivated by political considerations, the shoring up of white supremacism, is not to imply that by employing poor whites they were acting altruistically, a theme given much currency by Mitchell and his authorities. Mitchell himself cites the fact that "upon the whole, the return upon investment in Southern cotton mills has exceeded that upon factories in the North" (*Rise of the Cotton Mills*, p. 152 n. 214, citing *US Census of Manufactures, 1990*, "Cotton Manufacture," by Edward Stanwood, pp. 28–9; Mitchell provides many instances at pp. 261–5). Vann Woodward objects to the emphasis on the altruism of the cotton mill entrepreneurs (*Origins of the New South*, p. 133).

127. D. A. Tompkins, "Cotton Mill, Commercial Features," in *The South in the Building of the Nation*, 2:109–10. Cited in Mitchell, pp. 27–8 n. 40.

128. Mitchell, p. 134 n.162.

129. *Reports of the US Industrial Commission (1901)*, Vol. XIV, *Review of the Evidence*, p. LII (52). Just as the British Protestant investors in the Industrial Revolution in Belfast followed the practice of "keeping jobs for one's own co-religionists" (J. C. Beckett, *Belfast – the Making of the City* [New York, 1966], p. 136) the Cotton Mill Campaigners similarly shored up the poor whites' racial privileges by excluding Negroes from jobs as mill operatives.

130. Cash, p. 179.

131. George Will, New York *Daily News*, 19 December 1989.

132. William Hayes Simpson, *Some Aspects of America's Textile Industry* (Columbia, South Carolina, 1966), pp. 8–12.

133. Mitchell, p. 224.

134. Woodward, pp. 224–5.

135. Mitchell and Mitchell, p. 136.

136. Ibid., p. 143. After Mrs Rosa Parks had held her place on the Montgomery bus, after the

passage of the Civil Rights Act of 1964, with its provisions concerning government contracts, and about the time James Baldwin was asking, "Tell Me How Long the Train's Been Gone?," Mrs Mamie Chance was hired as an operative, and James Douglas got a job as a fork-lift operator at the Erwin Mills in North Carolina. They were parts of a change that raised the proportion of African-Americans among textile mill production workers from 3.3 per cent in 1960 to 11.6 percent by 1969. David Griffin, Euro-American President of the Textile Workers Local 250, points out the importance of facing the issue of white supremacy: "Whites hate to organize. They want to 'get along' with management. But Negroes *know* it's not on *their* side. They've known that sort of thing way back to slavery times" (Reese Cleghorn, "The Mill: A Giant Step for the Southern Negro," *New York Times Magazine*, 9 November 1969). Perhaps President Griffin also mentioned why – the white-skin privilege – but if so, the author did not report it.

137. "The South after the war presented the greatest opportunity for a real national labor movement which the nation ever saw or is likely to see for many decades" (W. E. B. DuBois, *Black Reconstruction. An Essay toward a History of the Part which Black Folk Played in the Attempt to Reconstruct Democracy in America, 1860–1880* [New York, 1935], p. 353).

7 The Sea-change

1. This famous phrase is credited to a speech made by Senator William H. Seward of New York in 1858: "An irrepressible conflict between opposing and enduring forces ..."

2. The term adopted was "persons bound to service" (Article I, Section 9.1). James Madison opposed the use of "slave" and "slavery" because he "thought it wrong to admit in the Constitution the idea that there could be property in men" (*The Debates in the Federal Convention of 1787 which Framed the Constitution of the United States of America, reported by James Madison, a Delegate from the State of Virginia*, 2 vols, edited by Gaillard Hunt and James Brown Scott [1908, Prometheus Books reprint], 2:469).

3. "As population increases poor laborers will be so plenty as to render slaves useless," said Oliver Ellsworth of Connecticut. Charles Pinkney of South Carolina, however, still secured the postponement of the importation of African bond-laborers until 1808 (ibid., pp. 2:444, 2:467).

4. Jeannette Mirsky and Allan Nevins, *The World of Eli Whitney* (New York, 1952), p. 66; Roger Burlingame, *Machines That Built America* (New York, 1953), pp. 44–6.

5. Lewis C. Gray, *History of Agriculture in the Southern United States to 1860*, 2 vols (Washington, 1932; 1956), 2:1026.

6. Robert William Fogel and Stanley L. Engerman, *Time on the Cross: The Economics of Negro Slavery* (Boston, 1974), p. 61.

7. Ibid., pp. 68–70; Robert William Fogel, *Without Consent or Contract: The Rise and Fall of American Slavery* (New York, 1989), p. 64.

8. Thomas Prentice Kettell, *Southern Wealth and Northern Profits* (New York, 1860; Alabama, 1965), pp. 159–60. For all the partisanship of Kettell's point of view, the passages quoted here are confirmed by Fogel (p. 71). Kettell's work was intended as a riposte to Hinton Rowan Helper's *The Impending Crisis of the South*, first published three years earlier, aimed at contrasting the sluggish Southern economy with that of the bustling free-labor North (Hinton Rowan Helper, *The Impending Crisis of the South* [New York, 1857; 1963]).

9. Fogel and Engerman, p. 70.

10. Kettel gives an index of the increase in labor productivity that, despite its obvious inexactitude, indicates a steady rise in the intensity of plantation labor. There were 9 African-American bond-laborers for every 10 bales of cotton produced in 1860, whereas in 1800 the ratio was 240 for every 10 bales (*Southern Wealth and Northern Profits*, p. 159). Lewis Gray seems to suggest that the overall increase in cotton productivity was largely due to the extension of cultivation to new lands in the Lower South, along with some minor improvements in production technique and fertilization (Gray, 2:708–10). The undisputed relative scarcity of bond-labor and the extraordinary efforts made to scrape up supplementary labor for the cottonfields from other spheres of activity leaves no room for doubt that there was an intensification of exploitation of plantation labor.

11. Fogel and Engerman offer a quantification of this super-exploitation of plantation bond-labor, under the heading of "non-pecuniary disadvantages" (pp. 235–45).

12. See Eric Williams, *Capitalism and Slavery* (Chapel Hill, 1944), pp. 200–207.

13. *The Pro-slavery argument, as maintained by the most distinguished writers of the Southern States* (Philadelphia, 1852; 1968), pp. 124, 127.

14. See William W. Freehling's analytical summary of the geography of the intramural political divergencies among the politicians of the slave states (William W. Freehling, *The Road to Disunion*, 2 vols (Vol. II forthcoming), Vol. I, *Secessionists at Bay, 1776–1854* (New York, 1990), pp. 17–18.

15. "I hold that ... the relation now existing in the slaveholding States between the two [i.e., the Euro-Americans and the African-Americans], is, instead of an evil, a good – a positive good" (John C. Calhoun, speech in the United States Senate, 6 February 1837 [*Register of Debates*, 24th Cong., 2nd sess., cols 2184–8]). "It is impossible to place labor and capital in harmonious or friendly relations, except by the means of slavery, which identifies their interests" (George Fitzhugh, *Cannibals All! or Slaves Without Masters* [1857], in Harvey Wish, ed., *Ante-bellum Writings of George Fitzhugh and Hinton Rowan Helper on Slavery* [New York, 1960], p. 125). "Our new Government['s] ... foundations are laid, its cornerstone rests, upon the great truth, that the negro is not equal to the white man; that slavery – subordination to the superior race – his natural and normal condition. ... This, our new Government, is the first in the history of the world based upon this great physical, philosophical, and moral truth" (Alexander H. Stephens, Vice-President of the slaveholder Confederacy, speaking at Savannah, Georgia, 21 March 1861, quoted in Michael P. Johnson, *Toward a Patriarchal Republic: The Secession of Georgia* [Baton Rouge, 1977], p. 135).

16. See Henry Clay to Richard Pindell, 17 February 1849, in *Candidate, Compromiser, Elder Statesman, January 1, 1844–June 29, 1852*, edited by Melba Porter Hay and Carol Reardon (Lexington, Kentucky, 1991), Vol. 10 of *The Papers of Henry Clay*, 10:574–81. For the fullest statement made by Clay on the subject of abolition and "colonization," see his speech in the Senate on 7 February 1839 (*Works of Henry Clay*, edited by Calvin Colton, 6 vols [New York, 1897], 6:140–59).

17. The reader will notice that of all United States cities only New York is given particular attention here. By way of apology, I offer the following considerations: New York was the largest city, and the main center of finance and commerce; New York was the most important single city in the North politically, because of its size and because of its distinction as perfecter of machine politics, in service to the slaveholders through the Tammany Hall–National Democrat axis; New York City contained the largest concentration of Irish-Americans and, for various reasons, as a whole they served as the most important political base of the Democratic Party, the main national organization of the slaveholders.

18. Richard B. Morris, ed., *Encyclopedia of American History*, 6th edn (New York, 1982), p. 488.

19. Gray, 2:931.

20. Philip S. Foner, *Business and Slavery: The New York Merchants and the Irrepressible Conflict* (Chapel Hill, 1941), pp. 1–5.

21. The volume of Southern imports was insufficient to make economical use of the ships returning from delivering bulky cotton cargoes to England. It was cheaper to pay the Northern middleman whose import volume sufficed to fill the returning ships.

22. Amy Bridges, *A City in the Republic: Antebellum New York and the Origins of Machine Politics* (New York, 1984), p. 44.

23. Kettell, p. 127. In tabulating the North–South balance of trade, included in this total are customs duties entering the Northern economy, professional services, and tourism, totaling about $100,000,000. Kettell, a former editor of the Jacksonian *Democratic Review* and a devout believer in chattel bondage, was seeking to counter the effect of Hinton Rowan Helper's *The Impending Crisis of the South*, which argued a contrast between an economically sluggish Southern economy and the productive vigor of the free-labor North.

24. Brother Basil Leo Lee, *Discontent in New York City, 1861–1865* (Washington, DC, 1943), pp. 131–5.

25. Message of Mayor Fernando Wood, Annual Report to the Common Council, 7 January 1861, in *Proceedings of the Board of Aldermen of the City of New York*, Vol. 81 (New, 1861), pp. 12, 24–6.

26. Iver Bernstein, *The New York City Draft Riots: Their Significance for American Society and Politics in the Age of the Civil War* (New York, 1990), p. 143.

27. Ibid.

28. "[N]o man acquainted with the history of the country can deny, that the general lead in the politics of the country, for three-fourths of the period that has elapsed since the adoption of the Constitution, has been a southern lead," said Daniel Webster (*Congressional Globe*, 31st Cong., 1st sess. [7 March 1850], p. 478). "The South, so far from having become an abject minority ... has controlled the Government ... for 60 out of the 72 [years] of our national existence" (Alexander H. Stephens, shortly before his election to the post of Vice-President of the Confederate [slave] States of America; cited by Rudloph von Abele, *Alexander H. Stephens: A Biography* [New York, 1971], p. 186).

29. *Congressional Globe*, 29th Cong., 2nd sess., Appendix (8 February 1847), p. 316. This is part of a direct quotation from one of Randolph's speeches against the Missouri Compromise. It was cited by David Wilmot at the time of the controversy over the inclusion or exclusion of slavery from California, where under the Mexican government slavery had been abolished a quarter of a century earlier.

30. See Theodore William Allen, *Class Struggle and the Origin of Racial Slavery, the Invention of the White Race*, a pamphlet (Hoboken, 1975; originally published, with abridgement of footnotes, in *Radical America*, 9:40–63 [May–June 1975]. See Volume Two of the present work for a full treatment of the subject.

31. See also William J. Grayson, "The Hireling and the Slave," in *The Hireling and the Slave, Chicora, and Other Poems* (Charleston, 1856).

32. *Congressional Globe*, 35th Cong., 1st sess., Appendix, pp. 68–71 (4 March 1858).

33. George Fitzhugh, *Sociology for the South, or The Failure of Free Society* (1854; 1960 reprint).

34. Ibid., p. 263.

35. The translation was always cleansed, however, of the less sympathetic second half of the generalizations voiced by Calhoun, Hammond, et al. It would obviously have been inappropriate for involving the laboring-class Americans on the side of the slaveholders to have them dwell on the political economy preached by Calhoun, namely that "the non-producing classes" would always appropriate the larger share of the social product whether produced by bond labor or wage labor: as it was in the beginning, was then, and ever should be (*Register of Debates*, 24th Cong., 2nd sess., cols 2184–8; 2186 [6 February 1837]). Discretion likewise would omit Hammond's thesis that wage labor and bond labor were merely variations in form of the "mudsills of society," necessary to "all social systems ... to do the menial duties, to perform the drudgery of life" (Hammond, *Congressional Globe*, 35th Cong., 1st sess., Appendix, p. 77 [4 May 1858]). Virginia lawmaker Benjamin Watkins Leigh in the same vein declared that while a "racial" distinction had to be observed, nevertheless, however "white" they might be, the "peasantry," dependent on "their daily labor for their subsistence," could never be admitted into "political affairs" (*Proceedings of the Virginia State Convention of 1829–1830* [Richmond, 1830], p. 158, cited by Freehling, p. 173).

36. "[T]he progress of machinery is so fast diminishing the profits of hand-labor as to render ... escape ... necessary to our existence." From an editorial addressed to Feargus O'Connor, Irish leader in the Irish liberation struggle and in the British Chartist movement, who had urged Americans to support the abolition cause. The letter was signed by "A Member of the NY Society for the Abolition of ALL Slavery" (*Working Man's Advocate*, 22 June 1844).

37. Ibid. See also Arthur M. Schlesinger Jr, *The Age of Jackson* (Boston, 1945), pp. 425–6.

38. Open letter from George Henry Evans to Gerrit Smith, a wealthy abolitionist (*Working Man's Advocate*, 6 July 1844; emphasis in original).

39. Ibid. For other examples of this tendency see Herman Schlueter, *Lincoln, Labor and Slavery* (New York, 1913), pp. 60–67, 72–3. Schlueter has the dubious distinction of founding the "Marxist" white-apologist school of American labor historiography. Schlueter interprets the growing "white labor" hostility toward abolitionism as a manifestation of "awakening class

consciousness" on the part of the increasingly "organized" European-American workers (pp. 46–7).

40. Open letter from George Henry Evans to Gerrit Smith, *Working Man's Advocate*, 6 July 1844.

41. Lee, *Discontent in New York City, 1861–1865*, pp. 143–4. Lee cites the president of the Painters Union, who scorned abolitionism because "the slaves in the South, where he had lived, were fed and clothed better than many thousands of white mechanics in New York City."

42. Henry Clay to Richard Pindell, 17 February 1849, in *Papers of Henry Clay*; 10:580.

43. Letter to Jacob Gibson, 25 July 1842, in *Works of Henry Clay*, 4:464.

44. Henry Clay to Calvin Colton, 2 September 1843, in *Works of Henry Clay*, 4:476–7.

45. Florence E. Gibson, *The Attitude of the New York Irish Toward State and National Affairs, 1848–1892* (New York, 1951), pp. 116–17. Two years after the Emancipation Proclamation, a Fourth of July "Address to the Workingmen of the United States," issued by the Workingmen's United Political Association of New York, espoused the slaveholder interest as the ally of the European-American worker, whose war-intensified miseries, it said, stemmed from the abolitionist effort to put Negro workers on an equal plane with white workers (Lee, pp. 142–3).

46. Wilbur H. Siebert, *The Underground Railroad from Slavery to Freedom*, with an Introduction by Albert Bushnell Hart (New York, 1899), pp. 341–2; Morris, *Encyclopedia of American History*, p. 758.

47. W. P. Garrison and F. J. Garrison, *William Lloyd Garrison, 1805–1879: The Story of his Life as Told by his Children*, 4 vols (New York, 1889), 3:51 n. 1. This footnote of the Garrisons is rich in detail and references.

48. W. E. Burghardt DuBois, *John Brown*, centennial edition (New York, 1962), pp. 280–86.

49. Aptheker cites William Lloyd Garrison as saying that 400 out of the *Liberator*'s 450 first-year subscribers were African-Americans, and that three years later, in 1834, African-Americans still accounted for three-fourths of the paper's 2,300 subscribers (Herbert Aptheker, ed., *A Documentary History of the Negro People in the United States* [New York, 1951], p. 108).

50. *Frederick Douglass' Paper*, 2 and 16 February 1855 (cited by Leon F. Litwak, *North of Slavery* [Chicago, 1961], pp. 160–61).

51. Karl Marx, *Capital: A Critique of Political Economy*, Vol. I, *The Process of Capitalist Production*, translated from the third edition by Samuel Moore and Edward Aveling (Chicago, 1906), Chapter VII, Section 7.

52. "Seventeenth Annual Meeting of the Massachusetts A. Slavery Society," *Liberator*, 1 February 1849. This resolution was offered by Charles Stearns, who "supported it in some very earnest remarks respecting the suffering of many of the laboring people of the North." Despite one tangential comment, tending to blame the workers' suffering on excessive drinking, especially among the Irish, the motion was passed without dissent. The record shows that resolutions were not routinely passed, as exampled by those on Free Soil and the religious connection.

53. See p. 138.

54. "I hear many expressions of sympathy for us in this City, and in case of an attempt to coerce us, I believe we can safely rely on much material aid from here, and especially from the Irish" (from a letter by Charles C. Spencer of Mississippi, *New York Times*, 14 December 1860: Spencer was in New York expressly to assess support for Southern secession from the United States; three days later an anonymous Irish-American disputed Spencer on the Irish and the Union, though not on the question of "Slavery or the wrongs [done to] the South" [*New York Times*, 17 December 1860]).

55. Despite the fact that pre-twentieth-century Irish emigration statistics are considered "notoriously unreliable" (R. F. Foster, *Modern Ireland, 1600–1972* [New York: Viking, 1988; Penguin Books, 1989], p. 345), especially for the period before 1840, emigration looms so large in Ireland's story that commentators are obliged to attempt to quantify it. In the period 1841 to 1861, emigration was more than 2.6 million, of whom two-thirds, 1.7 million, went to the United States. (This does not include the secondary migration of those whose first stop was Canada.) Irish emigration and United States immigration statistics seem comparable. (Total population and emigration figures are given in *A New History*, Ancillary Volume II, *Population, 1821–1971*, edited by W. E. Vaughan and A. J. Fitzpatrick [Dublin, 1978], Tables 13, 53 and 54). The total number of Irish immigrants entering the United States between 1820 and 1860 was just under 2

million, of whom $1\frac{3}{4}$ million arrived between 1841 and 1860 (United States Department of Commerce, Bureau of the Census, *Historical Statistics of the United States, Colonial Times to 1970* [Washington, DC, 1975], p. 106, Series C-92. Compare Foster, pp. 345, 354–5; Cormac O Grada, "A Note on Nineteenth Century Emigration Statistics," *Population Studies*, 29:143–9 [March 1975].)

56. Cecil J. Houston, *Irish Emigration and Canadian Settlement* (Toronto, 1990), p. 77. In 1861, Catholics made up 78 per cent of the 5.8 million total population of Ireland (*A New History*, Ancillary Volume II, Table 13).

57. *Historical Statistics of the United States*, p. 118. *A New History*, Ancillary Volume II, Table 3.

58. Eighth Census of the United States, 1860, "Population," p. 609, in Robert Ernst, *Immigrant Life in New York City, 1825–1863* (New York, 1949), p. 198. In 1855 more than half the city's population was foreign-born. See also Bridges, *City in the Republic*, p. 41.

59. David Noel Doyle ("The Irish in North America, 1776–1845," in *A New History*, 5:720–21) without attempting to document his argument, appears to challenge the traditional belief implied in the low dispersal ratio of Irish-Americans shown here. Doyle states flatly that "there was no over-concentration in seaboard slums." However, he makes exceptions for "the famine decade and its aftermath," which would include the period from 1845 to 1860, and for the protracted period of economic stagnation, 1837–43. Those periods together cover the majority of the period with which the present chapter is concerned. (Compare Carl Wittke, *The Irish in America* [Baton Rouge, 1956], pp. 24–6; and John Francis Maguire, *The Irish in America*, [London, 1868, New York, 1968], pp. 214–35].)

60. The percentages in columns A and B are based on *Annual Reports of the Commissioners of Immigration of the State of New York, from the Organization of the Commission 5 May 1847 to 1860 Inclusive* ... (New York, 1861), Appendix, p. 288; and Eighth Census of the United States, 1860, "Population," p. 609, in Ernst, pp. 188, 198.

61. John R. G. Hassard, *Life of the Most Reverend John Hughes, DD, First Archbishop of New York, with Extracts from his Private Correspondence* (New York, 1866), p. 17. The poem was published in the Gettysburg, Pennsylvania, *Centinel*.

62. Ibid. pp. 42–4. See Appendix K for the full text of the poem.

63. Ibid., p. 45. Shortly after entering upon his new career, Hughes heard from French refugees accounts of the Haitian Revolution that left him with "an exaggerated fear of Negro insurrection." It would be wrong to simplify the matter; still it is not to be ignored that thirty years later, in the middle of the Civil War, in arguing against Negro emancipation Hughes sought to reason from his encounters "as a young priest with refugees from the Dominican massacres" (Madeleine Hook Rice, *American Catholic Opinion in the Slavery Controversy* [New York, 1944], p. 120; Rice cites Hughes to the editor of the *Journal des Débats* in *Metropolitan Record*, 1 March 1862).

64. In an article written in 1976, Douglas C. Riach pointed to half a dozen issues regarding internal Irish affairs that had a negative impact on the development of the abolitionist front in Ireland ("Daniel O'Connell and American Anti-slavery," *Irish Historical Studies*, 20:3–25 [March 1976]). Of particular importance was the difference over the attitude to be taken toward offers of assistance by American slaveholders. Young Irelander critics, said Riach, "insisted that O'Connell, in pursuing an abolitionist course, was damaging Ireland's interest." In a subsequent article, Riach found that the issue of American slavery became "an important source of discord within the Repeal Association" (Douglas C. Riach, "O'Connell and Slavery," in Donal McCartney, ed., *The World of Daniel O'Connell* [Dublin and Cork, 1980], p. 184). More recently another Irish historian, Maurice O'Connell, contributed an informative treatment of the subject, including a review of discussions in the Repeal Association, in the columns of *Nation*, the organ of the Young Irelanders, and in the Irish Confederation, the Young Ireland breakaway organization formed in January 1847 (Maurice R. O'Connell, *Daniel O'Connell, the Man and His Politics* [Dublin, 1990]). The Young Irelanders saw the Irish cause as dependent upon working the Anglo-American contradiction in such a way that the American slaveholders would somehow create an opportunity to free Ireland from British rule (see Chapter 8 n. 42, for John Mitchel's defense of this strategy in *Nation*). Therefore, they argued, it was at least folly to antagonize the slaveholders.

The findings of Riach, O'Connell, and other Irish historians, leave no room for doubt that in the wake of Clontarf, the opposition to O'Connell's leadership became more definite and articulate, and that much of it took the form of criticism of O'Connell's abolitionism as a sacrifice of the interests of repeal. Yet, after all is said and done, the contrast in the relative strengths of abolitionism among the Irish in Ireland and among the Irish-Americans seems unmistakable. Riach's generalization ("O'Connell and Slavery," p. 185) regarding the state of Irish opinion on abolitionism – that "many" in Ireland objected to it – could hardly serve to describe the prevalence of anti-abolitionism among Irish-Americans. Nor would the Young Irelanders in the United States have felt as Young Irelanders in Ireland did, that "Had they neglected to condemn slavery they would have handed O'Connell an important debating point" (Maurice R. O'Connell, *Daniel O'Connell*, p. 130). To note the Young Irelanders' challenge at home to O'Connell's abolitionism does not negate the fact of the "sea-change" effect, the explanation of which is the concern of this study.

65. *Liberator*, 3:179. Charleston, South Carolina *Courier* article reprinted in the "Refuge of Oppression" column in the *Liberator*, 11: 41.

66. In a speech to a "monster meeting" of 400,000 at Mallow, near Cork, on 11 June 1843, a speech that came to be called "The Mallow Defiance," O'Connell declared that "Irishmen would soon have to choose between living as slaves and dying as freemen" (L. A. McCaffrey, *Daniel O'Connell and the Repeal Year* [Lexington, 1966], p. 82).

67. Except as otherwise noted, the citations of O'Connell's pronouncements are taken from a collection of excerpts of his speeches published in the *Liberator*, the organ of the Massachusetts Anti-slavery Society, 25 March 1842.

68. Speech before the London Anti-slavery Society, 12 May 1832. Riach cites a single exception, having to do with the parliamentary debate over the terms and time allowed for the "transition" from slavery to full emancipation in the British West Indies ("Daniel O'Connell and American Anti-slavery," pp. 4–5).

69. In two London speeches: at the British India Society on 6 July 1839, and at the anniversary of the British and Foreign Anti-slavery Society on 24 June 1840.

70. Oscar Sherwin, *Prophet of Liberty: The Life and Times of Wendell Phillips* (New York, 1958), pp. 631–2. O'Connell's allusion was to Psalm 137, verses 5 and 6. The citation is from Phillips's 6 August 1875 oration on the occasion of a celebration of the centennial of O'Connell's birth (Wendell Phillips, *Speeches, Lectures, and Letters*, 2 vols [Boston, 1894], 2:406–9).

71. London Anti-slavery Society speech, 24 June 1840.

72. Speech before the Glasgow Emancipation Society, September 1835.

73. In 1847, the remittances to Ireland from the United States amounted to £200,000 (about a million dollars); over the next seventeen years, the remittances averaged over £380,000 per year. Most of the money sent at Christmas and Easter "came from Irish laborers and servant girls" (Wittke, *The Irish in America*, p. 51).

74. Rice, pp. 79, 100. Rice cites a Boston *Pilot* editor, who drew no fine distinctions between abolitionism and Free Soilism, warning its predominantly Irish readership in 1851: "wherever you find a free-soiler, you find . . . a woman's rights man" (p. 100).

75. Speech to the British Anti-slavery Society General Meeting, 23 April 1831; excerpted in the *Liberator*, 25 March 1842.

76. Garrison and Garrison, *William Lloyd Garrison*, 1:373, 379. The exclusionary vote had been taken on 12 June. O'Connell replied to Mott's letter of criticism on 20 June.

77. William Lloyd Garrison, letter to G. W. Benson, 22 March 1842, in Garrison and Garrison, 3:50.

78. Rice, p. 85.

79. Gilbert Osofsky, "Abolitionists, Irish Immigrants, and the Dilemmas of Romantic Nationalism," *American Historical Review*, 80:889–912 (October 1975), p. 897.

80. Madden (1798–1886) had struggled against the obstructionism of the plantation owners when he served as a magistrate overseeing the dismantlement of the slavery system in Jamaica under the terms of the Emancipation Law passed by the British Parliament in 1833 (Henry Boylan, ed., *Dictionary of Irish Biography* [New York, 1978]). He became best known perhaps for a history of the Irish rebellion of 1798, *The United Irishmen: Their Lives and Times*, the first two volumes of which were published in 1842. See Appendix L for the text of the Address.

81. *Liberator*, 18 December 1841 (Osofsky, pp. 895–8).

82. William Lloyd Garrison to Benson, 22 March 1842, in Garrison and Garrison, 3:50.

83. Letter dated 1 February 1842 from Maria Weston Chapman (The *Liberator*, 1 April 1842).

84. Osofsky, p. 903. Osofsky refers specifically to the campaign against "the pro-slavery position of the Repeal Associations" in the United States.

85. Ibid., pp. 904–5; Doyle, "The Irish in North America, 1776–1845."

86. Robert Francis Hueston, *The Catholic Press and Nativism, 1840–1860* (New York, 1976), p. 30.

87. *Report of the Proceedings of the National Repeal Convention of the Friends of Ireland in the United States of America held in Philadelphia, February 22nd and 23d, 1842* (Philadelphia, 1842), pp. 9–11.

88. O'Connell at the weekly meeting of the Loyal National Repeal Association, Dublin, around 1 October 1843 (*Liberator*, 10 November 1843).

89. I am indebted to the kindness of Professor Maurice O'Connell, now living in retirement in Dublin, for my copy of the Cincinnati repealers' letter. See Dublin *Pilot*, 12 April 1844, British Museum Library, Newspaper Library, Colindale, London.

O'Connell's written reply was published in the *British and Foreign Anti-slavery Reporter*, 15 November 1843. The manuscript, dated 11 October 1843, is at University College Library, Dublin (McCaffrey, p. 74 n. 39).

8 How the Sea-change was Wrought

1. *Liberator*, 8 April 1842.

2. See: Joseph M. Hernon, "Irish Sympathy for the Southern Confederacy," *Eire–Ireland*, vol. 2, no. 3, pp. 72–85; and Joseph M. Hernon Jr, "Irish Religious Opinion on the American Civil War," *Catholic Historical Review*, 4:508–23 (January 1964). "The clergy in Ireland adopted the temporizing tactics of the Catholic clergy in the United States on the slavery issue", *Irish Religious Opinion*, p. 511. "Confederate agents in Ireland played upon the religious sensitivity of Irish Catholics in order to influence public opinion" (ibid., p. 515).

3. John O'Connell, letter to James Haughton of the Hibernian Anti-slavery Society, 27 January 1842 (*Liberator*, 25 March 1842).

4. According to James Canning Fuller (*Liberator*, 8 April 1842).

5. Letter dated 17 October 1841 (*Liberator*, 18 March 1842).

6. Asenath Nicholson, *Ireland's welcome to a stranger*, cited in George Potter, *To the Golden Door: The Story of the Irish in Ireland and America* (Boston and Toronto, 1960), p. 21.

7. Douglass, writing from Belfast to Garrison in America, 1 January 1846 (*Liberator*, 30 January 1846).

8. Frederick Douglass, *Life and Times of Frederick Douglass, Written by Himself: His Early Life as a Slave, His Escape from Bondage, and his Complete History*, revised edition (1892; New York and Toronto, 1962), p. 237. Ten years before, the year before Douglass escaped from slavery, O'Connell (apologizing for his conceit) had expressed the hope that in the United States "some Black O'Connell might arise among his fellow slaves, who would cry, 'Agitate, Agitate' till the two millions and a half of his fellow-sufferers learned the secret of their strength" (speech to the Glasgow Emancipation Society, September 1835; excerpted in the *Liberator*, 25 March 1842).

9. "Nearly all the Irish journals were strongly political, and each was a stalwart supporter of the Democratic party.... Influenced by the authoritarian traditionalism of Irish Catholicism, the papers rejected all schemes for the reformation of society.... Above all, the Celtic journals gave vent to the ... hatred of abolitionists" (Robert Ernst, *Immigrant Life in New York City, 1825–1863* [New York, 1949], pp. 150–53). See also: Robert Francis Hueston, *The Catholic Press and Nativism, 1840–1860* (New York, 1976); Florence E. Gibson, *The Attitude of the New York Irish Toward State and National Affairs, 1848–1892* (New York, 1951).

10. These Young Irelander publications (such as the *Nation*, the *Citizen*, and the *Irish News*) were extremely white-supremacist in their policies, and therefore they were objectively auxiliaries of the avowedly Catholic press in respect to the slavery question. They are refracted by Ernst as "left-wing"!

All the more honor is due, then, to those Irish-Americans who kept faith with O'Connell and

Irish abolitionism. The present writer has encountered their names only incidentally in the research for this work. Perhaps some other student – even some priest or heroic nun, such as those who have stood up for the peasants and workers even when not fully supported by their Church, or who marched or were Freedom Riders in the 1960s, or who stand up for women's rights to reproductive choice and to their right of ordination; or independent scholars, their consciousness raised by the Ulster civil rights demonstrators marching and singing "We Shall Overcome"; or some doctoral candidate – will search them out in the newspaper archives, letters preserved, forgotten memoirs, etc., and dedicate a volume to their memory and their message for today. If they do, they will surely give consideration (warts and all) to such immigrants as James Canning Fuller, the Garrisonian; Michael Sheehy, staunch abolitionist made to suffer privation on that account; Judge Doran, Philadelphia anti-slavery repealer, praised by O'Connell; lecturer Mason Jones (was he a resident or only a visitor?), booed from the stage for glorifying the "Universal Emancipation" principle. Perhaps room will be found for Confederate General Patrick Cleburne who in 1864 advocated arming African-American bond-laborers and giving them freedom.

11. See, for example, Hughes's lecture at St Patrick's Institute in Pittsburgh, 27 June 1856, on "the relationship between the civil and religious duties of the Catholic clergy" (*Complete Works of the Most Reverend John Hughes*, edited by Lawrence Kehoe, 2 vols [New York, 1866], 2:144–8].

12. Third Pastoral of the Province of Cincinnati, May 1861; cited, along with a number of others to the same effect, in Madeleine Hook Rice, *American Catholic Opinion in the Slavery Controversy* (New York, 1944), p. 94, and n. 32.

13. Rice, p. 96, citing *Speech delivered in the House of Representatives on Tuesday, Feb. 10, 1857*, p. 19.

14. *Freeman's Journal*, 4 June 1853, cited in Hueston, p. 212 n. 45.

15. Speaking in Baltimore in 1856, Archbishop Hughes stated that Catholics were being converted to Protestantism in America at more than three times the rate of conversion of Protestants to Catholicism (lecture on "The Present Condition of the Catholic Church in the United States," delivered at a meeting of the Catholic Friend's Society, in *Complete Works ... of John Hughes*, 2:128).

16. David J. Alvarez, "The Papacy in the American Civil War," *Catholic Historical Review*, 69:227–48 (April 1983), p. 231.

17. John R. G. Hassard, *Life of the Most Reverend John Hughes, D.D., First Archbishop of New York, with Extracts from his Private Correspondence* (New York, 1866), p. 384.

18. For a discussion of the schismatic pressures arising within Protestantism, see John R. McKivigan, *The War against Proslavery Religion: Abolitionism and the Northern Churches, 1830–1865* (Ithaca, 1984), pp. 82–90.

19. *Catholic Mirror*, 25 January 1850; cited in Rice, p. 101.

20. *Letters of the late Bishop [John] England to Hon. John Forsyth on the Subject of Domestic Slavery, to which are prefixed copies, in Latin and English, of the Pope's Apostolic Letter, concerning the African Slave Trade, with some Introductory Remarks, etc.* (Baltimore, 1844).

21. Ibid., p. iii.

22. Ibid., pp. 108–9.

23. Indeed, during the Civil War, especially after the Emancipation Proclamation was issued, differences over abolition did surface within the United States hierarchy (ibid.).

24. Hassard, pp. 215–16. Hughes's description of his attitude on this occasion seems consistent with his practice at home, where he is quoted as saying, "I will suffer no man in my diocese that I cannot control. I will either put him down, or he shall put me down" (Henry J. Browne, "Archbishop Hughes and Western Colonization," *Catholic Historical Review*, 36:257–85 [October 1950], p. 284).

25. Hassard, p. 216. Hassard's understated observation was that, "[T]he bishop's sentiments on the slavery question had undergone some change since Leander wrote verses for the Gettysburg *Centinel*." Incidentally, apparently during this same trip, Hughes heard O'Connell's Repeal address at a Donnybrook "monster meeting" which he estimated at "not less than two hundred thousand" (ibid).

26. The letter, with accompanying documents, dated New York, 30 March 1858, was sent to a friend in Rome for translation and eventual submission to Vatican officials (Hassard, pp. 389–90, emphasis in original).

27. Ibid., p. 351.

28. Ibid., p. 212.

29. Ibid., pp. 392–3. Richard J. Purcell says, "In no way was Hughes more mistaken than in his opposition to the Irish movement westward in the [eighteen] fifties" (*Dictionary of American Biography*: "Hughes, John Joseph"). See Browne, p. 283. Browne makes allowance for Hughes's stand as being purely the expression of a concern for protecting the flock from malign influences (p. 284).

30. John Francis Maguire, upon returning to Ireland after a visit to the United States, was moved to write: "... it is not within the power of language to describe adequately, much less exaggerate, the evil consequences of this unhappy tendency of the Irish to congregate in the large towns of America," which tendency he calls a "fatal blunder" (John Francis Maguire, *The Irish in America* [London, 1868; New York, 1968], pp. 214, 218. Maguire devotes a full chapter to documentation of the abominable conditions under which the Irish of the laboring class were condemned to live in New York).

31. Hassard, pp. 435–6. Historian Lee Benson observes that about 1854 "Catholic leaders reversed the policy of nonalignment" with any particular party (Lee Benson, *The Concept of Jacksonian Democracy: New York as a Test Case* [Princeton, 1961], p. 191).

32. *Complete Works of ... John Hughes*, 2:220–22.

33. Brother Basil Leo Lee, *Discontent in New York City, 1861–1865* (Washington, DC, 1943) p. 156.

34. *Caucasian*, 12 October 1862.

35. Lee, p. 142.

36. See the story of the Good Samaritan in Luke 10:30–34. Horace Greeley, editor of the *New York Tribune*, used this allusion to make the same charge against Archbishop Hughes just four days before the beginning of the 1863 anti-draft riots (*New York Tribune*, 9 July 1863, cited in Albon P. Man, "The Church and the New York Draft Riots of 1863," *Records of the American Catholic Historical Society of Philadelphia*, 62: 33–50 [March 1951], p. 46).

37. For a modern historian's criticism of Elijah P. Lovejoy on this ground, see the unsigned article, "Elijah P. Lovejoy as an Anti-Catholic," *Records of the American Catholic Historical Society of Philadelphia*, 62:172–80 (September 1951).

38. "Reply of the Repeal Association to the Address from Cincinnati," *British and Foreign Anti-slavery Reporter*, London, 15 November 1843. The way to "disarm" such anti-Catholics, he said, was "not by giving up to them the side of humanity," but by taking "a superior station of Christian virtue" as fighters "for the freedom of all mankind."

39. Massachusetts Anti-slavery Society, *Tenth Annual Report*, 1842, Appendix 8, cited in Oscar Sherwin, *Prophet of Liberty: The Life and Times of Wendell Phillips* (New York, 1958), p. 154. See also Aileen S. Kraditor's account of the Protestant in-fighting (*Means and Ends in American Abolitionism: Garrison and His Critics on Strategy and Tactics, 1834–1850* [New York, 1967; Vintage books edition, 1970], Chapter 4, "Religion and the Good Society").

40. William Darrell Overdyke, *The Know-Nothing Party in the South* (Baton Rouge: Louisiana State Press, 1950), pp. 198–9.

41. Alvarez, "Papacy in the American Civil War," pp. 234, 239.

42. Douglas C. Riach, "Daniel O'Connell and American Anti-slavery," *Irish Historical Studies*, 20:3–25 (March 1976) pp. 18–20. John Mitchel, writing in the Young Irelanders' *Nation* saw the "opportunity" for Irish independence in "a war between England and the United States." He defended this strategy against those who thought it cowardly to expect others to deliver the main blow (*Nation*, 6 and 13 December 1841, cited in William Dillon, *Life of John Mitchel*, 2 vols in 1 [London, 1888], 1:102).

43. Dillon 1:115.

44. Ibid., 2:43–4.

45. Quoted in Robert G. Athearn, *Thomas Francis Meagher: An Irish Revolutionary in America* (Boulder, 1949), p. 17. During the Civil War, Meagher switched affiliations, served as an officer in the Union Army, and made scathing attacks on the pro-slavery politics of those whose views he had formerly shared (see p. 198).

46. This strategic approach to Irish independence was taken up by the Irish Republican Brotherhood, or Fenians, as they were more commonly known, when they were organized in 1858. In 1866 and again in 1870, the American Fenians launched quixotic "invasions" of Canada. On

the first occasion, a few hundred Irish-Americans crossed the Niagara River and bravely fought an engagement with the local militia, but were forced to flee back to United States territory. The 1870 attempt was likewise defeated, and the US Marshal in Vermont arrested those who returned across the border.

47. Kerby A. Miller, *Emigrants and Exiles: Ireland and the Irish Exodus to North America* (New York, 1985), p. 335.

48. See p. 143 ff for the main lines on which the white-skin privilege system was reinstituted after the Civil War.

49. *Statutes at Large of the United States of America, 1789–1873* (17 vols, Washington, DC, 1850–73), 1 Stat. 103. The volume and page citations, and date of final passage of subsequent pre-Civil War immigration and naturalization laws are as follows: 1 Stat. 414 (29 January 1795); 2 Stat. 153 (14 April 1802); 2 Stat. 292 (26 March 1804); 3 Stat. 258 (22 March 1816); 4 Stat. 69 (26 May 1824); 4 Stat. 310 (24 May 1828).

In 1870, after passage of the Fifteenth Amendment, "the naturalization laws [were] ... extended to aliens of African nativity and to persons of African descent." Thereafter, until at least 1924, the law still bore its phraseological birthmark in the curious formulation giving the right of immigration to "... aliens being free white persons, and to aliens of African nativity and to persons of African descent" (United States Department of Justice, *Administrative Decisions under Immigration and Nationality Laws*, Vol. II [January 1944–August 1947], [Washington, 1948], p. 254). On 6 May 1882 the so-called Oriental Exclusion Law was enacted barring entry to the United States by any Chinese, except diplomats and individuals bearing special Chinese government certificates (22 Stat. 58). By a series of extensions this bar to Chinese entry remained in effect until 1943, when the first Chinese quota was established permitting the entry of 105 persons per year. Similar white-supremacist immigration bars were put into effect against Japanese, as being persons "ineligible to citizenship."

In 1922, the Supreme Court denied the appeal of a Hindu who argued that by anthropological classification he was a "Caucasian." The Supreme Court held that, although the book definition of "Caucasian" included Hindus, "the statutory words, 'white persons' ... [were] 'words of common speech, to be interpreted in accordance with the understanding of the common man ...'" Hindus were therefore to be excluded under that interpretation, because "Hindus could not merge into the mass of our population ... so as to [be] recognized as white" (*Administrative Decisions under Immigration and Nationality Laws*, Vol. II, pp. 254–5; the case citation is *United States vs. Thind*, 261 U.S. 206 [1923]).

50. Jackson, letter to his Vice-President-elect Martin Van Buren in November 1832, regarding a number of persons under consideration for appointment to office (*Correspondence of Andrew Jackson*, edited by John Spencer Bassett, 7 vols [Washington, 1926–35], 4:489).

51. Arthur M. Schlesinger Jr, *The Age of Jackson* (New York, 1945), pp. 45–7.

52. Leon F. Litwak, *North of Slavery* (Chicago, 1961), pp. 74–6.

53. Gustavus Myers, *A History of Tammany Hall*, 2nd edn (New York, 1917), p. 143.

54. United States Department of Commerce, Bureau of the Census, *Historical Statistics of the United States, Colonial Times to 1970* (Washington, DC, 1975), p. 106.

55. See p. 101.

56. Dixon Ryan Fox, "The Negro Vote in Old New York," *Political Science Quarterly*, 32:252–75 (1917), pp. 255–7.

57. The last of the restrictions on poor-white suffrage were removed by the New York Constitutional Convention of 1826 (Fox, p. 263).

58. The distinction attempted in this thesis between simple slavery and *racial* slavery, a *form* of racial oppression, is highlighted by the attitude of Federalist Philip Hone, who was an anti-abolitionist and yet a vigorous champion of equal voting rights for free African-Americans (see Fox, p. 265). What the slaveholders understood better than Hone did was that slavery in the United States could be maintained only as *racial* slavery, as a form of racial oppression of African-Americans, free as well as bond.

59. Fox, pp. 262 n. 5, 263–71.

60. Ibid., p. 274.

61. Amy Bridges, *A City in the Republic: Antebellum New York and the Origins of Machine Politics* (New York, 1984), p. 43.

62. Fox, pp. 273–4.

63. See Potter, *To the Golden Door*, Chapter 6, "The Irish as 'Ready Made' Democrats."

64. Myers, pp. 128–9; Man, "Church and the New York Draft Riots of 1863," p. 96.

65. Ernst, pp. 163–4; Myers, p. 132.

66. Myers, pp. 129, 133, 135.

67. Ernst, *Immigrant Life in New York City*, p. 163.

68. Myers, p. 141; Albon P. Man Jr, "Labor Competition and the New York Draft Riots of 1863," *Journal of Negro History*, 36:375–405 (October 1951), p. 378.

69. The purpose of annexation was to counter the limitations imposed by the Northwest Ordinance and the Missouri Compromise of 1820, by extending slavery to a vast territory, of 249 million acres, equal to more than one-sixth of the total area of the United States prior to that time.

70. Riach, "Daniel O'Connell and American Anti-slavery," pp. 18–19.

71. Letter to the London *Morning Chronicle*, 1838, reprinted in the *Liberator*, 25 March 1842.

72. William W. Freehling, *The Road to Disunion*, 2 vols (Vol. II forthcoming) Vol. I, *Secessionists at Bay, 1776–1854* (New York, 1990), p. 359.

73. See pp. 164–5.

74. *Works of Henry Clay*, edited by Calvin Colton, 6 vols (New York, 1897), 4:495 (letter of Frelinghuysen to Clay, 9 November 1844). See also Ambrose Spence to Clay, 21 November 1844 (p. 501), and Adam Beatty to Clay, 24 December 1848 (p. 517).

75. Letter dated New York, 6 December 1860, published in the Charleston (South Carolina) *Mercury*, and republished in the *New York Times*, 14 December 1860.

76. "Far more vehement than the clergy on the slavery question, especially after the issuance of the Emancipation Proclamation, were the newspapers conducted by Catholics. In fact, the editors of the Catholic *Metropolitan Record* and the *Freeman's Journal and Catholic Register* played leading parts in the movement to encourage violent resistance to the draft" (Man, "Church and the New York Draft Riots," pp. 49–50). Man adds, however, that "when the agitation bore fruit in the draft riots, the clergy of New York, headed by Archbishop Hughes, worked to restrain the mobs."

James McMasters, editor of the *Freeman's Journal*, was the chief representative of the New York forces who plotted with Confederate agents to exploit the discontent with the draft to seize New York City on election day in 1864 (John W. Headley, *Confederate Operations in Canada and New York* [New York and Washington, 1906], pp. 222–3, 265, 270). See also Gibson, *Attitudes of the New York Irish*, pp. 170–71.

77. The Union forces having sustained heavy battle losses, and the terms of volunteer enlistment expiring for many soldiers, on 1 March 1863 the Federal Congress passed a Conscription Act. "White" men between the ages of twenty and forty-five were subject to conscription, selection to be by lottery. Any man whose "number was up" who had the means could escape by paying $300 or by furnishing a substitute enlistee for himself. It was, of course, a raw assertion of bourgeois class privilege, and tended to give the war itself, at the heart of which was the abolition of chattel bond-servitude, the image of "a rich man's war and a poor man's fight." The draft lottery in New York City, set for mid-July, was taken as an opportunity by the anti-abolition forces to strike a mortal blow at the possibility of a Union victory. That blow took the form of the Draft Riot (sometimes described as a succession of riots) which lasted five days, during which eleven African-Americans were lynched in an atmosphere of bloodthirsty white-supremacism. The rioting was finally ended by Federal troops. (See: Adrian Cook, *The Armies of the Street; the New York City Draft Riots of 1863* [Lexington, Kentucky, 1974]; Iver Bernstein, *The New York City Draft Riots: Their Significance for American Society and Politics in the Age of the Civil War* [New York, 1990].)

78. *Proceedings of the Board of Aldermen of the City of New York*, Vol. 81 (New York, 1861), pp. 25–6.

79. Gibson, *Attitudes of the New York Irish*, pp. 116–17, 170.

80. Hassard, *Life of . . . John Hughes*, p. 439.

81. Lee, *Discontent in New York City*, p. 156.

82. *Leader*, 15 June 1861.

83. Theodore Maynard, *The Story of American Catholicism* (New York, 1941), p. 354; Rice, *American Catholic Opinion in the Slavery Controversy*, p. 123; Hassard, p. 437.

84. Hassard, p. 436. Rice, pp. 120–21.

85. Myers, *History of Tammany Hall*, p. 196.

86. Rice, pp. 124–5.

87. Myers, p. 196.

88. Quoted from the *Caucasian* in Lee, p. 138. Lee suggests that the event listed next in this chronology was "Perhaps the desired response . . ."

89. Man, "Labor Competition and the New York Draft Riots," pp. 389–90; Lee, pp. 139–40. Their citations are from the New York *Tribune*, 5, 6, 8 and 24 August 1862, and 24 January 1863.

90. Lee, p. 157.

91. *Caucasian*, 12 October 1862.

92. Lee, p. 102.

93. Man, "Church and the New York Draft Riots," p. 47; Thomas F. Meehan, "Archbishop Hughes and the Draft Riots," *United States Catholic Historical Society Records* (1899–1900), 1:171–90. In this impromptu speech, there was none of the sternness he had employed against the promoters of western colonization, or the Protestant New York School Board. When the crowd cried, "Let the nigger stay South," Hughes gave no apparent direct reply; he merely continued, "I am not a legislator. Everything is in the hands of the supreme people of the United States, and the majority of them, whether they make a blunder or not, must govern" (Meehan, p. 182).

94. Man, "Church and the New York Draft Riots," p. 47. Lee, p. 142.

95. See for example: Man, "Labour Competition and the New York Draft Riots," pp. 404–5; Man, "Church and the New York Draft Riots," p. 47; Gilbert Osofsky, "Abolitionists, Irish Immigrants, and the Dilemmas of Romantic Nationalism," *American Historical Review*, 80:889–912 (October 1975), p. 900; Rice, p. 84; Carl Wittke, *The Irish in America* (Baton Rouge, 1956), pp. 125–6.

96. Ernst, *Immigrant Life in New York City*, p. 105.

97. Philip Bagenal, *The American Irish and Their Influence on Irish Politics* (Boston, 1882), p. 73, cited in Florence E. Gibson, *Attitudes of the New York Irish*, p. 16.

98. Natives feared the added competition would drive wages down from $1.50 a day to a shilling or twenty cents (Myers, *History of Tammany Hall*, p. 134).

99. William Forbes Adams, *Ireland and Irish Emigration to the New World, from 1815 to the Famine* (New Haven, 1932), p. 379. Adams attributes the decline of the nativist movement to the massive immigration of Irish Catholics coupled with the political power available to them through "manhood suffrage."

100. *St Louis Leader*, 10 November 1835, cited in Rice, p. 101.

101. Bridges, *City in the Republic*, p. 41. Ernst, p. 199.

102. Ernst, p. 61.

103. Figures as presented by Ernst, pp. 214–15. Native-born European-Americans certainly added to the competition for jobs, but they are excluded here because, according to Ernst, comparative data are not available for them.

104. The Belfast parallel is again most striking. The Irish political scientists Budge and O'Leary comment upon the chronology of the anti-Catholic riots in Belfast in the period 1813 to 1912: "It is easy to postulate economic factors as the underlying cause," they observe, but they note that these outbreaks correlate not with economic cycles, but with political, for example electoral, cycles. "Moreover," they add, "the general facts in respect of the years when major riots occurred do not support an interpretation in terms of job-competition" (Ian Budge and Cornelius O'Leary, *Belfast: Approach to Crisis, a Study of Belfast Politics* [London, 1973], pp. 89, 91–2).

105. Ernst, p. 107.

106. Man, "Labor Competition and the New York Draft Riots," pp. 397–8.

107. Ibid., citing the *New York Tribune*, 13, 14, and 16 April 1863.

108. Ernst, pp. 107–8.

109. Ibid., pp. 104–5.

110. Man, "Labor Competition and the New York Draft Riots," pp. 376–7.

111. The Lorillard and Watson tobacco factories referred to above are cases in point. Negroes were well-entrenched in laborer and service occupations "before the spurt in immigration in the decades of the [eighteen] forties and fifties" (ibid., p. 376).

112. William Hartman, "The New York Custom House: Seat of Spoils Politics," *New York History*, 34:149–63 (April 1953), 34:149–50.

113. *Leader*, 15 June 1861 (emphasis in original).

114. *Leader*, 25 August 1862.

115. Gibson, *Attitudes of the New York Irish*, p. 90.

116. Albon P. Man Jr, "The Irish in New York in the Early Eighteen-sixties," *Irish Historical Studies*, 7:87–108 (1950–51), p. 100.

117. Gibson, pp. 116–17.

118. Man, "Labor Competition and the New York City Draft Riots," p. 401.

119. Henry C. Haynes, *The Negro at Work in New York City* (New York, 1912), pp. 46–7; cited in Ernst, *Immigrant Life in New York City*, pp. 230 n. 60, and 235 n. 37. Haynes shows a decline from 18,600 to 15,000 in 1860. The African-American population of Brooklyn, however, increased from 2,000 in 1840 to 5,000 in 1860. If Haynes's 1860 number is for Manhattan only, it is considerably higher than that given by Ernst himself at p. 199 and by Bernstein (*New York City Draft Riots*, p. 267), both of which cite the US Census to show that the number for 1860 was about 12,500.

120. It is ironic that Ernst, whose work provides such valuable materials for the study of the myth of "labor competition," seems to have remained a captive of it. To a reference to "a possible fear that Irish labor would be overwhelmed by the competition of emancipated Negroes," Ernst appended a note saying, "I have no evidence of the fear of possible competition from colored workers, but this is a reasonable assumption" (Ernst, *Immigrant Life in New York*, pp. 153, 279 n. 4).

121. *Historical Statistics of the United States*, p. 106.

122. Lee, p. 140, citing *Tribune*, 16 April 1863 and New York *World*, 28 August 1862.

123. Man, "Labor Competition and the New York Draft Riots," p. 387, citing the New York *Tribune*, 4 August and 7 November 1862.

124. See Chapter 6.

125. W. E. B. DuBois, *Black Reconstruction, An Essay toward a History of the Part which Black Folk Played in the Attempt to Reconstruct Democracy in America, 1860–1880* (New York, 1935), p. 20.

126. Athearn, *Thomas Francis Meagher*, p. 134.

127. Doyle, "The Irish in North America, 1776–1845," in *A New History*, 5:687.

Index

Mallow Defiance 291 n.66
Malthus, Thomas Robert (1766–1834) 277
n.90
Maroons 6, 13
marriage 33, 41–5, 55–6, 82–3, 89, 243 n.46,
264 n.128; "race" laws against
intermarriage: of Protestants to Catholics
83; of "whites" to Indians or Negroes 83,
89
Marx, Karl (1818–83) 29, 143, 149, 166, 254
n.57, 277 n.94, 289 n.51
Mary I (Mary Tudor) *see* English monarchs
Maryland Provincial Supreme Court 89, 90
Massachusetts Anti-Slavery Society 166, 173,
291 n.67
Maynooth (Royal College of St. Patrick
founded at Maynooth, County Kildare,
1795) 100, 110, 269 nn.58, 59
Meagher, Thomas Francis (1823–67) 179,
184, 198, 295 n.45
Mexican War 159, 188
Mexico 69, 159, 170, 189
migrants 21, 145–6
militia 13, 94, 264 n.6
Missouri Compromise (1820) 159, 163, 296
n.69
Mitchel, John (1815–75) 179, 184, 196, 294
n.42
Monaghan (County) 121, 273 n.12
"monster meetings" 291 n.66, 294 n.25; as
"Emancipation" and Repeal strategy 103,
106–7, 109, 269 n.81
Morgan, Edmund S. (author, *American
Slavery/American Freedom: The Ordeal of
Colonial Virginia*) 6, 16–20
Moryson, Fynes (1566–1630) 62, 253 n.45
Mountjoy, Charles Blount, 8th Baron
(1563–1606) 62, 63, 91, 117; executes
famine strategy in Ireland 64, Appendix F;
his task remains "unperfect" 65
"Mulatto" (intermediate social stratum) 12–14
Munster (Province), plantation in 59, 61, 76,
115, 123, 128, 129, Appendix D

NLU *see* National Labor Union ("white")
Nat Turner's Rebellion 84, 165, 262 n.94
National independence, as an Irish purpose 96,
104, 107, 126, 133
National Labor Union ("white") 142–3, 149;
Address of (1866) 142
national oppression 23, 28, 36, 115, 241 n.11;
British option for 92, 96, 97, 107; British
"praetorian guard", Irish garrison as
symbol of 112, 271 n.135; British West
Indies parallel 112–14
National Repeal Conventions of the Friends of

Ireland (1842, 1843) 173
nativism, "Know-Nothing" anti-Catholic
bigotry: Catholic Americans beset by 183;
draws on Ulster heritage 192; its decline
explained 297 n.99; regarded as less
threatening than Abolitionism 193
naturalization 184–5, 185–6, 192
Negro Exodus of 1879 144, 145–7, 148,
150–52, 157, 282–3 n.57, 283 n.59
Negro National Labor Union 142, 149, 281
n.41
Negroes *see* African-Americans
Nine Years War *see* Tyrone War
Norman Conquest of England (1066) 40
Norsemen 38, 246 n.88

O'Connell, Daniel "The Liberator"
(1775–1847) 32, 99, 102, 130, 161, 166,
243–4 n.53, 290 n.64, Appendix J;
Abolitionist leader 169–73, 177, 180–81,
183, 188–9; ambivalence toward the
peasantry 100, 102, 104–6, 267 n.47, 270
n.97; and the "Catholic Emancipation"
campaign 99–100; and Repeal of the
Union 97, 102–3, 105, 106, 267 nn.38, 40;
foe of racial oppression and white
supremacy 169–70, 174–6, 178, 199;
bourgeois dread of revolution 100, 105,
265 n.20, 270 n.106; Parliamentary
politician 100, 108–9, 112, 267 n.40, 270
n.105, 271 n.135
O'Connell, Morgan 270 n.94
O'Connor, Feargus (1794–1855) 288 n.36
O'Donnell, Neil Garve 254–5 n.80
O'Donnell, Red Hugh (1571–1602) 60, 255
n.86
O'Donnell, Rory, Earl of Tyrconnell
(1575–1608) 116, 117, 255 n.86
Offaly (County), "Plantation" in 59, 67
O'Neill, Hugh, Earl of Tyrone (1540–1616)
58, 60, 65, 116, 254–5 n.80, 255 n.86
Orangeism and the Orange Order 103, 269
n.87; rally to defend Protestant privileges
94, 126; key to British victory in 1798
127; succeed in delaying "Catholic
Emancipation" 95
O'Reilly, Mulmorie Og (d. 1618) 254–5
n.80
"Oriental exclusion," immigration laws 295
n.49
Othello 5–6, 7

Parliament, Anglo-Irish: authorized to
legislate independently of British
Parliament 57, 84, 93–6, 125, 276 n.72